ESSENTIALS
for Child Development Associates
Working with Young Children

ESSENTIALS
for Child Development Associates
Working with Young Children

Carol Brunson Phillips, *Editor*

The CDA Professional Preparation Program
Council for Early Childhood Professional Recognition

Acknowledgments

For immeasurable assistance in conceptualization—
Teresa Rosegrant and Sue Bredekamp

For review and conceptual direction—
Barbara T. Bowman, Janice E. Hale, and Jan McCarthy

And, for oversight and general counsel—
J.D. Andrews

Copyright © 1991 by the Council for Early Childhood Professional Recognition
1341 G Street, N.W., #400, Washington, DC 20005
202-265-9090   CDA Candidate Connection 800-424-4310

This Early Childhood Professional Preparation Program was prepared under the editorial direction of Carol Brunson Phillips, Ph.D., Executive Director, Council for Early Childhood Professional Recognition.

Contributing writers—Jan Brown McCracken and Sharon Cronin

Editorial consultants—Catherine Corder and Kathy Spencer

Design/production—Melanie Rose White

Photographs

Nancy P. Alexander, *51, 97, 119, 141, 188, 258, 291, 392, 401, 421, 422, 427, 428, 452, 460, 511, 525, 532*

Faith Bowlus, *42*

Blakely Fetridge Bundy, *347*

Nina M. Chieffo, *408*

Cleo Freelance Photography, *cover, 203, 406, 461, 475, 516*

Jim Cronk, *393*

Larry G. Cumpton, *8*

Gail Denham, *323*

Anita Windham Ehart, *221*

Episcopal Child Day Care Center, Inc., *465*

Cheryl A. Ertelt, *325*

Loren Fogelman, *369*

Diane Crafts, *311*

Bruce Grossman, *319*

Jeffrey High, *239, 353*

Bruce Jennings, *148*

Joanie Keller-Hand, *227*

Robert Koenig, *283, 453*

Valerie Beardwood Kunze, *413*

Toni H. Liebman, *4*

Janice Mason, *282, 492*

Esther Mugar, *198, 318*

Cheryl Namkung, *303*

Elisabeth Nichols, *205*

Marilyn Nolt, *146, 232, 358*

Bm Porter/Don Franklin, *306, 471*

Wendy Press, *332*

Rick Reinhard, *456*

Florence Sharp, *333, 470*

South Carolina ETV, *292*

Michaelyn Straub, *192, 493*

STRIX PIX—David S. Strickler, *110*

Subjects & Predicates, *3, 7, 19, 57, 82, 102, 143, 155, 278, 286, 288, 289, 297, 330, 357, 382, 383, 385*

Michael Tony—TOPIX, *85, 150, 208*

Tyroler & Cooper, *87*

Library of Congress Catalog Card Number: 91-71482
ISBN 1-879891-00-X
Printed in the United States of America.

Contents

Unit 3. Ways to set up a safe, healthy environment to invite learning   101

Unit 4. Positive ways to support children's social and emotional development   187

Unit 5. Steps to advance children's physical and intellectual competence   273

Unit 6. Keys to establish productive relationships with families   343

Unit 7. Putting it all together as an early childhood professional working with preschoolers   379

How you use this book

Unit 8. Preparing for final assessment as a Child Development Associate   464

Unit 7. Putting it all together as an early childhood professional providing family day care   484

Unit 8. Preparing for final assessment as a Child Development Associate   515

How you use this book

Most likely you are eager to become a Child Development Associate. It represents a big step in your early childhood education career.

You even may be tempted to skip this section so you can get started on your CDA. Go ahead and leaf through each unit to get an idea of what you will be doing with these materials during your CDA work. Then come back here to get the overall view of how this book fits into the next year of your life and beyond.

You probably read most books once and then put them on your shelf. On rare occasions you go back to look up something. This book is different. It contains **essential** information about what competent teachers of young children *do*. Some of the information and ideas probably will be familiar to you. Other ideas may be new or different—even contrary to what you always believed about teaching.

Before you complete your Child Development Associate Professional Preparation Program (CDA P₃), you will use this early childhood studies curriculum in three different ways:

1. On your own

CDA Candidates begin their work in real-life settings—work in family child care homes and other group programs for young children. Whether you are already working with children or have selected a site to work in just to prepare for your CDA, you begin this first phase of your CDA Professional Preparation Program (CDA P₃) by working on your own to learn more about yourself, your program, and the children you teach.

During the next 6 months, you will study at your own pace, and must set aside a regular time to do so. You will need at least 2 to 4 hours each week to think about ideas, to try out new techniques, to watch the videotape for each of the six units, and to find information that applies to your program and the children you teach. You will also talk with your *Field Advisor* at least once a week to discuss ideas, ask questions, and review your progress.

You are required to complete the six units in this book, which review what we know about young children and how we can help them grow and enjoy learning in the best ways. Begin with

Unit 1 and continue to work in order through Unit 6 because each section builds upon the last one.

Contained in the first six units are *self-study activities* for you. They are practical, hands-on experiences. As you do them, you will be looking for answers to questions YOU have, and you will learn more about your profession, the children with whom you work, and about the best ways to teach.

Essentials is designed to become the backbone of your professional resources. Write in it. Check the checklists. Make notes in the margins. Tear out pages to add to a specific folder.

As you work during the self-study phase, you will begin to build your *CDA Professional Resource File.* You will write about the things you do with children and families and why you do them. You will also gather many things to help you in your teaching: curriculum ideas and resources, phone numbers, regulations, teaching strategies, and observations of children's progress. Make this book—and your growing CDA Professional Resource File—work for you. You will use this book all year and beyond: during your self-study work, again when you meet in the CDA Seminar, and while you put everything you are learning into practice. Much of it will be used again and again all during your teaching career—it contains the basics for good professional practice.

A videotape is also recommended for each unit of study to help you see many of these ideas in action. A Viewer's Guide is enclosed with the tapes. Think about the questions in the guide as you watch each unit of the tape. You can view these videos with your Field Advisor if you would like, and discuss together what you have seen.

Your CDA Field Advisor will keep in touch with you once a week to guide and verify your progress during this first phase of study. Now is the time to ask questions . . . to search for information you can use . . . to collect ideas. Get yourself off to a good start!

2. With a small group

When the second phase of your study begins, you will join other CDA Candidates who have also completed their self-study materials. In these *CDA Seminars* you, your *Seminar Instructor,* and other CDA Candidates will discuss your experiences as you work in a real-life child care setting. You will continue to use *Essentials* along with other reading assignments and exercises.

Expect lots of lively discussions to bring to life the ideas you have read about here. Your Seminar Instructor will also help you broaden your horizons and give you opportunities to learn even more about young children.

Attend regularly and get involved in each session! Follow through with your assignments. Your participation will enable you to make satisfactory progress toward earning your CDA. Your expanding Professional Resource File will be another indication of how much you are learning.

At the end of this phase, you and all other CDA Candidates are required to document what you have learned. Your Seminar Instructor will give you the date for your *CDA Early Childhood Studies Review*, a written summary to verify your knowledge about the basics needed to teach young children.

3. As you work with children

After you complete your Seminar, you will continue to apply what you have learned, and prepare to demonstrate your skills with children. During this last phase, your Field Advisor will work with you to complete the last units in this book. You will continue to build your CDA Professional Resource File and you will be formally observed as you demonstrate your competency as a teacher of young children.

Your *Field Advisor* will distribute a Parent Opinion Questionnaire to parents in your group to determine their opinion of your work.

A CDA *Council Representative* — the person who will verify that you can put what you have learned into practice — and your CDA Field Advisor will support you throughout this period.

The entire CDA Professional Preparation Program is designed to help you see what you are doing well, to identify where changes are needed, and to know how to make changes that are best for children and their families. You will demonstrate your competency to meet children's needs in two ways.

During this year, you will put what you know into **writing**. You will make notes in this book,

build your Professional Resource File, and complete your CDA Early Childhood Studies Review.

You will put what you know into **practice**, too. You will share ideas with your CDA Seminar group, demonstrate appropriate strategies as you work with children, respond to parents' needs, join a professional organization, read to keep current with the field, attend conferences, and stand up for the needs of children.

To help you keep track of your efforts, a CDA progress record is provided in the back of this book. Each time you complete a unit of this book, or other major milestones in each of these three phases, you can check it off. You are to be congratulated on a job well done!

What if you have a question about the CDA Training and Credentialing process? You have several places to turn. You can call the *CDA Candidate Connection*, CDA's toll-free number, 1-800-424-4310 from 9:00 a.m. to 5:00 p.m. (Eastern Time) weekdays to get a quick answer to your question. Your CDA Field Advisor or Seminar Instructor may also have the information you need.

How do you make changes in your work with children? If you are a family child care provider, you probably can make improvements in your program as you see fit. If you work in Head Start, a nursery school, or other center-based program, it may not be possible for you to make changes without first discussing them with your supervisor. You may work in a shared space so someone else must be included in your decisions. Talk about your new learning opportunity with everyone involved. When your supervisors and co-workers share your commitment to making your program the best it can be, you can work together to make improvements.

Explain to the parents what you are doing. They will be proud to have you caring for their child! Parents are thrilled that their children are cared for by people who take their work so seriously. Be sure to explain to them what you are doing and how it will affect their children.

By the time you are awarded your CDA Credential, your CDA Professional Resource File should be brimming over with materials. Each day with young children and their families is filled with challenges. Begin now to prepare yourself to meet them!

Carol Brunson Phillips, Ph.D.
Executive Director
Council for Early Childhood
Professional Recognition

Introduction to the early childhood profession

**ELCOME!** You have made an important decision about your career with young children. You want to become a Child Development Associate, a CDA. As you follow the steps required to earn your CDA Credential—studying on your own, joining Seminar discussions, and applying what you know with young children—you will see how exciting and challenging it is to be a teacher.

When you have successfully completed your CDA Professional Preparation Program, you will be awarded your CDA Credential. Your skills as a primary caregiver for young children will be confirmed by this nationally recognized professional credential.

For some of you, the CDA program materials may be a review of how young children grow and learn. Many of the teaching strategies and guidance techniques will be familiar.

For others, this is your introduction to the early childhood education profession.

Regardless of your experience or formal train-ing in the field, we hope you discover some fresh, interesting ideas and information you can use in your work.

Parents, teachers, and other professionals have spent many years gathering information about how young children grow. They have looked at what teaching techniques are most effective. They have searched for ways to encourage children to learn self-discipline.

Now, as a CDA Candidate, you are making a commitment to become a professional early childhood educator. Whether you call yourself a family child care provider, a teacher, a classroom assistant, a caregiver, or some other title, you are choosing a career of work with children from birth through 5 and their families.

What you do with children during the day is somewhat like being a parent, but it is also very different. You are preparing to become a CDA because you want to be a good early childhood educator—a very special type of teacher of young children.

Let's start your CDA Professional Preparation Program with a look at the real world: Why do you want to teach? What kind of person is a good teacher of young children? How is a teacher different from a parent? What is a day in the life of a CDA really like?

Part 1

Why do you want to work with young children?

You are already working with young children, either in a center program or in your home. Before you started to take care of children, you probably thought about what you wanted to do with your life. You may have tried other jobs first.

But something drew you to early childhood education. You surely have several reasons why you decided to work with young children. **You will be a better teacher if you know what motivates you—why you want to teach. Write your reasons here.** Be honest with yourself.

Many of you probably wrote at least one of these reasons:

- I love children.
- I always wanted to be a teacher.
- Many of my family members have been teachers.
- Young children are . . . so cute . . . so energetic . . . so curious . . . so much fun.
- Children like me.
- I want to help young children . . . who have different abilities (such as deaf, emotionally impaired, chronically ill).
- I want to reach out to families who are . . . struggling to get out of poverty . . . trying to deal with difficult circumstances.

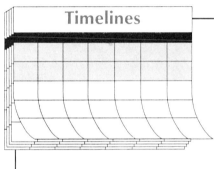

Timelines

You will need about 2 weeks to complete your study of Unit 1. During this time you must

1 Prepare for conferences with your Field Advisor to discuss three topics (becoming a CDA, who early childhood educators are, and legal requirements).

2 Complete two assignments (an interview with an early childhood education professional, and contact two national associations) and two entries for the Professional Resource File.

3 Complete two assignments for Seminar (visit an early childhood program, and locate state/local child care licensing requirements).

4 View the accompanying videotape using the Viewer's Guide.

- There aren't enough good teachers . . . for children who speak my first language . . . who speak a language common in our community.
- This is my way to help make the world a better place to live.
- Teaching is the perfect part-time job for a busy mother.
- Child care was an easy course at my school.
- Children's early years are the most important time of their lives. I want to make those years as good as possible.
- I want to be in charge of children who will listen to me. (Older children are hard to handle.)
- I need to make some money.

Now it is time to take an honest look at your reasons for wanting to work with young children. As you consider them, remember, young children are very vulnerable. Their parents trust you to provide good care. Children thrive only in a

If you really are committed to learning more about the best ways to work with children and families, you will surely make a positive difference in their lives. Becoming a CDA is an excellent step for you to take!

stable, predictable, loving environment.

Educators can help children and families change and improve their lives and our society. You need to know a great deal about young children, families, and yourself. Becoming a teacher cannot be taken lightly.

Some of the reasons we listed here are not very good reasons for choosing teaching as a profession. These reasons may ignore the needs of children or families. Some are misinformed ideas about what being a teacher of young children is really all about.

Try to be objective when you think about your reasons for wanting to work with young children.

If you want to become a teacher for sound reasons—if you really are committed to learning more about the best ways to work with children and families—you will surely make a positive difference in their lives. You probably have done a lot of thinking about how children's lives are special because of what you do. Becoming a CDA is an excellent step for you to take! Let your Advisor know why you are convinced this is the career for you.

What if you are not really sure whether your reasons are good enough? If most of your reasons seem questionable, now that you see them in writing, **you may want to spend more time considering your future before you make a definite commitment to teaching.** *Why Teach? A First Look at Working with Young Children* (Hendrick, 1987) is an interesting book that might help you decide whether a career as a teacher is right for you.

Try out your wings in something else, give

yourself more experience with young children, or talk about your reservations with your Advisor before you get further training.

Maybe your motives for being a teacher seem selfish or pretty weak, now that you see them down on paper. Teaching is a difficult job. There is a lot to learn. **You may want to reconsider your decision before you continue to work on a CDA Credential.**

The book, *Careers with Young Children: Making Your Decision* (Seaver, Cartwright, Ward, & Heasley, 1984) **might help you think about related careers. Discuss your reservations about becoming a teacher with your**

CDA Field Advisor. Rather than wasting your time preparing for a job that isn't suited to *you*, find a career counselor who can help you determine what kind of work fits you best.

Children deserve only the best care. Being a CDA can help you become a *superior* teacher. Do some hard thinking about your life. When you are sure working with young children is for you, you are ready for Part 2 of your CDA studies.

Part 2

Will you be a good teacher?

You probably have a few doubts about whether you can be a **good** teacher. In fact, your desire to improve is probably what drew you to the CDA program—you want to become better! Let's think for a minute about how teachers are different from parents and who a good teacher *really* is.

Your image of a teacher probably comes from your memories of what school was like for you: You remember that teachers . . . tell classes what to do . . . make children behave and sit quietly . . . spend a lot of time preparing work sheets and bulletin boards . . . correct papers and give grades. But this is *not* what a good early childhood teacher does.

Life is much more active in an appropriate program for young children! Early childhood

Your role as a caregiver is not quite the same as a parent, but children do feel loved and protected in your care.

Well-trained early educators

- move about the room to offer assistance,
- help children expand upon an idea,
- take notes about children's individual development,
- help young children learn to solve their own real problems rather than solving problems for them,
- give children opportunities to succeed,
- strengthen children's appreciation for their own and others' languages and cultures,
- allow children to be as independent as possible, and
- help children learn to control their own behavior and make good decisions for themselves.

educators plan and set up a rich, inviting environment filled with toys, equipment, and themes so children can learn through play. Children learn best with hands-on, real-life experiences. Children select their own activities and take as much responsibility as they can handle. They work alone or in small groups, talk with each other in their home languages, make choices, and pursue their ideas. The room hums with activity!

Early childhood teachers also change diapers, feed children, clean up messes, assist children with dressing, perform simple first aid, and administer medicine. Yes, teachers of young children do many of the same things parents usually do. But they also do much more.

Your image of parents also probably comes from your own experiences: Parents love their children . . . raise their children based on the values of their own culture . . . are disciplinarians . . . have hopes and dreams for their children.

Parents buy clothes, set bedtimes, and bring you soup and crackers in bed when you don't feel well! Parents think their child is the most important child of all.

As you have probably already found in your work with young children, whether it is in your own home or other group program, your role as a caregiver is not quite the same as a parent. You are not as emotionally invested in each child and don't show favorites—but children do feel loved and protected in your care.

Like parents, you want children to be proud of who they are, the traditions they share, and the abilities they have. You want children to learn to be self-disciplined and to be self-motivated. You too have dreams for children when they need you.

All through this book you will see how working with young children is **different**: Early childhood educators are different from teachers you had in elementary school. We are also different from children's parents.

Perhaps you remember the adults you looked up to as a child. You probably had a favorite teacher, a special grandparent or relative, or a neighbor who was dear to you. Why did you enjoy being with that person?

Jot down some of the qualities that made the person special to you.

mother - gentleness &
nuturing
Grandma's - stories
cultural back'ground

HOW we teach is just as important as WHAT we teach.

Children copy what we do and say.

Or perhaps you have always liked children—they just seem drawn to you and you to them. **Why do children find you appealing? Make a list of qualities that describe you.**

Compare your description of your favorite person—or of yourself—with this list of traits of good teachers of young children. You probably will find several matches. **You may have some other important ideas that are not included here. Add them to the list.**

As you work on your CDA during this next year, keep in mind that what you are learning is helping you to become the kind of teacher you want to be!

Good early childhood teachers

- **respect children, parents, and staff**—each person is valuable. We all are proud of our heritage and skills. Yet we all have biases about other people: Some of us are uncomfortable around children whose abilities are different and others harbor resentment about skin colors, languages, or cultures. We may hold stereotypes about rich or low-income families. Even a child's hair style or earrings may offend us.

  Unless you are willing to figure out what your biases are and to work to change them, you will not be a good teacher.
- **accept diverse ideas**—there are many good ways to look at and do things. Good teachers prepare children to live and work in a pluralistic society. Each family has its own ways. Cultural groups have their own preferences and languages.

  Our lives are richer when we appreciate each other's diversity and get along together. You and the children stand up for what is fair for people.
- **act warm and caring**—children **know** you care about them by what you do and what you say. A beaming smile, a loving hand, and genuine affection bring out the best in young children. Good teachers demonstrate affection in ways that are consistent with children's culture.
- **are flexible**—you can change direction at a moment's notice. Many of children's best learning opportunities happen without advance planning.
- **really listen**—you pay attention to what children say with words and through their behavior. You talk *with*, not at, children.
- **show enthusiasm**—you laugh with the children. You share life's big and little delights. What a wonderful world it is!
- **have lots of energy**—teaching is hard work. You carry heavy furniture, hold children,

Good early childhood teachers

- respect children, parents, and staff
- accept diverse ideas
- act warm and caring
- are flexible
- really listen
- are honest
- show enthusiasm
- have lots of energy
- are creative
- are patient
- remain calm
- are curious
- have a great deal of inner strength
- use knowledge, not opinion, when they teach
- are constantly learning
- know their strengths and weaknesses

walk about the room and outdoor play area, deal with strong emotions.

- **are creative**—you love new ideas—yours and children's.

- **are patient**—children cannot be rushed. Growing up takes a long time. There is so much to enjoy and learn!

- **remain calm**—you don't get upset easily, even when everything seems to be going wrong!

- **are curious**—you are eager to learn more about children. You want to give children just-right learning opportunities.

- **have a great deal of inner strength**—children can rely on you to help them weather life's storms.

- **use knowledge, not opinion, when they teach**—you read professional journals and books, attend workshops, participate in groups that work on behalf of young children, and learn from your own experiences.

- **are constantly learning**—good teachers always want to improve.

- **know their strengths and weaknesses**—no teacher is perfect for all children, but good teachers know the types of children and families with whom they are most effective and those that are not a good match for them.

What qualities do you think make a good early childhood teacher?

constant improvement
good listener, honesty & respect
enthusiasm & patience
recognizing value of each child
inner strength & commitment

Do most of these traits describe you? Or do you really want to work on being this kind of person? Are you willing to try to figure out how your cultural perspective affects your teach-

As you work toward becoming a CDA, you will change: Teaching will look different to you.

ing? Then you are probably in the right profession. Let's see what might happen once you become a CDA working with a group of young children.

Part 3

What is a day in the life of a CDA like?

Perhaps you are a Head Start volunteer or assistant. You may be a family child care provider. Or maybe you work in a nursery school or a child care program. Most likely you are a parent or plan to become one. No matter what your experience with young children, as you work toward becoming a CDA, you will change: **Teaching will look different to you.** You will have more questions. You will be a livelier person. You will see how much more you can learn about young children.

The following glimpse into a CDA's typical day may bring back fond memories of yesterday or today. So much of what happens in this example is the same in any program for young children—whether you operate a family child care home, work in a part-day program, or teach in a full-day center.

This review of a teacher's day may help you see how much work you really do. It could point out how many decisions you have to make. It might even make you smile.

The *left columns* (on pages 9 to 16) show

what you might expect your day to be like after you complete your CDA—you will probably take more responsibility than you have now.

The *right columns* contain some basic skills and information you need to know to offer the best program for children—what you must know to be more professional. You will learn more about these ideas while you work on your CDA.

Add your own questions to each section of this list so your CDA Field Advisor or Seminar Instructor can help you find answers.

Starting on the next page are some typical activities in a group program. Are you ready for days like this?

How do you watch children's behavior for clues about growing and learning?

A typical day for a CDA

Many CDAs work in all-day programs in centers, so let's pretend you do. All good group care for young children is very similar regardless of the number of hours children are there or of the setting.

What happens during a typical day for a CDA

 You arrive for work early on a cold January day. You and the teachers for the other 4-year-old group have picked up on children's curiosity and decided the basic theme for the next couple of weeks is children's senses: sight, hearing, taste, touch, smell.

You check the special activity list you have planned for the day and then begin to mix tempera paints. You put away most of the 5-piece puzzles and bring out some with 6 to 10 pieces. You find the cassette tape of Puerto Rican folk dances and locate the maracas and other instruments. You make sure you have easel paper and a marker ready to write a shopping list with the children.

What you need to know to handle the situation

Knowledge about child growth and learning is essential.

What do you look for in children's behavior to help you plan?
What activities and ideas are most appropriate for children?
How do you select good toys and materials?

You must know enough about other cultures to make them an authentic part of children's everyday experience.

Which foods are most nutritious?
How can you help children use written and spoken languages?

"Good morning!" calls the Program Director. "It looks like your group has a busy day ahead."

"We do indeed," you respond. "Please come to dance with us around 11:30."

How do you work as a team with your supervisor?
Why are visitors important?

What happens. . .

Children begin to arrive. "Mrs. Williams!" shouts Armando as he pushes open the door, his father close behind him. "Look at my fast new sneakers!"

"They look like speedy running shoes, Armando. When we go outdoors this morning, be sure to show all of us how you can run in them."

Six children have arrived. When Mrs. Blair brings her daughter Sadhana, she asks to schedule a conference. Sadhana is afraid of the dark. What should she and her husband do?

"We do need to talk soon, don't we, Kathy? Being afraid must be hard for Sadhana and for you. When is a good time for us to get together?"

Your assistant Michael arrives and together you quickly review the plans for the day. Then each of you moves about the room. The children are all busy during free play. You pause to get out the dinosaurs for a group at the sand table, to put an arm around a child who looks discouraged, to write names on artwork.

Suddenly you hear Luke shout, "Brandon, I was using those blocks. You can't have them!" His arm is in the air, ready to strike.

What you need to know. . .

Greet each child and each parent every day.

Children thrive on individual attention.

Cooperation, rather than competition, is a key teaching method.

Why was the function of the sneakers, rather than their appearance, emphasized?

How can you help parents resolve problems?
When should you refer them somewhere else?

Parents should always feel welcome. You all work together.

How can you work cooperatively with other staff members?

Children learn through PLAY. Teachers set up the materials.

What do teachers do during free play?
How can you respond to children's questions to encourage their efforts? What do you say about children's artwork?

DISCIPLINE — *What is it?* What it is not. . .

What happens. . .

You tell the children, "It's time to be finishing your work so we can clean up in 5 minutes."

The group soon settles down on the carpet with their favorite finger play, "Five Little Pumpkins." First the children volunteer for jobs during the week: water the plants, feed the gerbils, wash the paint brushes. Their names are on cards that go in slots on the job board. You and the children decide what vegetables to stir-fry for lunch tomorrow. You write the shopping list.

Kelly, watching from her wheelchair, says, "Hey Armando, let's run together!" and down the hill they go, laughing.

Everyone comes in, breathing dragon "smoke" in the cold air. Coats, hats, mittens — all go into each child's cubby.

Bathroom time again. Then the children select a book to read and sit on the large carpet. When everyone has returned, Michael reads *Peter's Chair* while you check with the other head teacher about next week's field trip to the local dairy. When you return, the children are eagerly sharing their experiences about new brothers or sisters. Two children wiggle over to you and snuggle under your arms.

What you need to know. . .

How can you change from one activity to another without wasting your time or the children's time?

What makes a successful circle time?
How do you help children love to read?

Math is a natural — money, measuring, time, shapes, and other important number ideas come up all the time.

How can you help children solve their own problems?

Children with different abilities should be included in regular classrooms whenever possible — *every* child has *some* special needs!

How do you keep lost boots and mittens to a minimum?

How do teachers read books to a group of children? What kinds of questions will get children to discuss story ideas? What is a good book?

Families should always be part of the children's day.

Mutual planning with other staff is essential.

Field trips open up new worlds. *How do you make them successful?*

Teachers are generous with affection.

What happens. . .

Dance time! The tape is playing. Each child has an instrument, scarf, or hat. "Come in," you call when the Program Director opens the door. "You must have heard the beautiful sounds coming from our room. See what lively dancers we have."

The children know lunch is ready—they smell it and besides, Amanda, the community lunch volunteer, has just arrived. Children wash their hands.

With one adult at each table, children and adults serve themselves from containers on the table. The conversation is animated. "Hey Danusia, I'm going to visit my Pop-pop this weekend," announces Jason.

You and your assistant each take about half of the children. Michael's group will wash their hands so they can fix snack, while the children in your group work on puzzles.

One of their favorite puzzles is a Matroshka. You make a mental note that Daniel seems to have difficulty with an 8-piece puzzle.

Children in Michael's group talk about whether their favorite apples are the color rojo, verde, or amarillo, and remember their trip last fall to the orchard.

"Now is a good time to go to the bathroom. Each person must wash their hands before snack. Who is ready?" You make sure children wash their hands thoroughly. Trays of apple slices, chunks of cheese, and a handwoven African basket full of whole-wheat crackers are on the table.

What you need to know. . .

Have you noticed that the day's activities alternate between busy/loud and restful/quiet? *Why?*

Real experiences with many cultures happen every day—not just on holidays or with foods.

How do you talk with children?
Adults always respect each other.

How can you work with volunteers?
Lunch: *How should it be served? What should you talk about?*

Small groups are best.
Activities are tailored to children's needs and interests.
How do you watch children's behavior for clues about growing and learning?

Handwashing is health in action. *How should staff and children do it?*
How can children's home languages be naturally incorporated into daily activities?
What are some attractive, culturally relevant ways to serve snack?
How do you help children build on their experiences?

What happens. . .

Both classes of 4-year-olds put on their warm coats to go outdoors. Many children need help with their zippers, buttons, mittens, and hats.

The teachers spread out to supervise different activities: riding vehicles, climbing equipment, sand box, and hoops.

You remember to ask Armando to show how he can run in his new shoes. A small group of children gather around. Armando beams with delight as he dashes across the playground.

Soon children begin to wake up. Cots, blankets, and pillows are put away. Trips are made to the bathroom.

The first children to arise help prepare snack. "Oops, I spilled some juice!" Chris says matter-of-factly. A sponge is handy, and Chris wipes up the puddle.

When children finish snack, they can choose from quiet activities in one area: small games, table blocks, or pasting. It's not long until everyone is up, all the lights are on, and the room is once again humming with activity.

What you need to know. . .

Why is outdoor play included every day?

Pay attention to children on the playground. This is no time to socialize with other adults.

What are some good outdoor play activities?

ALWAYS keep your promises (or explain why you can't) — children must be able to trust you.

How do you handle long transitions?

What do you need to know to select a good variety of activities?

What happens. . .

Children select what to do: they paint, roll and pat the dough clay, and open the grocery store in the dramatic play area. It has only been a few days since the grocery store was set up and the children still like to write grocery lists, stock the shelves with their families' favorite foods, push their dolls in the shopping cart, and check out with the scanner at the cash register.

What you need to know. . .

Pretend play is essential for young children.

"It's snowing! It's snowing!" chant a growing number of excited children. Although outdoor time isn't scheduled for another half an hour, you check with the other teacher of 4-year-olds and agree that catching snowflakes is an experience you don't want the children to wait for. Everyone excitedly gets their coats, hats, and mittens on again.

Predictable routines and good organization make the day go smoothly.

How can you take advantage of instant learning opportunities?

What is science for young children?

Outdoors, children search for the shovels. They make trails of footprints in the first flakes that stick to the ground. Everyone has a great time.

Be flexible to take advantage of a learning opportunity.

Teresa has had an ear infection. You locate her medicine in the refrigerator, measure out the correct amount, and make sure she swallows it all as you comment, "How much better you feel now that the medicine is helping your ears get well!" You mark her record that she received her medicine.

Children's health must be protected.

What happens. . .

After lunch, the children carry their plates to the cart, put their napkins and paper cups in the trash, brush their teeth, and put on their coats for a walk. "When you have your hearing ears turned on, your coats zipped, and your mittens tight, our group will be ready to leave," Michael calls. The children walk through the neighborhood, pausing to listen to the sounds of mid-day.

What you need to know. . .

Children can be responsible for appropriate tasks.

Why take simple field trips?
How do you keep the curriculum theme woven through the day's activities without it becoming monotonous?

When everyone returns, coats, hats, and mittens are put away again. It is naptime so the lights are dim and everyone uses soft voices. Amanda put the cots out while the children were out. Children go to the bathroom and then get their blankets and pillows from their cubbies. The adults move slowly from cot to cot, tucking one child in, talking softly to another, rubbing a back.

Naptime: *How do you get everyone to have a good rest?*
How do you keep cots and bedding clean?

While the children rest, the teachers take a short break to re-energize. They relax with a book, meditate, or sip a cup of coffee. Others make last-minute checks of the grocery store field-trip permission slips. You jot down the mental notes you made during your busy morning.

How do you change mental notes into written notes into ACTION?

What do you plan? What isn't planned?

How do you meet your own needs during breaks?

Wet mittens are spread out to dry and chilly fingered children return indoors. The late afternoon staff begin to arrive and you prepare to leave for the day. You gather your notes and say goodbye to each child and teacher. "¡Adios! Goodbye!" But the activity continues in the room.

How do you coordinate schedules?
How should staff come and go?
What are some good late-in-the-day activities?
How do you help children get ready to go home?

What happens. . .

When it is almost time for the parents to arrive for their children, a teacher alerts those children that it will soon be time to go home. Just as you are walking out the door, Felicia's father rushes in, saying to her in Spanish, "Please hurry, we need to pick up Mommy. We're going to the play at Miquel's school."

You wearily climb onto the bus for the snowy ride home, welcoming the opportunity to sit in the relative quiet!

If you work in a center, you probably have had busy days much like this.

If you run a family child care program there is even more to keep up with: You may be interrupted with telephone calls (you may want to invest in an answering machine) and your own children may return during the day. Instead of the bus ride, you may face cleaning your house before your family comes home.

Regardless of the setting in which you work, you will be exhausted and need a break before you can enjoy an evening with family or friends!

Now you have seen how much responsibility a CDA has for planning and supervising daily classroom activities. This is a good time for you to go see another program in action, and to watch the video for Unit 1.

Schedule a visit to another early childhood program. Try to visit one that you have never seen before and that is as different as possible from the one in which you work—a family child care home, a nursery school, Head Start, or a full-day program.

What you need to know. . .

How can you talk with parents who are in a rush? In their home language?

REST YOUR WEARY BONES.

Spend 1 or 2 hours watching what happens. Perhaps you can use a lunch hour. If you just can't manage to take off more than an extra hour or two, at least visit a co-worker's classroom or a neighbor's family child care home.

After your visit, go back through the typical day described here and check the activities that were similar to what you saw. You probably observed free play, outdoor play, snacks/lunch, naptime, and transitions. Then think for a bit about what it would be like to be a teacher or a child in that program.

Jot down some of your impressions here.

How I would feel if I were a teacher in the program I visited:

How I would feel if I were a child in the program I visited:

_____

_____

_____

_____

_____

_____

_____

What did you see that was similar to your program (or similar between different programs)?

_____

_____

_____

_____

_____

_____

_____

What was different from your program (or different from the other programs you observed)?

_____

_____

_____

_____

_____

_____

_____

You and your Field Advisor can discuss your observations and talk about any questions you may have about the variety of early childhood programs.

If you are not now working full-time with young children, you may have time to visit or even volunteer in several different types of programs. You need to have a really good feel for what happens with young children, and you just can't get it from reading. Use extra paper to write your responses to the same questions for each program.

If you can't schedule a visit, interview a family child care provider, group teacher, or program director. Ask her or him to describe a typical day. Perhaps a copy of the parent contract, statement of program goals and philosophy, or other written materials will help you visualize what happens in the program. Then go back and see whether you can answer the questions about the program.

Each time you visit another program or talk with someone else in the field, you gain a new perspective on what teaching is all about. Most likely you either feel good about your own work or are eager to improve. You either gain new ideas or discover that what you do is so much more creative. **When your Seminar group of CDA Candidates meets, you will see how much you can learn from each other as professionals.**

Part 4 of this unit and the accompanying videotape will give you an even better picture of just what teachers of young children do and how CDAs fit into the broad picture of the entire field of early childhood education.

Who are early childhood educators?

Many teach young children

You probably remember busy days like the one you read about in Part 3. Some are *more* hectic—there could have been an earthquake evacuation, a playground accident, a prospective parent visit, a substitute assistant teacher, or all of these!

Think back to the description of the CDA's day. Try to remember the day you visited another program. Review what you saw on the video. Did you see how some of the qualities of a good teacher were put to use? Now let's pull together all of the information you have gathered so far to see what good teachers do.

Teachers of young children . . .

. . . prepare the environment to create learning opportunities—you set the stage for children to learn through play:

You prepare art supplies for children to use in their own ways.

You select toys and materials that present problems for children to solve.

You plan field trips to familiar and interesting new spots.

You read picture books and have paper and markers so children can write their own stories.

You extend children's play by posing open-ended questions or introducing props used in many cultures and jobs.

You choose many types of music to listen and move to.

You give children quiet places to be alone, and other spaces to be together with their friends.

. . . have reasonable expectations—you know how children grow and learn, so you know wha⁺ each child in your group is trying to understand and do.

You know that children work on different skills during each age range.

You are aware of the strengths and weaknesses of each child.

You know the values of the culture(s) within the group and your community. You know when children need support and when you can stretch their thinking. Self-concepts are built in positive ways each day.

. . . offer appropriate activities—you select themes and activities that are a good match for children's development and experiences. Projects have just enough challenge for children to be successful.

What teachers of young children do

- prepare the environment to create learning opportunities
- have reasonable expectations
- offer appropriate activities
- provide time for children to be with each other and with loving adults
- are eager to learn more about children and teaching

. . . **provide lots of time for children to be with each other and with loving adults**—children learn how to get along well with people when they play with and solve problems with others. They also need time alone.

. . . **are eager to learn more about children and teaching**—you are ready to adopt sound new ideas about teaching. You want those ideas to be based on research, theory, and practical experiences of others who keep children's long-range development in mind. You are not easily misled by self-proclaimed experts.

You learn at least some key words in each language spoken by the families in your program.

You become better at working with parents. You stand up for what you know is fair for children and families.

Early childhood educators have lots of different jobs in various places. One goal of our profession is to ensure that the care and education of young children is in the hands of people who are well trained.

Early childhood education is more than teaching

Because you are on your way to becoming a CDA, this year of study concentrates on teaching young children. However, as you probably are aware, not everyone in our field teaches children. Regardless of what you do, there are many issues you need to know about that face our profession.

Let's take a brief look at the broader early childhood field.

Enjoy the variety of careers

Early childhood educators have lots of different jobs in various places.

Some teach young children or assist lead teachers. Others direct programs, plan curriculums for children, and supervise staff. Many others train teachers in colleges, workshops, and through books, journals, and videotapes, for example.

Working with parents, such as home visitors do, is another major area of our field.

Still others are researchers, finding new insights about how children grow and learn.

Some write children's books or produce children's television. Others may develop learning materials, design special clothing or equipment for differently abled children, or set up a variety of recreation programs for young children.

Many people are involved in government, perhaps in licensing child care or working on legislation to improve the lives of children and families.

Some work in educational sales or as consumer advocates.

Others work "outside" the field but need training in early childhood education or child development, such as medical staff, children's librarians, and social workers.

Where you work can also vary. Some early childhood educators work in offices, some in stores, some in churches, some in universities, some in their own homes. You have a lot of choices!

To be qualified for most of these positions, you must have a credential, such as the CDA, or a diploma such as an associate or bachelor's degree. Others require even more years of college training, such as advanced degrees. Many also require experience in teaching young children.

Although it is possible to be hired to work with young children while you are still in a training program, one goal of our profession is to ensure that the care and education of young children is in the hands of people who are well trained.

The National Association for the Education of Young Children (NAEYC) has identified four early childhood professional development levels. (See page 21.) Each level requires an increasing amount of education and/or experience. NAEYC is seeking agreement from the field on these, so keep up with new ideas about professional development and experience as they are published.

Each of these levels also varies greatly in salaries paid. You are probably aware that most paychecks in early childhood education are small compared to the amount of work and responsibility. Advocating for better salaries and working conditions is part of being a professional, too.

Get to know your colleagues better. **Interview someone who is in the field but works in a different type of job.** Perhaps you have met or heard about a person with an interesting career through your local early childhood association. You might choose a curriculum specialist, or a program director, or someone who writes books for children or parents. Consider someone from a cultural group different from yours, or who works with children speaking a home language other than English.

Your Field Advisor can help you locate people and figure out what to ask in your interview. Here are some questions you might talk about. Add your own questions to this list. **Then write the person's responses here after your interview.**

Interviewee _____

_____

Type of work _____

_____

_____

_____

Questions begin on page 22.

NAEYC Early Childhood Professional Categories

Early Childhood Professional Level I

Step 1   Successful completion of a program conforming to the Council for Early Childhood Professional Recognition's CDA Model Curriculum OR completion of a comprehensive training program that prepares an individual to successfully seek the CDA Credential.

Step 2   CDA with a total of 30 professional units* in ECE/CD and 1 year of early childhood work experience.

Early Childhood Professional Level II

Step 1   Successful completion of an associate degree from a program conforming to NAEYC guidelines for associate degree granting institutions OR an associate degree plus 30 units of professional studies in early childhood development/education including 300 hours of supervised teaching experience, preferably in an accredited program.

Step 2   Above plus 10 additional professional units in ECE/CD and 2 years of early childhood work experience.

Early Childhood Professional Level III

Step 1   Successful completion of a baccalaureate degree from a program conforming to NAEYC guidelines for baccalaureate programs OR a baccalaureate degree with 45 professional units in early childhood development/education including 300 hours of supervised teaching experience, with 150 hours each for two of the following three age groups: infants and toddlers, 3- to 5-year-olds, or primary grades.

Step 2   Above plus 15 additional professional units in ECE/CD and 3 years of early childhood work experience.

Early Childhood Professional Level IV

Step 1   Successful completion of an advanced degree program meeting NAEYC guidelines for advanced degree programs.

Step 2   Above plus 20 additional professional units in ECE/CD and 5 years of early childhood work experience.

Professional unit defined as 16 classroom hours or 1 semester hour of college-level coursework.

What are some of the challenges of your work?

Always keeping the child interested
Proper discipline for certain situations that occur.

What do you find most rewarding?

Watching the children learning & growing in all the positive ways

What do you find least rewarding?

How can we work together to make lives better for young children?

Flexibility and awareness
Always moving in a positive direction

What education and experiences are needed to do your job?

Everything

There are so many different types of early childhood educators. **Make a list here of other people that you would like to talk with in our field—either their names or job titles.**

Sometime while you are working on your CDA, you may have a chance to get to know these people. One of them may be your Seminar Instructor. Another might be your Council

Representative. Still others may be active in your local early childhood association. We all learn so much when we share ideas with other professionals.

Advocate for better wages and working conditions

Early childhood educators are proud professionals. However, as an occupational group our wages and working conditions are less than ideal.

In 1989, a large national study of child care teaching staff showed the following:

- Nearly all child care teachers are women.
- Over half earn $5 an hour or less.
- A third receive no paid holidays or vacation.
- Only 1 out of 10 receive paid sick leave.
- Each year, 40% of child care teachers leave their jobs for work in other occupations.

The national organization that conducted this study, the Child Care Employee Project in Oakland, California, believes that if all child care teachers became advocates for improved wages and working conditions, this situation would change. This organization has developed written materials to help accomplish this goal. NAEYC has also organized a campaign called "The Full Cost of Quality" to help develop advocacy strategies. NAEYC suggests as a start, you ask some questions to help find out what salaries and benefits are provided in early childhood programs in your community.

What are average starting wages?

NAEYC's Full Cost of Quality campaign

How do they compare with the wages received by other professionals in the community who have similar levels of educational preparation and responsibility?

_____

_____

_____

Is there a career ladder that provides opportunities for career advancement and encourages individuals to continue to work with children?

_____

_____

_____

Is there health insurance? Ample sick leave?

Are there retirement benefits?

If you need help in getting this information, ask your Field Advisor. It is important to be active in helping improve the status of the profession, a topic explored again in Unit 7.

Meet legal requirements

Every state has its own laws about standards for early childhood programs and teacher qualifications.

For programs. In some states it may be mandatory for every group program and family child care home to be licensed.

In other states, family child care registration is optional, the number of children enrolled may make a difference, or some group programs may be exempt from licensing (such as Head Start, church programs, or those sponsored by school districts).

You need to know just how your program, or any other place you might want to work, fits into the whole picture of the regulation of programs for children from birth through age 5.

Talk with the program director where you work or volunteer, or call your local social services or health department, to find out about your local and state laws.

What state and/or local agencies regulate group programs in your state? Who regulates family child care programs? Write the agency name(s), address(es), and phone number(s) here.

Group programs

Family child care

Which group child care programs in your state must be licensed?

_____

_____

_____

_____

_____

_____

Which programs are excluded?

_____

_____

_____

_____

_____

Contact the agency that regulates group programs. Ask for a copy of your state's group program licensing requirements.

Look through every section and especially study the sections about the curriculum and teaching materials. Do the requirements seem very strict? Or could almost any program meet the standards?

_____

_____

_____

_____

_____

Call or write the agency that governs family child care providers in your state or county. Ask for a copy of those regulations.

Save your copies of these regulations for your Professional Resource File. (You will begin to build this file after you have met with your Field Advisor.)

Regardless of the type of program you work in, you need to know about family child care. Most families who use out-of-home care still prefer family child care, especially for very young children.

Does your state or county regulate family child care providers? _____

_____

_____

Do the standards seem easy to meet or fairly strict? _____

_____

_____

If you work in Head Start, read through all the *Head Start Program Performance Standards.* List here some of the strengths and weaknesses your Head Start program has in meeting these standards.

_____

_____

_____

_____

_____

Perhaps you work in a program that is supported at least in part by another agency that also has regulations to be met—maybe the program is housed in an elementary school or church, or you receive Children's Aid Society funds.

Find out from your program director what additional requirements your program must meet. Jot them down in this space.

For teachers. Just as requirements for programs differ by state, so do regulations about teacher qualifications. For example, a lead teacher in some states might need a 4-year college degree in early childhood education or a related field and even a year or 2 of experience, while in other states less training is required.

In many states, people can only be responsible for a group of children if they are 18 or older. It is fairly common that people who work with young children cannot have a criminal record.

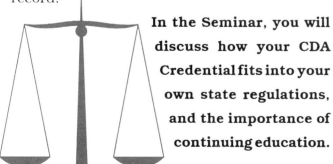

In the Seminar, you will discuss how your CDA Credential fits into your own state regulations, and the importance of continuing education.

Observe professional ethics

Perhaps you feel that requirements for teachers and programs are unnecessary or that they just cause endless paperwork and red tape. Maybe you are uncertain about the value of child care regulation. You may find it hard to understand how anyone could want to take advantage of young children. Perhaps you feel that government should not interfere with child care.

It might help you to see the value of mandatory licensing if you think in these terms:

Laws governing teachers and programs for young children offer at least a minimum level of consumer protection.

Cats and dogs need rabies shots. Ice cream vendors must have a license. Even your car is registered. Surely children, who are so precious and vulnerable, deserve to be protected!

Parents, teachers, programs, and governments can work together to provide good care for our most vulnerable citizens.

Conscientious teachers and programs welcome regulation and want to help their states work toward laws that will help to ensure only the best care for young children.

Legal requirements have been a controversial topic for many years and will be just one of the ethical issues you must face in our field. Some other typical problems, with no easy solutions, might be these:

- What do you do when parents ask you to spank their children?
- How do you handle suspected child abuse?

- How do you treat confidential information innocently passed on by a child that could be damaging to the parents?

- What should you do if your program has more children than its license allows?

You will have the opportunity to learn more about how to deal with issues such as these during your CDA Seminar.

As a CDA, you are expected to agree to the CDA Statement of Ethical Conduct and NAEYC's Statement of Commitment printed at the end of Unit 1. This statement is just the beginning of your commitment to the well-being of young children. All during your career, you will struggle with ethical dilemmas similar to the ones you will touch on during your CDA training.

Fortunately, you are not alone in your struggle to do what is right for children. Professional organizations such as those listed on page 29 are working to improve the quality of staff and programs for all young children.

The best way to keep up with professional issues is to be a member of an association. You may not be ready to join yet, but **write to one or two of the groups listed on page 29 and ask them to send you information.**

You will be off to a good start on finding the right association for you. **Name the two associations you have contacted.**

_____

_____

Save the information you receive from them in your Professional Resource File.

You have now completed Unit 1 of the self-study phase of your work toward your CDA. Turn to page 387 of these materials. There you will find your CDA progress record. Check off the box for the Unit 1 Self-Study.

You know that work with young children is not an easy job. Teaching—whether in a group program or as a family child care provider—is much more enjoyable and much more professional when you know a lot about children. You need to know about children in general and about those you work with in particular.

The next unit of *Essentials* will summarize for you what generations of people have learned about how children grow. Children's development unfolds before your eyes every day when you know what to look for!

Resources for more information

"Careers in early childhood education." Washington, DC: National Association for the Education of Young Children, 1983.

"Critical questions: What you should know about your child's teachers." (1990). Oakland, CA: Child Care Employee Project.

Early childhood teacher education guidelines: Basic and advanced. Washington, DC: National Association for the Education of Young Children, 1990.

Feeney, S. (1987). Ethical case studies for NAEYC reader response. *Young Children, 42*(4), 24–25.

Feeney, S., Christensen, D., & Moravick, E. (1987). *Who am I in the lives of children? An introduction to teaching young children.* Columbus, OH: Merrill.

Feeney, S., & Sysko, L. (1986). Professional ethics in early childhood education: Survey results. *Young Children, 42*(1), 15–20.

"The full cost of quality in early childhood programs: What you should know, what you can do." Washington, DC: National Association for the Education of Young Children, 1990.

Guidelines for early childhood education programs in associate degree granting institutions. Washington, DC: National Association for the Education of Young Children, 1985.

Head Start program performance standards. Washington, DC: Head Start Bureau, U.S. Department of Health and Human Services, 1984.

Hendrick, J. (1987). *Why teach? A first look at working with young children.* Washington, DC: National Association for the Education of Young Children.

Katz, L.G. (1984). The professional early childhood teacher. *Young Children, 39*(5), 3–10.

Modigliani, K., Reiff, M., & Jones, S. (1987). *Opening your door to children: How to start a family day care program.* Washington, DC: National Association for the Education of Young Children.

NAEYC Model of Early Childhood Professional Development. Washington, DC: National Association for the Education of Young Children, in press.

"NAEYC position statement on licensing and regulation of early childhood programs in centers and family day care homes." Washington, DC: National Association for the Education of Young Children, 1987.

Seaver, J.W., Cartwright, C.A., Ward, C.B., & Heasley, C.A. (1984). *Careers with young children: Making your decision.* Washington, DC: National Association for the Education of Young Children.

Whitebook, M., Pemberton, C., Lombardi, J., & Galinsky, E. (1990). *From the floor: Raising child care salaries.* Oakland, CA: Child Care Employee Project.

Willer, B. (1989). *The growing crisis in child care: Quality, compensation, and affordability in early childhood programs.* Washington, DC: National Association for the Education of Young Children.

Worthy work, worthless wages. Oakland, CA: Child Care Employee Project, 1989.

Membership and resource organizations

**Association for Childhood Education
   International**
11141 Georgia Avenue, Suite 200
Wheaton, MD 20902
301-942-2443

Child Care Employee Project
6536 Telegraph Avenue
Suite A201
Oakland, CA 94609
415-653-9889

**National Association of Bilingual
   Education**
Union Center Plaza
810 First Street, N.E., 3rd Floor
Washington, DC 20002-4205
202-898-1829

**National Association for the Education of
   Young Children**
1509 16th Street, NW
Washington, DC 20036
202-232-8777   800-424-2460

National Association for Family Day Care
1331-A Pennsylvania Ave., NW
Suite 348
Washington, DC 20005
800-359-3817

**National Black Child Development
   Institute**
1023 15th Street, NW, Suite 600
Washington, DC 20005
202-387-1281

**National Center for Clinical Infant
   Programs**
2000 14th Street North, Suite 380
Arlington, VA 22201
703-528-4300

National Child Care Association
1029 Railroad Street
Conyers, GA 30207
404-922-8198   800-543-7161

National Head Start Association
1220 King Street
Suite 200
Alexandria, VA 22314
703-739-0875

OMEP National Committee
1341 G Street, NW, Suite 400
Washington, DC 20005-3105
202-265-9090

Southern Association on Children Under Six
P.O. Box 5403 Brady Station
Little Rock, AR 72215-5403
501-663-0353

National Association for the Education of Young Children

Statement of Commitment

As an individual who works with young children, I commit myself to furthering the values of early childhood education as they are reflected in the NAEYC Code of Ethical Conduct. To the best of my ability I will

Ensure that programs for young children are based on current knowledge of child development and early childhood education.

Respect and support families in their task of nurturing children.

Respect colleagues in the field of early childhood education and support them in maintaining the NAEYC Code of Ethical Conduct.

Serve as an advocate for children, their families, and their teachers in community and society.

Maintain high standards of professional conduct.

Recognize how personal values, opinions, and biases can affect professional judgment.

Be open to new ideas and be willing to learn from the suggestions of others.

Continue to learn, grow, and contribute as a professional.

Honor the ideals and principles of the NAEYC Code of Ethical Conduct.

NAEYC Code of Ethical Conduct

Preamble

NAEYC recognizes that many daily decisions required of those who work with young children are of a moral and ethical nature. The NAEYC Code of Ethical Conduct offers guidelines for responsible behavior and sets forth a common basis for resolving the principal ethical dilemmas encountered in early childhood education. The primary focus is on daily practice with children and their families in programs for children from birth to 8 years of age: preschools, child care centers, family child care homes, kindergartens, and primary classrooms. Many of the provisions also apply to specialists who do not work directly with children, including program administrators, parent educators, college professors, and child care licensing specialists.

Standards of ethical behavior in early childhood education are based on commitment to core values that are deeply rooted in the history of our field. We have committed ourselves to

- Appreciating childhood as a unique and valuable stage of the human life cycle
- Basing our work with children on knowledge of child development
- Appreciating and supporting the close ties between the child and family
- Recognizing that children are best understood in the context of family, culture, and society
- Respecting the dignity, worth, and uniqueness of each individual (child, family member, and colleague)
- Helping children and adults achieve their full potential in the context of relationships that are based on trust, respect, and positive regard

The Code sets forth a conception of our professional responsibilities in four sections, each addressing an arena of professional relationships: (1) children, (2) families, (3) colleagues, and (4) community and society. Each section includes an introduction to the primary responsibilities of the early childhood practitioner in that arena, a set of ideals pointing in the direction of exemplary professional practice, and a set of principles defining practices that are required, prohibited, and permitted.

The ideals reflect the aspirations of practitioners. The principles are intended to guide conduct and assist practitioners in resolving ethical dilemmas encountered in the field. There is not necessarily a corresponding principle for each ideal. Both ideals and principles are intended to direct practitioners to those questions which, when responsibly answered, will provide the basis for conscientious decisionmaking. While the Code provides specific direction for addressing some ethical dilemmas, many others will require the practitioner to combine the guidance of the Code with sound professional judgment.

The ideals and principles in this Code present a shared conception of professional responsibility that affirms our commitment to the core values of our field. The Code publicly acknowledges the responsibilities that we in the field have assumed and in so doing supports ethical behavior in our work. Practitioners who face ethical dilemmas are urged to seek guidance in the applicable parts of this Code and in the spirit that informs the whole.

Section I: Ethical responsibilities to children

Childhood is a unique and valuable stage in the life cycle. Our paramount responsibility is to provide safe, healthy, nurturing, and responsive settings for children. We are committed to supporting children's development by cherishing individual differences, by helping them learn to live and work cooperatively, and by promoting their self-esteem.

Ideals

I-1.1—To be familiar with the knowledge base of early childhood education and to keep current through continuing education and in-service training.

I-1.2—To base program practices upon current knowledge in the field of child development and related disciplines and upon particular knowledge of each child.

I-1.3—To recognize and respect the uniqueness and the potential of each child.

I-1.4—To appreciate the special vulnerability of children.

I-1.5—To create and maintain safe and healthy settings that foster children's social, emotional, intellectual, and physical development and that respect their dignity and their contributions.

I-1.6—To support the right of children with special needs to participate, consistent with their ability, in regular early childhood programs.

Principles

P-1.1—Above all, we shall not harm children. We shall not participate in practices that are disrespectful, degrading, dangerous, exploitative, intimidating, psychologically damaging, or physically harmful to children. *This principle has precedence over all others in this Code.*

P-1.2—We shall not participate in practices that discriminate against children by denying benefits, giving special advantages, or excluding them from programs or activities on the basis of their race, religion, sex, national origin, or the status, behavior, or beliefs of their parents. (This principle does not apply to programs which have a lawful mandate to provide services to a particular population of children.)

P-1.3—We shall involve all of those with relevant knowledge (including staff and parents) in decisions concerning a child.

P-1.4—When, after appropriate efforts have been made with a child and the family, the child still does not appear to be benefiting from a program, we shall communicate our concern to the family in a positive way and offer them assistance in finding a more suitable setting.

P-1.5—We shall be familiar with the symptoms of child abuse and neglect and know and follow community procedures and state laws that protect children against abuse and neglect.

P-1.6—When we have evidence of child abuse or neglect, we shall report the evidence to the appropriate community agency and follow up to ensure that appropriate action has been taken. When possible, parents will be informed that the referral has been made.

P-1.7—When another person tells us of their suspicion that a child is being abused or neglected but we lack evidence, we shall assist that person in taking appropriate action to protect the child.

P-1.8—When a child protective agency fails to provide adequate protection for abused or neglected children, we acknowledge a collective ethical responsibility to work toward improvement of these services.

P-1.9—When we become aware of a practice or situation that endangers the health or safety of children, but has not been previously known to do so, we have an ethical responsibility to inform those who can remedy the situation and who can keep other children from being similarly endangered.

Section II: Ethical responsibilities to families

Families are of primary importance in children's development. (The term "family" may include others, besides parents, who are responsibly involved with the child.) Because the family and the early childhood educator have a common interest in the child's welfare, we acknowledge a primary responsibility to bring about collaboration between the home and school in ways that enhance the child's development.

Ideals

I-2.1—To develop relationships of mutual trust with the families we serve.

I-2.2—To acknowledge and build upon strengths and competencies as we support families in their task of nurturing children.

I-2.3—To respect the dignity of each family and its culture, customs, and beliefs.

I-2.4—To respect families' childrearing values and their right to make decisions for their children.

I-2.5—To interpret each child's progress to parents within the framework of a developmental perspective and to help families understand and appreciate the value of developmentally appropriate early childhood programs.

I-2.6—To help family members improve their understanding of their children and to enhance their skills as parents.

I-2.7—To participate in building support networks for families by providing them with opportunities to interact with program staff and families.

Principles

P-2.1—We shall not deny family members access to their child's classroom or program setting.

P-2.2—We shall inform families of program philosophy, policies, and personnel qualifications, and explain why we teach as we do.

P-2.3—We shall inform families of, and, when appropriate, involve them in policy decisions.

P-2.4—We shall inform families of, and, when appropriate, involve them in significant decisions affecting their child.

P-2.5—We shall inform the family of accidents involving their child, of risks such as exposures to contagious disease that may result in infection, and of events that might result in psychological damage.

P-2.6—We shall not permit or participate in research that could in any way hinder the education or development of the children in our programs. Families shall be fully informed of any proposed research projects involving their children and shall have the opportunity to give or withhold consent.

P-2.7—We shall not engage in or support exploitation of families. We shall not use our relationship with a family for private advantage or personal gain, or enter into relationships with family members that might impair our effectiveness in working with children.

P-2.8—We shall develop written policies for the protection of confidentiality and the disclosure of children's records. The policy documents shall be made available to all program personnel and families. Disclosure of children's records beyond family members, program personnel, and consultants having an obligation of confidentiality shall require familial consent (except in cases of abuse or neglect).

P-2.9—We shall maintain confidentiality and shall respect the family's right to privacy, refraining from disclosure of confidential information and intrusion into family life. However, when we are concerned about a child's welfare, it is permissible to reveal confidential information to agencies and individuals who may be able to act in the child's interest.

P-2.10—In cases where family members are in conflict, we shall work openly, sharing our observations of the child, to help all parties involved make informed decisions. We shall refrain from becoming an advocate for one party.

P-2.11—We shall be familiar with and appropriately use community resources and professional services that support families. After a referral has been made, we shall follow up to ensure that services have been adequately provided.

Section III: Ethical responsibilities to colleagues

In a caring, cooperative work place human dignity is respected, professional satisfaction is promoted, and positive relationships are modeled. Our primary responsibility in this arena is to establish and maintain settings and relationships that support productive work and meet professional needs.

A—Responsibilities to co-workers

Ideals

I-3A.1—To establish and maintain relationships of trust and cooperation with co-workers.

I-3A.2—To share resources and information with co-workers.

I-3A.3—To support co-workers in meeting their professional needs and in their professional development.

I-3A.4—To accord co-workers due recognition of professional achievement.

Principles

P-3A.1—When we have concern about the professional behavior of a co-worker, we shall first let that person know of our concern and attempt to resolve the matter collegially.

P-3A.2—We shall exercise care in expressing views regarding the personal attributes or professional conduct of co-workers. Statements should be based on firsthand knowledge and relevant to the interests of children and programs.

B—Responsibilities to employers

Ideals

I-3B.1—To assist the program in providing the highest quality of service.

I-3B.2—To maintain loyalty to the program and uphold its reputation.

Principles

P-3B.1—When we do not agree with program policies, we shall first attempt to effect change through constructive action within the organization.

P-3B.2—We shall speak or act on behalf of an organization only when authorized. We shall take care to note when we are speaking for the organization and when we are expressing a personal judgment.

C—Responsibilities to employees

Ideals

I-3C.1—To promote policies and working conditions that foster competence, well-being, and self-esteem in staff members.

I-3C.2—To create a climate of trust and candor that will enable staff to speak and act in the best interests of children, families, and the field of early childhood education.

I-3C.3—To strive to secure an adequate livelihood for those who work with or on behalf of young children.

Principles

P-3C.1—In decisions concerning children and programs, we shall appropriately utilize the training, experience, and expertise of staff members.

P-3C.2—We shall provide staff members with working conditions that permit them to carry out their responsibilities, timely and non-threatening evaluation procedures, written grievance procedures, constructive feedback, and opportunities for continuing professional development and advancement.

P-3C.3—We shall develop and maintain comprehensive written personnel policies that define program standards and, when applicable, that specify the extent to which employees are accountable for their conduct outside the work place. These policies shall be given to new staff members and shall be available for review by all staff members.

P-3C.4—Employees who do not meet program standards shall be informed of areas of concern and, when possible, assisted in improving their performance.

P-3C.5—Employees who are dismissed shall be informed of the reasons for their termination. When a dismissal is for cause, justification must be based on evidence of inadequate or inappropriate behavior that is accurately documented, current, and available for the employee to review.

P-3C.6—In making evaluations and recommendations, judgments shall be based on fact and relevant to the interests of children and programs.

P-3C.7—Hiring and promotion shall be based solely on a person's record of accomplishment and ability to carry out the responsibilities of the position.

P-3C.8—In hiring, promotion, and provision of training, we shall not participate in any form of discrimination based on race, religion, sex, national origin, handicap, age, or sexual preference. We shall be familiar with laws and regulations that pertain to employment discrimination.

Section IV: Ethical responsibilities to community and society

Early childhood programs operate within a context of an immediate community made up of families and other institutions concerned with children's welfare. Our responsibilities to the community are to provide programs that meet its needs and to cooperate with agencies and professions that share responsibility for children.

Because the larger society has a measure of responsibility for the welfare and protection of children, and because of our specialized expertise in child development, we acknowledge an obligation to serve as a voice for children everywhere.

Ideals
I-4.1—To provide the community with high-quality, culturally sensitive programs and services.

I-4.2—To promote cooperation among agencies and professions concerned with the welfare of young children, their families, and their teachers.

I-4.3—To work, through education, research, and advocacy, toward an environmentally safe world in which all children are adequately fed, sheltered, and nurtured.

I-4.4—To work, through education, research, and advocacy, toward a society in which all young children have access to quality programs.

I-4.5—To promote knowledge and understanding of young children and their needs. To work toward greater social acknowledgment of children's rights and greater social acceptance of responsibility for their well-being.

I-4.6—To support policies and laws that promote the well-being of children and families. To oppose those that impair their well-being. To cooperate with other individuals and groups in these efforts.

I-4.7—To further the professional development of the field of early childhood education and to strengthen its commitment to realizing its core values as reflected in this Code.

Principles

P-4.1—We shall communicate openly and truthfully about the nature and extent of services that we provide.

P-4.2—We shall not accept or continue to work in positions for which we are personally unsuited or professionally unqualified. We shall not offer services that we do not have the competence, qualifications, or resources to provide.

P-4.3—We shall be objective and accurate in reporting the knowledge upon which we base our program practices.

P-4.4—We shall cooperate with other professionals who work with children and their families.

P-4.5—We shall not hire or recommend for employment any person who is unsuited for a position with respect to competence, qualifications, or character.

P-4.6—We shall report the unethical or incompetent behavior of a colleague to a supervisor when informal resolution is not effective.

P-4.7—We shall be familiar with laws and regulations that serve to protect the children in our programs.

P-4.8—We shall not participate in practices which are in violation of laws and regulations that protect the children in our programs.

P-4.9—When we have evidence that an early childhood program is violating laws or regulations protecting children, we shall report it to persons responsible for the program. If compliance is not accomplished within a reasonable time, we will report the violation to appropriate authorities who can be expected to remedy the situation.

P-4.10—When we have evidence that an agency or a professional charged with providing services to children, families, or teachers is failing to meet its obligations, we acknowledge a collective ethical responsibility to report the problem to appropriate authorities or to the public.

P-4.11—When a program violates or requires its employees to violate this Code, it is permissible, after fair assessment of the evidence, to disclose the identity of that program.

Copyright © 1989 by the National Association for the Education of Young Children. Reprinted with permission.

Ways to study how children grow and learn

Part 1

Why do you need to know how children grow and learn?

Family picture albums. Baby books. Children's heights marked on the door each birthday. Nearly every family keeps a record of how its members grow and change. Have you looked at your family pictures lately? How did your family look 5 years ago? What a difference a short time makes!

You know young children grow so fast! Babies seem to change overnight. Preschoolers keep outgrowing their clothes. As a parent, teacher, or family child care provider, you may watch whole families of children grow from infants into responsible young people.

You have been watching how children grow all your life. Now you want to become a Child Development Associate. As you work toward

your CDA, you will become even more curious about how children develop.

If you want to be a good teacher, you must know what you can reasonably expect of the children in your care. Otherwise, how will you know what activities to plan . . . what toys to choose . . . how to handle "difficult stages" . . . how to foster children's self-motivation . . . how to nurture culturally important behaviors . . . how to help children feel good about themselves . . . how to help children develop self-control . . . how to answer parents' questions . . . and how to improve your work?

All around the world, people have been studying how children grow and learn. Some of these people are parents. Many are professors at universities. Others are teachers. What they have observed will help you become a better teacher.

We have condensed some of the most important information about how children grow and learn in the chart in Part 2 of this Unit. All of the ages given are approximate — some children will achieve these milestones earlier, some later —

but most normally developing children will fall into the range listed.

Each part of the chart also has some extra space for you to fill in. There are probably other developmental milestones that are especially important to you or to the cultural groups with whom you work. Add them where they are appropriate.

This is your chart—make it work for you. Refer to these next few pages often. Use them as you watch the video for Unit 2. Keep the chart handy. Make a copy before it gets worn out. Everything you do with young children is based on what you know about how children grow and learn.

Part 2

What are the characteristics of children from birth through age 5?

You see growing up takes time

RUSH! RUSH! RUSH! Everyone seems in such a hurry for their children to be the first . . . the first to walk . . . the first to be out of diapers . . . the first to learn to read. What IS the hurry?

Every child is different. You know that, but how do you respond when a parent asks you, "Why doesn't my 5-year-old know his ABCs

yet?" or "All the other babies are crawling. What's wrong with my 9-month-old?" Don't worry about preparing children for kindergarten. Instead, use your energy to make sure the group has a really good year being 4- and 5-year-olds.

No one can hurry or do much to change children's natural growth patterns. Some children are well coordinated, while others have

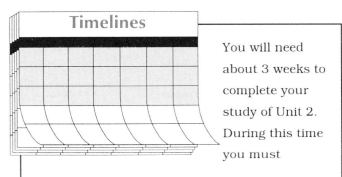

Timelines

You will need about 3 weeks to complete your study of Unit 2. During this time you must

1 Prepare for conference with your Field Advisor to discuss three topics (what are the characteristics of children from birth through age 5, value of and methods for observing children's behavior, and how observations of children and adult-child interactions can be used to teach appropriately).

2 Complete two assignments (add developmental milestones to the chart and try four observation tools), and three entries for the Professional Resource File.

3 Complete three assignments for Seminar (choose an observation tool to demonstrate, collect samples of developmental checklist/screening instruments, and resource agencies for developmental disabilities).

4 View the accompanying videotape using the Viewer's Guide.

less control of their changing bodies. Some children use lots of words right away, but others are content with just a few. Some children are friendly, and others are shy. Some can figure out problems quickly, yet others give up easily. Children may spurt ahead for a while in one area, while they seem to be "on hold" in another.

Children grow at their own pace, and that pace cannot be rushed. What can make a difference in children's growth?

- tendencies they inherit (some families have lots of tall people, for example),
- nutrition and good health (healthy foods encourage brains and bodies to grow),
- what families value (verbal and/or nonverbal expression), and
- what children have done (for example, if a child's home is on one floor, the child will have little practice with steps).

However, most of all, children need lots of time, lots of experiences, and lots of skilled people like you to become the best they can be. Respect each stage of development and have a good time with it. Children grow so fast!

You use developmental principles

Your chart is divided into seven major areas in which young children change rapidly:

- children show interest in others
- children become more aware of themselves
- children's muscles grow stronger and coordination improves
- children learn to communicate
- children become aware of the world
- children solve problems and use tools
- children express feelings

You may have read other books that put these categories together into four areas of development: *physical, social, emotional,* and *cognitive or intellectual/language.* There are many ways to look at different aspects of how children grow.

Whatever words you use to describe these areas, always remember that ***all of the categories overlap.*** For example, there is no one part of a child's brain or body reserved just for feelings. When children run, they use more than just muscles.

You must also keep one other point in mind: ***No child will ever develop exactly according to this chart.*** The areas of development overlap, and so do the age groups. We have sorted out just a few of the most important milestones that you can easily see in young children.

Your chart is divided into two columns:

- what children are usually like at each age
- how you can help children make the most of their age

Be sure to add other milestones that seem especially appropriate for the children with whom you work. There are many, many more than we could fit into this book!

These are just a few milestones to watch for as children grow and learn. The ages tell you when to expect normally developing children to begin to achieve these milestones.

Milestones of development—Birth through age 5

The early months (birth to 8 months)

What children are usually like at this age

Children show interest in others

Newborns like to look at people's faces. They love to hear people talk and sing. Within the first 2 weeks they can recognize and prefer the sight, smell, and sound of the person who takes care of them.

Babies soon smile real smiles. They look you in the eye and then look away. Smile back. Say, "What a wonderful smile you have!"

Older babies in this age range kick, smile, and/or hold out their arms when they know you are about to pick them up or to feed them.

Older babies love to play with people more than any toy.

How adults can help children make the most of this age

Hold babies close. Look at babies in the eye. Talk. Sing.

Talk to babies as you approach. Tell babies what you are about to do. Tell babies what you are doing. "Here I come. It's time for a clean diaper now. Here's the fresh diaper, just for you. . . ." Pick babies up. Carry on a conversation with babies in their home language while you hold them to feed them.

PLAY with babies. Dance. Take walks with the stroller. Show them what you are doing. Sing. Make up poems. Read stories. Play games like "Peek-a-Boo" and "This Little Piggy."

What children are like

Children become more aware of themselves

Babies may suck their fingers or hands. Soon they watch their hands in fascination.

Babies may move their hands in front of their faces as if to protect themselves when something comes close.

When you touch them, babies look to the place where they were touched.

Older babies in this age range reach for toys. They begin to grasp them with their fingers.

Older babies can clasp their hands together and wiggle their fingers. They hold onto their toes. They watch themselves in a mirror.

Older babies try to make things happen: squeak a toy, push a ball.

How adults can help

Give babies time to play. Comment on what they are doing. "Look! You've found your hands. Dos manos! Your two hands can do so many things. They can. . . ." Use the child's home language.

Be careful not to startle very young babies. Older babies may enjoy some surprises when they feel safe.

Touch babies gently to see how they respond.

Offer toys that are easy for tiny fingers to grasp: texture balls, rattles with narrow handles, spoons.

Talk with babies as they explore their bodies. Place an unbreakable mirror at babies' eye level. Talk about what they see.

Provide toys that babies can rattle, squeak, roll, or push. Firmly but safely attach large jingle bells to booties or wrists. Babies will be thrilled at the sound when they shake their arms or legs.

What children are like

Older babies in this age range usually begin to prefer being around people they know. Adult strangers may frighten them. This is called stranger anxiety. It is a great way to know that children are on target in their emotional and intellectual development.

How adults can help

Make sure babies get to know many friendly people. When you come up to strangers together, help babies feel secure. Talk with babies positively when they are afraid of strangers. Never be critical of such a natural event, such as saying, "Oh, come on, Grandma wants to hold you. What a bad boy to be so scared of Grandma."

Help parents understand that, although this is a difficult period, with experience and time children will again become friendly and will know that their parents will return after they leave.

It is probably not a good idea to put babies in new child care arrangements while they are afraid of strangers. It may be harder for them to adjust.

Give babies plenty of safe, comfortable space to crawl.

What children are like

Children's muscles grow stronger and coordination improves

Young infants have many complex reflexes (natural reactions): They search for something to suck; they hold on when they are about to fall; they turn their heads to breathe better; and they avoid bright lights, strong smells, and pain.

Babies put their hands and every object into their mouths. They begin to reach for everything.

Near the end of this age range, babies love to hold onto and let go of objects again and again. They look at things closely.

Very young babies begin to lift their heads. Later they hold them up. Within the first few months babies roll over. Later they sit up without support. They soon can transfer objects from one hand to another. As they near the age of 8 months, they may begin to creep or crawl.

How adults can help

Watch to see which reflexes babies use.

Safety first: Give babies items that are too large to be swallowed and that can be chewed on safely: rubber dolls or animals, soft plastic household items, plastic or fabric books, fabric toys. Keep objects within babies' reach. Wash toys often so germs don't spread. Offer new items as babies lose interest.

Give babies items that can be dropped without harm.

Safety first: **Before** babies are ready to try to sit up or roll over, make sure they will not hurt themselves when the day arrives. Never leave babies unattended. Roll babies gently back and forth so they feel comfortable with the motion. As soon as babies begin to try to creep or crawl, babyproof every area: cover electrical sockets, latch doors, close off stairways. However, give babies plenty of comfortable space to crawl—a carpeted floor is especially good. Large, firm cushions are fun to crawl on.

What children are like

Children learn to communicate

Babies cry to tell you they are in pain or distress. Sometimes it is impossible to figure out why they cry.

Babies smile or coo to get you to pay attention.

Babies smile at voices. They look intently at faces.

Babies use sounds and movements to express interest or to make things happen.

Older babies begin to babble, both when they are alone and when they are with other people. Later at this stage, they begin to combine babble sounds. They recognize their names, names of familiar people, and names of favorite objects. They may laugh heartily. They listen intently to conversations.

Children become aware of the world

Babies may use a pacifier or suck their thumbs.

How adults can help

Respond quickly but calmly to cries. If you make babies wait, they will cry more when they are older. Try to figure out what might be making babies cry and comfort them.

Smile and respond reassuringly!

Keep talking as long as the child is interested.

Pay attention to what babies tell you. Watch what they do. Some babies drop their food on the floor or push the bottle away when they are finished eating. On the other hand, if babies are showing pleasure, keep up the activity. This is how babies begin to associate sounds with language.

Baby talk is unnecessary. Children will imitate what they hear. Talk about everything using the child's home language in simple, clear sentences.

Allow babies to suck their thumbs or to use a pacifier to comfort themselves.

What children are like

Infants will follow a slowly moving object with their eyes.

About midway during this period, infants will reach for and then begin to hold onto toys.

When older babies drop a toy, they will look for it briefly.

At around 8 months, infants can identify objects from various viewpoints. They will be able to find a toy when they watch you hide it under a blanket.

Children solve problems and use tools

Babies notice their own hands.

Young babies can grasp a rattle when they can see both their hand and the rattle.

Within a few weeks, babies hit or kick something to make a sight or sound continue.

Babies use movement to show you what they want: If they are riding the horse on your leg, they might keep bouncing when they want you to continue giving them a ride.

How adults can help

Hold a bright or black and white object within babies' view and move it slowly from side to side. Hang mobiles above cribs. Prop up books accordion-style on the floor next to babies.

Provide toys babies can hold—rattles with handles, spoons, bracelets.

Play babies' favorite game: "Drop and Pick Up Toys." Talk while you play.

Move babies around to different viewpoints and heights—different rooms, on the floor or cushions, in a crib, and carry them. Play "Peek-a-Boo" with toys hidden by a diaper or blanket.

Talk with babies as they look at their hands.

Put toys within babies' reach.

Hang bells or other objects that make noise above babies' legs so they can kick them. Securely and safely tie jingle bells on babies' ankles or wrists.

Resume any activity when babies indicate they want to continue.

What children are like

How adults can help

Children express feelings

Tiny babies clearly tell you when they are uncomfortable (they may cry or wiggle) or when they are happy and comfortable (they smile, have a contented look).

Pay attention to what babies tell you and follow through to continue the pleasure or get rid of the discomfort (change the diaper, feed the baby).

Babies soon show they prefer to be with the person who usually takes care of them (mother or other primary caregiver) by kicking, smiling, or waving their arms when that person approaches.

Show how delighted you are to be with baby!

When babies are uncomfortable, most can be comforted by familiar adults.

Find out what comforts each baby best.

Babies in the middle of this range smile at people. They enjoy social contact.

Give babies the chance to know people of many ages and cultures. At the children's eye level, hang realistic pictures of people who look the same as and different from the children and families in the group.

Babies make belly laughs.

Babies think lots of things are funny. Experiment to find out what.

Babies fuss when they no longer have a favorite person or toy.

Always say goodbye when you leave a child and make sure parents say goodbye when they leave. This builds trust. Gently explain why the person left, that they will return, and that you understand. Then move on to a new, interesting activity.

Offer a new toy to replace the one that is missing.

What children are like	How adults can help

What children are like

By the end of this period, babies show several emotions: pleasure, anger, anxiety or fear, sadness, joy, excitement, disappointment, exuberance.

Sometime around the age of 7 months, many babies become afraid of strangers (stranger anxiety).

Other milestones. . .

How adults can help

Talk with babies about their feelings. Notice how each baby expresses feelings just a little differently.

Help parents understand this is a normal reaction and should be treated as a sign that the baby is growing up and learning more.

These are just a few milestones to watch for as children grow and learn. The ages tell you about when to expect normally developing children to begin to achieve these milestones.

Crawlers, waddlers, and walkers (8 to 18 months)

What children are usually like at this age

How adults can help children make the most of this age

Children show interest in others
Children may be unhappy when they are with people they don't know well.

Gently introduce strangers. Use as few substitute caregivers as possible in programs.

Babies get to know each other over toys during play.

Some toys are more fun when two children play—rocking boats, balls, toy telephones. Have enough of each toy so children don't have to share.

Waddlers use actions to ask you to do something they want (hand you a wind-up toy, bring you a book).

Have toys that adults can use with children—books, dolls, musical instruments. Do what the child asks you to do.

Older waddlers begin to show a great deal of interest in children their own age.

Give children plenty of time to get to know their friends while they play.

Babies listen intently to everything you say.

Use language you want children to repeat: speak in their home language, no baby talk, no offending words.

Children become more aware of themselves
Babies recognize their own names.

Use children's names often.

What children are like

Babies love to look in mirrors—they smile at themselves, watch themselves move.

Older waddlers know they can make things happen. At the same time, they are not yet aware of what it means to be responsible for their own actions.

Almost-toddlers begin to show they have a strong sense of self. They try to direct the actions of others and frequently say "no" to make sure they have some say about what happens to them.

Older children begin to identify parts of their bodies.

Near the end of this age range, children begin to use me, you, and I when they talk.

How adults can help

Place unbreakable mirrors securely on the wall at children's height.

Tell and show children what happened as a result of what they did. "When you dropped this book, it fell on Kendra's foot. It hurts when a book falls on your foot. How can we help Kendra feel better?"

Give children two good, real choices of things they like: "Would you like some green beans or a piece of cheese?"

Talk with children about parts of their bodies. "See what strong legs it takes to climb up our mountain!" Use fingerplays and songs with actions that include body parts. Talk and sing in the children's home languages. Ask parents to show you simple games from their culture.

Use these words correctly when you talk with children. Show pleasure at new words. Accept children's grammar without correcting them— just repeat it using the correct words.

What children are like

Children's muscles grow stronger and coordination improves

Older infants sit well in chairs, but want to do so only for a short time.

Babies begin to pull themselves up and to stand while holding onto furniture.

Waddlers begin to walk when they hold your hand. Then they walk alone.

Waddlers begin to throw objects.

Climbing up stairs on all fours is a great accomplishment during this period. Going down is more difficult.

Older infants can hold a marker and scribble on paper.

Almost-toddlers can stoop, trot, and even walk backward for a few steps.

How adults can help

Provide comfortable, stable, child-sized chairs. Children enjoy figuring out how to get up and out of chairs.

Have sturdy, securely anchored low tables, shelves, chairs, sofas, and other furniture for children to hold onto while they cruise.

Hold babies' hands when they walk. Rejoice at the early steps!

Keep plenty of soft balls handy to roll, push, drop, and throw.

Climbers with stairs on one side and a slide down the other are great.

Offer children wide, water-based markers and large sheets of plain paper.

Have enough open space for children to move around in. Go outdoors, too. Give children different surfaces for walking: carpet, grass, linoleum, sand.

What children are like

Children learn to communicate

Waddlers understand many more words than they can say. They will look toward objects when you say their names or do actions when requested (if they feel cooperative). Some children may be learning more than one language.

Older babies create long babbled sentences. Soon they use 2 or 3 words clearly.

They shake heads no.

Babies are interested in picture books. They point to objects.

Older children in this age range use sounds instead of crying to get your attention.

How adults can help

Talk with children at every opportunity. Check to see which words they understand. "Where is the piñata?" "Who can find the ball?"

Discuss with parents how you can best support their child's acquisition of two languages.

Carry on a conversation with babbles—take turns talking.

Respect children's "no" when possible.

Provide bright, colorful board books with pictures of familiar objects. Read them together. Ask baby, "Where is the. . .?"

Notice how each child uses a different way to get you to listen or come. Be sure to respond as quickly as possible.

Allow children to feed themselves with a spoon as much as possible.

Ways to study how children grow and learn

What children are like

How adults can help

Children become more aware of the world

Waddlers carry blocks and try to stack them.

Provide blocks in various shapes and sizes.

If you hide a toy under 1 of 2 diapers while babies watch, they can find the toy.

Play hiding games.

These babies are persistent in looking for a hidden toy.

Play searching games.

If a ball rolls under the couch, babies of this age walk around the couch to get the ball.

Make sure your play area has a table or sofa for something to roll under. Have lots of balls to chase and find.

Waddlers help you dress them by pushing their foot into shoes, their arms into sleeves.

Take time to give children the chance to help dress themselves.

Children solve problems and use tools

These older babies continue to move a wind-up car even when it has wound down, or search for the winder on a music box.

Have a few wind-up toys. No battery-operated ones, though. Child-propelled ones are best.

Waddlers bring a stool to reach something.

Use a low, lightweight stool.

Children this age push away things they don't want.

Pay attention to what children want or don't want. Respect their preferences.

Finger foods are great for self-feeding.

Serve bits of fruit, crackers, little chunks of meat, and as many finger foods as possible.

Children creep or walk either to get something or to move away from something they don't like.

Notice what children like and don't like.

What children are like

Older children are even more help in dressing themselves.

Children begin to feed themselves less with their fingers and more with a spoon.

Children begin to drink from a cup without spilling all of it.

By the end of this period, most children feed themselves with a spoon.

Children express feelings

Children are affectionate with loved ones. They hug, smile, run toward, or lean against favorite people.

Older babies are usually upset when they leave their primary caregiver.

Babies begin to show they are angry at people or things. They show their negative feelings by crying, hitting, and grabbing, for example.

How adults can help

Let children do everything they can to dress themselves, but don't let them get frustrated with little buttons, buckles, or snaps.

Allow children to feed themselves with a spoon as much as possible.

Keep a sponge handy. Use cups with lids to start. Only put a little bit of liquid in the cup.

Don't interfere when children are learning new skills such as feeding themselves with a spoon — it may take longer, but children have to do it themselves if they are going to figure it out.

Use lots of hugs. Respond warmly to their affection.

Come up with a ritual that will help ease daily separations. Perhaps first say "good morning" or "buenos días" to the teacher, hang up coats, then walk to the door together, and wave goodbye from the window.

Respect children's anger and negative feelings and help them find constructive ways to deal with them. "You are really mad because you can't play in the water longer. I know you loved it so much. Here is a towel to dry your hands and arms. . . . Let's see who is playing in our hideaway—I hear footsteps on the ramp. Do you?"

Ways to study how children grow and learn

What children are like

Waddlers and walkers are so proud of their new accomplishments.

These older babies show how intensely they are attached to their parents.

Children approaching toddlerhood assert themselves.

Other milestones. . .

How adults can help

Clap hands and be excited along with the children when they learn a new skill.

Give children time to show affection.

Continue to offer real choices so children begin to feel they have some control over what happens to them.

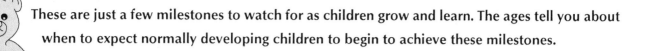

These are just a few milestones to watch for as children grow and learn. The ages tell you about when to expect normally developing children to begin to achieve these milestones.

What children are usually like at this age

Children show interest in others
Toddlers know you are watching them.

Children this age often get upset if other people are in the way when they want something immediately.

At this age, children are just beginning to see that other people have rights and privileges. Sometimes they may share. Most of the time they won't.

Playing with other children becomes more fun.

The benefits of cooperation are evident for the first time: together children can lift a heavy laundry basket, for example.

How adults can help children make the most of this age

Talk with children about what you notice. "I see how easily you put those beads on the string. Would you like some other shapes to string?"

Talk with children about their feelings. Help them find other ways to get what they need. "I know you want to push the fire truck, but Nicole has it now. Shall we ask her if she will be done soon? Or would you like to play with the ambulance?"

Always treat children and co-workers respectfully. Share with others. Children learn to treat others by watching and listening to what you do and say.

Make sure the day has plenty of time for children to play together if they choose to do so.

Encourage activities that require cooperation—rolling balls, carrying a basket of toys, setting the table for snack.

What children are like

Children identify with others of the same sex, age, and race.

Children are becoming increasingly aware of others' feelings.

Children at this age begin to show some self-control in their relationships with others and in meeting their own needs.

Children who are almost 3 years old enjoy activities with two or three other children for short periods of time.

Children become more aware of themselves

Toddlers frequently say "NO!"

Toddlers feel very powerful and creative. They want to explore everything.

How adults can help

Help children be proud of who they are. "How wonderful that your eyes are dark brown! And Marina's are bright blue."

Help children be aware of how what they do affects other children. "Tasha is worried that you will take all the clay and she won't have any left to play with. How can we work it out so you both can play with the clay?"

Commend children when they begin to control themselves. "Jason, how kind of you to wait until Rashad is finished washing his hands."

Keep group times short and involve children actively: do fingerplays, read short stories, play simple group games ("Ring Around the Rosie"). Select some in each of the languages spoken by children in the group. Don't expect all children to join or stay in the group the entire time.

Keep your requests to a minimum. Be prepared to accept "NO!" Offer choices that do not include "NO!" "Which would you like to wear, your red sweater or your blue sweatshirt?"

Give children appropriate chances to have some say about what happens to them: Offer choices of good things to do or eat. Provide activities that guarantee children's success. Have plenty of things to explore, indoors and out.

What children are like

Children begin to define themselves as good/bad, attractive/ugly, and other notions about their value as a person.

During this period, children begin to control their own behavior.

Toddlers use names for themselves and others.

By now, children usually can identify 6 or more of their body parts.

How adults can help

Always focus on children's positive qualities. Sometimes their behavior is not acceptable, but the children are learning self-control. Help them control their behavior by explaining, "Here, we don't hit other children. We talk about how we can solve our problem." Never say, "You're a bad boy." Children live up to (or down to) our expectations.

Support children when they try to control themselves. Point out how proud they feel when they do.

Use children's names frequently.

Continue to use fingerplays, songs, mirrors, and dress-up clothes to help children naturally learn parts of their bodies in their home languages.

Continue to offer new toys, activities, people, and events for children to learn about, and watch their vocabularies grow!

What children are like

Children's muscles grow stronger and coordination improves

Toddlers scribble with markers or crayons

Children at this age walk up and down stairs. They soon will jump off the lowest step.

Twos love to kick balls. They stand on one foot. Older twos may begin to stand and walk on their tiptoes.

Toddlers thread large wooden beads on shoestrings.

Most twos can draw a shape that looks like a circle.

Older children in this age range walk up stairs with one foot on each step.

Older 2-year-olds begin to use scissors.

Late in this stage, children begin to draw back and forth with a crayon.

How adults can help

Provide thick, watercolor markers and wide crayons. Offer large, blank sheets of paper.

Have a set of steps made for children to practice walking up and down them.

Schedule plenty of time for children to choose to work on these skills during play. Use a rubber ball. Play soft music for children to walk on tiptoes.

Tie a knot at one end of the shoestring so beads don't slip off.

Patterns and models of circles are unnecessary. Watch children's own drawing and see circles begin to appear.

Take pride with children when they master steps.

Use blunt-end children's scissors. Make sure some are left-handed. Show children how to carry them. Remember, children's first attempts to cut will be difficult and frustrating—do not expect children to cut on lines they draw until they have had lots of practice at about age 4.

Place blank paper on the floor for children to draw on. Never draw models for children to copy.

What children are like

Sometime during this period, most children will develop daytime toilet control.

Children learn to communicate

Around the age of 2, children may begin to speak in sentences. They usually prefer their home language, but will understand and speak other languages if they have meaningful interactions with speakers of the other language.

Toddlers sit for a short while to listen to a story.

As many as 200 words may be in a toddler's speaking vocabulary. Children learning two languages at the same time become aware that the languages are separate.

Children at this age begin to tell stories and play pretend games.

The uses of many household items are familiar to most children in this age range.

How adults can help

Help children learn to use the toilet when they are interested and when their bodies are ready. Keep the experience a positive one that children can be proud of. Never punish or humiliate children for toileting accidents.

Use more words and longer sentences when you talk with children. Listen for new words. Encourage children to be bilingual by using language in speaking and labeling artwork, for example.

Tell stories to 3 or 4 children with a flannel board or picture book for all to see.

Continue to offer new toys, activities, people, and events for children to learn about—and watch their vocabularies grow! Use both languages in a natural way.

Invite children to tell some stories that begin "Once upon a time. . . ." Encourage children's pretend play by providing everyday props such as kitchens, clothes, miniature people and animals, and small vehicles such as buses and boats. Select typical items from several different cultural groups.

With a small group, begin cooking experiences: spread peanut butter on crackers, cut fruit for a salad, break lettuce for tacos.

What children are like

Children's sentences become longer and more complicated as they approach the age of 3. They begin to talk about what happened during the day.

Children become aware of the world

Toddlers can identify some objects by touch.

Children begin using words about time, such as *tomorrow* and *yesterday*. Toddlers may ask "Is today tomorrow?"

Group members figure out who is missing.

Toddlers become increasingly independent: "Me do it!" "¡Yo puedo hacerlo!"

Older 2-year-olds dress themselves by putting on hats, socks, or slippers.

Children solve problems and use tools

When children this age play with a ring-stacking toy, they don't even try objects that have no holes.

How adults can help

Make what you say interesting! Listen to what children say!

Use a large, soft bag with 3 familiar objects inside. Have children put their hands in and figure out what they are holding without looking. Encourage them to use their home language.

Talk briefly with older twos about what happened yesterday and what you plan to do tomorrow.

Once in a while, ask the children to figure out who is absent. They usually just tell you anyway.

Give children many opportunities to do things themselves—wash tables, put mittens out to dry, park tricycles. They may need reminders to follow through.

Allow time for children to dress themselves as much as they can.

Give children items in addition to the rings and see what they do with them.

What children are like

Children can sort objects into two groups (such as hard and soft or green/verde and red/rojo).

Toddlers can help dress and undress themselves.

Children express feelings
Toddlers frequently are aggressive.

Children in this age range shift moods rapidly. One minute they are stubborn, the next minute they are cooperative.

Fears of the dark or monsters may appear for the first time.

During this period, children begin to have more control when they express emotions.

Children are increasingly aware of their own feelings and those of others.

How adults can help

Use real opportunities to sort (classify): "We need a pile of knives and a pile of forks." "This shelf is for cars and that shelf is for trucks."

Be patient while children learn to dress—soon it will take less of your time.

Help children control their own anger and aggression. Keep them safe from hurting themselves and never allow children to hurt each other.

Wait for children to calm themselves. Gently hold them if necessary.

Help parents understand that imaginary fears are natural at this age. Suggest ways to work with fearful children. A children's book, talking, dramatic play, or other techniques may help.

Compliment children about how grown up they are acting when they control their emotions appropriately.

Continue to treat everyone with respect and to comment on what you are doing. "Let's get all of our puzzles put on the shelf so that we are ready to sing when Mr. Adams joins us."

Ways to study how children grow and learn

What children are like

Twos are proud of what they make and do.

As they near age 3, children talk more about their feelings. Their feelings are often expressed in pretend play (playing house, for example).

Children at this age begin to develop a true concern for others.

Other milestones. . .

How adults can help

Put children's names on their artwork. Hang children's work at their eye level. Notice when children concentrate, work hard, or stick to a task for an especially long time.

Set up familiar play settings—medical offices, grocery stores, and other places children know. Have props common in their cultures for them to use.

Continue to show your concern and commend children when they are considerate of others. "How thoughtful of you to tell Jamie you are finished at the easel."

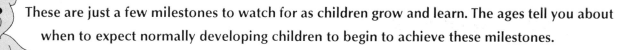

These are just a few milestones to watch for as children grow and learn. The ages tell you about when to expect normally developing children to begin to achieve these milestones.

Young preschool children (2 1/2 to 4 years)

What children are usually like at this age

Children show interest in others

Young threes prefer to play alongside another child or with one or two others.

Friendships are beginning but are often short-lived, especially early in this age range. Sometimes they center on silly activities.

Threes may share when given the opportunity. Sometimes they can wait for a short while for a turn.

Threes are increasingly less willing to hold an adult's hand while walking.

Older threes are affectionate with younger children. They may begin to select special friends in their own age group.

How adults can help children make the most of this age

Have many individual activities and materials children can do side by side. Also offer some things that require cooperation.

Support children's friendships. One good way is to help children treat each other as friends.

Allow sharing to develop spontaneously. Forcing it will **not** work. Children share when others are generous with them and when they do not feel the need to protect their possessions. Keep the need to wait to a minimum.

Keep an alert eye so children do not dart or wander away from you outdoors.

Give children opportunities to play with children from a wide range of ages.

What children are like

Children become more aware of themselves

During this year, children develop a firm sense of their sex, age, language, and culture.

Threes can spend fairly long times at tasks they choose: play in sand, build with blocks, paint, follow an obstacle course.

Children this age will test their skills. Sometimes they are cautious and at other times they may overestimate their abilities, especially if they are in a group with older children.

Threes are beginning to develop some self-control. They may still be easily frustrated.

Young preschoolers are very proud of their achievements and begin to feel independent.

The ideas of ownership and sharing are beginning to be understood.

How adults can help

Share children's pride in who they are. Respect each child. Incorporate their home language, cultural objects, and familiar activities as a natural part of every day.

Plan the schedule to allow large blocks of time for independent play. Offer a wide range of activities. Expect children to repeat activities again and again.

Adult supervision, especially on the playground, is essential. The area should be as safe as possible and positive rules should be set up.

Help children become more aware of how their behavior affects others and how friends treat each other. Eliminate as many frustrating situations as possible (do not expect children to wait quietly in line or sit at tables doing what you want them to do).

Share in children's pride. Allow time for children to be independent—to dress themselves, clean up, prepare snacks.

Respect children's personal possessions and constructions. Compliment children when they share. Point out how good it feels to share with friends.

What children are like

Young preschoolers can brush their own teeth and hair, unbutton and unzip clothes, and wash their hands and faces.

Children's muscles grow stronger and coordination improves

Toileting accidents may happen occasionally, especially at night. Food and art supplies sometimes get spilled.

Threes love to use their large muscles. They become stronger and their coordination improves greatly during the year. They can jump, paint with a 1-inch brush, begin to alternate feet when climbing stairs, do a forward somersault, kick a ball, hammer nails, and build increasingly higher towers.

Small muscle coordination increases. Drawings are more deliberate. Threes can lace shoes, button, and zip.

Children learn to communicate

Children can say their own names, express what they want using "I can . . ." and indicate when they need help or don't know something.

How adults can help

Reserve enough time for children to take care of their personal needs.

Treat accidents matter-of-factly. Have extra clothes on hand. Ask children to help clean up the mess and to change their own clothes.

Provide climbers, tricycles, balls, and lots of space and time to run, jump, and gallop.

Toys such as pegboards, beads to string, and construction sets are essential. Children's drawings are more controlled but still should never be expected to "look like something." Never ask "What is it?" Occasionally, threes will give names to their artwork. Write the name in the child's language.

Allow lots of time for children to talk and express their needs and wishes.

What children are like

Three-year-olds frequently ask, "What?" "Who?" "Why?" and "How come?" They use language to solve problems and figure out how the world works.

Vocabularies grow rapidly. Threes use words to describe and explain. If they hear other languages, they will increasingly become bilingual.

At this age, children begin to understand how words can be spoken and then written down to be read again.

Children at this age can listen to longer stories.

Children begin to recognize musical melodies, match a few tones, and move in reasonably good time to music.

Children become aware of the world

Three-year-olds are curious. They want to experiment with cause and effect. They take things apart with glee.

They draw figures with heads and bodies.

How adults can help

Give clear, understandable explanations to children's questions. Use the child's home language whenever possible. Expect children to talk a great deal to each other and with you. Encourage bilingualism. Use one language at a time. Limit translating. Talk to children in a second language at a little higher level than they talk to you.

Provide opportunities for children to use language in culturally relevant ways: poems, nursery rhymes, records, games, stories, field trips.

Have children tell you a story that you write down for them. They can then draw pictures to illustrate if they want. Sometimes children will draw first, then ask you to write their story.

Gradually increase the length and complexity of stories you read and tell.

Provide many musical experiences in which children participate by singing, playing, and dancing. Select music from many cultures.

Provide children with materials to manipulate: blocks, sand and water (with cups to pour and other tools), puzzles, things that come apart.

Provide open-ended art materials so children can express their own ideas of what things look like.

What children are like

How adults can help

Dramatic play becomes more involved. Frequent themes include work and family.

Add new props for dramatic play: office items, other dress-up clothes. Take field trips to expand children's experiences within and beyond their own cultures. Include pretend people (with tan, brown, black, and white skins) and animals in the block area.

Children at this age cannot yet distinguish real from pretend. Fact and fantasy are interrelated.

Frightening stories or television programs may be upsetting. Talk with children about what could happen and what is just pretend. Reassure them that you will keep them safe.

Children may begin to recognize the names of some letters or numerals, but they do not yet understand what they mean.

Use letters and numerals as they come up in real situations rather than teaching the ABC song or how to count out of context. Write children's names on their artwork and label their cubbies. Use the child's home language. Cook, address Valentines, count for table setting, make lists, notice the time, talk about birthdays—these ways make letters and numbers real.

During this period, children become increasingly aware of likenesses and differences.

Offer a wider variety of objects and ideas for children to compare: 4 or 5 different measuring cups, dolls with realistic ethnic features and skin colors, food with a variety of colors and shapes. Begin to talk with children about how unfair it is to treat people differently just because of their skin color or language.

Children may become more aware of immediate time.

Begin to remind children that they have only 5 minutes until it is time for some new activity. Talk about what you plan to do tomorrow or did yesterday.

Ways to study how children grow and learn

What children are like

At around this age, children can put their own toys away if they are supervised as they do so.

Children solve problems and use tools

Children want to do everything possible for themselves: dress, eat, go to the bathroom, brush teeth, wash hands. They may need assistance, however, with more complicated tasks.

They can do puzzles with between 5 and 10 pieces.

Threes can choose from two or three alternatives. They can choose what they want to do during free play.

Threes can usually count as high as 5 or 10, and can count from 3 to 5 objects.

Children are increasingly able to use tools: draw with markers or crayons, use cookie cutters with clay, hammer nails into soft wood, play simple musical instruments, balance blocks. They may name what they are making.

How adults can help

Invite children to help clean up together so they can find things when they need them the next time.

Watch children and give them time to take care of their own needs. Dressing is more difficult than undressing. Ask whether children need assistance.

Make sure you have puzzles with 4 to 12 pieces available so children can select the puzzle that best matches their skills.

Give children real choices: "Would you like to listen to a tape or build with the table blocks?" Be open to their suggestions for activities.

Provide opportunities for children to count small groups of objects if they are interested: "Let's see, how many shoes do we need to put on this doll? . . . Uno . . . dos . . . We need two shoes. Dos zapatos."

Rotate tools and equipment available. Select **real** carpentry tools and **real** musical instruments (maracas, tambourines, bells) so children can use them successfully. (Real ones last much longer too.)

What children are like

Children express feelings

At this age, children may cry, suck their thumbs, hit, or use other toddler-like behaviors when they are afraid or upset.

Children this age have a delightful sense of humor.

Three-year-olds can be very affectionate.

Other milestones. . .

How adults can help

Never ridicule children for immature behavior. Comfort them and give them the chance to get themselves under control before returning to the group.

Watch to see what your children think is funny and use these ideas to make your classroom or home a joyful place to be. Silly songs, funny faces—what delights your children?

Provide lots of hugs and kisses every day, just as you do throughout the early years.

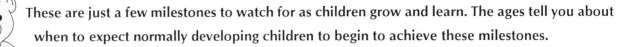

These are just a few milestones to watch for as children grow and learn. The ages tell you about when to expect normally developing children to begin to achieve these milestones.

Older preschoolers (older 3-year-olds to 5-year-olds)

What children are usually like at this age

Children show interest in others

Preschoolers love to play together with two or three others—with blocks, at the sand or water table, in pretend play. They also still need time alone.

Children are developing real compassion for each other. Friendships are more lasting. At the same time, prejudices may arise unless children are helped to appreciate each other and to recognize what is fair for everyone. Children gradually have fewer disagreements and are quick to apologize for their behavior.

How adults can help children make the most of this age

Provide lots of small group, child-directed activities. Have a quiet, private space where children can go to be by themselves. Limit larger group activities to a few minutes each day.

Continue to be compassionate with the children and to compliment them on their ability to understand how others feel. Support friendships. Treat children with respect so they will do the same with others. Talk about differences and differently abled people in an honest, nonfrightening way to help children appreciate how each person has unique qualities. Make culture a daily part of classroom experiences. Choose bias-free books. Model the behavior you expect from children. Encourage children to stand up for what is fair.

What children are like

Sharing and taking turns are becoming more common. However, preschoolers may also be bossy at times and call each other names and criticize each other.

Children become more aware of themselves

During this period children may be silly, boisterous, and use shocking language.

Preschoolers are quite independent and have definite preferences. They want to do things that interest them.

Children are easily discouraged and enjoy receiving praise.

How adults can help

By the end of this period, children can be expected to willingly take turns and share IF adults are generous with them and allow them to share as they are ready. Create opportunities for cooperation. Continue to demonstrate how to treat people in a friendly way.

Explain "In our program we are all friends. Friends are kind to each other. We use only friendly words." Use children's humor: Riddles and nonsense words may be fun. On the other hand, don't reward the use of bathroom language by giving children who use it lots of attention. Explain that those words are not used in the program because they hurt people's feelings.

Provide many opportunities for success. Help children develop a sense of pride in their language and heritage as well as their own actions and accomplishments.

Allow children to handle responsibilities they are capable of: pour their own juice, wash their hands, hang up their coats, and other similar tasks. Respect children's preferences. Support their internal motivation to do well—rewards are not needed beyond children's own sense that they are trying and making progress (awarding stars or candy for good behavior, for example, is unnecessary). Talk to each child individually every day.

Ways to study how children grow and learn

What children are like

Older preschoolers are gaining greater control over their own behavior. They can wait for short periods of time. They grow in respect for each other's belongings.

Children in this age range are increasingly able to follow a leader or act as a leader.

Children near the end of this age range usually know their first and last names, left and right, their address, and their phone number.

Children's muscles grow stronger and coordination improves

During this period, children test their rapidly improving physical skills. They are proud of their abilities.

Large-muscle skills are expanding and becoming more refined. Skipping and hopping may appear. They are good at riding tricycles. Skills are usually used as part of a game. Children become able to bounce and catch a ball, walk backwards, jump over a low obstacle, balance on one foot.

How adults can help

Continue to help children control their own behavior. Plan the day so waiting is kept to an absolute minimum, not just because children can't wait but because it is a waste of their time.

Children can be leaders and followers naturally throughout the day—during dramatic play, outdoors, on field trips, and during music, for example.

Use natural opportunities to help children learn about themselves—play games, talk, write letters or notes, look at pictures of the people who came before them, put names on artwork.

Offer many increasingly difficult large- and small-muscle activities and ample time to pursue them. Keep competition to a minimum—make any comparisons friendly and focus on how well every child did.

Allow plenty of time for children to use their large-muscle skills: obstacle courses, sawing, large hollow blocks.

What children are like

Small muscles continue to be more coordinated. Children's artwork begins to resemble real objects. Most children can make a drawing that looks like a person with facial features. Children can use scissors, glue, small beads, and paintbrushes with more skill. They can cut with a dull knife and string small beads. Near the end of this period, they start to tie shoes—usually the final step in being able to dress and undress independently.

Children in this age range can do puzzles with 10 to 20 pieces.

Construction skills become increasingly refined.

Children have usually settled on a preference for using their right or left hand.

How adults can help

Continue to offer a variety of art materials and blank paper. Never use coloring books or drawings for children to color. Give children opportunities to tell you about their artwork, but never ask "What is it?" Let children cut what they choose rather than trying to follow lines you draw for them. Do more elaborate cooking and woodworking projects. Provide smaller items for older children to use such as doll clothes with tiny buttons and sewing cards. Use more difficult finger plays.

Set out puzzles with a wide range in the number of pieces. Floor puzzles may appeal to older children in this age group.

Have a variety of construction toys—small plastic blocks, interlocking shapes of various types, unit blocks, and hollow blocks. Introduce sewing (with large yarn needles, yarn, and nylon net or burlap) and other small-muscle skills to older children in this age range.

Have left-handed scissors. Help children learn how to hold and use markers and other writing instruments properly. Never force children's hand preference.

What children are like

Children learn to communicate

Interest in written and spoken language increases. Children become curious about letters and words. They begin to match letters with those in their names. In bilingual programs, they use both languages with ease.

Vocabularies are growing with every experience. Sentences become more complicated. Children understand more words than they say. They are persistent in asking, "Why?"

Conversations become long and involved.

Children enjoy making up their own stories which are usually a mixture of make-believe and real.

How adults can help

Have lots of books, magazines, telephone books, and signs in several languages for children to use. Respond to children's questions about letters and words. Write down the stories children tell you. Older children can write their own when you help them with spelling. If older children notice that certain letters have certain sounds, encourage them to try their own spelling—and don't "correct" it. Use upper and lower case letters appropriately when you write. Keep paper and pencils or markers in every area of the room for children to use.

Provide lots of materials and experiences for children to learn new words and see new outlooks: field trips, props, songs, visitors, puppet stories. Be sure to help children see how many varied ways there are to find answers to questions: asking people, looking in books, experimenting.

Allow lots of time for children to talk among themselves about what they are doing: dramatic play, art activities, outdoors.

Encourage them to tell their own stories.

What children are like

Older preschoolers can retell long stories quite accurately.

Some children at this age, who have learned English as a second language, may want to only speak English to the point of rejecting their home language. They are able to pick up on biases surrounding them about their language, culture, or skin color. They may feel like they have to choose between speaking English or their home language and culture.

How adults can help

Give children a chance to use the flannel board, puppets, or other dramatic play methods to recreate stories. Encourage children who wish to do so to retell stories to the group. Watch that the stories do not contain stereotypes or distort the facts (such as presenting only the viewpoint of the new settlers at the first Thanksgiving).

Provide positive models of people speaking their language and of their culture in the program activities.

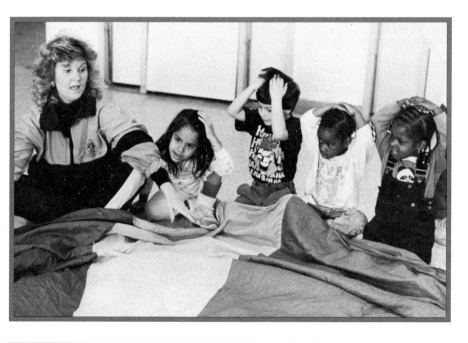

Help children understand how people are alike and different. Each of us is special and valuable.

What children are like

Music becomes more sophisticated: Children like singing games, want to dramatize songs, and make up their own songs (often silly ones). They are increasingly able to sing melodies on pitch and move in time to the beat.

By the end of this period, children may want to copy or write their own names, other important words, and even stories. Through these experiences they take important steps in learning to read.

Children become aware of the world

Preschoolers want to use real adult things.

Preschoolers want to save all of their artwork and other projects and increasingly are able to carry over themes from one day to the next.

How adults can help

Offer an ever-wider range of musical experiences including lots of songs with words in other languages, more complicated actions, and more real instruments from several cultures.

Keep paper and markers or pencils handy. Let children write whenever they are interested. Never force them to write or trace letters.

Offer real objects for children to use: tools, money, ways to carry things (briefcases; straw, paper, or fabric bags; baskets), eating and cooking utensils, typical clothing, and similar everyday objects from several cultures.

Put children's names on their work. If a block construction is prized, for example, offer to make a sign asking others to leave it standing for a day or two. Make the sign using as many languages as are spoken by children in the program.

What children are like

Children at this age become curious about differences and similarities in people and their lifestyles. They generally choose friends of their own sex.

Interests of preschoolers expand to include topics such as transportation, dressing up, community helpers, and different forms of music.

Preschoolers are still trying to understand what is real and what is make-believe.

Children want to take more responsibility for doing errands. Older 5-year-olds may be able to cross all but the busiest of streets by themselves if they have practiced the proper procedures with an adult over an extended period of time.

How adults can help

Help children understand how people are alike and different: eye color, hair, clothing, where we live, what we eat, members of families. Each of us is special and valuable. Discuss what is fair and accurate (for example, sharing, standing up for what's right, songs drawn from a specific culture) and what isn't (playing cowboys and Indians, stereotyped drawings in books or on greeting cards). Decorations and materials all through the room should include art, music, and other authentic everyday objects from a variety of cultures.

Add new topics as children express interest.

Talk with children about what could happen and what is just pretend. Halloween masks may still be too frightening for some children.

Give children more responsibility as they are ready. Follow safe crossing procedures. Perhaps set up streets for pedestrians and riding vehicles on the playground.

What children are like	How adults can help

What children are like

Children solve problems and use tools

Preschoolers are increasingly able to figure out how things work and fit together. They are curious and want to try different ways to do things. They can sort objects using more than two categories. Cutting and pasting become favorite activities.

Children usually are able to resolve differences between themselves with words.

Children are naturally interested in shapes, colors, and textures.

Children gradually learn to count up to 20 and may be interested in printing numbers up to 5. They begin to compare sizes and weights of objects and can identify basic shapes.

How adults can help

Bring in all kinds of objects for children to explore: an old toaster with any dangerous parts removed, a clock, hole punchers—anything safe for eager learners. Ask children to think of a variety of ways to solve problems: "What ideas do you have for using these yogurt tops that Kai's mother saved for us?" Involve children in making repairs. Stock up on paste and glue!

Encourage children to use words to work out problems that arise during play. "Meaghan, you and Sadao both want to use the funnel in the sandbox. What solution can you two agree on?"

Use the names of shapes and colors in natural ways: "What shape of blocks do you need to make a ramp for your truck?" "Your blue shoes match the blue in your shirt. See how they are alike?" Provide lots of textures through cooking, woodworking, clay and finger paint, and clothes for pretend play, for example.

Continue to encourage the use of number and quantity in real experiences such as measuring, distributing or dividing items, and matching. Count and compare in each of the languages spoken by the children in the group.

What children are like

Typewriters or computers, woodworking tools, and other items to use for hands-on projects are of great interest and children develop skills to use them well. Projects may extend over several days.

Children express feelings

Preschoolers still have intense feelings: fear, joy, anger, love. They may still need an adult to help them manage their strong feelings.

Children ages 4 and 5 are easily encouraged or discouraged. They may show off and demand attention.

Children at this age usually are able to say goodbye to their parents with little difficulty if they have had previous group experience.

Other milestones. . .

How adults can help

Introduce more complicated cooking projects, new carpentry tools, a cash register, and other items as children are ready to use them. Take care to save their projects from day to day.

Accept children's feelings and help them find a safe way to express them. "You are really mad that your beautiful tower was knocked over. How angry you are! Let's sit here for a while until you feel calm enough to talk with the children who destroyed it." Children's books may help them see how others have faced and resolved problems such as divorce, moving, death, disabilities, learning a new language, a new baby in the family.

Provide lots of opportunities for children to be successful and take leadership roles.

You may even need to remind children to say goodbye—often they want to plunge right in to the day's activities.

Ways to study how children grow and learn

Whew! Those milestones of development contained a wealth of information. Much of it you may already have known. It is a good reminder, though, about how children's bodies change, that children learn from whatever they do, and that how adults treat children can make a big difference in how children treat others.

Perhaps you noticed in this chart that early childhood professionals focus on what children **can** do. So many people these days are concerned about rushing children to get them ready for the toddler group, or for preschool, or for kindergarten, that they lose track of the natural process of development.

Children need to practice, to consolidate what they have learned, and to have many real experiences with a wide variety of people and objects. From now on, you will think in terms of what children can do and how you can make the most of that particular day for that particular child. It may be a whole new way of teaching for you, but it is the best way!

Be sure you are familiar with the **range** of development for every section on the chart. If you work with 5-year-olds, this information points out just how many things children have learned in a few short years! If you work with infants, look through the next section as a reminder of how quickly they will change.

If you haven't already done so, go back to the developmental chart. Lots of items are missing. Fill in at least two milestones in each age range that are particularly important to you and the cultural groups you work with.

When you are finished, show your additions to your Advisor as part of your next conference. Later, we will look in some detail at how you will use all this information to answer questions you have about children and how you work with them.

Information about how children develop is used for many different purposes. Some child development professionals use it to help spot developmental problems. These highly trained educators, physicians, therapists, and psychologists have specialized skills to identify and help children who are not developing normally. We will talk later in this unit about how to make use of their assistance.

Other professionals also use this information to help parents understand their own children. Pediatricians, for example, often give materials to new parents so they will know what to look for as their children grow.

Schools and libraries also have books and pamphlets about children's growth and development, some written for parents, and others written for professionals. You should become familiar with some of these for they will always be important to your work. Even after you become a CDA, you will continue to build your own knowledge about children's development by reading professional literature. And as you work with parents, you will always be ready with ways to help them understand their own children.

Whenever you see pamphlets or articles about the way children grow, pick them up

and read through them. Find a few that would be useful to parents and add them to your Resource File. Think about how these other resources are similar to and different from your CDA materials and other professional literature.

Part 3

How do you collect information about children's development?

In order to be a good teacher, you need to know about children's patterns of growth and development in general. And you will be a better teacher if you use this information to really know the children in your group. You need to know what they can do, their interests, their languages and cultural heritages, their strengths and weaknesses, how they think, and what skills they are learning.

Once you know each child well, you can combine all you know to teach appropriately, to evaluate children's growth, and to assess your own work.

Know what range of behaviors to expect. Help children make the most of each age.

There are many ways to learn more about individual children. We have included several practical methods here. You can adapt each of

Every day, watch how . . .
• children show interest in others
• children become more aware of themselves
• children's muscles grow stronger and coordination improves
• children learn to communicate
• children become aware of the world
• children solve problems and use tools
• children express feelings

these to fit your style and your questions about children. Try each method at least once to get a feel for how it works. You will use these methods again and again in your CDA Seminar and each day as you teach young children.

You observe children in your group

What a thrill it is to see a child's first steps! To watch a child learn to cut with scissors! To enjoy playing with a child who can throw and catch the ball!

A big part of your day is spent watching children grow and learn. You probably even take pictures of what happens. Maybe your program requires you to fill out some forms. You most likely save some of the children's artwork to show parents at your next conference. Perhaps you keep a diary of some of the fascinating things children have said or done.

Now that you are on your way to becoming a **professional** early childhood educator, you will want to begin to use these and other methods to more systematically record what you see.

Your notes will help you answer questions about whether your children are making progress, what their strengths and weaknesses are, what they need, how well you teach, and whether children reach the goals you have for them. As you talk with your CDA Field Advisor, ask questions about your observations.

Whenever new children join your group, you will need to find out what they can do, what they like, and much more about them. Every fall, or whenever you have a new group, you will need to take notes about each child so you can choose the right activities and materials to put out. As a teacher, you will constantly study children to see whether they are growing and learning at an appropriate pace. You will always need to record what children do.

There are several ways you can take notes and organize them. The method you use depends on what you are trying to figure out. You need to match your questions with the best way to find the answers. Here are some ways you can keep track of what children do. Perhaps you have other methods that work for you.

As a teacher, you will constantly study children to see whether they are growing and learning at an appropriate pace.

Ways to study children
- Keep a diary of your observations.
- Write about a specific incident.
- Record information on a chart.
- Interview children.
- Use developmental assessments.

Read through the next 7 pages, and try out four techniques for studying children. Then select one recording tool that will be helpful to you in answering a specific question you have. During the next conference you have with your Advisor, you can talk together about your experiences in using these observation tools.

Keep a diary
Each day, jot down something special about at least two of the children in your care. Use a small notebook for each child, a three-ring binder, or notecards—whatever suits you. Just write down the day and what happened like this:

March 4 – Today Brandon (20 months) crawled through the tunnel on the playground for the first time. He had been watching two other children coming out of the end for about 5 minutes before he did it himself.

May 15 – Allison poured her juice without spilling a drop. She's been trying so hard all month.

When you look back on your notes, you will see just how much children learn when you're together. When you compare children's ages and skills with the information on the chart, you might see areas to emphasize. Or you might get some ideas for new activities to pick up on children's interests.

As a first step, think about two of the children in your care and write here what they did today.

Date _____

Who did what? _____

Date _____

Who did what? _____

You have just started an informal diary! **In this next week, decide how you want to organize your notes and begin to keep your diary every day. After a week, look back to see what you can learn about these two children's development or what you need to change in your teaching.**

Continue to make daily notes for a full 2 weeks. Bring your diary to your next meeting with your Advisor so she or he can check your progress and answer any questions. You will use your diary notes to complete the exercises in Part 4 of this unit.

Write about a specific incident

Keeping track of what happened at certain times can help you answer specific questions about children's behavior. Many teachers find it helpful to occasionally sit down with a pen and paper, watch children, and write down details about what they see happen.

Perhaps you want to see what happens when you place 5-month-old Lindsay, sitting in an infant seat, in front of a mirror for the first time in your family child care home. You might write something like this:

September 2, 11 a.m. – Lindsay (5 months) turns her head toward the mirror right away. She _reaches out with her arms and waves them around. Smiles. Kicks her feet. Watches herself for at least 5 minutes._

As children grow older, your observations may include more than one child. For example, a 4-year-old boy seems to fight a lot when he is in a small group. Your notes about what he does with a group might read like this:

January 12, 9:30 a.m.: Seth, Melissa, and Brandon in the block corner.

Melissa: "Let's make a river with boats."

Brandon: "OK. Here, the river can start on this side." He takes the longest blocks from the shelf and places them on the floor.

Melissa carries more blocks and puts them next to Brandon's.

Melissa looks up to see Seth watching them: "Hey, Seth, don't you want to play boats with us?"

Seth does not answer her. He slowly walks over to the shelf with the boats. He picks up a barge, climbs onto the riding truck, and then rams into the river.

Brandon screams: "Seth, DON'T DO THAT! You are messing up our river!" . . .

(_Note:_ Do you want to jump in and rescue the river before Seth demolishes it? It is tempting, but by now you know that whenever possible children should be given the opportunity to solve their own problems.)

By writing down several brief samples of just what happens in your classroom with Seth and the other children, eventually you may be able to piece together why he acts this way, and what you can do to help him be a more friendly player.

When you write down examples like this of what you see, be sure to

1 Note the date and time.

2 Include the names of all the children involved.

3 Write where the incident happened.

4 Jot down what children said and exactly what they did. Try not to use words that jump to conclusions about why children behave the way they do. For example, in the situation above, instead of writing that Seth didn't want to play or that he was mean, we wrote what he **did**.

5 Do not get involved—just watch (unless someone or something is about to get hurt, of course).

Write a description of an episode with the children in your care: Choose a particular child to watch or choose an activity area to observe. Take your pen and paper, and watch quietly on the sidelines. Write down what happens here:

Date and time

Place

Children _____

_____

_____

What the children said and did

_____

_____

_____

_____

You may need to collect several of these observations in order to practice writing about exactly what happens. Save your notes so you can discuss the observation with your Field Advisor.

Do you know which activities are most popular in your program?

Use a chart

You want children to take advantage of all the learning opportunities you offer. But do children ignore some activities and use other areas all the time?

The only way you can know for sure is to keep a count. For example, if you want to know how many children use clay or paste each day, keep a pad handy, and make a mark whenever a child enters that area:

WEEK September 25

	M	T	W	T	F
ACTIVITY					
Clay	II	I	IIII	III	II
Paste	III	II	ЦHI I	II	IIII

Do you know why so few children used these art materials on Tuesday? And what made them so appealing on Wednesday? Did you put out some new magazines to cut or bring in some fancy cookie cutters?

What activities do children seem to ignore in your program? Or which ones seem the most popular? Use this chart to find out:

WEEK _____

	M	T	W	T	F
ACTIVITY					

Based on what you saw, how can you make the less popular activities more appealing? Or should they be replaced with more appropriate materials?

Try out your ideas if you get a chance.

Another type of tally can help you see which activities each child uses. Sometimes children get in a rut and do the same thing every day. To find out whether children are playing in a variety of activities, use a chart like this:

Each time these children did these activities:

WEEK April 25

CHILDREN Nikki   Roberto   Chaka

ACTIVITY	Nikki	Roberto	Chaka
Read books	I	II	IIII
Blocks	III	I	II
Do puzzles	IHT I	I	IHT
Pretend play	III	IHT I	I
Games	II	III	I
Easel	IHT	I	III
Water play	IIII	II	

What might this information tell you about each of these children? Do some prefer to play alone? Which one likes messy things? Who prefers to play in groups?

Are there some children in your group who seem to do the same things day after day? Pick two or three children and keep track of what they do. **Fill in this chart to record what these children do for a week.**

WEEK

CHILDREN

ACTIVITY

What does this information tell you about these children? Who needs to be encouraged to branch out into other areas (maybe girls are reluctant to play with trucks)? Are some different or more difficult materials needed (perhaps more materials are needed in the child's home language)? **Use what you are learning to improve your teaching, and discuss what you have learned with your Advisor.**

Interview children informally

Did you ever just sit down and chat with a child in an effort to learn something about the child? You can learn so much just by casually talking together!

Sometimes you might be fairly direct about what you would like to know. If you are direct, ask questions that require more than a yes, no, or a "right" answer—but don't pry or your conversation may come to a sudden halt.

Better yet, pick up on children's cues and make comments children can respond to: "You seem to be having trouble finding something of interest to do this morning." "You brought your doll to school today." Choose a comfortable place and see what you can learn so you can be a better teacher.

As you talk, you may find out all kinds of things: what is bothering a child, where she or he would really like to visit on the next field trip, or discover an idea that is confusing for the child. A conversation might go something like this:

Date: October 28

Child interviewed: Alexandra, age 3

Question: Alex will soon be having minor surgery. How can you help her deal with this potentially frightening experience?

Conversation:

"Alex, when you have finished looking at your book, please come sit next to me for a few minutes." Alex continues to read for a few minutes, then brings the book with her.

"That must have been a good book you were read-

You can learn so much just by casually talking with a child.

ing—you had it for a long time," you comment.

"I know. I was looking at the pictures."

You want to know more, so you elaborate on your comment. "They must have been special pictures. You were concentrating hard."

"It's about a hospital. I'm going to a hospital."

"It *is* only a few days until your operation," you note.

"This weekend I get to visit the hospital," she volunteers.

You ask, "What kinds of things will you see there?"

And so the conversation continues.

Based on what you discuss, you may want to put out some medical props in the pretend play area. Perhaps talking with the children about Alex's absence will help them understand her situation. Maybe after the surgery the children could take a field trip to a clinic, or a nurse could talk with them about ways to stay healthy. You need to know a lot about your children to select just the right activities to make every experience a positive one.

You may learn more than you expect when you really listen to children in this way. Children may tell you personal things about their families, may announce what they bought for a birthday gift, or may reveal that a parent dislikes someone at work.

As a professional you must keep any information confidential, unless you suspect child abuse. Child abuse must be reported (see Unit 3). Always respond with respect to whatever children say.

In addition to talking, you might ask children to do a specific task. This can also give you information about their skills or understanding.

For example, you might give a toddler a puzzle with more pieces than have been available. If the child completes the puzzle with only a bit of struggling, it could be time to put some of the easier puzzles away. Or you might ask a child to build a block model and ask another child to make a building just like it. That could help you see how well she can use objects in space.

Think about what questions you have, and whether you might find an answer by interviewing or asking children to show you what they can do.

Think of a question about a child that might be answered through an interview. Write the question here:

Then think about what questions you might ask or what activity might give clues about what you would like to know to be a better teacher. Write how you could talk with the child here.

When you have a chance, conduct your interview and jot down what happened.

DATE

CHILD

ACTIVITY OR QUESTIONS FOR THE CHILD

CHILD'S RESPONSES/SOLUTIONS

What did you learn about this child? How can you use this in your teaching? Use what you have learned to improve your work with the child.

Now that you have tried out four (4) different ways of studying children, pick one you would like to demonstrate to other CDA Candidates.

- **Choose a question that you have about a child or children.**
- **Study the question using any technique you think is appropriate.**
- **Prepare to share your example in your CDA Seminar. You should be able to tell the group what you did, how you did it, and why you chose the specific technique. (Be prepared to answer questions too!)**

You make developmental assessments

Before we leave the topic of ways to study children, there is one other important tool to know something about — developmental assessments. These include the many types of checklists, tests, and rating scales used to evaluate children's abilities and progress. When used properly, some of these can be helpful in answering questions about growth. They also can help identify children with exceptional talents or with learning or physical disabilities.

However, you should *always use checklists, tests, and rating scales with caution,* just as you use the developmental chart in this chapter with care. Some checklists simply aren't accurate. Some don't consider childrearing differences among cultures, languages, and income levels.

Before you use any checklist, ask some questions about it: What is it for? How is it supposed to be used? What will the results be used to do? Why was this checklist selected? What training do you need to use and interpret it properly?

If you have any questions about a child's development that you can't answer, it is not a good idea to guess. It is best to refer the child to a specialist who knows about the issues. Specialists are trained to select the best type of test for each child.

If you work in a program where developmental checklists or other screening instruments are used, **collect some samples to bring with you to your CDA Seminar. Find out how they**

are used so that you can discuss them in Seminar.

The more you know about children, the less you will want to rely on someone else's criteria for evaluating children. Your own observations—made with one of the methods you have just used—are much more valuable in planning your curriculum and teaching strategies. Become increasingly familiar with these and other appropriate ways to observe children and record their behavior. **Choose one sample of your favorite observation tool for your Professional Resource File. Put in two copies—one blank and one filled in with a sample observation.**

Part 4

How do you use information to teach appropriately?

Tamile, 5½ months, is just beginning to sit up steadily. You need to find some good places to let her feel she is part of the action.

At 14 months, Andrew insists on feeding himself. How can you be sure the finger and spoon foods are healthy foods?

It seems as if every toddler in your group wants to do everything for themselves. What responsibilities can they handle?

None of your 3-year-olds will sit still for a story. Why?

Nikki is almost 5 and soon will be a big brother. How do you help him feel good about it?

Your day is filled with problem-solving opportunities just like these—how do you help children become the best person they can be? You can make it happen. You know that children learn best through play. You know the general characteristics of children at that age. You know what your particular children have mastered.

This may seem hard to believe: When children are offered a few good choices, they choose activities that are just challenging enough for them. Children usually ignore items that are "old hat" for them—toddlers rarely pick up teething rings, for instance. Children may also ignore a toy that is too strange. Instead, they generally choose an activity that looks interesting and yet not too difficult.

In good programs, children choose what they're going to do many times every day. New children who are not used to having choices about what to do (perhaps their former teacher told them what to do every minute) may be overwhelmed. But soon they will feel comfortable making their own selections during free play.

Sometimes children want to *practice* what they have already learned. A baby who has just mastered step climbing will do it over and over again. Preschoolers will write their names several times on a page just for the joy of being able to do it.

Using your daily diary notes, what are some of the children in your group practicing?

scissors - cutting

decision making

computer - ABC's

Sometimes children prefer to *try something new*. They always seem drawn to the fresh dough clay, the new dump truck, or the book you just checked out from the library. Novelty — but not too much — often appeals to children. You probably have seen a child who would rather play with the box than the toy inside.

On the other hand, children may not use an easel or a bowling game if they have never seen one used before. Children also are generally more willing to try new things when they know they usually are successful in what they do.

List something new that someone in your group tried this week:

At other times children will be ready to *combine something familiar with something new*. An older toddler who has enjoyed drawing with markers may be intrigued with some brightly colored chalk. A preschooler who has mastered hammering nails may want to start to saw some boards.

What did you see a child do this week that combined something old with something new?

As you observe and teach, you will see it's true: Children learn best when they select the activity — **IF** you make the right materials available. Your role as a professional early childhood educator, then, is to set the stage for children to grow and learn.

To find the right match between children, activities to offer, and your teaching strategy, you

1 consider what you know about child development,

2 watch children to see what they can do,

3 figure out what they will be moving on to next,

4 choose the materials children need, and

5 plan how you will guide the activity (time to allot, showing how to use something for the first time, number of children who can participate at one time).

You use this way of thinking many times each day. In fact, the process is so important it even has a name. As a well-informed teacher, you decide what is **developmentally appropriate** for children—fitting activities and interactions with children's developmental needs.

To find the right match between children and activities you

1 consider how children grow and learn,

2 watch children to see what they can do,

3 figure out what they will be moving on to next, and

4 plan the materials you need and how you can guide the activity.

What happens if an activity isn't developmentally appropriate? You have wasted the child's time, your time, and the materials. Children may be bored and do the activity halfheartedly or walk away. Or they may feel like failures and give up. They may take out their frustration through disruptive behavior. Children won't become the best they can be.

What happened with your group this week that probably was not developmentally appropriate?

What activities did you offer that were good matches for your children?

It is not easy to decide what makes a good match for children. Most of the rest of this book will help you find solutions to questions you have about what **is** developmentally appropriate for children. **You are probably not sure about some activities or discipline techniques, for example. Write a few of your concerns here.**

You can look for the answers to your questions in the coming units, and by talking with your Field Advisor and Seminar group.

Every day you plan how to spend your day with children. For every activity or interaction, ask yourself, is this developmentally appropriate for these children?

This is probably the most important question you can ask as a teacher. There are many activities and strategies that are appropriate for young children. There are also many common projects and techniques—worksheets, coloring books, and drill, for example—that are not appropriate.

Hang the poster (page 95) as a reminder to ask yourself this question whenever you plan an activity or talk with a child. Throughout this book we will help you plan and do your best for young children.

You use this information to evaluate children's growth and your work

Sometimes you want to confirm that children are flourishing. They are delightful, curious children who seem healthy and happy.

At other times you are concerned that a child may be lagging behind. Or a child's behavior seems stalled at a younger level.

Sometimes you are sure children have disabilities that have gone undetected.

In all these cases, you can use your knowledge of child development and your observations of particular children to help you decide what to do next.

When children are doing well, you will want to share the good news with their parents. If you suspect a problem, you may want to first discuss your concerns with your supervisor or the program director. Your notes will help you explain why you think the child should be referred for further testing or screening.

There are probably one or two children you work with who seem to be doing exceptionally well. You may have others in your group who seem to have some type of problem.

Which children will you concentrate on first as you begin your systematic observations?

_____

_____

_____

_____

What type of recordkeeping will help you find out what you want to know?

_____

_____

_____

_____

We will first look at keeping track of children's successes. Then we will examine how you can use screening to find out which children have some type of problem.

Follow up on children's activities

Your observations of children can help you decide whether you are really doing a good job and how you can improve even if things are going well.

Look back on your diary. Did you write mostly positive things or did you see mostly problems?

Do any patterns show up—such as do the children have a hard time sitting still when you have them together as a group?

Are some activities ignored while others are always in great demand?

Take a good hard look at what you felt was so important that you wrote it down. Congratulate yourself on things that went well. Where were you successful?

Ask yourself how you can make the children's hours with you an even more beneficial experience. What areas seem to need improvement?

You may have expressed some concerns about one or more children's physical, intellectual, social, or emotional development. Let's look now at how you, your program director, and the children's parents can work together to identify any disabilities.

Screen children for possible disabilities

Parents are usually the first to notice a problem with their own child. Sometimes, however, the caregiver may be the first to suspect a problem. Regardless of where the concern first comes up,

it is important to work openly and honestly with the parent, and to rely on the help of experts in deciding what to do.

Every community has services for children who have mild, moderate, or severe problems or disabilities. These individuals or agencies usually also have expertise in diagnosing handicapping conditions.

Some offer screening services for programs for young children. Some organizations may be willing to check annually each child's hearing, dental, and sight problems. These kinds of screenings should be done each year, regardless of whether you suspect any problems.

Other types of screenings can be conducted, too, depending on the child's need.

Find out the names of agencies to contact for expertise in developmental disabilities if you should ever need assistance for a family in your program. List the phone numbers and include brochures about each agency or service in your Professional Resource File for easy reference. Your Field Advisor will assist you if you need help, and you will share your resources with other CDA Candidates during Seminar.

Teachers' observations of children and/or information parents give you in a conversation or conference usually help you decide when to call in expert help. Your daily records and special observations, and those parents make, also help determine what type of screening is needed.

So always take care to keep dated notes, to record information accurately, and to keep your notes organized. Then, when a problem is suspected, you can provide your program director or other expert with good solid observational information from which to start the screening process.

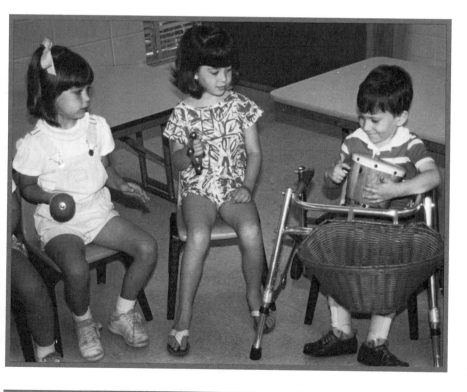

All children have different abilities. With a few exceptions, most children can benefit from attending the same program. This strategy is called *mainstreaming.*

If developmental problems are identified early, and remedial action is taken immediately, you greatly increase the child's chances for overcoming the problem and going on to future successes.

Just as you are likely to play a role in spotting a possible developmental disability, you are also likely to work with children who have already been diagnosed as having handicapped conditions. All children with developmental difficulties have a legal right to attend an appropriate educational program. At one time, it was believed that children with handicaps should all be in separate classes. Today, however, we realize that all children have different abilities. With a few exceptions, most children can benefit from attending the same program.

This strategy is called **mainstreaming**—children with special needs and regular needs are both enrolled in the same program. That way, children can learn in the least restrictive environment. If you work in Head Start or nearly any other program with large numbers of children, yours is probably already a mainstreamed group. If you are a family child care provider, you may have already considered having a child with special needs in your group.

There is a large body of specialized information to help you make good decisions about working with these children. Some will be discussed throughout *Essentials*, but most of it you will gather on your own as the need arises with individual children. One excellent resource for caregivers working with preschoolers is the series published by the Head Start Bureau in Washington, D.C. (U.S. Department of Health and Human Services, 1978). The series consists of eight manuals, each specialized for the following handicapping conditions.

1. Children with Emotional Disturbance
2. Children with Health Impairments
3. Children with Hearing Impairment
4. Children with Learning Disabilities
5. Children with Mental Retardation
6. Children with Orthopedic (Physical) Handicaps
7. Children with Speech and Language Impairments (Communication Disorders)
8. Children with Visual Handicaps

Much of *Essentials* contains ideas you can use to improve your work with children. Before we look at some specifics about what is appropriate—and what is not appropriate—let's see if what you have already learned can help you decide how to answer some typical questions parents will ask you about your program.

Part 5

What questions can you expect about what you do?

Parents want their children to have the best experiences they can, especially in their early years. When parents first visit, or after their child has been enrolled, they may ask questions like the ones that are listed here.

Other staff may also ask you to explain what

you do. Think about how you would respond to these questions. You will find answers in the next few units of this book and in the videos.

1. Why do you plan for children in your program to play so much?
2. How do you get children to share?
3. Why do the boys and girls use the same bathroom?
4. Why does each child need a cubby?
5. Why do you insist parents always say goodbye to their child—even babies?
6. Why are meals served family style?
7. Where are the coloring books and worksheets?
8. Aren't you just wasting learning time when you change diapers or wait for children to dress themselves?
9. How do you get children to respect other cultures/languages, people with disabilities, different ages, and the opposite sex?
10. Will my child get confused learning two languages at once?
11. How do you make children sit still for stories or show and tell?
12. Why don't you teach the alphabet?
13. When will my toddler learn to count?
14. How soon can you toilet train my child?
15. Why do children go off by themselves or do things in small groups? Why don't you teach everyone something at the same time?
16. Why don't you do the same things with children every year? It's so much work to think up new activities.
17. Aren't you just a baby sitter?
18. Will my child be ready for kindergarten?

You can probably think of other similar questions. Write them here.

_____

_____

_____

_____

If you don't find the answers to your questions here or in the videos, talk with your CDA Field Advisor or bring them up when you join your CDA Seminar group. See if together you can find out what is developmentally appropriate for young children.

By now, you should have watched the videotape to accompany Unit 2. Keep thinking about the questions in the Viewer's Guide. You will probably want to come back to this unit and its accompanying video to refresh your memory again and again throughout your teaching career.

This marks the end of your second unit of early childhood study toward your CDA Credential. Turn back to page 387 and check off your progress—this unit was really a giant step forward!

Now, let's deal with some specifics about curriculum planning and teaching. The next unit will review how to set up a safe, healthy, learning environment—your CDA Competency Goal I.

Resources for more information

Ames, L.B., Gillespie, C., Haines, J., & Ilg, F.L. (1979). *The Gesell Institute's child from one to six.* New York: Harper & Row.

Bredekamp, S. (Ed.). (1987). *Developmentally appropriate practice in early childhood programs serving children from birth to age 8* (expanded ed.). Washington, DC: National Association for the Education of Young Children.

Characteristics of preschoolers: Vol. I—Birth through 2, Vol. II—Ages 3 and 4. [Videotape—30 min.]. Early Childhood Consultants, Inc., P.O. Box 800065, Roswell, GA 30075-0001, 1-800-634-2307, ext. 246.

Cohen, D., Stern, V., & Balaban, N. (1981). *Observing and recording the behavior of children* (3rd ed.). New York: Teachers College Press, Columbia University.

Hendrick, J. (1984). *The whole child: Early education for the eighties* (3rd ed.). St. Louis: Times Mirror/ Mosby.

Looking at young children: Observing in early childhood settings [Videotape] (1988). Developed by the Center for Early Education and Development, University of Minnesota. Distributed by Teachers College Press, P.O. Box 939, Wolfeboro, NH 03894.

McCracken, J.B. (1990). "El juego es fundamental." Washington, DC: National Association for the Education of Young Children.

Meisels, S.J. (1987). Uses and abuses of developmental screening and school readiness testing. *Young Children, 42*(2), 4–6, 68–73.

Miller, K. (1985). *Ages and stages: Developmental descriptions & activities birth through eight years.* Marshfield, MA: Telshare.

Schickedanz, J.A., Schickedanz, D.I., & Forsyth, P.D. (1982). *Toward understanding children.* Boston: Little, Brown.

Ways to set up a safe, healthy environment to invite learning

"NO! Don't touch that glass jar. You could break it."

"Which cookie would you like for snack?"

"How many times have I told you to stay away from those stairs?"

"Are you sure you want to draw? I'll have to get the crayons out of the cupboard for you, then."

OR

"These plastic stacking cups are for you. What can you do with them?"

"You may put these raisins on your celery stuffed with cream cheese if you like."

"Our rocking boat turns over like this so you can climb up and down the steps."

"All of the markers, crayons, and paper are here on this shelf. Help yourself whenever you are ready to use them."

Children learn wherever they are. They learn from what they do and see. They learn from what they eat and smell. They learn the languages they hear spoken. They learn how to treat others by the way they are treated. Your attitude determines their attitude.

How you set up your classroom, your family child care playroom, your play yard, or any space you use with the children makes a big difference in what children learn about themselves, about other people, and about the world around them.

If you want children to be safe and healthy . . . you need to make their play areas safe, all of you must practice good hygiene, and you must serve only nutritious foods.

If you want children to feel good about themselves and their friends . . . you must give them plenty of opportunities to succeed and to play in harmony.

If you want children to enjoy learning . . . you select good toys, arrange materials in an appealing way, and encourage children to be curious.

In this unit of your CDA early childhood studies, you will look objectively at **where** and **how** you work with children. Much of what you do most likely already works well. You probably would like some things to work better. Maybe your room arrangement seems to encourage children to run. Perhaps children in your program get sick frequently. Maybe children become bored easily with the materials you have.

We will help you identify what works, and what doesn't, in all types of programs for young children. Unless you are a family child care provider, you may not be responsible for all these items, but you do need to know there are a lot of things to think about when you teach.

The first part of this unit will help you create a safe environment. Then we will outline good health and eating practices. Finally, we will give you some guidelines to apply when you plan your schedule, arrange and decorate your room, and buy new learning materials. Throughout this unit, we will suggest appropriate teaching topics and ideas for children's activities, too. The video for Unit 3 will help you see how programs in many different settings can successfully apply these concepts.

As a result of this unit, we expect you to make changes. Whatever you change, your goal should be to create an enjoyable, challenging, and age-appropriate place for children to learn. Not only will the children benefit, but teaching will be much more pleasant when the children are happily engaged in learning.

Timelines

You will need about 3 weeks to complete your study of Unit 3. During this time you must

1 Prepare for conference with your Field Advisor to discuss four topics (keeping children safe, staying healthy and well-nourished, planning environments that promote play, and choosing appropriate learning materials).

2 Complete four assignments (take a first-aid class, complete the nutritional values chart, sketch space arrangements, and complete the Environment Checklist), and three entries for the Professional Resource File.

3 Complete four assignments for Seminar (identify uncomfortable topics, prepare meal/ snack plans, sketch space arrangements, and rate children's books for stereotypes).

4 View the accompanying videotape using the Viewer's Guide.

Your goal should be to create an enjoyable, challenging, and age-appropriate place for children to learn.

What you learn in this unit will help you feel confident when you demonstrate your knowledge and competency for Goal I: To establish and maintain a safe, healthy, learning environment.

Part 1

How do you keep your children safe?

Safety is not an option. It is essential in any good program for young children. **Look at your copy of your state and local regulations for your program. Most of those standards probably deal with safety. Refresh your memory by reading every safety requirement you must meet.**

Go sit on the floor in the middle of the children's play area. Pretend you are a child. How does it feel to be so short? Can you reach everything you want to play with? What can you get into that you shouldn't?

Crawl around the room and sit in each area. As you do so, write down what you see that doesn't work very well for young children. Maybe the puzzles are on such a high shelf that the pieces always fall out when a child takes them down. Are the sockets covered? Can children get at dangerous substances easily? Are your knees getting dirty? **Make a list here of everything that is a potential danger or nuisance to children.**

Now go out to your playground, back yard, park, or wherever you take children to play outdoors. Sit on the ground and look around for possible hazards. Write down what you see.

Scattered all through this chapter are sections of a checklist for you to use. As you go through it, you will put a check next to items that describe your facility or program. Those without checks will be the areas you can work to improve. **Your Field Advisor will verify that you have accurately completed all sections of the checklist.**

✔ Environment checklist: Safety

This first part contains some of the most basic safety concerns you should watch for. If you didn't notice each one of these items during your first survey, go back and look again.

Put a check next to items that describe your program. Add anything else you feel is particularly important for safety in your program. Your location, climate, or ages of the children make a difference. Refer to this checklist often just to be sure you haven't overlooked something.

_____ You meet every state or local requirement for a safe program.

_____ Adults protect children from themselves and each other—children may not hit, bite, or otherwise hurt people or things.

_____ All accidents and any first aid you give to children are reported to the appropriate staff (in a center) and to the children's parent.

Safety indoors

_____ The floors are clean and in good repair. Floors are not slippery.

_____ All areas are well lighted.

_____ There is enough space for children to move around without constantly bumping into each other. Your state requires _____ square feet of indoor space per child. Your program has _____ square feet per child.

_____ Furniture and toys are sturdy enough to withstand constant use by children.

_____ Furniture, toys, and materials are appropriate for the age of the children (child-sized chairs and tables, blunt-end scissors).

_____ Furniture, toys, and materials are in good repair—no sharp edges, no peeling paint, no loose parts.

_____ Electrical sockets are covered, extension cords are used only behind heavy furniture, electrical appliances are out of children's reach except when under close supervision (such as cooking).

_____ Radiators, ovens, fans, and space heaters are out of children's reach.

_____ Your water is not hotter than 110° F.

_____ Dangerous substances (such as toxic plants, balloons, plastic bags, cleaning products, matches, and medicine) are not accessible to children. Poisons and medicines are stored in a locked cabinet.

_____ You require a parent's signature to give medication. You maintain a log of when which medicines were administered to which child.

_____ Smoke detectors are located properly. You check them monthly to be sure they work.

_____ Fire extinguishers are easy to reach. You practice how to use them at least once a month.

_____ Emergency evacuation procedures are posted. You practice how to leave the building quickly with the children at least once a month. Diagrams and pictures are used to make procedures clear. Instructions are in every language spoken by any staff member or parent.

_____ Emergency telephone numbers are located next to each telephone. One telephone is in the room where the children play most. Symbols or other languages are used on the list so any parent or staff member can easily locate a number.

_____ Easy entry and access is available for disabled staff, children, or parents. Handrails are installed as necessary.

_____ Room arrangements, equipment, and furniture are adapted as needed so children with disabilities can participate in as many activities as possible.

_____ Children can come and go from your center without major safety concerns: there are no steep steps, parking is nearby and ample.

_____ If your program uses buses, they are regularly inspected, drivers are well trained, and safe procedures for loading and unloading are followed.

_____ Children are always supervised by adults—indoors, on the playground, in the yard, on walks and field trips. You anticipate potential problems and take steps to avoid them.

_____ Children are only released to authorized people. Parents must sign a list of those who are authorized.

_____ Children know indoor safety rules. They are taught these rules in a way that does not frighten them. They are helped to understand why the rules are necessary. Pictures, demonstrations, and children's primary languages are used when explaining rules.

_____ A well-stocked first-aid kit is easy to get to.

In addition, if you care for babies or toddlers:

_____ Babies are never left unattended on a diaper changing table, in their bath, or in a wading pool.

_____ Cribs have all their slats. Slats are no farther than 2 3/8 inches apart (2 inches apart in Canada).

_____ Cribs were made after 1978 (no lead paint).

_____ Crib sides are put up for naps.

_____ No pillows or heavy blankets are used.

_____ Toys are too large for children to swallow.

_____ Walkers, highchairs, swings, strollers, and other equipment are sturdy, clean, and in good repair.

_____ Bottles are never warmed in a microwave oven (because of the uneven temperatures that may result).

_____ Stairways are accessible only to adults.

Other indoor safety checks for my program:

Safety outdoors

_____ Children have enough space to run around without bumping into each other or the equipment. Your state requires _____ square feet of outdoor space per child. You have _____ square feet of outdoor space per child.

_____ The play area is free of debris. It is fenced and/or located away from traffic. There are no poisonous plants growing in the area. There is no standing water. Sand is covered when not in use to keep animals out.

_____ Traffic patterns are set up so children are not likely to run in front of or behind moving equipment such as swings.

_____ Equipment is clean, sturdy, and in good repair.

_____ Equipment is securely anchored.

_____ Children have a variety of types of equipment to use for different types of play: riding toys, climbing apparatus, sand to dig in.

_____ Some surfaces are hard (for riding vehicles) but most are soft (grass). Sand, bark, or other soft materials are underneath any equipment where children might jump or fall.

_____ Children with disabilities can use most areas of the playground.

_____ Shade is available.

_____ Children know the rules for playing safely outdoors. Rules are explained with diagrams, pictures, demonstrations, and in children's primary languages.

_____ When crossing streets, children must be accompanied by an adult. Everyone uses appropriate crossing precautions.

_____ When children ride in cars or buses, they use age-appropriate safety seats and/or belts. You have a policy that parents are expected to use these daily.

_____ An adult monitors each area of the playground at all times. Teachers do not use outdoor play time to talk among themselves. Unauthorized adults on the playground are asked to leave immediately.

Other outdoor safety checks for my program:

_____

_____

_____

You make safety a daily experience

Safety is much more than a hazard-free environment. Safety is what happens every day. This means setting some developmentally appropriate rules for children's behavior and teaching children how to be responsible for their own safe behavior.

Set up a few safety rules

Most likely you already have safety rules for children to follow in your program. **Write your rules here:**

_____

_____

_____

Here are some tips about safety rules. **Compare these guidelines to your own rules.** Rules work best when they are stated in terms of what children should do, when there are just a few rules, and when they match the ages of the children in your group.

If you put rules in terms of what children **should** do, children are much more likely to follow them.

Look back at your rules. How many tell children what to do (rather than what not to do)? _____ Do you often have trouble getting children to follow your rules? _____ If so, could it be that they don't know what they are supposed to do?

It is also important to have only a few important safety rules so children don't feel overwhelmed with too many. These are some basic rules that many programs for young children find helpful:

- We walk indoors.
- We take good care of our bodies.
- We are kind to other people.
- We take good care of our things.

These rules will need to be adapted to the ages of the children in your care. Younger children may need specific rules such as these:

- People are for loving. People are not for biting or hitting.
- We climb on the cushions and the climber, not on the sofa.

Somewhat older children may need specific rules such as these:

- Tricycles are only for riding on our playground roads. We never crash tricycles into anything.
- Sand is for sifting and pouring. Sand hurts when you get it in your eyes.

Older preschoolers will probably welcome the opportunity to set up some of their own rules. They might include this rule:

- One person may walk on the balance beam at a time.

If you work with older children, tell them you are thinking about rules. Ask them to make suggestions for rules that will help everyone in the group be safe. Write some of their suggestions here.

Children also need to know why a rule is necessary. Discuss with children why your group has rules. Children will surely ignore the rules if they don't know why the rules are needed. Even when children can tell you why it's not safe to stand on chairs or climb on tables, frequent reminders may be necessary. Sometimes posters with pictures will work for preschoolers.

Use safe behaviors

Of course, all the rules in the world and the safest equipment will not prevent accidents. **You also need a lot of common sense and a careful watch over children.**

Perhaps a child drops a bit of peanut butter spread on a banana on the floor. You notice it and ask the child to clean it up before someone slips. Another child can watch that no one else steps in the mess while it is being cleaned up.

Or you see that a bolt on the steering wheel on the playground is loose and the steering wheel wobbles. You tighten it up or ask the person responsible to do so before any more children are allowed to use it.

You must constantly check the environment and children's behavior. Catch accidents before they happen!

Most of all, not only do you set rules, but you follow them, and you always use safe behavior yourself. You buckle up when you ride or drive in your car. You pull electrical cords from the socket by holding the plug, not the cord. You cut away from yourself when you use a sharp knife to make carrot sticks for snack. You **don't** go dashing across the street with a note a parent left behind!

Children follow your example. When you do something safe—such as carrying scissors by the blades and walking slowly, for example—you point out to the children what you are doing and why. It won't be long until children will remind you when you are being unsafe.

Incorporate safety into the daily curriculum

Fire Prevention Week. Mr. Yuk. *We Love You—Buckle Up!* Community helpers. These are familiar themes for teachers of young children.

But how effective is it to talk about fire safety just 1 week each year? Children are constantly growing and learning new things. Safety needs to be a natural part of their daily lives. Children need to try out safety ideas in their play all the time—driving a fire truck, pretending to be doctors, or playing captain of a boat, for example.

While you may want to emphasize a topic for a week or two, you certainly want safety to happen in your group every day. Whenever you teach safety—which is constantly—keep these general guidelines in mind:

- Your purpose in teaching safety should be to **help children learn safe behaviors.** Fear is not a good teacher. Children shouldn't be taught in ways that intentionally frighten

them. Instead, you want children to learn what to do to take care of themselves and their friends and family.

- The topics and the way you present them should **make sense to children**. Before you decide how to teach about a topic, talk with the children to find out what they already know. Ask open-ended questions: Who knows why we . . . ? What would you do if . . . ? Some topics are very abstract, such as electricity, yet children can learn how to be safe around electrical cords and appliances. They will learn more about how electricity works when they are much older.

- Activities and materials should **be as realistic as safely possible**. Children need to sit in safety seats and use safety belts. They need to cross streets again and again in the company of an adult. They need to use a disconnected telephone to practice dialing or pushing the buttons for the emergency number. Then, when children listen to stories, watch movies, and talk about being safe, these activities will make sense because children remember their **real** experiences.

Here are some specific teaching tips on favorite and appropriate safety topics for young children. **For each topic, jot down other ideas you have so you can share them later with your CDA Field Advisor.**

Everyday safety. Even the safest program has potential hazards for active children. A high tower of blocks crashes down on someone's head. Paint spills beneath the easel and someone slips. Waddlers fall down repeatedly as they learn to walk.

How do you reduce these risks? You always think how to make your home or classroom a safer place to be. You watch children and see what happens, then make changes. Perhaps a height limit needs to be set for block structures. Maybe soap flakes will thicken the paint so it doesn't drip. A flatter carpet might be safer for waddlers to practice walking. Always keep your eyes and ears open for safety's sake!

List some of your everyday concerns for indoor safety:

Fire safety. Fire fascinates children. Its colors are pretty. It crackles. No wonder fires kill or injure thousands of children every year.

How do you help children learn to respect fire? Birthdays are good times to bring up fire safety in a natural way. Why do adults light the birthday candles? What happens to the match and candles after they burn?

Fall is a good time to talk about fire safety, when families rake leaves, light fireplaces, and heat their homes. Summer, too, with bonfires, fireworks, and barbecue grills, offers yet another opportunity.

Children's dramatic play is an excellent way for them to work through their ideas about fires.

Preschoolers can learn to give matches they find to an adult so younger children won't accidentally start a fire. They can learn not to touch anything that has a fire in or near it—a stove, kerosene heater, campfire—so they won't get burned. They can learn and practice how to STOP, DROP, and ROLL, should their clothing catch on fire. They can memorize and practice dialing your local emergency number. Children of all ages can follow your program's procedures for a fire drill.

Children's dramatic play is an excellent way for them to work through their ideas about fires. The block corner should have a firetruck. Add some old pieces of hose, a medical kit, a blanket, and other similar props to the dramatic play area and let children explore their ideas about what happens in a fire.

If their play seems limited to siren noises, help them expand their play by asking questions such as "And then what happens when the firefighters arrive? What equipment do firefighters use?"

A visit to the fire station can be a fun and learning experience for children. If you plan it with the children's development in mind, this popular field trip is appropriate for preschoolers.

Talk with the firefighters ahead of time about the general principles of teaching about safety to young children. Ask whether children can climb into the driver's seat of a fire truck, try on boots and a helmet, or attempt to lift a hose — *real* experiences.

Your primary emphasis, however, should be on what children and grown-ups do to be safe with fire and why they do it.

In addition to your fire department, there may be other local resources for teaching fire safety. Perhaps the school PTA, your library, or a civic organization has a program or some books. Be sure to use only the parts of them that seem appropriate for young children. Select stories that include men and women from various ethnic groups as firefighters.

Make a list here of other appropriate ideas you use to help children be fire safe.

_____

_____

_____

_____

_____

Crossing streets safely. Accidents involving motor vehicles are the leading cause of death for young children. You know how quickly a child chasing a ball can dart into the street. From the time children begin to crawl you can introduce ideas about keeping safe wherever there are cars or trucks. Find out what the children in your group know — just take a walk and see what children want to do when you approach the street. Then you will know where to begin.

Here are some things young children can learn about crossing streets:

- Walk only on sidewalks (or in the opposite direction of traffic on the edge of the road if there are no sidewalks).
- Always cross streets with an adult.
- Watch for cars about to leave the curb.
- Stop and look for cars coming from all directions before crossing streets or alleys.
- Take frequent walks to practice safe street crossing procedures.

> **A word of caution is in order here.** Many businesses, civic groups, and community leaders have teaching ideas, sometimes even complete curriculums, for teaching about safety topics.
>
> Many of these curriculums are not appropriate for young children. Some may try to scare children. Others may consist primarily of lectures or coloring books, rather than real experiences. Many fail to recognize that children learn primarily through play.
>
> **You must rely on what you know about how young children learn when you select these materials.** You may want to use only one or two good parts of such material.

Children may also enjoy using toy cars and miniature people as part of their pretend play. If crossing guards or police officers are familiar, children enjoy wearing orange belts or vests to play street crossing on the playground. As always, emphasize what children should do and make the activities real. Then, when children are in elementary school, they will be ready to learn to cross streets by themselves. An excellent source of suggestions for teaching about crossing streets is the preschool curriculum, *Walk in Traffic Safely (WITS)*.

Add your ideas for teaching street safety here.

Safety seats and belts. Every state has regulations about child safety restraints. However, every parent and teacher should use the proper restraints for children — and themselves — even if it is not required by law.

Children are often injured in low-speed accidents around town, because adults too often find excuses not to use proper restraints. Holding a child in your lap is no protection at all — in fact, it will only cause more injury in case of an accident, because the adult's heavy body would crush the child or the child would be thrown out the window.

How do children learn to be safe when riding in a car, van, or pickup truck? By parents and teachers giving them the experience of using a proper seat for every ride. Children who are expected and accustomed to riding in these seats do so willingly.

Infant seats face to the rear. Toddler seats face forward. There are special car booster seats for preschoolers. All of these seats are held in place with the car's safety belt. The child is held in place either by the car's belt (on booster seats) or by a separate belt system attached to the seat.

Your first step, then, is to find out which children regularly ride in safety seats. That will help you determine how much you need to work with parents and what you can do to help children feel comfortable using safety seats. How many of the children in your program are buckled up each day?

Next, bring the experience of safety seats into the programs. You may want to borrow a seat or find one at a garage sale. Make sure it is the right type for the children in your group. If you are a family child care provider, you may need more than one for children of different ages. Put the seat in your play area so children can sit in it and see for themselves how good it feels to be safe.

If your program's policy does not specify that children arrive and leave in safety seats, find out what you can do to change it. Make sure your program's field trip policy includes a statement such as the one here:

Whenever transportation is provided for children in this program, they will be properly restrained. Adults driving or riding in the vehicle will also be properly restrained.

A number of other appropriate activities are suggested in the economical curriculum package *We Love You—Buckle Up!* **What ideas do you have to encourage parents and children to buckle up?**

_____

_____

_____

if they see someone who needs help in the water. Show children where to find lifeguards or other adults.

Check with your Red Cross or other water safety group in your community to find out what resources they have to help you teach children water safety.

Make a list here of water safety behaviors you can incorporate in your teaching:

_____

_____

_____

Water safety. Children can drown in just a bit of water—a kitchen sink, wading pool, or toilet, for example. Although young children are never waterproof, even if they can swim, we can help them know what to do to be safe around water. Babies and toddlers need constant supervision and should never be left alone in a bath, at the beach, or even at a classroom water table.

Toddlers and young preschoolers can make sure an adult is watching before they climb into a wading pool or splash in a big puddle. They can learn to walk (not run) near water.

Young children love to play boat. They can fish, search for treasure, or sail away to a sunny island. Build on this interest. They enjoy buckling up in life preservers before they climb into a boat.

Older preschoolers can also learn what to do

Electrical safety. Most of us don't understand how electricity works, but we certainly should know and share with the children the need to be cautious with it.

As you watch and listen to the children in your group, you will probably see that crawling infants, waddlers, and curious toddlers would stick their fingers or anything else into a socket if they could. Therefore, every socket must have a cover.

Preschool children are still not capable of using electrical appliances alone, but with proper supervision they can learn how to plug something in and remove it from the socket. They can learn how to keep their fingers on the dials when they turn on the radio or television. They can learn not to touch electrical appliances that get hot—curling irons, heaters, electric skillets, toasters. Cooking projects are excellent times for helping children learn electrical safety when using appliances.

Write down some of your ideas for teaching children electrical safety.

Care with hot and cold. Most children have probably accidentally been burned and will tell their friends how much it hurt. Others may have had their fingers stick to an ice cube or a frosty window. Start with children's experiences as a base for helping them figure out what things are too hot or too cold to touch.

Use warm and cool items that are safe to touch so children can feel the difference. For example, at lunch children could feel how warm their pizza is and how cool their milk is — take advantage of what naturally happens in the classroom rather than setting up an artificial experience.

Weather plays a big part in children's lives because it determines what they wear and what they play outdoors. Many infants and toddlers especially will require sunscreen to avoid burning even when they are outdoors for short periods of time. Shade should always be available on part of your outdoor play area so children can play in comfort in the summer.

Drinks of water should be offered frequently.

In the winter, frostbite is a danger in cold climates. On bitterly cold, windy days you may need to stay indoors and find some vigorous games or activities. Usually children, even infants, can go out to play for at least a few minutes, though. Make sure they are warmly dressed but not so bundled up that they get hot and sweaty if they are active.

Older children may enjoy dressing up in clothes for hot or cold weather — in the opposite season. What fun a picnic at the beach would be in the middle of the winter! Doll clothes and dress-up clothes can also be seasonal.

What other ways do you have to help children understand hot and cold?

Riding vehicles (tricycles, low bikes, scooters) safely. Another major cause of accidents for young children are cars in driveways that run over children who are riding or skating. Children are usually so short the driver cannot see them or the child appears suddenly from behind a tree or another car.

Every good early childhood program has an assortment of riding vehicles. While your riding area is well supervised and away from traffic, children can still learn riding precautions to use when they ride on their own sidewalks.

Some programs even set up a miniature road with stop signs to help children develop good driving skills! At the very least, you will want children to learn not to drive their vehicle into another person or object.

Children should learn what to look for when a car is about to move: a driver climbs in, the engine goes vroom, lights may come on. With practice, while taking walks or riding on the sidewalk, children can identify these vehicles, and explain what they need to do to be safe around them: stop at every driveway or alley to look for a car that might move, never ride up a driveway unless an adult is with you.

This topic is another excellent one to involve the children's parents and other community resources. In addition, *Children Riding on Sidewalks Safely* (CROSS) is a curriculum package for helping young children develop safe riding habits.

What kinds of activities can you think of to help children stay safe when they ride?

_____

_____

_____

_____

_____

_____

_____

Poison and medicine safety. In every program for young children, both poisons and medicines should be kept in a locked cabinet. Although you store these dangerous substances the same way, you handle discussions about them in two entirely different ways.

Poisons are presented as chemicals that are dangerous for your body—they can make you feel awful or even die. Children cannot always know what is dangerous, so they should be told, in the language most familiar to them, never to put anything into their mouth unless they ask an adult first.

Medicines, on the other hand, are chemicals that help our bodies get well when we swallow or apply the right amount. Children should never be misled into thinking medicines (or vitamins) are treats. Rather, if children have difficulty swallowing pills or liquids, mix them with drinks or food. The emphasis should always be on getting or staying well by taking good care of our bodies.

When children must be given medicine, it should be given to them by a teacher who speaks their primary language, with whom they feel comfortable, and according to written instructions from parents. The dosage and time of administration is written immediately on the child's medical record.

Children can also learn poison and medicine safety while playing doctor or hospital. Provide a variety of types of props: a stethoscope, bandages, crutches, prescription pads—whatever you can find that will allow children to pretend.

You and your program's health consultant probably have several other suggestions to help young children avoid poison and accept medicine when it is prescribed. **Write those ideas here.**

List some ways your playground safety could be improved.

Playground safety. Children need to use playground safety every day. The design of your playground can either make it easy or difficult for children to be safe. The checklist earlier in this unit is a good place to start to identify areas for improvement. Whenever possible, change the playground to make it safe rather than coming up with another rule for children.

Even when the areas are as safe as possible, your constant attention is needed on the playground. This is no time to socialize with other teachers.

Playground rules are used every day, not just on special occasions, so it is essential that children understand why you have the rules. Explain rules clearly, in children's primary language, when they are first introduced.

Each time you talk with a child about a rule, gently remind her or him about the reason. "Rachel, sand is for digging. Sand is not for throwing. It can get in people's eyes. Sand hurts our eyes very much."

Safety—and strangers. This topic is a broad one. It can cover everything from what a child should do when lost in a store, to reporting abuse. No other topic arouses so much emotion. We all want children to be safe from physical or emotional abuse, but we don't want them to be so scared they avoid making new friends or refuse to talk with someone they can trust, either.

Much of what you decide to do about this topic will depend on your community and the feelings of the parents of the children in your program.

As a professional, your role is to help children grow up to become adults who feel good about themselves and who can make wise decisions. The tone of your voice, your posture, and what you say and do will all affect children.

Helping children know what to do when they are lost is a fairly simple problem compared to some of the other issues that fall in this category. Generally it is sufficient to read a good children's picture book that shows how a child handles the problem: Find a person who works in the store. Ask a police officer, zoo worker, or security guard for help. Stay where you are and wait for your parents to find you. After the story, children may want to act out what to do, draw pictures, or dictate stories about a time when they were lost.

Many materials have been developed to help children know what to do when approached by a stranger who makes them feel uncomfortable. An additional focus is needed, however, for we know that the greatest danger to very young children may actually be from people they know who abuse them either physically or emotionally.

Therefore, your primary goal will be to help children feel cared about, protected, and free to be honest about their feelings when they talk with you. They must know that they can trust you to take good care of them.

As part of this process, you can do and say things to inspire children's confidence and build their self-esteem. For example, you want children to be proud of their bodies and their functions so you never make them feel ashamed of themselves. Dressing and using the toilet are excellent times to help children begin to learn proper names for their body parts. You can also help preschool children understand that the parts of their bodies covered by their swimming suits are private.

In addition, even young preschool children can begin to learn the difference between good touches and uncomfortable touches. They can learn how to say no to those touches that make them feel strange. Children also need to be told what to do when this happens: Tell an adult you trust.

Select carefully from the children's books, films and videos, puppets, and other curricu-lum materials that are available so you choose only those that are appropriate for young children and sensitive to the cultures of the families with whom you work.

This is one topic you may want to discuss at length with your supervisor, the director, your licensing worker, or your CDA Field Advisor.

List here some of the concerns you have about how to help children deal with these harsh realities of life:

_____

_____

_____

_____

_____

You also need to know what to do if you see signs of potential child abuse. Knowing what those signs are and what to do about them will be discussed in Unit 4, Part 4 of *Essentials*. For now, it is important to know that each state requires that educators report any possible case. **Find out who you report your concerns to, and write the name and number here:**

_____

_____

Copy this information on your emergency telephone list, if it is not already there. Also add it to your Professional Resource File.

If the suspected child abuse case is confirmed, you will want to seek the advice of a professional, such as a social worker or psychologist, about how to help the child and family handle such a delicate situation.

Now that we have covered some basic safety themes, are there others you have used or plan to use? **Make a list of them here:**

You are prepared for emergencies

What would you do if a child in your program
- choked on a sandwich?
- fell and hit her head?
- was stung by a bee?
- got cut badly on a tricycle?
- burned himself on a hot pan?
- complained of ear pain?
- had a seizure?
- chewed on some plant leaves?

Old home remedies, common sense, and a first-aid kit are not enough.

As part of your training to become a CDA, you are expected to take a first-aid course so **that you will know what to do for these and other common types of accidents.**

Contact your local Red Cross or other group and enroll in a class as soon as possible. You will be required to submit a copy of your certificate of completion to the Council before you can complete your CDA assessment. Keep a record of your class and the original certificate in your Professional Resource File.

Record the dates of your class here

Safety is so easy to take for granted. Sometimes it seems like such a bother. But accidents happen in a flash. You must always be on your toes with young children!

Part 2

How do you and your children stay healthy and well nourished?

You have probably heard a lot about how diseases spread easily in group care for children. While outbreaks of illness can happen, children and teachers in good group care programs can improve their chances for staying well. How? You, the parents, and the children all work together. These are the main steps you must take:

Stay well!

- Make sure all children are properly immunized. Keep child and staff health exam records current. Promptly and properly report contacts with contagious diseases.
- Keep the environment clean.
- Use good hygiene. Children and staff wash their hands thoroughly. Teachers who change diapers follow recommended procedures. Children feel proud when they are learning to use the toilet.
- Serve only nutritious foods.

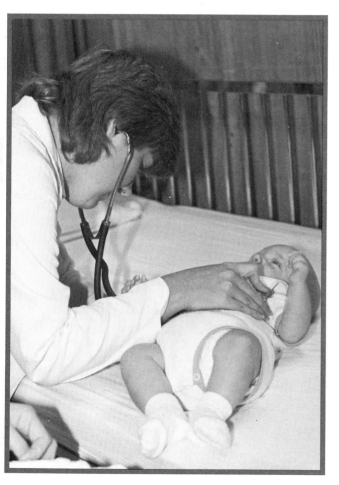

Children's health must be protected by the adults who care for them. Parents and staff share this responsibility.

Just as you did in the last section on safety, you need to locate your state's regulations and/or Head Start Performance Standards for health and food service. Keep your copy handy and refer to it as you work through this unit.

Use the next four sections of the environment checklist to think about the primary ways in which you maintain a healthy environment. If you work in a group program, you probably are not in charge of some of the items listed, but you do need to know about them. If you are a family child care provider, you are responsible for each one. Within each section, you will find ideas to present these health topics to children.

You monitor immunizations, health exams, and report diseases

Children's health must be protected by the adults who care for them. Parents and staff share this responsibility.

Start your study of this critical aspect of child care by checking which points in the following list are already followed in your program. Add others that are especially appropriate. Then, look at the items you have not checked. This is where you can begin to improve children's health—and your own.

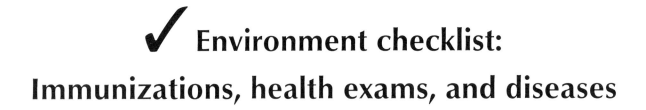

✔ Environment checklist:
Immunizations, health exams, and diseases

_____ Your program complies with all state, local, and program regulations regarding child and staff health.

_____ When you contact parents about children's health, you share information in their primary language.

_____ Children are immunized according to the schedule recommended by the American Academy of Pediatrics (see page 121) before they are admitted to your program.

_____ At least once a year, you check children's immunization records to be sure they are current. Boosters as needed are recorded.

_____ Before children are enrolled, they have a health exam. You use the form provided by your licensing agent or another similar form. The form is signed by a health care professional. The health record includes any health conditions (allergies or disabilities, for example) and emergency contact information.

_____ Health exams are repeated each year either on the anniversary date of the child's enrollment or some other convenient date.

_____ Your program keeps a copy of all health exam records.

_____ Your own health exam is repeated each year. You keep a copy in your program records.

_____ Whenever you or a child in your group is exposed to a contagious disease (pinkeye, impetigo, or chicken pox, for example) you immediately report it to your supervisor (in a group program) or make a note of it (in family child care).

_____ You give parents information, in their primary language, about the incubation period, symptoms to watch for, and health care when a contagious disease is reported.

_____ You watch for signs that children may not be feeling well as they arrive and throughout the day.

_____ You and the children use a tissue once and then discard it in a closed container.

_____ Your program has a written policy about when sick staff and children may and may not attend. When you or the children are sick you make no exceptions to this policy. This policy is given to parents upon enrollment. It is written in the parents' preferred language.

_____ You refer parents to medical services when appropriate. Whenever possible, the referral is made to a provider who can speak their language.

Other health practices appropriate for my program:

_____

_____

_____

_____

Many of us remember polio outbreaks. Some of us remember whooping cough. How fortunate we are that children can now be easily and quite safely immunized against these and other dangerous and contagious diseases. Parents generally are very cooperative about scheduling immunizations and health exams.

Recommended schedule for active immunization of normal infants and children

	DTP	Polio	Measles	Mumps	Rubella	Haemophilus**	Tetanus-Diphtheria
2 months	✓	✓				✓	
4 months	✓	✓				✓	
6 months	✓					(✓)	
12–15 months						(✓)	
15 months			✓	✓	✓	(✓)	
15–18 months	✓	✓					
4–6 years	✓	✓					
11–12 years*			✓	✓	✓		
14–16 years							✓

Childhood immunization means protection against eight major diseases: polio, measles, mumps, Rubella (German measles), whooping cough (pertussis), diphtheria, tetanus, and Haemophilus influenzae type b infections.

[Parents should] check the table and ask [their] pediatrician if [their] child is up-to-date on vaccines. It could save a life or prevent disability. Measles, mumps, Rubella, polio, pertussis, diphtheria, Haemophilus influenzae infections, and tetanus are not just harmless childhood illnesses. All of them can cripple or kill. All are preventable.

If [parents] don't have a pediatrician or family physician, [they can] call [the] local public health department. It usually has supplies of vaccine and may give shots free.

* Except where public health authorities require otherwise.

** As of March 1991, two vaccines for Haemophilus influenzae infections have been approved for use in children younger than 15 months of age.

( ) indicated in many circumstances depending on which vaccine for Haemophilus influenzae infections was previously given.

Reprinted with permission from "Immunization Protects Children." Copyright © 1991 American Academy of Pediatrics.

Comfort children who are ill

Sick children are cause for alarm in families. Parents are naturally concerned about their child's health, but also, children who are ill often cannot attend child care. As a result, parents often are forced to miss work, use leave time, and sometimes take a cut in their pay.

When children must stay home because of illness, be sensitive to the parents' needs, too. Explain that in the long run keeping sick children at home usually means fewer sick days for everyone. Since it is difficult to make other child care arrangements on short notice, if possible, keep a list of caregivers willing to provide sick child care.

Your program's policy for excluding sick children needs to be carefully set and reviewed often to keep it up to date with medical advances and as in tune with parents' and children's needs as possible.

Sometimes when a child is ill, you become frustrated. Perhaps your biases about children's families come up: Lice, scabies, worms, and other conditions may seem to you to be a result of poor parenting or inadequate health care. Discuss any concerns you have about dealing with parents with your health consultant or licensing representative. Learn all you can about these conditions—and you will find even children from all types of homes can suffer from them. Stay well informed about common childhood diseases so you can concentrate on taking good care of children who do not feel well.

How do you help a child who becomes ill during the day? Just as you always do, you treat the child with dignity, handle any messes matter-of-factly, and offer as much comfort as you can. While you wait for the parent to arrive, you probably will want to give the child a place to rest away from the others in the group. Sometimes a child will want to stay close to you—perhaps resting her or his head in your lap. Try to provide as much comfort and attention as you can because, besides not feeling well, sick children are sometimes frightened.

Other children in the group will see how much comfort you provide. They will be reassured that they too will be cared for well should they get sick. Children treat each other as kindly as you treat them.

Your health is extremely important, too. Working with young children is exhausting. The stress is constant. Runny noses, diarrhea, and earaches are almost daily occurrences. Be sure you take good care of yourself: Get plenty of rest, eat well, and stay calm!

What health areas do you want to improve in your program? List them here and follow through as soon as possible.

Dramatic play is the best way to help children learn about their health. Be sure you have plenty of props so they can relive their own experiences with being examined, immunized, and bandaged. Find some children's books, in English and other languages, to read together about what medical workers do. Field trips to a neighborhood clinic or a pediatrician's office might be helpful, too.

You keep the environment clean

Cleanliness is essential if you and the children are to stay healthy. If your environment is clean, dry, and filled with fresh air you greatly improve your chances of staying well. **Check each item on this list that applies to your program.**

✔ Environment checklist:
Keep the environment clean

_____ Your program meets all state and local requirements for sanitation.

_____ If you prepare and store food, all state and local regulations are met.

_____ Indoor and outdoor areas are clean, dry, and well lighted. Natural light is let in whenever possible.

_____ Preschool children are expected to clean up their own spills, paper scraps, and other minor messes. You supervise their efforts.

_____ You use paper cups or child-sized drinking fountains for drinking water.

_____ Trash is emptied daily.

_____ Bathrooms are cleaned daily with bleach solution (see page 125).

_____ Spills of body fluids (blood, urine, vomit, feces) are cleaned with bleach solution.

_____ You assign individual cubbies for children's personal belongings. If possible, each child keeps an extra set of clothing in her or his cubby (or you keep an extra set on hand). Each piece of clothing is labeled with the child's name. The child's name is easy to see on the outside of the cubby, and is written in both English and the child's home language.

_____ Dress-up clothing and accessories (hats, wigs, bridal veils) are washed or replaced weekly.

_____ Children's bedding is washed weekly. Only one child uses bedding between washings.

_____ Cots, cribs, and mats are washed whenever they are soiled. They are labeled with children's names.

_____ You ventilate indoor spaces with fresh air whenever possible. Windows that open have screens.

_____ Indoor heat and humidity levels are comfortable and healthy.

_____ You know where to find information on how to clean the environment in the event lice or other similar problems are discovered. **List your resource here:**

If you care for infants or toddlers:

_____ Infant equipment is cleaned with bleach solution (see page 125) twice a week.

_____ Toys that infants put in their mouths are washed with bleach solution (see page 125) daily.

_____ Bottles are never set down on the floor.

_____ Children's wet or soiled clothes are sealed in labeled, individual plastic bags so parents can launder them.

_____ Disposable diapers are thrown away in a container lined with a plastic bag and covered with a lid.

_____ Cloth diapers are sealed in individual labeled, plastic bags for parents to launder them.

_____ The diaper-changing area has one of these two types of covers:

    1. a plastic cover that can be washed with bleach after every diaper change, **or**

    2. a paper cover that is discarded after every diaper change.

_____ Several changes of clothing are available for children who are learning to use the toilet.

Other hygiene practices appropriate for my program:

If you did not check every item in this section of the checklist, take steps to make your program a healthier place to be. You may need to meet with your director to share this information and work out a plan to improve the cleaning in your program. Unless these guidelines are followed, you, the other staff, and the children are at risk for spreading illness.

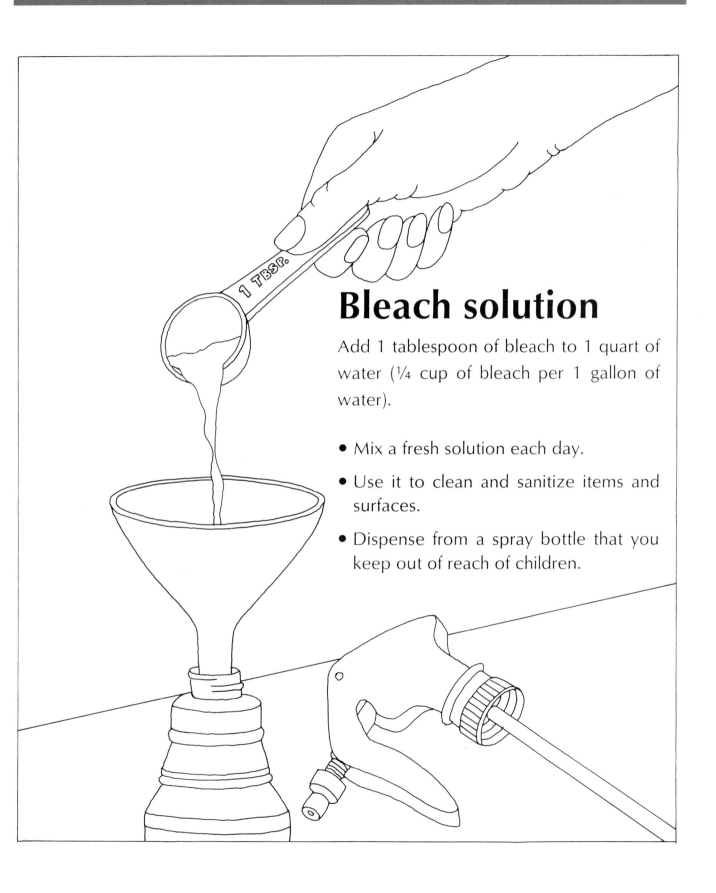

Bleach solution

Add 1 tablespoon of bleach to 1 quart of water (¼ cup of bleach per 1 gallon of water).

- Mix a fresh solution each day.
- Use it to clean and sanitize items and surfaces.
- Dispense from a spray bottle that you keep out of reach of children.

Preschool children can certainly help you in your efforts. You can label their cubbies with their name and a picture they can easily identify. This way, they can put their belongings away by themselves. They can use sponges and water to wipe up their own messes. They can put their trash in the wastebasket when they finish eating. They can change their wet clothing and put on dry clothes. These are good health habits they will use the rest of their lives.

On the right, list some other similar responsibilities preschool children can take to keep your area clean:

You take good care of yourself, other staff, and children

Many other good personal habits are also a part of your daily routine. Let's look at what you and the children can do to take good care of your bodies — and increase your chances to stay well.

✔ Environment checklist:
Children and staff take good care of themselves

_____ You and the children always wash your hands thoroughly before handling food and after toileting. Use liquid soap, running water, rubbing, and paper towels to dry your hands and turn off faucets (see the poster on page 128). Wash your hands after wiping a child's nose, a sneeze, or a cough. Hand lotion is readily available for staff.

_____ You all brush your teeth after eating. Individual toothbrushes are labeled. Brushes are stored in an open container. Bristles do not touch each other.

_____ At least one rest period/naptime is provided for older toddlers and preschool children.

_____ Children are shown how and expected to use good toilet habits: wiping properly, lifting and lowering the seat, aiming well.

_____ Children use their own hairbrushes, combs, and hats.

_____ Children and adults wear clothing appropriate for the weather.

_____ Children play outdoors at least once in the morning and once in the afternoon.

If you care for infants or toddlers:

_____ You wash your hands after diapering each child and before feeding a child.

_____ You follow the specific procedures for changing diapers (see pages 132 to 133) every time you change a diaper. Post procedures in every language spoken by the staff and parents.

_____ Children take naps on their own schedules—they sleep when they are tired.

_____ Children who are learning to take responsibility for using the toilet are treated with respect. They are never shamed or made to feel like failures when they have accidents.

Other self-care procedures appropriate for my program:

Teaching good personal habits

During their early years children are developing good personal habits to use all of their lives. They are learning to be proud of their bodies and their skills. Nearly every minute of every day will be an opportunity for children to learn and practice how to take good care of their bodies.

Handwashing. Most of us are lazy about handwashing—it seems like such a bother. But did you know that handwashing is the *one best way* to prevent the spread of disease? It's true.

Washing your hands thoroughly is more effective than anything else you do to keep the environment clean because so many types of diseases are spread by touching infected areas and then touching parts of your body or food.

If you wash your hands frequently, children will follow your example. You simply must wash your hands often—especially in the winter, when it will seem as if you are wiping a runny nose every minute. Use lots of hand lotion and keep telling yourself how well you and the children will stay.

"This is the way we wash our hands to stay healthy! Bubbles, lots of rubbing, rinsing, and dry with a towel." Children love to play in water, so with a little guidance about the correct technique, teaching handwashing is a cinch!

How to wash your hands

Use soap and running water

Rub your hands vigorously

Wash thoroughly backs of hands, wrists,
   between fingers, under fingernails

Rinse well

Dry hands with a paper towel

Turn off the water using a paper towel, not your
   clean hands

**Help children learn the proper way to wash
   their hands, too.**

Then just be there to supervise each time children wash their hands. **What else can you do to get children involved in handwashing?**

_____

_____

_____

_____

Toothbrushing. Most children think it's fun to brush teeth—if the adults who teach them make it fun. And how good it feels afterward!

Be sure you and the children brush teeth after snacks as well as meals, especially if you eat sweet or sticky foods such as dried fruits, cheese, or peanut butter. After your group finishes eating, make it part of your daily routine to brush your teeth.

Use an egg carton, turned over, with holes punched in each hill, to store the brushes. Make sure each brush is marked with the child's or teacher's name. Brushes should be replaced as they get worn or after someone has been sick. Cartons can be replaced weekly. Ask parents to save them for you.

Young children need to take good care of their baby teeth. If you work with older preschoolers, you even may get to share the delight of those first loose teeth. There are some excellent children's stories to read together about losing teeth. Maybe you will want to make a poster to record children's teeth lost or take pictures of those toothless grins. Remember, this is one clear sign that children are growing up.

Children are naturally interested in their teeth. You can find lots of ways to help children care for their baby and permanent teeth. Look at teeth in the mirror. Make a papier-mâché model tooth and use a large brush to practice brushing. Carve a jack-o-lantern with lots of strong teeth.

Find a dentist who is especially good with children and take a field trip to her or his office to help children feel more comfortable when they go for their checkups.

Children can also learn that what they eat can help keep their teeth healthy: drink lots of milk, avoid sweets and sticky things. Work with parents to encourage them to help children take good care of their teeth.

Professional organizations for dentists and hygienists sponsor a variety of activities. Find out what is available in your community. Select materials and activities that are appropriate and non-stereotypic for young children.

If possible, try to locate professionals in this field who are from some of the cultural groups or speak the language(s) of the children in the class.

List some special activities that you want to do with your children to help them learn to take good care of their teeth.

_____

_____

_____

_____

Get plenty of rest. Most children have such a good time playing that they don't want to take a nap. Infants, on the other hand, can fall asleep in the midst of the wildest commotion. Infants should always be allowed to sleep whenever they need to—adjust your schedule to theirs rather than expecting babies to adjust to you.

Watch toddlers and preschoolers, and try to follow their natural nap schedule as much as possible as well.

A good schedule for early childhood programs alternates quiet and active times throughout the day. Children need both.

After a busy morning, children are usually ready to take it easy for a while. Generally, naps will take place sometime shortly after lunch and a trip to the bathroom. Lights can be turned out to get children in the mood. Some teachers like to read a soothing story or play soft music. Some sing quietly.

What soothing techniques have you found work best for you and your children?

If you are a family child care provider, or even on the staff of many programs, naptime may be your only break. Be sure you get some rest, too!

Diaper changing. Diapers are a fact of life if you care for even one infant or toddler. Follow the steps on pages 132 to 133 to make it a safe and sanitary procedure.

How you treat children during diapering is also important. Don't view diapering as a drudgery or lost time. Instead, look upon it as a special close time for just you and the baby. Be playful and talkative. Explain what you are doing with the baby in gentle tones. Play "This Little Piggy." Point out the names of body parts: "What strong legs you have. You can really kick them hard." Use the child's home language whenever possible during these important times. Right from birth, children will begin to learn to respect their bodies and to feel good about themselves—if that is your attitude. Diapering is one of the best ways to make sure children learn pride in their bodies.

Toilet learning. Few milestones of life have received as much attention as learning to use the toilet! Most parents are eager to no longer have the expense and hassle of diapers. They want to brag to their friends about their child's early toilet habits. No wonder they are in a hurry for their child to learn to use the toilet. You and the child's parents must work closely together during this critical period.

Notice we call it toilet learning, not toilet training. That is because children learn to use the toilet just as they learn everything else:

They show interest, their bodies are mature enough, and loving adults set the stage for positive events.

Sometime between the ages of 2 and 3, most children want to be dry. Their interest is easy to notice. They may follow others to the toilet or even walk into the bathroom on their own. It may be time to take the hint!

Watch for children who stay dry for several hours and/or who indicate they are going to the bathroom by making a face, noises, or standing in a certain way. Your observations will give you the information you need to decide when a child is ready. Ask parents to help you look for signs.

Learning to use the toilet is a big step for children and parents. Few things you do with children require as much coordination and cooperation with parents. Few stages are treated with such high expectations.

Unless a child's body is ready, there is no way the child can successfully learn to use the toilet. Never, never, never fall for the crazy idea that a child can learn to use the toilet in one day. It simply is not possible. Physical, intellectual, emotional, and social maturity — and practice — are all necessary.

When children are "ready," they can learn to use the toilet independently. But what is often their biggest hurdle? Their clothes. Buckles, belts, buttons, tights, zippers — what a struggle! It's no wonder children end up putting on new dry clothes each time they go to the bathroom! You may need to ask parents to choose clothes that are easy for a toddler to take off quickly. Sweat pants, shorts, and clothes with elastic waists are great.

When clothes are no problem, children quite readily learn to lift the lid, sit down, wipe themselves, get dressed, and flush the toilet. Children may need to watch you demonstrate with a doll or see how a friend does it, but before long they remember every step. There are also several good children's books that you might read with one or two children at a time.

Potty chairs are probably the easiest for children to learn to use because of their just-right size. They are also difficult to keep clean. Slightly older children may benefit from a step stool firmly placed in front of the toilet. Select the type of arrangement that works best for the children, given the space and time you have.

How you set the stage for children to feel good about toileting makes a big difference. You have surely heard parents say things to their children such as "You bad boy. You got your pants wet twice today!" or "What a mess you made. Why do you create so much work for me?"

If you were a child, how would these comments make you feel? Rotten. Not worth much. A failure. Not what we want children to feel when they are growing up!

If you have ever made a child feel bad for having wet or soiled pants, resolve never to do it again. Instead, think of ways you can support children during this major challenge of their young lives. Most parents will follow your example. Explain to those who are less sensitive to their children's needs that the process will probably take longer and children may have other problems unless you both help children feel good about toileting.

What words should you use when you talk

How to change a diaper

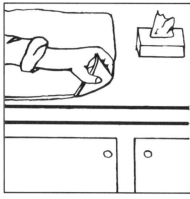

♥ **Check** to be sure supplies you need are ready. Place paper or other disposable cover on diapering surface.

♥ **Pick up** the child. If the diaper is soiled, hold the child away from you.

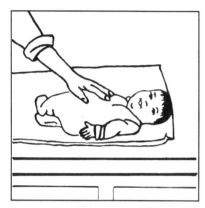

♥ **Lay** the child on diapering surface. **Never leave child unattended.**

♥ **Remove** soiled diaper and clothes. Fold diaper inward, reseal with tapes.

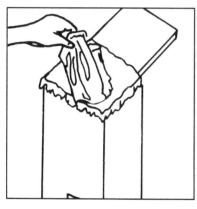

♥ **Put** disposable diapers in a lined, covered step can. Do not put diapers in toilet. Bulky stool may be emptied into toilet.

♥ **Put** soiled clothes or cloth diaper in a double, labeled plastic bag to be taken home.

♥ **Clean** the child's bottom with a moist disposable wipe. Wipe front to back using towelette only once. Repeat with fresh wipes if necessary. Pay particular attention to skin folds. Pat dry with paper towel. Do not use any kind of powder, as inhaling it can be dangerous. Cornstarch is not as effective as air or petroleum jelly.

♥ **Dispose** of the towelette or paper towel in a lined, covered step can.

♥ **Wipe** your hands with an alcohol-based disposable wipe. Dispose of it in the lined, covered step can.

♥ **Diaper or dress** the child. Now you can hold her or him close to you.

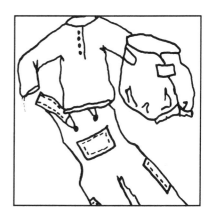

♥ **Wash** the child's hands. Assist the child back to the group.

♥ **Remove** disposable covering from the diapering surface.

♥ **Wash** the area and disinfect it with bleach solution made fresh daily.

♥ **Wash** your own hands thoroughly.

Ways to set up a safe, healthy environment to invite learning about toileting? Some experts suggest you use only *urinate, bowel movement,* or other technical terms. Very few parents feel comfortable with these words. You and each child's parents need to agree on the general method of toilet learning. In addition, you need to respect the parent's wishes for what they want to call toileting functions: *peepee, tinkle, go potty, poop...*the list is practically endless.

Try to be flexible and accept anything that is not offensive. Children in a group will generally all start using the same word—one that is fun to say, perhaps.

On the other hand, how do you handle crude language? Talk privately and calmly with the child: "We don't use words like that here. Those words offend some people." Then, if you don't pay much attention to such language it will be used less often.

Because toilet learning is so often abused by adults, let's review some things that an early childhood professional would never do when helping children learn these important self-control skills:

NEVER rush a child.
NEVER shame a child.
NEVER tease a child.
NEVER punish a child.

Instead, encourage toilet learning when children are mature enough. Help them feel good about their bodies and growing up. Praise is much more effective than ridicule.

Dressing. How grown up children feel to be able to get undressed and then dressed by them-

selves! Even before their first birthdays, babies delightedly pull off their own socks and shirts. They can push their arms through sleeves when they get dressed, too.

Children love to take clothes on and off—especially off. Give them plenty of opportunities with dress-up clothes that have large buttons, big zippers, snaps, and ample space to squirm around in. Buckle boots or large-laced work shoes are intriguing. Scarves can become saris or turbans. Clasps on purses are fun to latch and unlatch.

You can probably think of many more everyday objects from many cultures that give children the practice they need with dressing. You certainly do not need to make or buy special boards or books for this purpose.

The changing seasons also offer many opportunities to talk about weather, clothing, and what we each do to stay well. Rainy days, snow, wind—children love the variety in weather. Be sure you all go outdoors at least once in the morning and once in the afternoon. The fresh air is good for your health and invigorating to the spirit.

As children grow, make sure they take increasing responsibility for dressing themselves. Each day you go outdoors. Paint smocks may need to be hooked and unhooked. Finger plays such as "The Mitten Song" are perfect to assist toddlers as they gain these valuable self-help skills. Be sure you allow ample time for children to get themselves ready. And have hooks labeled with names for each child's coat and hat or swimming suit and towel.

The Mitten Song

Thumbs in the thumb place
Fingers all together.
This is the song we
Sing in mitten weather.

— Mary Louise Allen

Never do for children what they can do for themselves — and be sure to encourage children to help each other whenever possible. Dressing is an excellent way to learn cooperation.

List some new dress-up clothes you want to add so the children can practice dressing:

_____

_____

_____

_____

_____

Ask parents whether they have any of these items they could donate.

Body image. Everything you do with children is intended to build their self-confidence, to lead them toward more skills, and to foster their love of learning. Children's own bodies are one of the most fascinating learning tools you have.

Each child grows each day. Children love to look at their baby pictures and pictures of their families. Hang some on the wall at the children's eye level. Together, notice how children look a lot like their parents, grandparents, or others in their ethnic group. Compare the beautiful shades of skin colors.

Make charts to mark children's gains in weight and height. Children love to play with younger friends and help them learn new skills. In the process, the older children see just how much they really can do.

Two areas of child development that often are cause for discomfort with adults are children's growing awareness of themselves as girls or boys and masturbation. Sometimes children hold their genitals when they need to go to the bathroom. They are always curious about other children's bodies. Their curiosity is natural and healthy.

In good early childhood programs, young girls and boys share bathrooms because of the marvelous opportunity it presents for them to feel comfortable with other children and with their own sexual identity.

Bathrooms are excellent places to learn how our bodies work and what parts of our bodies are called. Help children feel good about their bodies. Talk about them in a natural tone.

Older children may compare their bodies. In one child care center, a boy bragged, "Ha, ha, I have a penis and you don't!" The 5-year-old girl quickly countered, "Yes, but I have a vagina and I can have babies when I grow up."

Children need to feel good about being a boy or being a girl. Help them see that each has its advantages. And that men and women can be parents, have jobs, and do household chores.

You will have many other natural opportunities to help children feel strong and competent as boys or girls. If necessary, encourage girls to use blocks and boys to nurture baby dolls or pets. Never assign tasks that require strong muscles, for example, to only boys. Cooking experiences are shared equally. Read only books in which boys and girls are viewed as equals. We'll talk more about this important issue of sexism in Part 3 of this unit.

Sometime during their first few months children discover how good it feels to touch their bodies. Masturbation during the early years is usually nothing to be concerned about. It is best to gently remind children who masturbate to do so in private.

If a child masturbates so frequently that many opportunities to play or rest are missed, you may have cause for concern. Bring your concerns to your supervisor or health consultant. Your observations about the child will be essential in determining how to handle any problem.

If you are embarrassed to talk about children's bodies with them, to help them feel good about being a boy or a girl, or to see a child masturbating once in a while before falling asleep, for example, **discuss your feelings with your CDA Field Advisor.** You will need to be able to deal with these topics comfortably in order to be a good teacher. Young children should never be made to feel ashamed of themselves and they will pick up your attitudes.

List any topics you want to discuss about children's bodies that make you feel uncomfortable:

You will have a chance to discuss these further during Seminar.

You eat healthy foods

One of the best ways to stay healthy and to feel good is to eat the most nutritious foods. Let's see how to fix and serve healthy snacks and meals in your program to contribute to children's overall health. Even if children only are in your group for a morning snack, it should be a nutritious one that helps them have a balanced diet for the entire day.

Why waste your money on sugar, salt, and other chemicals that don't contribute to children's healthy development? Sodas, cookies, and other treats do not promote growth and may even start children on the road to a lifetime of being undernourished and overweight.

Use this next section of the environment checklist to improve the quality of the foods you serve in your program.

✔ Environment checklist: You eat healthy foods

_____ You meet all state or program requirements for food service preparation and selection.

_____ You keep a list of children's food allergies in a prominent place and written in all languages spoken by parents and teachers.

_____ You plan snacks in advance. You see snacks as part of children's overall daily nutrition. You try to offer a wide variety of fruits, vegetables, proteins, milk products, and breads. You post the menus for parents to see.

_____ If you prepare meals for the children, you plan the menu in advance. Each meal includes a fruit, vegetable, protein, milk, and bread. You post the menus, in as many languages as needed, for parents to see.

_____ The foods you serve represent a wide variety of cultural preferences. You frequently serve favorite foods of families in the program. You respect dietary restrictions and parent preferences.

_____ If children bring their own lunches, you store lunches properly until they are eaten. You send leftovers home so parents will know what their children ate.

_____ You serve only real juices (no soft drinks, no sugary substitutes).

_____ Vegetables and fruits are fresh whenever possible.

_____ You select foods that are low in sugar, salt, and other added chemicals. You read and compare labels so you can choose those with the most food value.

_____ When canned fruits are used, you select only those packed in juice, not syrup.

_____ You serve child-sized portions. You prepare foods with lots of appeal to children: finger foods, colorful combinations, different textures.

_____ Plates, cups, and utensils are scaled to children's size. Glass is never used.

_____ You adapt utensils and menus as needed to help disabled children feed themselves as easily as possible.

_____ You encourage children to try a bite of a new food. They are never forced to clean their plates.

_____ You never use food as a punishment or as a reward.

_____ You serve meals group style. All of you eat the same thing. Children are given as long as they need to finish eating.

_____ Meals and snacks are pleasant times for friendly conversation.

_____ Children help prepare and cook food as often as possible.

_____ You model and expect children to use appropriate table behaviors: pleasant conversation, saying "please" and "thank you," and other manners specific to their culture.

_____ Foods are never wasted by using them as art materials.

If you care for infants or toddlers:

_____ You follow any directions given by the child's parents or medical care provider regarding breast milk, formula, or solid foods.

_____ Infants are always held in an inclined position when they are given a bottle. Bottles are never propped. You use feeding time to develop a close, warm relationship.

_____ You tell parents what their children ate during the day.

_____ When children begin to sit in a highchair or at a table, you feed each child individually. Children are never fed as if they were a production line.

_____ You help children learn to feed themselves by offering finger foods as they are added to the child's diet. You expect messes and do not criticize the child for making a mess. Ample time is allowed for self-feeding.

_____ Children learn appropriate table behavior as they are able.

Other nutrition practices appropriate for my program:

Learn principles of good nutrition

Food contains vitamins, minerals, and other substances that contribute to healthy growth. No vitamin pill can take the place of a wide variety of naturally good foods! One of the best sources of current information about food and nutrition is your county Cooperative Extension Service.

Locate their telephone number by calling the general information number under your county government listings. Call them to request information on nutrition for children. Ask for materials in several languages if you need them. If you have any children who are vegetarians, request information about the special requirements to prepare nutritious foods for vegetarians. You will probably be astounded at how much they can send you.

Start to use the information as soon as it arrives. **Post it on your bulletin board for parents.** Keep these materials in your personal files so you will use the ideas often. **Write the number here and add it to your Professional Resource File as well.**

Cooperative Extension Service:

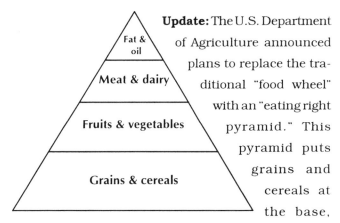

As you noted on the checklist, meals should always contain a fruit, vegetable, source of protein (meat or cheese, for example), bread, and milk. Snacks should always contain at least two of these items, and should contribute to the child's complete daily nutritional needs. The list below of especially good foods will help you get started with your selections.

You should get into the habit of reading labels, too, because even quite similar prepared foods can be very different in food values. You may be astonished at what is contained in different kinds of crackers, juice, or hot-dogs.

Update: The U.S. Department of Agriculture announced plans to replace the traditional "food wheel" with an "eating right pyramid." This pyramid puts grains and cereals at the base, fruits and vegetables on the next level, meat and dairy products in a narrow band near the top, and fat and oil in the smallest area. The shape emphasizes that some of the basic food groups are more important than others. You will discuss these new ideas about nutrition during your Seminar.

Select three or four items that you typically serve for snack. List the items on the chart on page 140. Read the labels and write down the per-serving levels of these common ingredients. Your Field Advisor will verify that you have completed this exercise.

Especially good foods

These foods are some of the best sources of balanced nutrition within each category. Young children should have one food from each category at each meal and one food from any two categories for snack.

Protein—Fish, poultry, meat, cheese, nuts (peanut butter), eggs, tofu

Breads—Whole grain, enriched breads, crackers, Melba toast; starchy vegetables (peas, beans, corn, potatoes); corn tortillas, breads; whole grain, enriched, cereals without added sugar; rice

Milk—Milk, cheese: cream, ricotta, hard, cottage; yogurt

Fruit—Bananas, nectarines, melons, cherries, berries, oranges, apricots, grapefruit, peaches, tangerines

Vegetables—Broccoli, cauliflower, spinach, carrots, Brussels sprouts, tomatoes, lima beans

---

Nutrition comparison of typical snack foods

Names of four typical snacks

Per serving levels of	1. _____	2. _____	3. _____	4. _____
Protein	_____	_____	_____	_____
Carbohydrates (sugar/starch)	_____	_____	_____	_____
Fat	_____	_____	_____	_____
Iron	_____	_____	_____	_____
Vitamin C	_____	_____	_____	_____
Vitamin A	_____	_____	_____	_____
Sodium (salt)	_____	_____	_____	_____
Calories	_____	_____	_____	_____

Which one offers the best nutritional value?

Next time you purchase foods or plan menus, check the labels first. Avoid large quantities of sugar, salt, and fat. Try to select whole grains, enriched flours, fresh fruits and vegetables, and other foods that offer the most nutrition for the money and the calories. Don't be misled by "health food" or "natural" claims—read the label and compare nutrition!

Here are some good ideas for snacks and lunches to get you off to a good start. Ask parents for suggestions to be sure you include familiar ethnic foods. Special provisions will need to be made for infants just beginning to eat solid food and for children who have allergies, special food requirements, or dietary prefer-ences. See whether parents can regularly come in and prepare foods from their culture with children. **Practice meal and snack planning by adding your favorite ideas to this list. You will share them with the others in your CDA Seminar.**

If you eat healthy foods, have a positive attitude about trying new foods, and use appropriate table manners, the children in your group will soon follow suit.

Yummy snacks

Celery stuffed with low-fat cream cheese or peanut butter
Fruit juice

French toast squares
Apple slices
Orange sections
Bagel quarters

Apple slices
Peanut butter

Carrot sticks
Yogurt dip with cinnamon or orange juice

Melted cheese
French bread squares or tortilla chips

Banana milkshake
Graham crackers

Deviled eggs
Broccoli trees

Your ideas:

_____

_____

_____

_____

_____

_____

_____

Favorite lunches

Macaroni and cheese

Broccoli

Baked apple with raisins

Milk or juice

English muffin pizza

Green beans

Peach slices

Milk or juice

Chicken taco with corn tortilla (chicken chunks,
lettuce, tomato, shredded cheese)

Banana

Milk

Tuna melt (whole-wheat bread, tuna, melted cheese
on top)

Greens

Melon chunks

Milk

Scrambled eggs

Stewed or sliced tomatoes

Orange slices

Milk

Your ideas:

Teach good habits with food

Your example is your primary teaching tool. If you eat healthy foods, have a positive attitude about trying new foods, and use appropriate table manners, the children in your group will soon follow suit.

Too often, children see parents or teachers gulp down a cup of coffee and a donut for breakfast, for example. Or we may reach for something in front of the children instead of asking to have it passed to you. All of us have bad habits either in what or how we eat.

List some of your bad food habits here.

Each week, choose one bad habit to get rid of, and then do it. You are only hurting yourself and the children you care for with your behavior.

Instead, resolve to set a good example for children.

Every person needs three healthy meals each day. Children need between-meal snacks. And babies need to eat whenever they are hungry.

If children arrive at your program without breakfast, talk with their parents. Find some way to work it out so children eat breakfast either before they come or after they arrive.

Some parents will send food, others may be willing to pay you an additional fee if you provide breakfast. Children and adults need to get their day off to a good start with a nutritious breakfast.

You may be eligible to be reimbursed for the food you serve. Does your program qualify for the Child Care Food Program? _____ Find out by contacting your licensing agent or state department of agriculture or education. Use local resources, too, to make sure you don't skimp on food to try to save money.

Your enthusiasm for good food will be contagious, but don't overdo it either, or children may wonder why the big deal. When children help prepare foods, they are often more willing to try them for the first time. They love to slice, spread, stir, and dip foods. How foods look and feel in their mouths make a difference too. Have a variety of colors, shapes, temperatures, and textures: Juicy fruit and crunchy crackers. Gooey peanut butter and cool milk.

Sources for food. Few children have an opportunity to learn where these foods come from — except the grocery store! Young children can get to know so much by visiting farms (in the winter, spring, summer, and fall) to see cattle, vegetable crops, fruits, dairy cows, grains. Watch dairy cows being milked. Visit a butcher shop. See grains ground into flour. Dig some potatoes. Shop at ethnic markets. Give children plenty of chances to see many types of food in different stages of growth and preparation.

Build on these field trips by growing plants

What attitudes about food do you want children to have?

outdoors in a small garden or in a sunny window. Read lots of books about foods.

List at least four places you can take children to help them better understand where their food comes from:

_____

_____

_____

_____

_____

_____

If possible, plan a field trip to each of them during the best seasons.

Settings for mealtimes. The atmosphere you establish at snack and mealtimes is very important. Doesn't a meal with candles and romantic music (or whatever your favorite setting) always taste better?

When children work with food, these are some things children learn. **Add others that you can think of to this list:**

- choose healthy foods from many cultures (health, social studies, self-esteem)
- write lists and read recipes (languages and reading)
- shop and spend money wisely (mathematics, economics, consumer education)
- measure, time, and divide foods (mathematics, sharing, cooperation)
- see how food changes when it is cooked, is mashed, or is mixed with other things (science)
- _____
- _____
- _____
- _____
- _____
- _____

We so often take eating for granted. Don't. Think about what you want children to learn. What attitudes about foods do you want them to have? Here are some appropriate goals for older toddlers and preschoolers when they eat. **You may have other goals as well. Add them to the list.**

- Children are encouraged to taste at least one bite of new foods. Sometimes they are surprised and like it!
- Children enjoy talking informally with their teacher and friends. Don't ask boring questions such as "What color are the peas?" or "What shape is the bread?" Instead, have a natural, pleasant conversation about topics the children bring up.
- Children become familiar with foods from many cultures, especially those of their friends in the group. Welcome a new child on the first day with a favorite food (ask the parents for suggestions when the child enrolls). Regularly serve typical foods from a variety of cultures—don't limit this opportunity to a few special occasions.
- Children serve themselves child-sized portions and are expected to eat only until they are full. Family style meals are more relaxed. Never force children to clean their plates. Give children the time they need to finish.
- Children learn respect for others at the table (by saying "Please pass...," "Thank you," and using other courtesies appropriate for their culture).
- _____
- _____
- _____
- _____
- _____

Talking about food preparation and eating is an important part of any early childhood program environment. These curriculum areas are just two of the many opportunities you have to plan, set up, and guide children's play to ensure that the environment invites them to learn. Now let's look at some others—how you schedule your day, set up your home or classroom, and choose materials for children.

How do you plan an environment that promotes play?

What do children love to do more than anything else? **PLAY!** And how do children learn best? **PLAY!**

Children's play looks so simple. It isn't.

Children's play doesn't just happen. You set the stage for children to learn through play. They need time to try out their ideas. They need a comfortable area in which to play. They need real things—good toys and equipment that they can use independently. And most of all they need an adult who knows how to make all of the pieces of the environment, the people, and the action fit together. Let's see how you make it possible for children to learn through play.

You select appropriate activities

We have already talked in general about how important it is to match children's development with the kinds of activities you offer. Now we will look at exactly how a professional early childhood educator decides what will happen each day. Let's start with the framework within which you structure each day.

Establish a schedule

Every program—half day, full day, home, center—needs a schedule. Not a rigid one. Not one that is ignored. But one that helps lend some sense of predictable rhythm to the day for you and the children.

Some of you work in programs where your schedule must be coordinated with others, perhaps so you can share playground space. Family child care providers, on the other hand, can probably set their own time frame.

Use this section of the environment checklist on page 147 to evaluate your schedule. As you have done before, continue to add any points to the checklist that are especially important for your program.

Through play,

children pursue their interests. . .discover how the world works. . .

communicate with others. . .see how it feels to act like other people. . .

practice familiar skills and learn new ones. . .cooperate and solve problems—

They **learn by doing**!

Play Today?

You say you love your children,
And are concerned they learn today?
So am I—that's why I'm providing
A variety of kinds of play.

You're asking me the value
Of blocks and other such play?
Your children are solving problems.
They will use that skill everyday.

You're asking what's the value
Of having your children play?
Your daughter's creating a tower;
She may be a builder someday.

You're saying you don't want your son
To play in that "sissy" way?
He's learning to cuddle a doll;
He may be a father someday.

You're questioning the interest centers;
They just look like useless play?
Your children are making choices;
They'll be on their own someday.

You're worried your children aren't learning;
And later they'll have to pay?
They're learning a pattern for learning;
For they'll be learners always.

—Leila P. Fagg

© 1975, National Association for the Education of Young Children. Reprinted by permission from *Young Children*, January 1975, p. 93.

✔ Environment checklist: Schedule

_____ You have a daily schedule. It is written in the home languages of the parents and teachers, and posted for parents.

_____ Your schedule is coordinated with all others who are affected by it or who share space with you.

_____ Children are aware that you follow a basic routine. They are told before it is time to change from one activity to another so they have time to wind up what they are doing.

_____ Children play outdoors at least once in the morning and once in the afternoon.

_____ Your schedule alternates between active and quiet times.

_____ You plan time for both individual and small group activities. Most activities involve individual play or groups of two or three children, not the entire group.

_____ The schedule is flexible to allow for children's needs and to take advantage of good learning opportunities when they come up.

_____ The schedule balances large-muscle and small-muscle activities.

_____ You plan for frequent, large blocks of time so children can have free play (children choose what to do).

_____ You have occasional, small blocks of time for teacher-led activities (story, music, introducing a new piece of equipment).

_____ You balance the use of two or more languages when teaching a second language, providing for the use of both first- and second-language development strategies.

Other schedule considerations for my program:

Here are two fairly typical schedules for older toddlers and preschoolers, one for a morning part-day program (a similar sequence could be followed in the afternoon), the other for full-day child care. Both of these schedules demonstrate how you put the ideas in the checklist into action.

Typical part-day schedule	
8:45–9 a.m.	Children arrive, greet parents
9–9:45	Free play
9:45–10	Story/music/finger plays
10–10:30	Outdoor play
10:30–10:45	Toilet, snack, brush teeth
10:45–11:30	Small group activity/free play
11:30–11:45	Review day, prepare to leave

For an afternoon-only program, a similar sequence could be followed.

Typical full-day schedule	
7–9 a.m.	Children arrive, greet parents, breakfast/free play
9–9:15	Daily plan/sharing/finger plays
9:15–10	Outdoor play
10–10:15	Toilet, snack, brush teeth
10:15–10:45	Small group activity/story/music
10:45–11:30	Free play
11:30–12	Clean up, toilet, food preparation
12:30–1:15	Outdoor play/games
1:15–1:30	Toilet
1:30–3	Nap/rest/quiet play for older children
3–3:30	Toilet, snack, brush teeth
3:30–4:15	Outdoor play
4:15–7	Free play/leave for day

For a program using more than one language with the children, additional scheduling considerations may be needed. If there is going to be a balance of the two (or three!) languages being modeled by the adults, specific times for them to occur may need to be planned. Although the specific strategy for any program should be determined by the needs and language backgrounds of the children, language usage should not be haphazard. The strategy might be flexible during the day or you may actually set aside times of the day or entire days to focus more on one language during that time.

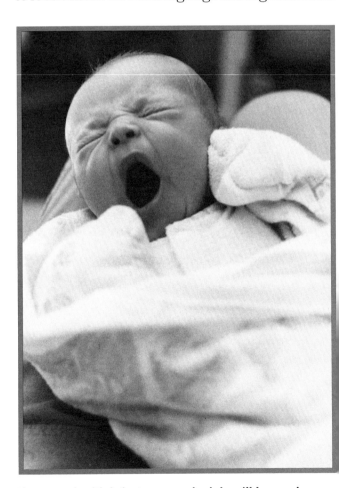

If you work with infants, your schedule will be much looser, but you will still want to establish some predictability.

Typical bilingual part-day schedule

8:45–9 a.m.	Children arrive, greet parents	Los niños llegan, recibe a los padres
9–9:15	Music, story sharing	Musica, compartiendo, cuentos,
9:15–10:00	Play in areas	Juego en las areas
10:00–10:15	First language Small group time	Primera lengua Tiempo de grupo pequeño
10:15–11:00	Outdoor play	Juego afuera
11:00–11:10	Second language Small group time	Segunda lengua Tiempo de grupo pequeño
11:10–11:40	Wash hands Lunch	Lavado de las manos Almuerzo
11:40–12:00	Toilet, leave	Hora del baño, salida

If you work with infants, your schedule will be much looser, but you will still want to establish some predictability. You will want to keep three factors in mind:

• each baby's personal rhythms for eating and sleeping,

• infants' tendency to play alone or alongside another child, and

length of time babies can maintain interest in an activity.

A full-day schedule for infants might be like this:

Typical infant program schedule

8–9 a.m.	Arrival, say goodbye to parents
8–9:15	Play/story
8–10	Diapering/bottles
8:30–11	Naps/individual play/diapering
10:30–12	Outdoor walk/play
11:30–1	Diapering/lunch/mid-day bottles
12:30–2:30	Naps/individual play/diapering
2–4	Bottles/outdoor play/diapering
3–5	Naps/songs/play/diapering
4:30–6	Play/bottles/leave

These schedules are just samples to give you some ideas. Regardless of the children's ages or the setting in which you teach, you probably need to juggle the availability of staff, children's needs, playground use limits, and many other factors. What are some of them?

First, young children want to be on the move. They like variety. Neither infants, toddlers, nor preschoolers should be expected to spend too much time in one place or on one activity. Not in line. Not in the highchair. Not on a carpet. Not at the table. They get fidgety.

They like to be involved. They want to be in on the action, not just a watcher. Infants nearly always head for the action, either with their eyes or by crawling or walking.

Toddlers rarely pay attention in a group for more than 4 or 5 minutes. Even preschoolers function best in small groups. While 5-year-olds might stay alert in a group of 10 or 12 children, they won't pay attention for much longer than 10 to 15 minutes.

Children like to be involved and in on the action, not just a watcher.

Second, young children get frustrated with rigid time restrictions. Because they need to be active, plan how you can help them make smooth transitions from one activity to another in your schedule.

Don't waste their time by insisting they stand in line to wash their hands, sit until everyone is absolutely quiet for a story, or wait while all the children get ready to go outdoors. If at all possible, break into small groups to avoid these time-wasters and help children move on to the next activity. Keep children involved in all of the daily routines.

Third, young children need individual attention. Be sure each day has time for you to talk with every individual child in the family's primary language. Greet the child personally, talk throughout the day about what the child is doing or thinking or feeling, and say goodbye at the end of the day. Small group times provide opportunities for interactions that address developmental skills at the child's individual level.

After you have considered all the factors, **write your preferred schedule in the space that follows. Use the codes to help you see how your schedule is balanced. Discuss your schedule with your Advisor**. Depending on how different it is from the one you follow now, you may want to gradually make changes. If you work in a group program and want to make some schedule changes that will affect other staff, check with your supervisor and the other teachers first. And talk about any changes with the children—preschoolers especially quickly come to expect that one activity will follow another!

My preferred daily schedule

In the column labeled *type of activity*, use these codes to indicate what is happening during that time: **A**—children are **active**, **Q**—children are **quiet**, **P**—children initiate **play**, **T**—**teacher** directs activity.

Time	Activity	Type of activity
		A Q P T

Plan for the day

Now you have a good idea of how to structure the children's day. How do you decide what happens within that day? Some teachers like to call this *curriculum planning*. That is fine if you consider that **curriculum is whatever happens during the day**.

Children learn through play—and they also learn from every other event: The janitor who comes to replace an overhead light, the snake that slithers through the door, a friend who just learned about moving to another town.

Of course, you can't leave the whole day, or even a few minutes, to the chance that something exciting might come up. Use this section of the checklist to help you think about how to plan what happens during your day with children.

 # Environment checklist: Activities and themes

_____ Your program has written goals that describe appropriate methods and topics for children's learning. Your goals are realistic and keep in mind cultural, language, and individual differences and special needs.

_____ You choose themes, and the activities that build upon them, to help reach those goals. Themes and activities pick up on interests children have expressed, on skills they are working on, or on typical developmental milestones.

_____ You choose topics that help children grow in their understanding of themselves, each other, and people of various ages, sexes, and cultural groups. Stereotypes are never portrayed. Cultural diversity and cooperation are always promoted. Children learn about cultures and languages daily, not just on holidays or as a tourist might, but through real experiences with real people and things. Children learn to identify what is fair and to stand up for their rights and the rights of others.

_____ You develop themes and activities so children feel good about themselves, their families, their culture and language, and their friends. You appreciate and plan for individual learning styles.

_____ You encourage children to ask questions, experiment, and figure out things on their own.

_____ You ask lots of open-ended questions (What would happen if. . .? or Why did this . . .?) rather than questions that have one correct answer.

_____ You encourage children's creativity. Models, coloring books, and patterns are never used. Children's artwork is never expected to look like that of another child.

_____ Activities for children involve **real, hands-on** experiences. (Paper and pencil tasks, movies, and demonstrations are not real, hands-on experiences. Butterflies, coins, fabric scraps, sand, dress-up clothes that represent many cultures and jobs, stethoscopes, and musical instruments are all real.)

_____ Activities busily involve children. Children spend very little time watching.

_____ If television is used, programs are selected for their appropriateness for children. You talk with the children about what they see and hear. Television is used for a very limited time each day.

_____ Children work individually or in small groups most of the time. Preschool children gather in larger groups for perhaps 10 minutes on an occasional basis.

_____ Children learn to appreciate beauty and diversity in the world around them (art, nature, music, literature) through daily, culturally authentic activities.

_____ If something more interesting happens, you do not force children to continue with what they are doing, but give them an opportunity to learn from whatever is going on.

_____ You take advantage of resources within the community: story hour at the library, puppet shows, community fairs, ethnic neighborhoods, to acquaint children with the interesting things and people around them.

_____ You present activities with enthusiasm to build children's interest and curiosity. You have a playful, cheerful attitude. You demonstrate respect for all peoples.

_____ You move about the room as children play. Children and their work are treated with respect and interest. You do not ask "What is it?"

_____ You support children's play rather than interfere and dictate what they do. For example, you show children how to use new materials appropriately, help children expand on a theme by offering ideas or props, ask open-ended questions to extend children's thinking ("Why do you think . . .?"), write names on artwork, and pick up ideas from children's play for other themes and activities.

_____ You see every minute of the day as a learning opportunity: for example, when children are diapered, snacks and lunch, and dressing; disagreements between children; everything that happens. You frequently find yourself asking: **What are children learning by doing this?**

_____ Field trips are well organized: You have permission slips from each parent, you carry a first-aid kit with you, adult chaperons are recruited, you visit the place first and talk with the staff to ensure the children's safety and that appropriate activities will be offered, children are prepared for what to expect, rules are reviewed in children's primary languages, safe transportation is arranged, follow-up activities are planned so children can build on what they have seen.

Other activity and theme considerations for my program:

Each of these items is a component of a good, developmentally appropriate program. They are so important that each of these ideas will keep coming up throughout this book, in your CDA Seminar, and in your teaching. Watch for them and make changes in your program as you keep learning more about what is best for young children.

Hang up the poster at the end of this unit to remind yourself to ask

> **What are children learning by doing this?**

Facilitate children's play

All through the day, you coordinate, supervise, and guide children's activities.

You set up the room or your home, help children choose what they want to do, talk with individuals or groups to support or expand their play, stay alert for any problems that may need your presence, and make notes about individuals and activities. You walk about the area, sit occasionally with a small group, and are constantly aware of what all the children are doing.

If you look back at the description of a CDA's typical day in Unit 1, you will see that this style of teaching is emphasized.

Notice that the teacher sets out materials before the children arrive and several times throughout the day.

During free play times, children can select what they want to do. If children have a difficult time choosing their own activities, the teacher suggests things that would seem to be of interest based on what she already knows about them. She shows them how to use any unfamiliar equipment.

While children play, the teacher moves about the room, stopping to chat with a group who are building with blocks, or watching a child engrossed in drawing at the easel. Perhaps some children are having a disagreement. Our teacher stands nearby but does not interfere unless they reach a standstill or someone is about to get hurt. Soon the children solve their own problems.

This style of teaching not only illustrates what **to do**, but also what **not** to do.

- Do not lecture to the entire group of children.
- Do not choose children's activities for them all of the time.
- Do not use work sheets, workbooks, coloring books, or other seatwork.
- Do not interrupt or interfere with children's play.
- Do not make children wait or line up.
- Do not carry on a lengthy personal conversation with another teacher. Do not ignore the children. Do not leave the children unattended.

You will learn more about this style of teaching in Units 4 and 5 and in the videos on developmentally appropriate practice. But for now, it is important to know that this style of teaching is built upon your understanding of each child and child development in general.

You have been observing children and getting to know them for a few weeks by now, so you probably have a good idea of what the children in your group can do and what their interests are. Perhaps you have found out what activities are used often and which are ignored.

On the following pages, summarize what you know about each child's abilities, interests, and any concerns you have.

You will use this information in this unit and in the next two to select some themes, to decide how to arrange your home or room, to choose the best learning materials, and to make decisions about daily activities. Use additional paper if you need it.

What do you know about the children in your group? What topics interest them?

What I know about the children in my group

CHILD'S NAME: _____

Abilities: _____

_____

Interests: _____

_____

Concerns: _____

_____

CHILD'S NAME: _____

Abilities: _____

_____

Interests: _____

_____

Concerns: _____

_____

CHILD'S NAME: _____

Abilities: _____

_____

Interests: _____

_____

Concerns: _____

_____

CHILD'S NAME: _____

Abilities: _____

_____

Interests: _____

_____

Concerns: _____

_____

CHILD'S NAME: _____

Abilities: _____

_____

Interests: _____

_____

Concerns: _____

_____

CHILD'S NAME: _____

Abilities: _____

_____

Interests: _____

_____

Concerns: _____

_____

CHILD'S NAME: _____

Abilities: _____

_____

Interests: _____

_____

Concerns: _____

_____

CHILD'S NAME: _____

Abilities: _____

_____

Interests: _____

_____

Concerns: _____

_____

CHILD'S NAME: _____

Abilities: _____

_____

Interests: _____

_____

Concerns: _____

_____

CHILD'S NAME: _____

Abilities: _____

_____

Interests: _____

_____

Concerns: _____

_____

CHILD'S NAME: _____

Abilities: _____

_____

Interests: _____

_____

Concerns: _____

_____

CHILD'S NAME: _____

Abilities: _____

_____

Interests: _____

_____

Concerns: _____

_____

Ways to set up a safe, healthy environment to invite learning

CHILD'S NAME: _____

Abilities: _____

_____

Interests: _____

_____

Concerns: _____

_____

CHILD'S NAME: _____

Abilities: _____

_____

Interests: _____

_____

Concerns: _____

_____

CHILD'S NAME: _____

Abilities: _____

_____

Interests: _____

_____

Concerns: _____

_____

CHILD'S NAME: _____

Abilities: _____

_____

Interests: _____

_____

Concerns: _____

_____

CHILD'S NAME: _____

Abilities: _____

_____

Interests: _____

_____

Concerns: _____

_____

CHILD'S NAME: _____

Abilities: _____

_____

Interests: _____

_____

Concerns: _____

_____

Writing down what you know about each child is hard work! But it is essential to help you be a better teacher. For now, we will just focus on children's interests to select some themes to concentrate on in the next few weeks.

Look back over your list. If you teach preschoolers, there is a good chance that topics such as these appear: dinosaurs, money, people who help us, animals, their names or other words, plants/food, transportation, water, numbers.

Toddlers often are interested in climbing, pushing, dumping, colors, dressing, stacking things, and messy things.

Infants and waddlers are interested in things such as rocking, sliding, crawling, dropping things, squishing things, watching themselves in mirrors, and making things happen.

List below any topics that are of interest to more than one child or topics that you know several children would be curious about.

_____

_____

_____

_____

_____

Keep your children's topics in mind as you go through the next two sections of this unit. Think about how you might set up your room so children can investigate these ideas. You might begin a list of materials for children to use, too.

You arrange and decorate the space

You probably have at least one room that the children in your care play in most of the time. You may also have rooms for sleeping, eating, and perhaps a special bathroom. Some programs are housed in churches, some in child care providers' own homes, some in schools, and some in spaces designed especially for young children.

Whatever your space is, even if it works well, improvements can usually be made. So few early childhood educators have ideal environments that we will assume you probably would like to make yours work better for your group. Perhaps it is noisy, or children seem to run a lot indoors, or some areas never seem to attract any children.

The design of and/or lack of space does make a difference in children's behavior.

What areas in your space seem to work well?

_____

_____

_____

_____

What problems have you noticed in your teaching environment?

_____

_____

_____

_____

This section of the environment checklist will help you think about some of the basic principles involved in designing a space for young children.

✔ Environment checklist: Use of space

_____ All state and local safety requirements are met (fire exits, windows, floor coverings, flammability, etc.).

_____ Your space is flexible so you can meet the needs of children or adults with physical or other disabilities.

_____ You can monitor children's play in every area while standing.

_____ Indoor areas are bright, well-lit, and appealing.

_____ Your space is designed to encourage a wide variety of age-appropriate, culturally relevant activities.

_____ You give each area outdoors a specific purpose: vehicle riding, swinging, climbing, sand.

_____ You assign each area of the room a specific type of activity: table toys, dramatic play, blocks, reading, science, messy activities (clay, paint, water, sand), private thinking space, music, large muscle, or other appropriate areas.

_____ You group quiet activities together and noisy activities together.

_____ You place related activities near each other: blocks and small transportation toys, for example.

_____ You have enough play areas so that children spread throughout the space without crowding.

_____ Some areas are hard (tables, chairs, vinyl floors) while others are soft (pillows, rocking chair, carpet).

_____ You have varied the areas so that some contain activities that have one obvious use (climber with slide) while other areas are more complex (large hollow blocks).

_____ You have made clear pathways for children to walk from area to area without walking through the middle of busy spaces. Furniture is used to mark off play spaces and pathways.

_____ Your pathways are short. You have no long hallways that invite children to run or yell.

_____ You frequently observe children to see how they use the space and make adjustments as children's skills and interests change.

_____ If your program is in your home, you arrange your space so that the space and belongings of family members are treated with respect.

_____ Your primary play space is convenient to sleeping areas (especially for infants), bathrooms, and outdoor exits.

_____ Labeling of areas or objects is done in English and the home language of the children. Different colors are used for different languages to reinforce that they are separate language systems.

Other space considerations in my program:

If these points help you see where you might change something, try it. You can always move everything back the way it was. Keep experimenting.

When you are fairly satisfied with your room arrangement, draw a rough sketch of your primary teaching space. Note doors and windows. Include major pieces of furniture. Mark the name of each activity area. Talk with your Field Advisor if you have any questions.

You will use this floor plan again in your CDA Seminar. And in case your ideas change as you learn more, we have included another page for you to draw a revised plan later.

Floor plan designed through self-study

Final floor plan at completion of CDA

Once your basic use of space is determined, you select the furniture and storage equipment for children's materials. Your observations of children will help you determine what should work well for them.

✔ Environment checklist: Furniture and storage

_____ All furnishings are sturdy, safe, and the appropriate size for the children in the group.

_____ Furnishings are adapted as appropriate to meet the needs of children or adults with physical or other disabilities.

_____ If children of different ages are in the same group, table and chair sizes are varied. Partitions or tables are used to help older children protect their projects from intrusion by younger children.

_____ Infant areas include rocking chairs, lots of cushions, mirrors, and other age-appropriate items. Children can crawl and walk about easily.

_____ You use low, open shelves for children's learning materials. Blocks, paper, puzzles, science materials, markers—every learning material is stored where children can reach it easily. Pretend kitchen appliances in the dramatic play area may have doors.

_____ You expect toddlers and preschoolers to return materials to the shelf where they found them. Every shelf is labeled with pictures and/or words in children's home languages.

_____ You never use toy boxes: fingers, heads, or arms can get caught; toys get lost and broken easily; children have difficulty finding what they want; and they never develop the habit of putting their toys away where they belong.

_____ Most of the furniture can be moved by one adult so that it can be rearranged easily. Large items are on casters or rollers with locks.

_____ You store preschool items with small parts (tiny plastic building blocks, for example) in see-through, unbreakable containers.

_____ Children can move chairs up to a table if they wish to sit down. Children are not expected to sit for most activities.

_____ Additional supplies are stored elsewhere rather than taking up valuable program space (in closets, under beds, in the basement).

_____ Toys and materials are rotated (some put away, others brought out) as children's needs, skills, and interests change.

_____ Special furniture is available to meet the needs of children with disabling conditions.

Other furniture and storage checks for my program:

With all these ideas fresh in your mind, this is a good time to "go shopping." Look back at what the children in your group are interested in, can do, or soon will be doing (pages 156–161).

Pull out some of your school-supply catalogs or borrow some from your director, public library, or family child care network. Look through the catalogs. Identify (or cut out pictures of) one or two pieces of furniture that you think would be good additions to your program. Explain why.

If your budget is tight (and whose isn't?) think of ways you could find, make, or improvise something similar. What could you do to get these items without spending a lot of money? Would a parent who is a carpenter be willing to make one if you supply the lumber? What about going-out-of-business sales, yard sales, sec-

ondhand shops, or consignment stores? **Your CDA Field Advisor may be able to help you think of alternatives, too.**

In addition to how the space is used and the furniture you select, the way you decorate your space can determine how welcome children feel. In fact, these seemingly small touches can make a big difference in the kind of atmosphere you create for children.

First impressions can be lasting. Just poke your head in the door of someone else's classroom or family child care home. What is the first thing that strikes you?

The environment checklist includes some pointers for decorating your teaching space, whether it be in your home or in another building.

✔ Environment checklist: Decorations

_____ Your teaching space sets a warm and welcoming atmosphere.

_____ All pictures, posters, signs, and accessories reflect and celebrate diversity within your program, community, and country: culture, ethnic groups, age, sex, language, family, and abilities.

_____ Children's artwork is hung at their eye level. Most of the room is decorated with their work. Each child's work is individual (no two look alike). A wide variety of work is posted—not just what you consider to be "the best."

_____ Pictures of children and their families are hung about the space at the children's eye level.

_____ Posters, pictures, plants, baskets, and other accessories are pleasing to look at. They radiate beauty and come from or authentically show many cultures.

_____ You avoid too many cartoon and other "cute" or commercial characters—children see enough of them elsewhere, and many of them depict stereotypes. Instead, you aim for variety with some photographs and some drawings of real people.

Other decorating points for my program:

_____

_____

_____

_____

_____

Take a look around your teaching area and think of some things you can do to spruce it up. When is the last time you added something new? Are your posters dogeared because they have been used year after year? Ask parents to bring in their old magazines. Find some new pictures. Choose some based on the children's interests you've observed. Hang children's latest artwork. **Write here what you did to spruce up your teaching area.**

_____

_____

_____

_____

You choose appropriate learning materials

By this time, you probably have some new ideas about changes in your space, furniture, and decorations. Now let's look at what fills your shelves and how appropriate the materials are for the children in your group.

When we talk about learning materials, we mean all of the toys, art supplies, puzzles, games, climbers, riding toys, and other equipment that children use.

This next section of the environment checklist corresponds with the milestones of development. Make sure you have at least some toys in each category for each age range you teach. We have left lots of space for you to fill in other appropriate toys—there are far too many to list everyone's favorites here.

✔ Environment checklist: Appropriate learning materials

_____ You select a range of materials that are appropriate for children from 6 months younger than the youngest child in the group to 6 months older than the oldest child. A broader range is provided if any of the children are disabled or have other special needs.

_____ Popular toys are available in duplicates, or even threes, so children can use them without waiting.

_____ Toys and materials are intended for children to **use** them, not to watch toys perform. There are no battery-operated toys.

_____ Children can choose from a wide variety of different types of materials that offer a balance of activities:

- small muscle/large muscle,
- quiet/active,
- short interest/extended play,
- cause-and-effect/creative,
- unlimited possibilities/one or a few solutions,
- messy/neat,
- loud/quiet,
- indoors/outdoors, and
- pretend/real.

_____ You make sure all toys, pictures, books, posters, and other materials authentically demonstrate acceptance of children's sex, family, race, language, and culture. You use the criteria in "Ten Quick Ways to Analyze Children's Books for Racism and Sexism" to evaluate all materials.

If you work with young infants (birth through 8 months):

Until children can move around by themselves, they do a lot of looking and listening, and rely on you to give them a change of scenery. Toys go straight to their mouths, so nothing should be so small they could swallow it. Infant toys have one or more of these qualities:

_____ Bright or contrasting colors (board books, pictures).

_____ Interesting designs (people's faces, mobiles, pictures, books, blankets).

_____ Movable parts (people, mobiles, balls, fish).

_____ Shiny, reflective surfaces (unbreakable mirrors on the wall at children's eye level, small ones to hold).

_____ Noisy parts (rattles, balls, voices, pots and pans, squeaky toys).

_____ Tactile surfaces (people, spoons, texture balls, cloth and rubber dolls or animals).

_____ "Chewable" materials—but not to be swallowed (teething rings or beads).

Teachers can also participate personally in infants' activities:

_____ Talk, sing, recite poems, play "Peek-a-Boo" and "This Little Piggy," move them from place to place for a different view, and most of all—hold infants.

Other good toys for infants:

If you work with crawlers, waddlers, and walkers (8 to 18 months):

At this age, children are delighted to be mobile. Their language skills are growing rapidly. They can increasingly use their hands to make things happen. Toys for this age have these qualities:

_____ Safely allow children to crawl over, under, and through (obstacle course of large cushions, empty boxes).

_____ Low items to hold on while walking (low table, cushions).

_____ Give chances to balance, rock, climb (rocking chair, climber, steps/slide combination, carpeted climbing space, rocking horse).

_____ Can be held and manipulated (cars, trucks, planes, boats, cardboard books with round edges, dolls, large cardboard blocks, unit blocks, puzzles with two to four pieces).

_____ Make noise or do something when manipulated (knobs to turn, buttons to push, squeaky toys, telephones, balls, maracas, bells, piano, pounding benches, stacking toys).

_____ Allow first opportunities to scribble (watercolor markers in dark colors and large blank pieces of paper).

_____ Allow children to copy familiar behaviors (purses, dolls with ethnic features and skin colors, cradles, dishes and pitchers, steering wheels).

_____ People who speak children's home languages to play games, talk, sing, and read with.

_____ Things to push or ride (low riding vehicles that are steerable but have no pedals, toy lawn mowers, pretend baby strollers).

Other good toys for crawlers, waddlers, and walkers:

If you work with toddlers and 2-year-olds:

Toddlers and 2-year-olds are becoming increasingly independent. They are more aware of others and like to imitate them. They are becoming more familiar with their community. They can do lots of things with their fingers and hands. They are very active. Therefore, toys for children at this age have these qualities:

_____ Come apart and go back together (puzzles with four to six pieces, sorting toys, large plastic building sets, stacking boxes or dolls).

_____ Can be dumped and refilled (buckets of spools or beads, containers with pieces inside).

_____ Sometimes require cooperation (balls, wagons).

_____ Require finer motor skills (spools or beads to string, blunt-end scissors, clay, tempera paints including brown and black with wide brushes at easels, watercolor markers, fat crayons, large sheets of paper, finger plays).

_____ Allow for jumping, throwing, kicking (climbers, balls, lots of space).

_____ Can be pushed, pulled, or ridden (low-riding vehicles that steer and have pedals, pull toys, shopping carts, large trucks).

_____ Let children pretend (dress-up clothes and accessories, medical props, baby care items, play food and appliances, dolls, small realistic vehicles, rubber animals).

_____ People who speak the children's home languages to read with, say poems, sing songs (picture storybooks, recordings).

Other good toys for toddlers and 2-year-olds:

If you work with children 2½- through 3-years-old:

Children at this age sometimes seem toddlerish and at other times very grown up. Much of their play is alone or with one or two other children, and they sometimes share. They are curious, are learning more about language, and are very active. Toys and materials for children this age allow them to

_____ Try out and practice new skills (dress-up clothes, watercolor markers and large sheets of paper, tempera paints, blunt-end scissors, clay dough, finger paints, paste, and glue).

_____ Use numbers and letters in real situations (you write down the stories they dictate, they distribute napkins for snack, you write their names on artwork, follow simple recipes, make lists and labels, read picture books that have simple stories).

_____ Play alone or with one or two children (small tables so children can work side by side with puzzles, pegboards, beads, art, table blocks, more dramatic play props, zoo and farm animals). Rarely use large group activities.

_____ Do lots of running, jumping, pushing, pulling, galloping, riding (balls, tricycles, large cardboard blocks, obstacle course, climber).

_____ Explore cause and effect (blow bubbles; unit blocks; sand and water with scoops, funnels, and cups; toys that come apart, latch, open, and/or close; rhythm sticks, drums, tambourine; construction sets with fairly large pieces).

Other good toys for children from 2½- through 3-years-old:

If you work with older preschoolers (older 3-year-olds through 5-year-olds):

Preschool children are increasingly able to plan what they want to do and carry out their plans. Their dramatic play is much more involved. They can play together in small groups for as long as 30 minutes or more. Early reading and math skills are growing daily. Friendships are more stable and they can take turns. Preschoolers are very aware of their sex, culture, and abilities. These are some of the qualities of toys for preschoolers:

_____ Allow children to play together cooperatively (large sets of unit blocks, dramatic play props for many different themes, simple board and card games, puppets, large empty boxes).

_____ Give opportunities to write and use numbers in real ways (you write stories or letters children dictate in their preferred language; children make lists, label projects; typewriters/computers; real hammer, nails, saw, and soft wood; more complicated recipes, shopping, cash register).

_____ Children can expand upon their own ideas (more art materials such as crepe paper, collage materials, chalk, papier-mâché, tape, thinner markers and crayons that include black and shades of brown; carpentry with real tools; more real musical instruments such as guitar, recorder, harmonica; cameras).

_____ Help children learn more about people and cultural diversity (various peoples depicted properly in music, art, more complicated picture storybooks, pictures, foods).

_____ Use more small muscles (tiny plastic construction sets; sewing cards; sewing with burlap or nylon net, yarn, and yarn needles; puzzles with many more pieces).

_____ Still have lots of activity (roller skates, balance board, Frisbee, plastic bat and balls, riding vehicles, beanbags, bowling pins).

Other good toys for preschool children:

As you look at this list, dollar signs may have flashed before your eyes! How can you possibly afford so many things?

The best toys for early childhood programs are those that can be used in more complex ways as children gain new skills. Unit blocks are a good example. Children can play with them from infancy through the elementary years. Although they are very expensive to buy, blocks are a good long-term investment.

You want to get the most for your money. Consider the life expectancy of major purchases. If you buy better quality riding vehicles, for example, they may last much longer than cheap imitations.

Children will use dramatic play items (ethnic dolls, doll beds, kitchen appliances), musical instruments, and many other items for years. Your cost actually may be far less for popular toys that span children's ages or for well-made toys that hold up under hard use.

Careful thought should be put into smaller purchases too. Slightly thicker paper may be a better investment because it doesn't tear so easily. Children will be more successful when they draw or paint. And remember, many toys are common household objects (pots and pans, measuring cups, funnels). Many art supplies are discards (meat trays, paper bags, fabric scraps, egg cartons).

How do you put what you've learned into practice?

Now it is time to apply all that you have learned so far in your CDA early childhood studies.

Look over everything you have in your classroom and begin to weed out those items that are inappropriate. What would you remove?

1. _____
2. _____
3. _____
4. _____
5. _____

Write down three things you can do to improve the quality of materials in your classroom.

1. _____
2. _____
3. _____

Children often tell us when activities are inappropriate. Remember when you did a tally of which activities were most and least popular (page 85)?

Now, think about the three most popular, and the three least popular, activities. Then try to figure out why children do or don't choose them, based on the activity qualities in the checklist. Are they appropriate for the children's ages? Have they been around, with no varia-

tion, for too long? Have you unwittingly encouraged only a few children to take part (such as suggesting carpentry for boys more often than for girls)?

Three **most popular** activities:

1. _____
2. _____
3. _____

Why?

_____

_____

Three **least popular** activities:

1. _____
2. _____
3. _____

Why?

_____

_____

Next, evaluate the books you provide for children. List five children's books that you regularly use in your group. Using the criteria in the following "Ten Quick Ways to Analyze Children's Books for Racism and Sexism," rate your books. *Circle "O" for OK*

or "S" for stereotyped next to the titles on your list. Jot down why you decided they were OK or stereotyped and be prepared to discuss your opinion with your Advisor.

1. OK S _____

2. OK S _____

3. OK S _____

4. OK S _____

5. OK S _____

Ten quick ways to analyze children's books for racism and sexism

Both in school and out, young children are exposed to racist and sexist attitudes. These attitudes—expressed over and over in books and in other media—gradually distort their perceptions until stereotypes and myths about minorities and women are accepted as reality. It is difficult for a librarian or teacher to convince children to question society's attitudes. But if a child can be shown how to detect racism and sexism in a book, the child can proceed to transfer the perception to wider areas. The following 10 guidelines are offered as a starting point in evaluating children's books from this perspective.

1. Check the illustrations

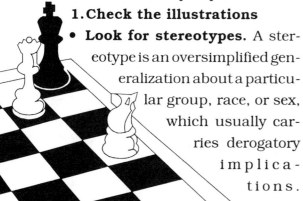

- **Look for stereotypes.** A stereotype is an oversimplified generalization about a particular group, race, or sex, which usually carries derogatory implications.

Some infamous (overt) stereotypes of Blacks are the happy-go-lucky, watermelon-eating Sambo and the fat, eye-rolling "mammy;" of Chicanos, the sombrero-wearing peon or fiesta-loving, macho bandito; of Asian Americans, the inscrutable, slant-eyed "Oriental;" of Native Americans, the naked savage or "primitive" craftsman and his squaw; of Puerto Ricans, the switchblade-toting teenage gang member; of women, the completely domesticated mother, the demure, doll-loving little girl, or the wicked stepmother. While you may not always find stereotypes in the blatant forms described, look for variations which in any way demean or ridicule characters because of their race or sex.

- **Look for tokenism.** If there are non-White characters in the illustrations, do they look just like Whites except for being tinted or colored in? Do all minority faces look stereotypically alike, or are they depicted as genuine individuals with distinctive features?

- **Who's doing what?** Do the illustrations depict minorities in subservient and passive roles or in leadership and action roles? Are males the active "doers" and females the inactive observers?

2. Check the story line

The Civil Rights Movement has led publishers to weed out many insulting passages, particularly from stories with Black themes, but the attitudes still find expression in less obvious ways. The following checklist suggests some of the subtle (covert) forms of bias to watch for.

- **Standard for success.** Does it take "White" behavior standards for a minority person to "get ahead?" Is "making it" in the dominant White society projected as the only ideal? To gain acceptance and approval, do non-White persons have to exhibit extraordinary qualities—excel in sports, get As, etc.? In friendships between White and non-White children, is it the non-White who does most of the understanding and forgiving?

- **Resolution of problems.** How are problems presented, conceived, and resolved in the story? Are minority people considered to be "the problem?" Are the oppressions faced by minorities and women represented as causally related to an unjust society? Are the reasons for poverty and oppression explained, or are they accepted as inevitable? Does the story line encourage passive acceptance or active resistance? Is a particular problem that is faced by a minority person resolved through the benevolent intervention of a White person?

- **Role of women.** Are the achievements of girls and women based on their own initiative and intelligence, or are they due to their good looks or to their relationship with boys? Are sex roles incidental or critical to characterization and plot? Could the same story be told if the sex roles were reversed?

3. Look at the lifestyles

Are minority persons and their setting depicted in such a way that they contrast unfavorably with the unstated norm of White middle-class suburbia? If the minority group in question is depicted as "different," are negative value judgments implied? Are minorities depicted exclusively in ghettos, barrios, or migrant camps? If the illustrations and text attempt to depict another culture, do they go beyond oversimplifications and offer genuine insights into another lifestyle? Look for inaccuracy and inappropriateness in the depiction of other cultures. Watch for instances of the "quaint-natives-in-costume" syndrome (most noticeable in areas like costume and custom, but extending to behavior and personality traits as well).

4. Weigh the relationships between people

Do the Whites in the story possess the power, take the leadership, and make the important decisions? Do non-Whites and females function in essentially supporting roles?

How are family relationships depicted? In

Black families, is the mother always dominant? In Hispanic families, are there always lots and lots of children? If the family is separated, are societal conditions—unemployment, poverty—cited among the reasons for the separation?

5. Note the heroes and heroines

For many years, books showed only "safe" minority heroes and heroines—those who avoided serious conflict with the White establishment of their time. Minority groups today are insisting on the right to define their own heroes and heroines based on their own concepts and struggles for justice.

When minority heroes and heroines do appear, are they admired for the same qualities that have made White heroes and heroines famous or because what they have done has benefited White people? Ask this question: Whose interest is a particular figure really serving?

6. Consider the effects on a child's self-image

- **Are norms established that limit the child's aspirations and self-concepts?** What effect can it have on Black children to be continuously bombarded with images of the color white as the ultimate in beauty, cleanliness, virtue, etc., and the color black as evil, dirty, menacing, etc.? Does the book counteract or reinforce this positive association with the color white and negative association with black?

What happens to a girl's self-image when she reads that boys perform all of the brave and important deeds? What about a girl's self-esteem if she is not "fair" of skin and slim of body?

In a particular story, is there one or more persons with whom a minority child can readily identify to a positive and constructive end?

7. Consider the author's or illustrator's background

Analyze the biographical material on the jacket flap or the back of the book. If a story deals with a minority theme, what qualifies the author or illustrator to deal with the subject? If the author and illustrator are not members of the minority being written about, is there anything in their background that would specifically recommend them as the creators of this book?

Similarly, a book that deals with the feelings and insights of women should be more carefully examined if it is written by a man—unless the book's avowed purpose is to present a strictly male perspective.

8. Check out the author's perspective

No author can be wholly objective. All authors write out of a cultural as well as a personal context. Children's books in the past have traditionally come from authors who are White and who are members of the middle class, with one result being that a single ethnocentric perspective has dominated American children's literature. With the book in question, look carefully to determine whether the direction of the author's perspective substantially weakens or strengthens the value of his/her written work. Are omissions and distortions central to the overall character or "message" of the book?

9. Watch for loaded words

A word is loaded when it has insulting overtones. Examples of loaded adjectives (usually racist) are savage, primitive, conniving, lazy, superstitious, treacherous, wily, crafty, inscrutable, docile, and backward.

Look for sexist language and adjectives that exclude or ridicule women. Look for use of the male pronoun to refer to both males and females. While the generic use of the word "man" was accepted in the past, its use today is outmoded. The following examples show how sexist language can be avoided: ancestors instead of forefathers; chairperson instead of chairman; community instead of brotherhood; firefighters instead of firemen; manufactured instead of manmade; the human family instead of the family of man.

10. Look at the copyright date

Books on minority themes—usually hastily conceived—suddenly began appearing in the mid-1960s. There followed a growing number of "minority experience" books to meet the new market demand, but most of these were still written by White authors, edited by White editors, and published by White publishers.

They therefore reflected a White point of view. Only very recently in the late 1960s and early 1970s, has the children's book world begun to even remotely reflect the realities of a multiracial society. And it has just begun to reflect feminists' concerns.

The copyright dates, therefore, can be a clue as to how likely the book is to be overtly racist or sexist, although a recent copyright date, of course, is no guarantee of a book's relevance or sensitivity. The copyright date only means the year the book was published. It usually takes a minimum of 1 year—and often much more than that—from the time a manuscript is submitted to the publisher to the time it is actually printed and put on the market. This time lag meant very little in the past, but in a time of rapid change and changing consciousness, when children's book publishing is attempting to be "relevant," it is becoming increasingly significant.

Reprinted with permission from the Council on Interracial Books for Children, Inc., 1841 Broadway, New York, NY 10023. Copies are available from the Council on Interracial Books for 10¢ each plus a self-addressed, stamped envelope.

The Council also publishes the *Bulletin* (eight issues a year), which reviews new children's books for the human and anti-human messages they convey.

Are the books you listed appropriate for children or do some of them perpetuate stereotypes and myths about people?

Save one sample of a book that is stereotyped to discuss with the other Candidates in your CDA Seminar. Read the OK books to the children in your care, if the books are age-appropriate.

Books—and other materials—that do not convey a respect for sex, age, race, abilities, language, culture, and families should only be used with preschoolers and/or their parents as special examples to spark a discussion about how pictures and stories are fair or unfair to some people. See the book, *Anti-Bias Curriculum: Tools for Empowering Young Children* (Derman-Sparks, 1989) for suggestions of ways to help children and adults recognize and deal with biases.

Use these criteria every time you choose books, posters, games, dolls, and other materials. Don't waste your money on items that perpetuate myths or inaccurate generalizations about people's heritage or abilities.

Now let's go shopping again! You know where you would like to make some improvements.

Pretend you have $200 to spend on new learning materials for your classroom. Using all the information you have about children's interests, the most and least popular activities in your program—how would you spend it?

In the spaces provided below and on page 182, write the items, their cost, and why you chose them here. Discuss your choices with your CDA Field Advisor.

ITEM _____

Cost _____

Why children in my group would benefit _____

_____

ITEM _____

Cost _____

Why children in my group would benefit _____

_____

_____

ITEM _____

Cost _____

Why children in my group would benefit _____

_____

ITEM _____

Cost _____

Why children in my group would benefit _____

_____

ITEM _____

Cost _____

Why children in my group would benefit _____

_____

ITEM _____

Cost _____

Why children in my group would benefit _____

_____

ITEM _____

Cost _____

Why children in my group would benefit _____

_____

ITEM _____

Cost _____

Why children in my group would benefit _____

_____

Well, you are on your way to being a great teacher of young children! You are making the kinds of decisions that teachers must make and you are making them based on your own observations and understanding of the needs of the children in your own group. You have set up a splendid teaching area equipped with marvelous materials.

If you have not already done so, be sure to see the video that accompanies Unit 3. Think about the questions raised in the Viewer's Guide and talk about them with your Field Advisor if something is puzzling to you.

Now we will turn from a focus on **where** to **what** happens in your interactions with children. Be sure to check that you have completed Unit 3 in your self-study section on your CDA progress record.

Resources for more information

American Red Cross child care course: First aid in the child care setting. Washington, DC: American Red Cross, 1989.

American Red Cross child care course: Preventing infectious diseases. Washington, DC: American Red Cross, 1989.

Berlfein, J. (1986). *A classroom with blocks* [Videotape]. Washington, DC: National Association for the Education of Young Children.

Children riding on sidewalks safely (CROSS). Washington, DC: National Association for the Education of Young Children and the U.S. Department of Transportation, 1990.

Davidson, J. (1980, May). Wasted time: The ignored dilemma. *Young Children, 35*(4),13–21.

Dental health curriculum. Washington, DC: Head Start Bureau, 1986.

Derman-Sparks, L., & the A.B.C. Task Force. (1989). *Anti-bias curriculum: Tools for empowering young children.* Washington, DC: National Association for the Education of Young Children.

Goodwin, M.T., & Pollen, G. (1980). *Creative food experiences for children.* Washington, DC: Center for Science in the Public Interest.

Greenman, J. (1988). *Caring spaces, learning places: Children's environments that work.* Redmond, WA: Exchange Press.

Greensher, J., Shelov, S., & Schaeffer, K. (1988). *Baby alive.* [Videotape]. Produced in cooperation with American Academy of Pediatrics. Port Washington, NY: Action Films & Video, Ltd.

Health and safety. (1986). Bank Street's Family Day Care Cassettes. Bank Street College, 610 W. 112th Street, New York, NY 10025.

Health in day care: A manual for health professionals. Elk Grove Village, IL: American Red Cross, 1987.

How seriously do you take the soaps? *Young Children, 42*(5), 69, National Association for the Education of Young Children (1987, July).

Ideas that work with young children: Tire hazards, woodworking, and crib safety. *Young Children, 41*(5),17–18, National Association for the Education of Young Children, (1986, July).

Kendrick, A., Kaufmann, R., & Messenger, K.P. (1991). *Healthy young children: A manual for programs.* Washington, DC: National Association for the Education of Young Children.

Koblinsky, S., & Behana, N. (1984, September). Child sexual abuse: The educator's role in prevention, detection, and intervention. *Young Children, 39*(6),3–15.

Kritchevsky, S., & Prescott, E., with Walling, L. (1977). *Planning environments for young children: Physical space* (2nd ed.). Washington, DC: National Association for the Education of Young Children.

Lansky, V. (1986). *Koko Bear's new potty.* New York: Bantam.

Lice aren't nice. *Young Children, 42*(3),46, National Association for the Education of Young Children (1987, March).

Lovell, P., & Harms, T. (1985, March). How can playgrounds be improved? A rating scale. *Young Children, 40*(3),3–8.

McCracken, J.B. (1987). "Merrily we roll along." Washington, DC: National Association for the Education of Young Children.

McCracken, J.B. (1990). "Playgrounds: Safe & sound." Washington, DC: National Association for the Education of Young Children.

National Black Child Development Institute. *Child Health Talk,* quarterly publication.

Stewart, I.S. (1982, July). The real world of teaching 2-year-old children. *Young Children, 37*(5), 3–13.

"Toys: Tools for learning." Washington, DC: National Association for the Education of Young Children, 1985.

Transportation manual—Us in a bus. Washington, DC: Head Start Bureau, 1985.

Walk in traffic safely (WITS). Washington, DC: National Association for the Education of Young Children and the U.S. Department of Transportation, 1990.

Wanamaker, N., Hearn, K., & Richarz, S. (1979). *More than graham crackers: Nutrition education & food preparation with young children.* Washington, DC: National Association for the Education of Young Children.

We love you—Buckle up! Washington, DC: National Association for the Education of Young Children and the U.S. Department of Transportation, 1984.

Williams, L. R., & De Gaetano, Y. (1985). *Alerta, a multicultural, bilingual approach to teaching young Children.* Menlo Park, CA: Addison-Wesley.

What are children learning by doing this?

Positive ways to support children's social and emotional development

HOW WONDERFUL IT IS to see children who genuinely care about others . . . who are persistent when they learn new skills . . . who celebrate their successes . . . and who have loving adults to help them deal with their strong emotions!

At every age and at all times, children need adults to help them be secure, loving, self-motivated, successful people. They will be better prepared to deal with life's challenges and problems.

Much of the time, children are a joy to be around. They want to please us, they try hard, they are loving and generous. Sometimes children's behavior can be frustrating—they bite, scream, don't pay attention, or are afraid of monsters.

> Lakeisha (18 months) sees her friend Paige fall. She rambles over to Paige, pats her gently on the back, and says, "OK, OK."

> Three preschoolers are making French toast. Yuichi wants to flip his piece over, but he is quite awkward at it. Ms. Silva shows him how to hold the turner, slide it in under the bread, then turn his wrist and the spatula to flip the toast.
>
> Yuichi lifts a piece out of the pan and puts it on a plate. He tries to turn the next piece of bread, and, after some difficulty, manages to flip it.
>
> Yuichi and Ms. Silva smile at each other.

> Two 3-year-olds both want to play with the same toy and one hits the other. Mr. Olesen says to the children nearby and to the child who hit, "It's so important to let people know how you feel—so important. Use words to tell him how you feel. . . . Yes, tell him instead of hitting."

In this unit we will talk about how to encourage the pleasant, friendly behaviors, and how to deal with the natural, sometimes difficult behaviors you face every day.

First we will think about what kinds of people we want children to be—not just today, but tomorrow, in elementary school, and as adults. These goals for children's social and emotional growth will be based on **their** developmental needs and on what will serve them best all their lives.

Then we will talk about guidance and discipline—what strategies work to support

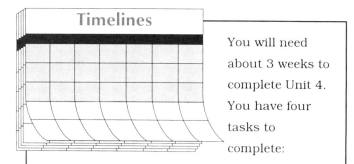

Timelines

You will need about 3 weeks to complete Unit 4. You have four tasks to complete:

1 Prepare for conference with your Field Advisor to discuss seven topics (what kind of people we want children to be, discipline, creating feelings of security, supporting families and cultures, fostering friendships, dealing with difficulties, and helping families cope with life's stressful events).

2 Complete two assignments (observe children at play and develop plans to build social and emotional skills) and five entries for the Professional Resource File.

3 Complete five assignments for Seminar (explore culture you grew up in, expand knowledge of other cultures and lifestyles, identify ways to deal with everyday expressions of bias, develop techniques for staying calm when children are out of control, and learn procedures for reporting child abuse).

4 View the accompanying videotape using the Viewer's Guide.

Word list

Anti-social—Acting in ways that hurt (feelings or physically) other people.

Cognitive—Thinking or intellectual development.

Oppositional—When two people cannot cooperate or agree.

Pro-social—Acting in ways that help people get along better.

Regress—Go back to less mature behaviors.

Reinforce—Encourage a behavior through praise or attention.

Young children may be outgoing and friendly, withdrawn and quiet, or somewhere in between. All through life, individual differences account for some of our behaviors.

children's self-control and long-term development. We will look at some of the typical challenges children face as they make friends, figure out who they are, and grow up. And we will see how you can help children handle extreme stress—new babies in the family, separation and divorce, moving, disabilities, hospitalization, death, and abuse.

Part 1

What kind of people do we want children to be?

"What a bad boy you are!"
"That's a good girl."

When we say things like this to children, what are we really telling them?

Not much. And a lot.

When we aren't specific about what was bad or good, we are labeling **the child** as bad or good. And before we know it, most children will begin to live up to our labels.

Children are neither bad nor good. Their **behavior** may range from appropriate to not appropriate, and even that depends on the situation.

Picture a child running and making fire engine noises. That behavior is entirely appropriate on the playground or in the back yard. It may be fine in the basement of your family child

care home or in the all-purpose room. It is not appropriate at the library.

Successful teachers do not think of children's behavior as either bad or good. They look at children in a different way. They realize that all through childhood, children are learning to control their behaviors.

Our first step in knowing how to help children learn to control their own behavior is to know how they grow and develop. Then we can give a lot of thought to the kind of people we want children to become.

You understand what children are like

As we saw in Unit 2, many people around the world have studied children. We know how development unfolds and how children's experiences affect their behavior. Based on this knowledge about children, we can make wise decisions about how we interact with them.

Know individuals

Babies radiate their own personalities. They tend to act in certain ways. Some infants are easy, some difficult, and some a little of both. Young children may be outgoing and friendly, withdrawn and quiet, or somewhere in between. All through life, individual differences account for some of our behaviors.

Know age-appropriate development

Many behaviors are natural as children grow up. Most infants struggle with separation anxiety. The notorious "terrible twos" are an important stage of development for toddlers. You are already familiar with these from your study of the chart of developmental milestones in Unit 2 and from your experience with children.

Turn to the section(s) of the chart that includes the ages of the children in your group. Look at the three parts that deal mostly with social and emotional development: *children show interest in others, children become more aware of themselves, children express feelings.*

Think about your experiences with children at this age. In your own words, write one paragraph describing some other typical social or emotional behaviors:

Know how to treat children

Much of children's behavior is learned. They copy the way they have seen other people act: relatives, neighbors, friends, or characters on television shows or in movies. They might learn to yell, hit, and criticize. Or they might calm themselves down, talk about their feelings, and solve problems constructively.

Most of the time, young children act the same way they are treated. Your attitude, discipline strategies, and the way you plan the learning environment can make a tremendous difference in what children are like.

Jeffrey always hits when another child doesn't give him what he wants immediately. You've seen his mother hit him when he doesn't instantly obey her.

Dhruv quietly moves about the room and works independently. His father is an engineer who spends many hours in his home workshop.

Two children in the group flit from activity to activity, use loud voices, and usually play superheros. They watch lots of cartoons on TV.

Maria is always able to keep herself busy. While others are bickering over toys, she can be found sitting and looking at picture books. You can see that Maria has done this many times before.

These examples point out why you and the children's parents need to work together to provide the kinds of experiences that lead children to become happy, well-adjusted people.

You have dreams for children

All parents have hopes and dreams for their children. Those dreams should enable their children to become all they can be—happy, productive members of our society.

Each time you talk with children's parents, you learn a little more about what they hope for their children. They probably selected your early childhood program because you share many of the same dreams for their children.

Perhaps you want . . .

. . . children to feel proud of themselves, their families, and their culture.

. . . children to feel competent.

. . . children to be curious — eager to learn and try new things.

. . . children to gain increasing control over their own behavior.

. . . children to see themselves as fair, kind, cooperative, friendly people.

. . . children to sense that their talents, language, and learning styles are respected.

. . . children to feel secure but not overprotected.

. . . children to feel independent but not overwhelmed with responsibility.

. . . children to know they can talk about their feelings. They trust adults who listen and understand.

. . . children to develop their own inner strengths.

Each family and cultural group emphasizes slightly different areas of development. Add to this list some other goals you share with the parents of children in your care.

Perhaps you want . . .

. . . children to

. . . children to

. . . children to

Sometimes parents have expectations for their young children that you do not think are in children's best interests. Perhaps they want their child to read before the age of 3 or expect their toddler to sit quietly during long family dinners. Maybe they want their child to start preparing for the Olympics at the age of 4.

You need to be aware of parents' unrealistic expectations. **On the next page, list any unrealistic expectations held by the parents of**

children in your care or by other parents you know that you think are unrealistic.

Think about how you would discuss one of these with a parent. Later on in *Essentials*, we will discuss further ways of comfortably talking with parents about how they might rethink their expectations for their children's benefit.

For now, remember that parents look up to you for figuring out age-appropriate expectations and long-term dreams for their social and emotional development.

Long-term dreams for children's social and emotional development

Parents and teachers want children to

- have a healthy self-esteem,
- be competent,
- love to learn,
- control themselves,
- love others,
- appreciate their uniqueness,
- feel secure,
- be independent, and
- trust others.

Gain self-esteem

Some parents worry that their children will be braggarts or stuck up. So they constantly point out their children's weaknesses.

Other parents are ashamed of their families. Perhaps their families don't have much money. Or their family has more, fewer, or different members than others. Some families even try to cover up their heritage. They don't share their roots with their children. They may feel it is better not to teach children their home lan-

Children with positive self-esteem know from their own experiences that they are capable, loving, and fun-to-be-with people.

guage, but speak to them in English instead, even though it is their second and maybe even weaker language. They remember being punished for speaking their home language at school and they want to spare their children this pain.

As a professional, it will be a challenge to understand and help parents understand why children should feel good about themselves. Because **when children feel good about themselves they can make the most of their lives**.

Think about your own self-esteem. When you feel good about who you are, you are ready to take on almost any challenge. You can weather almost any storm.

Children are no different. Children with positive self-esteem know from their own experiences that they are capable, loving, and fun-to-be-with people. Their successful experiences begin at birth, when parents and others bolster healthy development. Self-esteem is the key to self-confidence!

Be competent

Did you ever watch a baby beam when she first claps her hands? Or a toddler glow when he zips his coat? Children have a natural pride in what they can do. When children know they are able to do things, they are motivated **from inside** to try more new things. Competent children become competent adults. Success leads to more success.

In contrast, if children feel like failures, they rarely have much interest in anything. Their feelings of competence can be easily destroyed if we don't notice and support their successes.

Love learning

Children's first group experiences determine how they feel about learning and school. In their early years, if they are forced to be quiet, or to sit for long periods, or are given tasks much too hard, by the time they get to elementary school, they will already hate learning!

However, if they can be curious, find delights in books written in their own language and that contain pictures that look like them, are given a chance to try out ideas through play, laugh together, solve their own problems, and feel loved and welcome, they will be eager to learn all through their lives.

Teachers of young children set the stage for children to love to learn. Learning is enjoyable and rewarding. Your attitude, the activities and materials you plan, and the way you treat children can make learning a positive experience—one that children will want to continue.

Control themselves

Discipline.

Punishment.

These are the words most often used to describe what we do to make children "behave" or "be good." But as we have already seen, children themselves are neither good nor bad, their behaviors are just appropriate or inappropriate, depending on the time and place.

Our goal is for children to be able to control themselves. Why? So they don't need an adult hovering over them to enforce every rule or to punish them for the least infraction. You probably have seen children who cower if you lift your arm to pick something up. Or who shake in fear when they have broken a rule. Or who lie about what they did because they are afraid of the punishment. These children have probably been disciplined in ways that don't help them develop healthy forms of self-control.

As a professional, you look at children's current and long-term development. The process for learning self-control **is** slow and gradual. Children need lots of help—some more than others. Helping children learn to control themselves takes time and patience.

But the rewards are many: Children become teenagers and then adults who feel good about themselves . . . are trustworthy . . . can make reasonable decisions . . . and are a joy to know! When you teach self-control you make an investment in children's futures.

Help children
want to control themselves
by finding appropriate ways
for them to express their feelings.

Love others

A person who is unable to love, or to show love in positive ways, is an empty shell. Children learn to love because they feel loved. They feel  safe and secure, physically and mentally protected by those who care about them. Children need to feel lovable before they can love others. These ideas may seem so ob-

vious, but love is something we show all the time—not just on Valentine's Day!

Appreciate their uniqueness

No two people are alike. Fortunately. What a boring world it would be!

Children need us to help them see what wonderful individuals they are—their own special looks, skills, personalities, tempos, likes, and dislikes. By helping children be happy with who they are, and who nobody else can be, we strengthen their sense of value as a person.

Feel secure

The security blanket the cartoon character Linus carries around makes the point clear: Children need to feel secure. Familiar things give them secure feelings. When they feel secure, they can do new and different things.

Kyle and his mother are spending his first day in preschool together. At first, Kyle sits with his mother, watching the other children.

He spots some children playing with airplanes, looks tentatively at his mother, and then walks toward the activity. He stands and watches. When a child says, "Do you want to fly this plane?" Kyle looks back at his mother, who smiles. He reaches for the plane.

Throughout the morning, Kyle occasionally walks back to his mother, who reassures him and comments on what he is doing. Then he returns to his play.

Kyle feels secure that this mother is there on his first day. He needs occasional reassurance from her, but he neither clings nor ignores her presence. All children need something familiar to feel secure.

Act independently

This seems to be a really tough area in our society. Some children are so overprotected they fail to learn how to handle even the smallest problems. Other children are given too much independence too soon and become overwhelmed with responsibilities far beyond what they can handle at their age. We need to strike an appropriate balance with children. We want them to be able to do things on their own. We want them to be able to make good choices. So the things we give them to do by themselves need to be tailored to their age and maturity level.

Once again, you must rely on your knowledge of child development and of the individual child to decide how best to foster the sense of independence.

Trust others

Growing up is so hard. Children need at least one understanding adult who can **really** listen to what they say. Someone who will not criticize, scold, judge, or turn off children's ideas. Children need someone with whom they can share their joys, their fears, and their dreams. They need someone they can count on to follow through on promises, who will treat children with respect.

You will undoubtedly be one of those people. Learn how to be a good listener and how to respond to children's work or thoughts.

All of these features of long-range development blend together to build children's **inner strength**—their ability to use their own re-

sources to get as much out of life as possible, both now and as they mature. Let's now look at how we can make all of these goals for children become a reality.

Part 2

How do you guide children's development of inner strength?

DISCIPLINE. Everyone wants children who behave. But some people's techniques for making this happen are not in children's best interests. Why? Because many discipline strategies aren't based on knowledge about child development.

When discipline systems depend upon adult control and punishment, they are inappropriate. When discipline systems are designed to **make** children behave—rather than to help children **want** to control themselves, they are inappropriate.

Systems that rely on threats or punishment may work in the short term, but they don't have many beneficial long-term effects. In fact, they may even stop children from learning to control themselves.

In this section of *Essentials*, we will concentrate on positive, specific, time-tested ways to help children learn to discipline themselves and get along with each other. These ways work. They are not quick fixes for problem children. Instead, they help children learn from experiencing the logical consequences of their own actions. When you use these techniques, you will feel good about yourself as a teacher. The children will feel good about themselves. And even skeptical parents will soon begin to see the value of this positive approach. Children will begin and continue to use prosocial behaviors that will last all their lives.

There are two basic steps in teaching with this child development-based type of discipline. First, you eliminate as many problem-causing situations as possible. Then, you always act in specific positive ways.

Always think:

> *What can I do to help children*
> *learn how to be in control*
> *of their own behavior?*

You plan to avoid problems

Whenever children build with blocks, someone always rides a tricycle through and bumps into the building.

Caitlin grabs the doll from Joshua. Soon Pallavi yanks it away from her.

Children wander aimlessly about the room during free play. When you suggest a puzzle, they begin half-heartedly, then dump the pieces on the floor.

While you read the story, several children fidget, loudly lift the Velcro strips on their shoes several times, and then get up and leave.

The parents want a graduation party for your Head Start children. You order diplomas, small caps and gowns, and prepare an hour-long program in which children sing, recite poems, and act out their favorite story: *Caps for Sale.*

Graduation is a disaster. Children get wiggly and wave heartily to their families. They barely whisper the songs. They forget their poems or refuse to even try. The play ends when the peddler's caps fall off and he bursts into tears.

You probably have had similar incidents happen with children. And you may have already figured out the reason. Why do you think children misbehaved in these examples?

Block wrecking:

Doll grabbing:

Puzzle dumping:

Story fidgeting:

Graduation chaos: _____

_____

_____

Often, children are not the cause of the problem at all. The environment, the schedule, or your expectations can cause conflict and disruption. We often unwittingly plan the day or set up the materials in ways that invite children to behave inappropriately. Let's explore how to avoid doing this.

Identify toys and materials

Children often fight over toys. If dolls are a popular item, for example, having enough dolls so infants and toddlers don't need to share will prevent conflicts. Your money will be better spent on duplicates of favorite toys than on lots of items children ignore.

Even preschoolers, who are becoming more able to share, need enough duplicates of toys to keep up their interest and avoid long waits for a turn. Children will share when they don't feel the need to protect things and when they are developmentally mature enough.

The children in the example probably dumped the puzzles because the clinking sound they made on the floor was more interesting than the puzzles. Perhaps they had done the puzzles many times already. Maybe the puzzles were too easy or too hard.

Rotate toys so children always have a varied selection. Just put some (that are too familiar or too easy) away for a while and bring out others.

Select those that are a good match for what children can do.

Be alert to children's boredom and skill levels. Think up interesting, new activities with different materials. Many things you use will be discarded items that cost nothing: egg cartons, packing chips, computer paper. Just make sure everything you offer is respectful of people and children's ability levels.

Which toys in your program are a source of problems? What could be done to reduce the problem?

_____

_____

_____

_____

Discuss your ideas with your CDA Field Advisor.

Make good use of group times

Most teachers seem to think circle time, sharing time, show-and-tell, or some other large group gathering promotes togetherness. Or that this is the only time children are learning because an adult is directing what happens.

But your experience probably has been that many group times are spent telling children to sit down, to pay attention, and to PLEASE stop playing with their shoes!

Circle time, long transitions, stories, and other large group times nearly always cause a problem for young children. Until children are about 3½ years old, stick to smaller groups. Four or five children are enough. Even with preschoolers, you will find more behavior problems the larger the group and the more time they are asked to sit still and pay attention.

If you want preschoolers to gather together, make the time short, keep the children involved, and don't be offended if children wander off. They probably will learn more from an activity of their choice than they will from tuning you out and disturbing the other children. Use this behavior as a clue that the child was bored and had enough sense to find something better to do!

Read stories to *small* groups so children can sit on your lap or next to you. Then you can informally talk about what happened, children can see the pictures, and they will experience stories as a pleasant, warm time with their teacher. Children's librarians can assist you in choosing stories that are of the right interest level and age level. In addition, they are a good resource to locate related items that can embellish a story session. Short songs, fingerplays and games that tie the session together provide a means of introducing some "active" time into a seemingly quiet time. What a great way to build a love of reading!

Follow Oralie McAfee's excellent suggestions (see page 199) for ways to have a more appropriate circle time with preschool children.

It follows that large, structured parties, such as graduation, beauty contests, or children's proms, are not developmentally appropriate for young children.

We need to keep our expectations realistic. Performances for an audience cause a great

Pick a group time activity that is appealing and appropriate for the children in your care.

Unit 4

deal of stress for young children. Children are not miniature adults or even teenagers, and their activities should be children's activities.

As professionals, we must never take advantage of children just to satisfy our needs or the needs of parents.

If you want to have a celebration, plan a picnic, a beach party, or some other event. Children can decorate, fix refreshments, and perhaps everyone can join in to sing "The Wheels on the Bus" and some other favorite songs. Anything much more structured or lengthy is sure to be a disaster.

Ways to make group time more appropriate for preschoolers

Before circle

- **Schedule** it to avoid distractions. Between other more vigorous, individual activities is best.
- **Plan** for children to move into and out of circle in an orderly way. (Gather children quickly so they don't have to wait, use open-ended activities such as finger plays while children gather, set up activities for a few children to go to at a time when they leave.)
- **Select** very interesting activities appropriate to children's development.
- **Plan** the order of activities so you can vary the pace.
- **Anticipate** problems. Sit near children who have the most difficulty.

During group time

- **Watch** to see what the children do and change your plans accordingly. If no one is paying attention, skip to something more interesting.
- **Tell** children how you expect them to behave and why.
- **Give** clear, simple instructions about what children are to do next.
- **Keep up** the momentum: show enthusiasm; whisper; use mystery, suspense, or humor; bring out props. Don't spend your time telling children to sit or listen. Do something so appealing they will want to be there.
- **Comment** on appropriate behavior. Ignore minor distractions.

After group time

- **Think** about what worked and what didn't. Don't make the same mistakes twice.

Note: Adapted from "Getting Past Two Little Pumpkins" by O. McAfee, *Young Children*, September 1985, *40*(6), 27. Copyright © 1985 by National Association for the Education of Young Children. Reprinted with permission.

What types of appropriate celebrations have you found were very successful?

easier for children to control their own behavior in appropriate ways.

What changes can you make in your space that will help direct children toward more appropriate behaviors?

Discuss your ideas with your Field Advisor.

Organize space

You probably had no trouble figuring out why the trike-riding children kept knocking down the block constructions: The block area was most likely in a traffic path!

As you saw in Unit 3, you can arrange your classroom or your family day care home play areas in ways that protect children's activities. When the area works well, you make it much

Watch for indications your actions have worked and discuss what happened with your Field Advisor.

Here are some tips on ways to make sure your environment doesn't cause clashes over the use of space:

- **Organize the area to separate activities.** Eliminate long pathways so children aren't tempted to run. Use physical barriers to show where running or bike riding should end. Place noisy activity areas (pretend play, vehicles, blocks) near each other so quieter activities (reading, art) are not disturbed.

- **Arrange space in ways that help children understand how it should be used.** Label children's cubbies and clothes so things don't get lost. Mark shelves with pictures and/or words so children can return items to their proper place.

You act in specific, positive ways with children

Equally important to planning materials, activities, and space to avoid problems is **how we act** with children. How you treat each child—how you communicate your acceptance of them as individuals—is the key to being a successful early childhood educator or parent. Nothing else you do for children will make them want to please you or will have as much impact on their sense of themselves as capable and loved human beings, now or in the future.

All of the techniques described here are based on what we know about the effects of various approaches on children's development. Don't just do what comes naturally, or teach the way you were taught. Practice these interaction strategies until they seem second nature to you.

As you do, you will feel good about yourself, for you will be using the most up-to-date, effective, and child-oriented methods for helping children learn to discipline themselves for the rest of their lives.

Create a secure feeling

There are so many things you can do to create a predictable, secure setting and thereby help children learn to control their own behavior. Besides being necessary for becoming disciplined and self-controlled, security is one of the basic building blocks for children's overall healthy social and emotional development.

Remember, you foster children's trust in you and people in general each time you interact with them! All of the following strategies for interacting with children help build that trust and this feeling of security as well. Each contributes to children's long-term development of a sense of acceptance and well-being.

Be there. Use substitutes infrequently. Your presence definitely gives the children a feeling of security and convinces parents that their children have consistent, reliable care.

Of course, there will be days when you are absent for illness, vacation, or other business, and substitute care has to be arranged. If at all possible, introduce your substitute on a day when you are there. Give children time to get to know the person. Then tell children in advance who will be taking your place if you know you will be absent. The sudden appearance of a new person can shake a child's sense of security, even in a familiar setting.

Greet children and parents warmly. Let children know you are happy to see them and that you look forward to an enjoyable day together. Let parents know their children will be safe and happy in your care.

"Hi, Kristy! I'm so glad you are here today. We missed you while you were sick. How do you feel, now?"

It is often hard for children to say goodbye and to be away from their loved ones. Respect those feelings. Their separation difficulties may be especially strong after weekends, vacations, and illnesses and at certain times in their development.

When children are reluctant for their parents to leave, say things such as this:

"I know you had such a wonderful weekend. You really enjoyed so much time with your family. Now it is time for them to go to work. Dad will be back to pick up this afternoon after nap. Let's both wave goodbye out the window."

During the day you will want to talk with children frequently about their families. Hang photographs of their families near the diaper-changing table, on the children's cubbies, or in some other conspicuous place.

Talk about what Mother, Dad, or other family members are doing while the children are with you. If you try to avoid the topic, children will wonder why you are ignoring their favorite people! Don't use the excuse that it will make children too sad or lonely. They have a right to miss their loved ones.

> Never say, "Be a big boy now. Don't cry. The day will be over before you know it." Treat children's feelings with respect. Their feelings are **real.**

In addition to saying hello with every arrival, you need to be sure to say goodbye when children and parents leave. Often, children are as reluctant to go home as they were to say goodbye in the morning — they are having such a good time! Parents may even need reassurance that this reaction is typical and that their children are not rejecting them — just that they have chosen such a good program for their children.

Plan to make this transition from program to home as smooth as possible. If all the children leave at the same time, your schedule can be planned so activities end together. Everyone says goodbye as their parents pick them up or they get on the bus.

If children leave at different times, select open-ended activities for the last part of the day. This way, children can save what they are working on for another day or can easily leave the activity without disrupting a group or missing something special. Art activities, construction toys, books, table toys, individual projects, and even outdoor play usually work well at the end of the day.

Just as you did in the morning, be sure to say goodbye to each parent and child. "Adios, Margarita and Julio. See you tomorrow! ¡Hasta mañana!" You give families a real sense of importance and belonging with a warm greeting and a warm goodbye.

If a child is coming into an already established program, before the child's first day, ask parents to visit the program with the child during a time when no other children are present. This gives the child a chance to look around, find the bathroom, and feel more comfortable about you and the environment.

On the child's first day, ask the new child and parent to arrive early. That way, the other children join the new child instead of the other way around. As the other children arrive, you can more gradually introduce the newcomer.

Keep children's needs a priority. Be especially responsive to the needs of babies by cuddling and picking up on their cues about their schedule. Talk with them softly in their home language to give them a chance to get used to your voice. Move gently and slowly so children can adjust to you. Watch the baby to get a feel for her or his personal style. At any rate, you probably won't want to introduce the Jack-in-the-Box or other surprise toys on the first day.

Show older newcomers their cubbies and where to hang their coat or store their lunch. You might also ask another child, perhaps one who is fairly outgoing, to be the new child's guide for the day or week. Give the newcomer a brief review of the day's schedule so she or he knows what to expect:

"First we all choose what we would like to play with, then we play outdoors, and when we come in we work on projects until lunch."

Then the new child can get involved in an activity so the other children join her or him. During the day, you may want to point out that:

"After we play outdoors this afternoon, your mother will be coming to pick you up."

Small things can mean so much to show new children they are welcome. Have their names already on their cubbies and cots or cribs. Hang their family photo with the rest of the children's.

Display books with characters who look or talk like they do. Skip name tags unless every-one is new. If everyone is new, ask the children if they could wear their name tags for just that day—most will want to when given the choice.

Frequently call new children by name, especially during those first difficult hours. Talk about what the children did during the day before they came to your program, using their home language whenever possible. Talk about their old and new neighborhoods—express a genuine interest in children's lives by listening rather than prying. Post pictures of their families. Hang their art work.

Use your observation skills to learn more about children's strengths and weaknesses so

Show children affection in the tone of your voice and by snuggling and hugging. Be generous with affection and touch, tailoring it to children's individual styles and their cultural preferences.

you can plan more appropriately for each one. Be sensitive to children's own pace—some will plunge right in, while others may need a week or two to feel more comfortable.

What strategies do you use to make children feel welcome on their first day in your program?

Show affection. Use a warm tone of voice and snuggle and hug. Be generous with affection and touch, tailoring it to children's individual styles and their cultural preferences.

Make sure you treat all children with respect: Use children's names often. Speak in children's home languages whenever possible. Never say "Hey, you!" or use nicknames that belittle children.

Do not back away from children you find unappealing in some way. Talk with a trusted co-worker to try to help you overcome any feelings of dislike you may have for a child.

Show that you enjoy children's company. If you don't want to spend time with children, or are feeling burned out, take a vacation. Children are too vulnerable to be cared for by someone who doesn't have their heart in their work.

Be sensitive about how you show affection to young children by knowing what is culturally appropriate. In some cultures, certain types of touch or eye contact, for example, may not mean the same thing as it does in your culture. Find out about the families in your group. Then use the positive ways they use with their children.

Be cautious about teasing and tickling. It's easy for children to perceive them as hostility. If you know the family well enough, you may decide to use some lighthearted teasing once in a great while—perhaps a surprise game of "Hide and Seek." Make sure you don't do it at the child's expense, however, and be sure to stop the instant you see it makes the child uncomfortable.

Be sure you help children know the difference between touches that feel good, and touches that make them feel uncomfortable. Help them understand that it is OK to say "Stop!" or "Don't do that anymore!" to an adult who makes them feel uncomfortable.

Make eye contact. When you talk with children look at them in their eyes, unless they are taught by their culture not to do so. Bend your knees, sit on the floor, or sit in a chair.

Never yell at children from across the room or outdoor play area unless it is an emergency. Remember the story about the boy who cried "Wolf!" If you yell at children all the time, they will soon tune you out and then when it really is an emergency they will keep right on ignoring you.

Start today to use this simple, but very

important, teaching technique of getting down to the child's level to make eye contact.

Respond quickly. Be sensitive to children's requests for assistance. An infant's cry should never be ignored. Go as quickly and calmly as you can to find out what is wrong or what the baby needs. Babies cannot be spoiled by too much attention. In fact, if you respond quickly to babies' cries when they are very young, they tend to cry less often and for shorter times when they are older. Respond calmly and lovingly.

Babies also are helped to feel secure in your care when you adapt to their schedules, then gradually guide them into more regular eating and sleeping patterns. Never make infants wait to eat if they are hungry or wake them up just because it's time to do something else, for example. Be sensitive to each baby's own rhythm.

It is sometimes difficult to respond appropriately when children either do not have the language skills or do not know what the problem is. Many times their cry for help is silent or comes out through antisocial behavior—biting, hitting, or withdrawal, for example.

Sometimes you will have to use observation, talk with parents, and the process of elimination to figure out why the child is crying or acting in unacceptable ways. We will look at some causes typical for misbehavior in the last two sections of this unit.

Whenever or however children ask for help, keep this key question in mind: **What can I do to help the child be in control of her or his own behavior?**

With older children, it may be is easier to figure out what's wrong because when they need help they usually ask for it. Familiar requests for help are "I can't . . ." or "This isn't working." Sometimes they show frustration by stopping before completing a project.

Whenever or however children ask for help, keep that key question in mind: **What can I do to help the child be in control of her or his own behavior?**

If you solve the problem by doing it yourself, children may feel like a failure. They begin to expect someone else to solve problems for them. They lose the chance to figure something out for themselves. They certainly won't learn to think about what they are doing, to try several solutions, and to feel the glow of success for having figured it out on their own.

Instead of taking over, give children an opportunity to take the next step on their own. Ask them what they are trying to do: "What did you want to do with the saw?" Or comment on what you see: "You seem to be frustrated with your progress, but I know you can figure this out."

Once you know the child's goal, you can help get to a solution, often by asking more open-ended questions to get the child to think through the steps involved. Questions with yes or no answers rarely are helpful. Instead, ask questions such as "What is giving you difficulty?" or "What do you think you need to do first (or next)?"

If the child seems to be at a real loss, you might suggest some solutions in the form of questions: "What do you think would happen if you tried a thinner piece of wood?" "How about using the vice to hold the wood?"

Children learn to cope with frustration best when they do as much as possible themselves to stick with something until they find a solution. Don't interfere with the learning process. Instead, find a way to help children figure out how to solve their problems. This technique works for all types of problems, including resolving disagreements between children.

Use this space to write down an example of how you supported a child who was figuring out a solution to a problem.

Respect children's choices. Children feel much more secure when they feel they have some control over what happens to them. They know they can make a difference, that they have some say in their fate, that someone has confidence in them—they feel trustworthy. Whenever a choice is possible, offer children **real** choices and accept their decisions. Just make sure that whatever the children choose, it will be a **good** choice! You wouldn't offer children a choice between chocolate ice cream or orange slices for snack, for instance. Nor would you offer a child the choice between wearing a swim suit or a snowsuit to play outdoors.

Instead, the choices you offer should be appropriate, similar, and they should matter to the child: healthy foods, similar types of clothing, appropriate activities.

The type and number of choices offered should depend on the child's maturity. Children can handle increasing responsibility as they grow older and gain practice in making decisions.

Let **infants** and **waddlers** choose which toy to play with or which color of sweater to wear.

Toddlers can select which activity to do or which fruit to eat for snack.

Older preschool children can select from three or four good options of what to do, eat, or wear.

Individual choices should also be part of your daily planning. Free play periods should include a variety of play options for children. Some activities would focus on small groups (blocks, dramatic play, cooking) while others would be more individual (art, puzzles, books).

Children's days should be filled with choices for them. Then they can select the activities that best match their interests and skills. That is when they will learn the most.

There is a special bonus in store for you when you offer children choices: **Children who feel they have some control over what happens to them usually will be much more willing to cooperate at other times.**

Two-year-olds have a reputation for always saying "NO!" But if you give them choices, rather than always insisting upon a specific behavior, children generally will be a lot less negative when something comes along about which they have no choice. If a toddler must wear a sweater to play outdoors, offer a choice: the red sweater or the blue sweatshirt.

Write here an example of a choice that you gave to a child and what the child did:

_____

_____

_____

_____

_____

_____

Encourage self-help skills. You don't want to rush children into too much responsibility, but the more things they do for themselves, the more they learn how to be in charge of their own actions. All through this book we have talked about appropriate self-help skills for young children: toileting, washing hands, brushing teeth, cleaning up spills, hanging up clothes, taking good care of and putting away toys, preparing food, and making choices.

Most children are eager to learn these skills and take responsibility for their own behavior.

Such skills increase their sense of security because they know they can count on themselves and they feel so grown up.

Take every opportunity to let children practice these skills—don't do the job for them. Let children perfect these real-life skills on real-life objects: children's own clothes or dress-up clothes, toys children use every day, meal times. Be sure to allow enough time for children to do it themselves.

Encourage children to help others learn skills, too. You have surely seen how catching it is when the first toddler learns to put on her coat.

Children should feel special everyday. They thrive on one-on-one contact and attention. Pay attention to each one during the day, and make it a point to talk with every child.

She lays it on the floor, collar toward her feet, sticks her arms in the sleeves, and flips the coat over her head and on! There is no easier or more fun way!

Notice children as individuals. Children should feel special everyday. They thrive on one-to-one contact and attention. Pay attention to each one during the day, and make it a point to talk with every child. A brief statement of fact such as "Hi, Jocelyn. I see you are using the lotto game," can open up a whole conversation on topics the child considers important.

How you interact with children lets them know how important they are to you. Perhaps you're all playing outdoors and a child kicks a ball. You enthusiastically note, "¡Qué fuerte pateaste la pelota!" "What a strong kick!"

Changing diapers and feeding infants are perfect times for you and the youngest children to get to know each other better. While doing these routine tasks, you can recite rhymes, poems, songs and fingerplays to the child.

Never let children feel like they are just one of the forgotten crowd. If you have trouble remembering whether you have talked to each child during the day, keep a tally on a card in your pocket.

Notice children's successes. Positive attention is much more effective than negative attention if you want children to act appropriately.

Many times, children are so needy for attention that they misbehave—that is a sure way to make most people notice them. Instead, ignore inappropriate behavior and catch children behaving appropriately!

"Casey and Nicole, you figured out a way to carry that heavy bucket full of water! The two of you are working so cooperatively. That's hard to keep walking together."

"Your baby looks so cozy all tucked in his bed, Rasheed. What a loving father you are."

"All the lids are on all the big plastic bottles! You got every one to match, Takenori and Ariel. You must feel so proud."

Children's self-esteem is given a big boost when you notice what they do. Sometimes this encouragement strategy is called **reinforcement**. When you comment on positive actions, you accomplish at least two things:

- You let children know which behaviors are appropriate: cooperation, sharing, finishing tasks, nurturing others, trying hard.
- You build their sense of pride for behaving appropriately.

Children live up to our expectations for them. Even the most difficult children will begin to control their behavior when they are given attention for acting appropriately. It won't happen instantly, but your efforts will be rewarded. Children will act more maturely. Parents will be thrilled!

Select one child in your group who could benefit from additional attention to successes. During one week, keep a diary of all the things you did to help that child feel more successful.

When you finish, discuss your strategies with your Field Advisor.

Support children's families and cultures

Our primary goals for children's long-term development include having a healthy self-esteem and feeling unique. Both of these concepts can be fostered when children's experiences in your care are built on respect for the cultural values of their own families and other families.

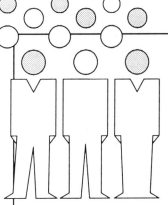

As an early childhood educator, you have responsibilities to support children's healthy development regarding their families and cultures:

- Children's individual development must be fostered within their own cultural group (concentrating on their values and lifestyles).
- Children must learn and experience the value of diversity (stressing individual and group differences and similarities, race, skin color, bilingualism, differing abilities).
- Children must be exposed to experiences that counteract bias and stereotypes.

Foster children's development within their own culture. Perhaps you are puzzled about what a culture really is and why it is important to consider for young children's total development. While you will be looking at these issues in depth during your CDA Seminar, you can start getting ready now.

Instead of thinking about other cultures first, it may help you to understand culture better if you start by thinking about your own culture. Your culture strongly affects how you work with young children. What culture did you grow up in?

What are some of the beliefs your culture holds . . .

. . . about infant feeding: breast/bottle, time, introduction of solids, crying, how much infants should be held?

. . . about how to handle toilet learning? At what age? Should it be different in any way for boys or girls?

. . . about spanking? Who should do it? Who shouldn't?

. . . about boys crying?

. . . about typical toys?

What other practices does your culture see as important in childrearing? **Ask your CDA Field Advisor to help you think of some and be prepared to discuss your ideas in your CDA Seminar.**

Childrearing practices are only one way that cultures differ. There are many others. Jot down some things your culture values in these areas. Add others that are especially important to you.

Language:

_____

_____

_____

_____

How you dress:

_____

_____

_____

_____

How you express affection:

_____

_____

_____

Holidays you celebrate:

_____

_____

_____

_____

_____

_____

Art preferences:

_____

_____

_____

Musical tastes:

_____

_____

_____

_____

What it takes to be pretty or handsome:

_____

_____

_____

Who is considered smart:

Skin color:

How girls should act:

Now think about some stereotypes that people hold about your culture. Write those here:

What then is culture? Culture mainly consists of a set of rules about how to behave. The rules tell us what values to hold and what ideas to believe in. All of the items on the lists here—and many more—are areas of behavior where cultures have rules. Most cultures have a long history, with roots in countries and civilizations that have grown and changed in response to resources and conditions.

Once you have a better idea of what your own culture is, you will see how your own culture influences what you do with children and how you have been taught about other people's cultures.

List all the cultures represented within the group of children you care for:

Your first step is to learn more about these cultures. How? You can talk with the children's families, read authentic materials (good children's books are a great resource), learn the language, add to your recipe collection, listen to some new types of music, or visit a museum or library, for starters.

Begin immediately to find out as much about these cultures as you know about your own, so you can use this information in your work with the children in your care. Before you can be an effective teacher, you need to learn as much as you can about the values, customs, struggles, contributions, and languages of these cultures. It is essential to know these in order to make your program culturally comfortable for the child. You must understand for example how cultural characteristics are so fundamental to children's ability to make sense out of the world — that they simply can't be ignored in the everyday interactions in the setting.

The following material on educating culturally different children by Barbara T. Bowman offers some valuable ideas for you to consider.

Educating language-minority children
by Barbara T. Bowman

Why can't all Americans just speak standard English? This plaintive question reflects the distress many citizens feel about the linguistic diversity in the schools. In many school districts, languages of Central and South America, Africa, and Asia mix with American dialects, creating classrooms in which communication is difficult. Across America, children are not learning essential lessons in school. In the next decade or two, the problem will become even more serious. Language-minority children will become the majority in public schools, seriously straining the capacity of those institutions.

In a nation increasingly composed of people who speak different languages and dialects, the old notion of melting them together through the use of a common language is once again attractive. Requiring all children to speak the same language at a high level of proficiency would make the task of educating them a good deal easier.

Unfortunately, what seems quite good in theory is often difficult to put into practice. In this instance, the interrelationship of culture, language, and the children's development may make a common language difficult to obtain.

Culture, language and development

Differences in the ways groups think and act are more than a matter of using different words or performing different actions for the same purposes. Differences in cultures are more substantial than whether members of a community eat white bread, corn pone, or tortillas. The behavior of people varies, and the beliefs, values, and assumptions that underlie behavior differ as well. Culture influences both behavior and the psychological processes on which it rests. Culture forms a prism through which members of a group see the world and create shared meanings. And a group's culture is reflected by the group's language.

Child development follows a pattern similar to that of culture. Major structural changes in children, such as language learning, arise from the interaction of biology and experience. Such changes are remarkably similar in kind and sequence among cultural groups. But the knowledge and skills — the cultural learning — the child acquires at various ages depend on the child's family and community.

Learning a primary language is a developmental milestone and a developmentally appropriate educational objective. However, the uses to which that language is put are determined by the culture. As the ideas from a child's social world are brought to bear through the guidance of the older members of the community, children come to share meanings with their elders.

Classroom discourse presents children with the challenge of learning new rules for communication. The use of formal language, teacher control of verbal exchanges, question-and-answer formats, and references to increasingly abstract ideas characterize the classroom environment, with which many children are unfamiliar. To the extent that these new rules overlap with those that children have already learned, classroom communication is made easier. But children whose past experience with language is not congruent with the new rules will have to learn ways to make meaning all over again before they can use language to learn in the classroom.

When teachers and students come from different cultures or use different languages or dialects, teachers may be unaware of variations between their understanding of a context and their students'; between their expectations for behavior and the children's inclinations. When children and adults do not share common experiences and beliefs, adults are less able to help children encode their thoughts in language.

Teaching children from different cultures

Teachers facing the challenge of teaching children from different cultural communities are hard-pressed to decide what constitutes an appropriate curriculum. If children from some groups are hesitant to speak up in school, how can teachers organize expressive language experiences? If children from some

groups are dependent on nonverbal cues for meaning, how can teachers stress word meaning? How can teachers test for mastery of the curriculum if children do not speak a standard language or use the same styles of communication? Cultural diversity makes it hard for teachers to assess each child's developmental status, find common educational experiences to promote growth, and measure the achievement of educational objectives.

Given the complex interaction between culture and development, is it possible to design a developmentally appropriate curriculum? If that question implies that the same curriculum can be used for all children, the answer must be *no*. However, the following developmental principles can provide a conceptual framework for teachers trying to bridge the gap between children's cultural backgrounds and school objectives.

Guidelines for teachers

First, teachers need to learn to recognize developmentally equivalent patterns of behavior. Before children come to school, they have all learned many of the same things, such as a primary language and communication styles. Although these developmental accomplishments may look different, they are developmentally equivalent. When a child does not respond to the social and cognitive expectations of

the school, the teacher should look for a developmentally equivalent task to which the child will respond. A child who does not separate buttons correctly can be asked to sort car logos or other personally relevant artifacts. A child who does not listen to stories about the seasons may be spellbound by a story about an ice skater. Teachers with doubts about the development of culturally different children should assume that the children are normal and look at them again, recognizing that their own vision may be clouded by cultural myopia.

Second, it is essential not to value some ways of achieving developmental milestones more highly than others. Asa Hilliard and Mona Vaughn-Scott point out that because the behavior of African-American children is so different from that of their white peers, African-American children are often judged to be deficient, rather than different, in their development. Young children who speak languages other than English, or who speak nonstandard dialects, are often reluctant to give up this connection to their group. When such children find that the way they talk is not understood or appreciated in school, they are apt to become confused or disengaged. And their rejection by the school presages their rejection of school.

Third, teachers need to begin instruction with interactive styles and content that is familiar to the children. Whether this entails speaking in the child's primary language, using culturally appropriate styles of address, or relying on patterns of management familiar to the children, the purpose is to establish a basis for communication. While fluency in a child's primary language may not be possible for many teachers, they can nonetheless become more adept at planning and implementing a culturally sensitive curriculum. Such a curriculum encompasses more than tasting parties, ethnic costumes, shopworn introductions to practices of people from different nation as or racial groups. In order to teach such a curriculum, teachers must come to grips with their own ethnocentricity.

Fourth, school learning is most likely to occur when family values reinforce school expectations. Parents and other community members must view school achievement as a desirable and attainable goal if children are to build it into their sense of self. Interpreting the school's agenda for parents is one of the most important tasks for teachers.

Fifth, when differences exist between the cultural patterns of the home and community and those of the school, teachers must deal with these discrepancies directly. Teachers and children must create shared understanding and new contexts that give meaning to the knowledge and skills being taught. Learning mediated by teachers who are affectionate, interested, and responsive has greater sticking power than learning mediated by an adult who is perceived as impersonal and distant.

Sixth, for children from different racial and ethnic groups, meanings of words, gestures, and actions may differ. Assessment of learning outcomes presents a formidable problem when children misunderstand the teacher's requests for information or demonstrations of knowledge and skills. Formal assessment should be delayed until teachers and children have built a set of new meanings.

A developmentally appropriate curriculum can never be standardized in a multicultural community. But thoughtful teachers can use principles of child development to make the new context of school meaningful and to safeguard the self-confidence of children.

Note: Adapted from "Educating Language-Minority Children" by B. Bowman, 1989, *ERIC Digest* (No. EDO-PS-90-1), Urbana, IL: ERIC Clearinghouse on Elementary and Early Children Education. Public domain.

Experience and value diversity. The world, our country, and your community are diverse. Perhaps some communities are more diverse than others, but diversity surrounds us: Not only culture or race, but people also have minor or more visible disabilities, religious preferences, and live in different family groups.

Your role is to help children build on their experiences by getting to know lots of other people, preferably first hand, and to live each day in a way that demonstrates how rewarding diversity can be to each person. You will also need to help children unlearn some of the stereotypes they have already formed.

There is a wealth of materials that can assist you in exposing children to all types of differences. These include books, artifacts, individuals, and materials.

The principle of valuing and accepting differences applies to every activity and conversation you have in your classroom or home. Your positive attitude about the value of people is essential if children are to gain a wider perspective about the world in which we all must live and work in harmony.

Look at the diversity within your community. What cultural groups will the children come into contact with? What other types of diversity will they experience?

As an early childhood educator, you must feel comfortable with your own attitudes about families who are different from the ones you grew up with, or who are different from those of the supposedly traditional nuclear family—a family with working father, mother at home with children rarely exists in the United States. Single parents, different custody arrangements, multigeneration families, and blended (step-) families are just some of the variations that nearly always are found in even a small group of people.

It is hard to do this by yourself, so **this will be one of the areas you work on in your CDA Seminar**. For now, we will see how you can integrate respect for children and their families—from many cultures, with disabilities, with various family members—into your daily work with young children.

Pictures of posters with Black, White, Asian, Indian, and Native Americans, showing both sexes, differently abled people, and all ages are an excellent start. Positive books about stepparents or living with grandmother are a good addition. Cooking ethnic foods is fine. Celebrating Hanukkah and Christmas and the Chinese New Year are a beginning. Trying out crutches and playing with puppets who have disabilities are good ideas. They are not enough.

If children are to get an accurate picture of what being human is all about, they need more than a tourist approach. Children need to do more than spend one week a year crawling into a tepee in order to gain concrete ideas about Native Americans yesterday and today. They need more than one brief movie about elderly people who are active in their community to really get to know how people age. Children need to **live with diversity**.

To offer a balanced approach, you need to incorporate languages, real objects, music, art, and many other aspects of people's experiences into your curriculum. This way, you will establish an atmosphere in which diversity is accepted and celebrated as a natural part of life.

Bring diverse individuals into the environment as guests or volunteers. Perhaps someone who signs or uses cued speech can teach all of you some basic communication skills to use with the deaf. Or children can feel books prepared in Braille. Visit a library with a teletype service. See how a Braille typewriter works. With every experience, children begin to appreciate how many ways there are for people to communicate.

Label materials or children's constructions

in more than one language. Use different color pens for each language. Provide books in a variety of languages. Read the stories to them, or invite a storyteller to bring a new dimension to the literature. Audio recordings also provide a new dimension to the stories and often have background sounds or music that provide additional depth. Recite poems in the language in which children feel most comfortable. Create finger plays. Perhaps the words will not be understood at first, but they can enjoy the pictures, action, and beauty of the language.

Languages. Language is children's window to figuring out the world.

Just try reading a story to a child using an unfamiliar language. You will get a puzzled look back. Using the same language that the child knows and understands is an essential part of every early childhood classroom.

Many children come to early childhood programs knowing languages other than English. Children easily learn a second language during their early years. They do best, however, when you help these children feel comfortable in using their home language, help them strengthen that language, and at the same time gradually assist them to also become fluent in English.

Opinions vary about the best way to achieve this. Some experts believe that translating everything doesn't work, because children soon learn to wait until they hear the language they know best and tune out on the other. Do some additional reading on this topic. Find out what works best for the children in your group.

If you don't speak the same home languages of the children in your group, what ways have you found to foster development of their home language?

_____

_____

_____

_____

_____

Real objects. Dress-up clothing can come from many cultures. Ask parents to contribute garments from their culture if possible. Make sure anything you purchase is authentic, not just a stereotype of what people in that culture wear. Clothes should also be primarily what people wear every day, not what they wear only on special occasions. Be sure to include many types of shoes, hats, and other accessories, too.

Also in the dramatic play area, you can incorporate models or pictures of ethnic foods, a variety of serving and eating utensils (Native American baskets, chopsticks), and different types of furniture (futon, cradle, hammock, rugs). Families can be composed of various members (mother or father and child only, combined families due to remarriage, grandparents, roommates). Crutches, canes, hearing aids, old glasses, and other devices can become as familiar as the doll cradle.

Dolls, puppets, and miniature people can portray people of both sexes from many cultures, and with varying ages and physical abilities. Every doll should have authentic features and clothing also. If you cannot find any to purchase, perhaps someone could make them. You may need to give some specific guidance to make sure they are appropriate for the cultures or physical abilities represented. "Kids on the Block™" puppet presentations are available through nonprofit organizations. These shows provide a realistic view on many disabilities in a very straightforward way.

One often overlooked aspect of culture is children's games. Every culture has its own games. Many games can be made with household objects or common items such as rocks. Some require no props at all, just a willingness to play. Preschool children enjoy games when the rules are tailored to their developmental abilities and the emphasis is on having fun, not on competition. Perhaps a parent or an elderly person in the neighborhood would be delighted to play some favorites with the children.

Remember (and remind parents too) that the library is a wonderful resource. Children's librarians are trained in child development as well as literature and other resources. They can provide children and families a positive introduction to a whole new world of information—through toys, books, audio and video materials. Libraries are publicly funded and **free** to everyone!

Most young children are very interested in various modes of transportation and construction. Select vehicles and tools from several cultures and time periods: sleds, boats, wagons, trains, rockets, shovels, and road graders.

If you are not sure where to locate books and other materials or to find some resource people to assist you, remember to check with your local library. Their job is to keep records of various community resources as well as collect and arrange many print and non-print materials.

What kinds of objects can you add to provide a better balance of multicultural experiences for young children?

_____

_____

_____

_____

Share your ideas with your Field Advisor and the other CDA Candidates in your Seminar.

Music. Music from many cultures is marvelous for developing an appreciation for different types of instruments, rhythms, expressions, themes, and languages.

While recordings are useful, it is hard for children to visualize who is playing the music and what the instruments look like. Try to obtain real instruments, such as drums, different types of bells, stringed instruments, or shakers, from several cultures. Demonstrate how sounds are made. Older children might even enjoy creating their own instruments.

After children have lots of experience with real instruments, they will be able to identify sounds in recordings. Singing children's songs or folk songs in both the original language and English is a marvelous way for children to explore language and music at the same time. Parents or grandparents are often thrilled to be asked to share some of their favorite childhood songs with the group.

Children are intrigued with different types of dance. Ask willing families to teach children some simple ethnic dance steps. Take small groups to a local performance. Watch a video of cultural dances. Just make sure the dances are authentic, not just a stereotyped idea of the real thing. Also, help children see that people in any culture dance once in a while, just as the children do, and not every day.

Keep everything in context and as authentic as possible so children can put things in proper perspective.

What kinds of musical experiences do you need to add to assure more cultural variety?

_____

_____

_____

_____

Talk about these ideas with your CDA Field Advisor.

Art. Children can also begin to appreciate how cultures express themselves through art. Museums and libraries are excellent resources for this. Don't limit your focus just to flat pieces or art from Western cultures.

Fabrics can be touched in clothing, rugs, hangings, pillows, or blankets. Preschool children can try their hand at simple weaving, quilting, and other textile arts. They are spellbound when they watch a sheep being sheared or wool being carded. Perhaps they could use food coloring to dye swatches of cotton. Compare the colors and textures of fabrics to children's hair and skin. What a wide array of beauty! The possibilities for using fabrics as a learning tool are limitless.

Carvings and sculpture—wood, stone, metal, clay—can be handled and appreciated when you choose sturdy pieces. Children can try to use similar techniques: Children can carve soap with plastic knives. Younger children can collect rocks. Older children can begin to work with wood.

Commercial clay substitutes or homemade doughs are fine, but children also need to experience the texture and feel of real clay. Dig it together if you can. Point out how the color of real clay is similar to some skin colors. After children have worked with clay for a while, try to find a potter willing to show how to use their potter's wheel. What a thrill!

Baskets, boxes, caned chairs, and pottery—all have intriguing cultural variations and children can use them, too. There are many other art forms like these that you will discover once you start talking with parents and seeking more information.

Painting can be done on paper, textiles, fences (with water and a big brush!), and faces. Many different types of media can be used: Craypas, crayons, tempera, finger paint, food coloring. Explore ways in which different cultures use the materials they have available to draw and decorate.

How can you broaden children's art experiences to reflect many cultural variations?

What other ideas does your CDA Field Advisor have to suggest?

Everyday living requires many diverse types of cooperation and work. Help children see how much variety there is. Once you get started thinking in terms of what children are already familiar with, and how similar activities occur in different ways among different families, you will wonder how you ever left out or skimmed over such an important facet of children's education!

What have you done to include cultures, different life styles, and people with disabilities in your teaching environment?

Be prepared to share your ideas about all the questions in this section with your Field Advisor.

Counteract bias and stereotypes. Just as with all other behaviors, young children copy others' ideas and attitudes. They may unwittingly repeat stereotypes they have heard or seen others express without fully understanding what they mean. It is important to help young children avoid these, even in their earliest experiences.

We all have biases—in fact, every culture and family is biased toward itself. That's part of having a healthy self-concept, to be proud of who we are. However, as an early children professional, you must also be aware that our biases can get in the way of doing your best with young children.

Good teachers spend a lot of time figuring out what stereotypes they hold about race, cultures, families, sexes, disabilities, or ages. Then we work to change our thinking. It's harder for some of us than others, especially when we have spent so many years cultivating our opinions.

What are some stereotypes or biases that you learned that you would like to change?

_____

_____

_____

_____

_____

You will discuss these in more detail during your CDA Seminar.

Stereotypes in the environment. Preschool children are forming important attitudes about themselves and others regarding sex and gender, age, abilities, and race. Unfortunately, stereotypes appear in every classroom, because they are so deeply embedded in our society. But there are strategies you can use to reduce the presence of these in your setting.

We have already looked at how to avoid children's books and other learning materials that contain biased attitudes about race and sex. These same ideas can be adapted to select classroom materials that avoid other stereotyped ideas about physical or mental capacity, family composition, and age.

The work of Barbara Sprung and Merle Froschl at Education Equity Concepts in New York has produced valuable resources for this effort, along with the work of the Council on Interracial Books for Children. Both organizations will put you on their mailing list if you write to them:

Educational Equity Concepts
114 E. 32nd Street
New York, NY 10016
212-725-1803

Council on Interracial Books for Children
1841 Broadway, Suite 500
New York, NY 10023
212-757-5339

Children who get along well can use the same strategies they are learning now to share, negotiate, and solve problems as adults.

Your example is the primary way children learn to be friendly and cooperative. You always treat children, their parents, and neighbors or other staff with respect.

Look around your classroom or family child care home. What evidence do you see of stereotypes? (race, culture, family, sex, age, or disability)

Try to watch the video, *Anti-Bias Curriculum,* while you are studying this section. The video will help you gain a more complete picture of the ideas we discuss here.

Interactions that reflect bias. You want children to learn to get along with each other better and to stand up for what is fair and right. Therefore, you need to notice when children's interactions reflect society's biases. If you ignore slurs and prejudices, children will perpetuate negative values and attitudes.

What if at Thanksgiving, a child asks whether the Indians are going to scalp people at your harvest feast? Or a child makes fun of another who wears braces on her legs? Or someone says girls can't play with blocks or boys can't cook? Or a child stares at an elderly neighbor on a morning stroll? Or a child comments, "Pink is my favorite color. Black is ugly." Children pick up stereotypes very easily from other people; in print from books, greeting cards, advertisements; and from movies.

How do you deal with instances such as these? This is one time when the principle of ignoring inappropriate behaviors does not apply. You must take direct action to counteract these unproductive and erroneous ideas.

Your goal is to help children feel comfortable when they (1) stand up for themselves and (2) insist that everyone respect the rights of others. Children need self-confidence and practice to develop these strengths.

Early childhood educators are irresponsible if we fail to prepare children to deal with the

Good early childhood teachers use an anti-bias curriculum:

Anti-bias curriculum is about preparing children for healthy, effective, cooperative, and peaceful living in a diverse, complex society and world. It is about strengthening children's self-identities and their abilities to respect differences and interact cooperatively with each other. It is about opening up choices. Consequently, anti-bias curriculum is also about challenging those conditions which prevent all children from achieving their full range of abilities and possibilities. This requires facilitating our own and children's critical thinking, problem solving, and developing skills for creating social change. In a word, anti-bias curriculum is about empowerment.

—*Louise Derman Sparks*

world's harsh realities. Just being around children from other cultural groups (or sexes, or ages, or with disabilities) isn't enough to ensure children will grow in their understanding of each other. Instead, we must show children appropriate ways to interact, teach them the truth about others, and involve them in solving problems based on what is fair.

Teaching children about what is fair is not something you set aside 10 minutes for each day. Questions and attitudes about differences between people come up frequently, and you can stimulate children's thinking even further by raising questions about physical and cultural differences and similarities, equipping your classroom with many objects that reflect diversity, and reading books about a variety of children and situations.

In addition, you will need to directly confront biases as they come up. How you deal with everyday expressions of bias such as these examples will be discussed in your CDA Seminar. Think about how you would respond in each situation and make some notes here:

"You're a sissy because you play with dolls."

On a field trip, children stare at a person in a wheelchair.

A child puts his fingers at the corners of his eyes, pulls his skin up, and brags, "Me Chinese brother."

A new child shrinks back in fear from a Black child when the group joins hands to play a circle game.

List two or three other incidents you have experienced that reveal prejudice among children. How did you respond?

Talk with your CDA Field Advisor about how you feel about your responses.

Responding to incidents such as these may be difficult for you. Perhaps you feel embarrassed to talk about prejudices with young children. Or perhaps you were raised to not notice skin color or disabilities because it wasn't "nice."

The following guidelines will give you the support you need to respond in ways that are comfortable for you and that are also professional:

- When a child is the target of bias, first offer comfort. Assure the child's safety. Listen to the child's concerns and express your understanding in a culturally appropriate way. Acknowledge the child's recognition that what was said or done was very unfair. Indicate you know how badly her or his feelings are hurt.
- Then talk with the child or children who hold the stereotypes. If a small group is involved, talk with each child individually, so you can get to know more about each child's thinking. If the entire group is affected (as in the example with the wheelchair) you may need to meet together.
- How you respond depends on the children's ages and the nature of the stereotype, but you never punish or ridicule the offending children. Instead, allow the children plenty of time to talk about the ideas, questions, or feelings that led to the incident.

A simple statement such as "You think Adam is a sissy because he plays with dolls" can open up the conversation. As the child talks you will have a better idea how to counteract the unfair attitudes. You will find more about talking with and listening to children in just a few pages from here, but we will provide some specific examples now because this is an area about which most people feel very uncertain.

- When you talk with children who have shown prejudice, you always relate what happened to people's feelings and what is fair.

"It hurts people when you make fun of them. We don't make fun of people here. Each person is valuable."

"Ideas like that are not fair to other people. In our school, we treat everyone fairly."

"Friends don't treat each other like that. Friends are kind to each other."

- Sometimes you must explain history or a child's physical condition. Do it as accurately, fairly, and simply as possible so children can begin to understand and see it in context. Always reassure children that they are safe.

"Native Americans were the first people to live here. Then strangers came and tried to take away their land. The Indians defended their homes and families. That was a long time ago. You don't have to worry about people being hurt like that any more."

- Children are often worried that they, too, could develop a handicap. Again, assure the child's safety.

"You are worried about your leg, too. But Anthony was in a bad accident. We are always careful. We will keep you safe."

When you meet with your CDA Seminar, you will practice other techniques to confront children's stereotypes.

Help children become friendly and cooperative

In addition to demonstrating respect for children and their families, there are many other ways children can learn to be friendly and cooperative. Children who get along well can use the same strategies they are learning now to share, negotiate, and solve problems as adults. You truly are working toward building a more peaceful world!

Your example is the primary way in which they learn to be friendly and cooperative. You always treat children, their parents, and neighbors or other staff with respect.

Foster children's friendships everyday. Within your program, you establish an atmosphere that is warm and welcoming. You have only a few reasonable rules about behavior:

- We treat each other in friendly ways.
- We cooperate with each other.

How do friends treat each other? They help each other, they talk pleasantly, they never hurt another person, they are kind and considerate, they are generous, they are courteous, they offer comfort.

Ask the children in your group how friends treat each other. Have a large piece of paper handy so you can write down their answers. This is an excellent language experience as well. Jot down their responses here:

_____

_____

_____

_____

Watch and you will see children who treat each other in friendly ways—if they have seen adults act like that. A baby might pat a crying child on the back. Toddlers may offer a friend their truck when they are finished. Preschoolers can be eager helpers for each other and younger children. Just keep your expectations in line with children's development.

The atmosphere you establish sets a tone of cooperation rather than selfishness or competition. Although infants and toddlers primarily play alone or beside other children, rather than with them, they still can be cooperative at times.

Friendships begin to develop in infancy. Babies might roll balls to each other or coo and reach toward one another. A child who can crawl or walk might take a toy to a nonmobile child. Toddler friendships are even more firm. A toddler might sit with another to look through a book or play hide and seek on the climbing structure.

Preschoolers are increasingly able to work together and form lasting friendships. They can choose a theme and carry it out at length in dramatic play or with construction toys. They might dance together, or offer assistance to a differently abled child on the playground, or pull each other in the wagon.

How do you foster friendly behavior and cooperation among children?

- Set up the environment to invite children to cooperate, play, and work together. Have enough space for three or four children to play in a small group. Set up enclosed areas such as lofts or climbers. Use double-sided easels. Establish teams to use computers. Pick interesting props to encourage dramatic play. Read books about cooperation, such as *Swimmy* (Lionni, 1968).

- Provide toys that are more fun with two or more children: blocks, rocking boats, balls, wagons, jump ropes, stethoscope, bandages, telephones—there are hundreds of items. Choose large puzzles with enough pieces so two or more children can work together, and put the puzzle on a small table with two or three chairs.

- Play games that support doing things together such as "Ring Around the Rosie" (everyone does the same thing) or bowling (one child bowls, one is the pin setter, another keeps score). Change the rules of games that seem too competitive—put out enough chairs for everyone to play "Musical Chairs." Just listening for when the music stops, finding a chair, and sitting in it is enough challenge for young children!

- Always be friendly and cooperative with children and other adults. Phrase directions and rules in a positive way: "Walk, please," rather than "No running." Help children see how their actions affect others. "When you dropped the briefcase, it hit Liliana on her foot. That hurt. She is crying. How can you help her feel better?"

You can foster children's friendships every day

Here are some suggestions for encouraging cooperation:

- Set up the environment to invite children to cooperate, play, and work together.
- Provide toys that are more fun with two or more children.
- Play games that support doing things together.
- Always be friendly and cooperative with children and other adults.
- Notice when children are friendly and cooperative.
- Encourage children to use words (rather than violence) to find solutions to their disagreements.

- Notice when children are friendly and cooperative. Let them know how proud they should be of their behavior. "Garrett, you were so kind to help baby Jassmin with her mittens so we could all go outdoors to play. Her smile is telling you 'thank you'."

  If there are unpopular children in your group, set up pairs with more popular children and watch how the unpopular child blossoms. Computers and games are an excellent way to help two children get to know each other better.

- Encourage children to use words (rather than violence) to find solutions to their disagreements. Help children feel good about their successes — and they will soon applaud others for theirs.

How do you encourage cooperation and friendly behavior with your group? What do you do to help unpopular children? List several of your strategies here.

_____

_____

_____

_____

Listen and understand. Being a child is not easy, although it may seem like it on those days when everything goes wrong for us! Children are trying so hard to figure things out, to do what pleases others, and to grow up. Each child needs at least one adult who will listen attentively and understand how the child feels. Children who can find words to describe their feelings are well on their way to controlling those feelings.

We can help children resolve their problems by listening to them, supporting their feelings, and helping them work through the problem.

Sometimes children are bothered by something and you don't know what. Sometimes they get into fights and give you two or more conflicting stories about what happened. Sometimes they are dealing with difficult times in their lives and need a comforting ear. In all these cases, we can help children resolve their problems by listening to them, supporting their feelings, and helping them work through the problem.

Really listening to children is not as easy as it might first appear. Many books have been written about how to listen to others. Listening is so important because you need to be aware of what children are thinking and feeling. Then, based on what you know, you can decide on the best action to help get the problem resolved. Lots of times, just listening is enough to help children work through their own difficulties.

We will cover some of the basics of listening here, and then in your work with children you can practice your skills. Don't wait to start using these techniques, though. It will feel awkward at first, and you might even be skeptical about the idea — but it does work, and you maintain everyone's dignity in the process.

Trust. You already know how important it is for children to be able to trust you. Children need to feel comfortable when they talk with you. Bend over, squat, or sit on a low chair so you are on the child's level and give your full attention to the child. Avoid distractions. And keep any secrets (unless you have a legal obligation to do otherwise, as in reporting child abuse).

Children's talking. When children have a disagreement, seem sad, or have done something inappropriate, it is very tempting to want to lecture, ask harsh questions, criticize, or give a lengthy explanation. STOP! You can't talk and listen at the same time. Say as little as possible so the child can talk. Keep the emphasis on finding out the truth about what happened and how the issue can be resolved.

Actions **and** *words.* Children use body language as well as spoken language to communicate.

Tyler is mad. He stomps over to you. "Kimberly hit me!"
    You take Tyler by the hand and walk calmly over to Kimberly.

These are the main principles of effective listening:

- Be someone children can trust.
- Let children do most of the talking.
- Pay attention to children's actions as well as their words.
- Accept whatever children say in a way that leads them to think more about the idea or solve the problem themselves.
- You guide what happens — you do not impose solution.

"Kimberly, Tyler is angry. He says you hit him."

"I did not hit Tyler," asserts 4-year-old Kimberly. But her eyes are on the floor and she is squirmy.

The children's body language tells you there is more to the story. Learn to read what posture, eye contact, tone of voice, and other actions. Tyler and Kimberly are usually cooperative. Tyler rarely gets angry enough to stomp. Kimberly is usually confident. So something must be up.

Further thinking. Talk further with Tyler and Kimberly:

"But Tyler says you hit him," you point out.

"Yes, she did, because I wouldn't give her the red marker," retorts Tyler.

You pause. Kimberly continues to look down and fidget, but says nothing. "Tyler says you hit him because he wouldn't give you the red marker," you repeat, and then wait again.

"Well. . . I asked him nicely first and he said 'No'," admits Kimberly.

What did you do to encourage children to tell what happened?

- You stated Tyler's version of what happened.
- You included Tyler in the discussion and gave him an opportunity to explain.
- You gave Kimberly time to think and respond to what Tyler said.
- You restated Tyler's account with more details.
- You waited for Kimberly to think. She then admitted she hit Tyler.

Kimberly did not feel threatened or belittled in the discussion, so she eventually acknowledged her inappropriate behavior. Now it is clear what happened.

What happens next. But now what do you do? Scold Kimberly? Call Tyler a tattle-tale? Make Kimberly apologize? Put Kimberly in time out? Insist that Tyler give Kimberly the red crayon? NO indeed. You think about what children are learning in the situation. You think about your long-term goals for children. And then you ask the children what they think should happen now.

Does asking the children what should happen next seem unteacherly to you? Are you frightened that you are not in control of the children? You are still there to **guide** what happens, but you don't impose a solution.

If children express solutions, listen to what they say and try to use their ideas to help settle things down. This way, they certainly are learning to control their behavior. And they are learning to live with the natural consequences of how they act.

Effective listening can work in many situations with children. You encourage children to state what happened or what they think. You give children time to respond. You keep the focus on the issue. The key is to keep children involved, not to take away from their feelings and actions by talking yourself.

You will use these listening skills many times each day. Begin immediately to practice, even though it may feel strange. The

next time you really listen to a child, jot down some notes about how the conversation went. Record here what was said as soon as you can.

_____

_____

_____

_____

Talk about what happened with your CDA Field Advisor.

Solve problems with a positive approach

Think about the basic skills we have just discussed to implement a positive approach to encourage children to learn to discipline themselves: you have developmentally appropriate expectations for children, you make sure the environment doesn't create problems, you create a secure feeling, you build their concepts of themselves and their families, you expect them to be friendly and cooperative, and you listen to them and understand how they feel.

Well, all these positive methods are fine, you say. But what do you do in a really tough situation where children are especially difficult or even completely out of control? Do you spank? Do you yell? Do you threaten? NO! You remain calm. You control your own anger. And you use similar, but more adult-structured strategies to help children bring their own behavior under control.

Sometimes children need to be redirected into another activity. Sometimes children need to find a more acceptable outlet for their feelings. And sometimes you need to isolate a child. Let's see how you implement these more controlling strategies in extreme situations, while still keeping in mind the goal of children's long-term development of self-control.

Threats can strike real fear in children's hearts and can ruin their sense of security with you.

NEVER, ever threaten to . . . flush the child down the toilet . . . burn a security blanket . . . lock the child in a closet . . . or otherwise endanger anything important to the child. Children need to know you will protect them from harm, physical or emotional. That requires your acceptance of them, even when they misbehave. Remember, your goal is to help children learn self-control.

Redirect the activity. Whenever possible, you want children to select their own activities, to follow their own ideas through, to figure out their own problems. There are times, however, when you need to firmly take the child by the hand and move her or him to something more productive.

Katie joins three other children at a small round table. They have been playing with the Legos™, have made some elaborate constructions, and the limit for that activity is three children. As soon as you see her enter the area, you walk over. The other children are reminding her that the area is full, but she doesn't look like she is ready to leave.

"Katie, the children are telling you there are already three people playing with Legos," you point out as you extend your hand. "Let's see what else you might like to do until they have finished. Would you rather use the unit blocks or work on puzzles?"

In this example, there are some important points. The children already knew the rules and used words to tell Katie. You respected what the other children were doing and didn't tell them to hurry, or ask one of them to leave.

At the same time, you gave Katie a clear signal that she must leave, but you did not force her to hold your hand. You offered two other acceptable choices that were somewhat similar to Legos. And you indicated that when the area was open she could play with the Legos. Katie may be disappointed, but she also learned that her rights would be protected in a similar situation.

How much happens in such seemingly simple interactions!

You can use this same technique of redirecting in other situations where the child's efforts clearly are not being productive or are disrupting others. At times like this, you need to be firm so that children know you are serious, but you don't need to lecture or belittle children.

Dana (age 2½) rushes up to three other toddlers who are coloring. He grabs a handful of crayons, scribbles all over one of the pictures, and is reaching for the next one.

"No, Dana! Don't mess up our pictures," one of the children cries.

You rush to the scene. You firmly ask Dana to put the crayons back where they belong. Then you ask the children if they have anything to say to Dana.

"I am mad at him."

"He messed up Sarah's drawing."

"He isn't my friend."

"We don't want him to play with us."

Dana seems unfazed by the children's complaints. You offer him a choice of throwing pillows or hitting some clay until he is ready to talk. He chooses throwing pillows.

Later, when he has calmed down, you can listen to Dana and perhaps learn why he is acting this way. Does he need attention? Is he angry about something? Was he just bored? When you listen you may find out and can take steps to help him solve his problem.

When have you found it necessary to redirect children into a more productive activity? List one or two of your own examples here.

_____

_____

_____

_____

_____

Talk with your CDA Field Advisor about your strategies and other ways you might have made the most of these learning opportunities.

Find acceptable outlets to express feelings. Pretend play is a natural way for children to express and work out their feelings in a secure environment. Sometimes, though, feelings are so strong—anger is so overwhelming or sadness is so consuming—that children need additional outlets.

Find safe ways that will enable children to feel protected by caring adults. If children are angry and need to physically take out their frustration, they may find a release by hitting or throwing pillows or cushions. Sometimes they pound their fists on a soft pad or stomp around outdoors. Clay is wonderful for pounding with fists or hammers.

If children are sad, they may just want some

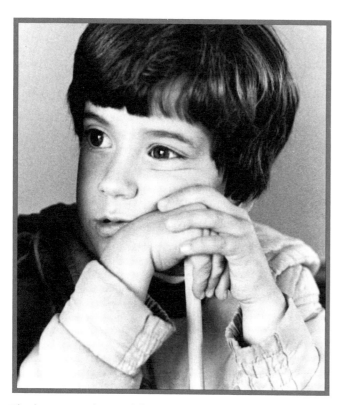

The better you know children, the easier it will be to help them channel their feelings into more acceptable behaviors.

private, quiet time. Or they may want to talk or write a letter. Or paint. Or read a book with you about a child facing a similar problem. Acting out stories is an excellent way to have children express a variety of feelings and understand the results of their behavior.

Group play in the classroom can on occasion cause all of the children to act wildly. Monsters, fires, and other emotionally charged topics can lead to harmful aggression, shrieking, or other inappropriate behaviors. When possible, you notice that the play is escalating and de-fuse it before the children's feelings become overwhelming.

If it suddenly erupts, your actions will help children regain their control and calm down. Act calmly but firmly. You may need to hold a hand or two. Speak quietly. Move slowly. Perhaps turn the lights out to restore the quieter, playful atmosphere. Or maybe going outdoors will help children channel their energy more appropriately.

You use your professional judgment to decide what methods will be most effective, but you always remain in control of yourself. The better you know children, the easier it will be to help them channel their feelings into more acceptable behaviors.

What are some ways you have helped children express their strong feelings?

Isolate a child out of control. You probably are familiar with an isolation strategy called *time out.* Lots of people use it whenever a child behaves inappropriately. In most time outs, children are removed from the situation, usually asked to sit on a chair away from the others, and told to think about what they did. A time limit may be given ("You can return to the group in 5 minutes.") or children determine when they are ready to play in a more friendly way.

But what do children learn in this kind of time out? And what are its long-term effects? Children learn that they only have to wait a few minutes until the problem goes away. They may spend the time figuring out how to get revenge. They usually have no opportunity to explain the situation from their viewpoint, so they may feel they were treated unfairly. They never even had a chance to negotiate or figure out a solution to the problem. And if they were bored or didn't like the activity, they found a sure way to get out of doing it!

Time out is usually just an easy way out for the adult. It is an escape for children, which doesn't help them learn self-control, and may even teach them things we don't want. Think for a minute about older children who are expelled from school because they are misbehaving. Often they don't want to be in school—and getting thrown out is just what they want! We don't want our discipline strategies to backfire like that.

Once in a while, though, you probably will need to ask a child to take some time out away from the rest of the children. But only in situations where the child is a danger to herself or himself or to others. If a child is flailing the arms and legs about, or hitting anyone in sight, or throwing toys, or otherwise completely out of control, she or he desperately needs to feel the security of control from someone else. When self-control is impossible, then the child needs some isolated time and space to regain her or his composure.

Sometimes a child will go with you willingly to a quiet place. On rare occasions, the child will be so out of control that you must **gently restrain** the arms and sometimes the head (to avoid bites). You need to remain very calm and feel very strong inside while you do this, because you want to protect the child's safety and your own.

Always leave the area with the child (making sure someone else is in charge while you are gone), and stay with the child until the episode is resolved. Go to a quiet place where the two of you can be alone. Sometimes gentle stroking of the hair or rubbing the back will help the child calm down. Sometimes a drink of water will work—or it might be thrown in your face or a crying child may choke on it. You use everything you know about the child to help you decide how to handle such an explosive situation.

After the child has calmed down, respect the child's wishes as much as possible. If the child would rather rest (lots of energy is used in such emotional outbursts) try to make her or him comfortable. Some children need to talk, while others are too embarrassed. Decide which is the best way to help the child maintain dignity and return to the group.

All through this unit, we have looked at positive ways to support children's growing ability to control themselves so they can lead happy, productive lives. You will use these strategies every day to help resolve typical developmental problems and to support children during stressful times.

How you guide young children toward appropriate behavior:

1 Plan to avoid problems with toys and materials, group times, and space.

2 Act in positive ways with children
- create a secure feeling
- support families and cultures
- help children become friendly and cooperative
- solve problems with a positive approach

Before we move on to some other aspects of social and emotional development, jot down any questions or ideas you have about children in your group who need some extra attention in one or more of the areas we have discussed. Write their names here, and list the strategies you intend to use to help them mature in a healthy way.

Self-esteem

Competence

Curiosity

Self-control

Friendly behaviors

Feeling special

Security

Independence

Trust

Inner strength

Talk with your CDA Field Advisor about your questions and plans.

Teaching young children is filled with dilemmas. There are rarely any clear-cut answers, especially when dealing with unique situations. **List some here that you have found particularly troublesome. Raise them for discussion in your CDA Seminar.**

How do you deal with the difficulties of growing up?

Sometimes it seems as if children are full of surprises! Never knowing what to expect is part of why we find working with children so appealing.

At the same time, much of their behavior is really pretty predictable, once we understand how they grow and learn.

You expect developmental hurdles

In this part of your study about children's development, you will see how we guide children as they deal with some of the expected social and emotional hurdles of growing up.

These hurdles include separation anxiety, oppositional behavior, egocentricity, shyness and aggression, sexual identity, and fears. If these terms sound unfamiliar to you, you will soon see that they are professional shorthand for behaviors that are very familiar.

Much of what you already have learned fits in with what we discuss here: the milestones of development and positive guidance methods that lead to self-discipline. Now we will build on what you already know, and try to put even more pieces of the puzzle of the whole child's development together.

Deal with stranger and separation anxiety

Jamie was such a darling baby. He cooed for his grandmother. He smiled at everyone in the grocery store. He didn't even mind when his parents left him with his family child care provider every day!

Then all of a sudden, he whimpered when he was handed to Grandma. He cried as he was pushed through the aisles of the grocery store. But worst of all, he wailed whenever Mom and Pop left him to go to work.

Grandma said, "Don't be strange, boy. I'm mad at you." Shopping was suddenly a chore. Leaving Jamie each day was pure torture for his parents — and a trying time for his child care provider as well.

What went wrong?

Nothing. Absolutely nothing. In fact, everything went right. Most babies, sometime between the ages of about 5 months and 3 years, become frightened of strangers. Babies know the familiar faces, voices, and smells of their parents, and they have developed strong feelings for them. Not even their regular child care provider — you — can quite take the place of their family. This momentous intellectual and social achievement should be celebrated! Baby is learning about people and is securely attached to the most important ones.

Of course, even when you know that stranger anxiety is a natural part of development, there will be times when it is difficult for you as a caregiver. You must deal with crying children each morning and you need to advise parents about a very perplexing aspect of development.

For example, parents often ask when the best time is to enroll their son or daughter in child care. Usually you will want to encourage parents to enroll their baby at a time other than the peak of the child's period of stranger anxiety. It is far more sensitive to the baby's feelings (and the parents') if children are enrolled before they develop stranger anxiety or after they have passed its most intense period.

When the child is already in your care and begins to exhibit a wariness of strangers, YOU may be the stranger, even though the child has spent a great deal of time with you. Parents need to feel reassured that the tears and screams last only a few minutes after they leave, and then children settle down to have a happy day.

Don't assume parents will take your word for this, especially first-time parents. A phone call to dismayed Moms and Dads may help later in the morning. If the children are old enough, encourage them to talk or at least listen to the parent's voice on the phone.

Most of all you need to be warm, understanding, and loving each day while babies adjust to the change of care. Welcome children and parents warmly. Speak in the language with which they are most comfortable. Make sure they go through their usual morning ritual and say goodbye.

But when the parents must leave, be confident in helping them do so. If any of you hesitate, the child may think that crying will convince a parent to stay. Instead, help the baby get involved in something interesting. Get out a bright ball, or a cuddly animal, or a musical toy. Sometimes a picture of children's families or a recording of parents' voices speaking in their home language will help ease the transition for the child.

You can help families deal with this puzzling stage. Suggest to parents that they give babies a while to warm up at their own pace with Grandmas, strangers, or babysitters. The parents can stay nearby during this "getting to know you" time. Soon most babies will be climbing into the visitor's lap.

Rather than criticizing children for their natural feelings, ("Don't be strange, boy. I'm mad at you."), encourage parents to find a way to tell their child how proud they are that baby loves Mom and Dad so much.

This is one of many early opportunities to use a positive approach to childrearing. Even the most difficult situations can be handled in a positive way that supports children's long-term development.

How do you help infants feel less overwhelmed by separation or stranger anxiety when they arrive each day?

_____

_____

_____

_____

_____

Tell your CDA Field Advisor how you handle these trying times.

Prepare for oppositional behavior

The "terrible twos." Everyone has heard of them. And most parents dread their arrival. Only those of us who know children and how they develop can really appreciate how wonderful the child's "NO!" can really be.

Our first step in dealing with 2-year-olds is to stop calling them terrible. How would you like to be labeled "thickheaded 30" or "fierce 40" or "flabby 50"? Such negative labels can damage children's self-esteem and may even be self-fulfilling (children become what we say they are).

Instead, look at this third year of life as one in which children blossom. They want to act grown up. They assert themselves. They have opinions and preferences. They want to do things for themselves. Do these descriptions sound familiar? Yes, those are some of our long-term goals for children's development. Children already are beginning to take control of their own lives. How wonderful to see they are indeed growing up!

Children at this age are filled with opposites: They want to be independent and in control, but they need a clear set of limits or they will be overwhelmed. They want to be powerful, and yet constantly run into something they can't do alone. Their feelings are strong, so they need someone they can rely on to help them verbalize and manage those feelings.

Right from birth, the balance of power over who is in control starts to slowly shift from the adult to the child. At first parents have all the power over everything children need. Then babies begin to hold their own bottles. Waddlers begin to walk where they want to go. And toddlers may refuse to eat their vegetables. Independence is what growing up is all about!

Many adults want to make sure their child still understands who is "the boss." With this attitude, the smallest incident can turn into a power struggle.

Two-year-old David is contentedly rolling small balls of clay. You give all the children the 5-minute signal before clean-up time, but when the time is up, David continues to play with the clay. When you ask him to put it away, he stubbornly refuses.

What should you do? You could force David to quit by putting away the clay for him and carrying him, kicking and screaming, outdoors to play. After all, you have a schedule and you want children to follow the rules. But what is David learning if you rip him away from the clay? He's learning that his feelings and interests don't matter.

Or you could threaten him, "Unless you put the clay away now, you won't be able to play with it tomorrow." But you already know that threats strike fear in children and don't help them develop long-term self-control.

What is a more professional approach? How can you avoid a power struggle and still respect the child and yourself? This is one possible solution:

"David, I can see that you are having a ball with the clay. You don't look like you are quite ready to quit yet. Would you like to take it outdoors with you? Or do you want to leave it out on the table so you can use it again when we come back inside?"

Instead of rigidly sticking to your rules, you offer the child a choice. Either choice is a good one and will accomplish your goals (get all children outdoors to play, respect children's interests, build self-control). And best of all, the power struggle never even took place. Both you and David get what you need.

Offering choices was an excellent way to let children of all ages exercise their growing decision-making abilities. Offer good, real choices, like those in the example, and children can't go wrong.

Of course, sometimes you cannot offer a choice. You will still have to say "no" in some situations. But when you do, be firm and fair, and whenever possible, offer an alternative.

"No jumping from the sofa. You could hurt yourself. Your car could break if you land on it."

"Sofas are to sit on. These are our jumping cushions. How can you jump from the red one to the blue one?"

Twos will test limits, so make sure your environment is safe and your rules are reasonable and simple. Children will soon learn that they get to make choices frequently, that you mean business when you say "no," and that the environment is arranged for them to try out their skills.

As fate would seem to have it, most children also are ready to learn to use the toilet sometime during this period of strong negativism. These two developmental milestones seem so incompatible. How can a child learn to use the toilet just when she or he is always refusing to do what adults want? No wonder toilet learning is a major—often dreaded—event and a power struggle to get the child to do what the parents want!

On the other hand, when toilet learning is seen as something the child wants—to be independent and have self-control—it clearly is a great match for the child's social and emotional development as well as physical development.

You and the child's parents may be more prepared to use effective methods to help their child with this task.

In all of these and other similar situations, once you realize what is happening—children are growing up—you will see that twos are really pretty terrific!

If you teach 2-year-olds, what can you do to be more in tune with their development?

How can you help parents look at the positive side of 2-year-old's negativism?

Your CDA Field Advisor will be interested to hear about your ideas.

Acknowledge children's egocentricity

A few years ago, many people in our profession thought that infants and toddlers never played together or made friends. They claimed that very young children were not capable of showing sympathy toward or warm feelings about other children. They thought young children could only see things their way.

Now we know better, thanks to teachers like you, parents, and researchers who took a closer look at how children act in real situations. Children generally do see themselves as the center of everything, but occasionally they can relate to how others feel.

If infants and toddlers have been treated kindly, know each other, and are in an appropriate environment, you probably saw them giggle together . . . hold hands . . . share . . . offer comfort when the other has been hurt—sometimes. They definitely are beginning to relate to and understand others.

Young children are not completely egocen-

Most very young children are content to play by themselves. This is called *solitary play.*

tric. They are, however, naturally self-centered. They know their own feelings and wants best, and have little idea about how what they do makes other people feel.

How terribly important it is to understand children's natural self-centeredness and how it influences the way they play, make friends, and get along with each other.

Types of play. Children's play looks so simple — it's just what they want to do all day. However, play is really a very complicated process through which children learn about the world, each other, and themselves.

Most very young children are content to play by themselves. This is called **solitary play.** Babies gaze at themselves in mirrors, shake rattles, and watch the fish swim. Of course, older children and we adults also occasionally enjoy time all to ourselves. Solitary play is what we do when we put together a jigsaw puzzle, read a novel, or tinker in the garage.

Watch a child of any age engaged in solitary play. What happens? How long does the child concentrate on the task at hand? Does the child talk to herself or himself or to others? What is the expression on the child's face like? Write a brief observation here:

Another typical form of play, one that is especially common during the late infant and toddler years, is called **parallel play.** Two children play side-by-side, for example in the sandbox or water table, each doing their own thing. At first glance they may appear to be playing with each other, but careful observation will reveal that they seem unaware of the other's presence. Older children and adults also engage in this type of play.

Find two or more children engaged in parallel play. What are they doing? How long do they continue? Are there any interactions between them? Write what happened here:

By the time children are preschoolers, we begin to expect more **cooperative play.** Children's social and intellectual development has matured enough so preschoolers can pretend to be someone else or stick with a game, sometimes for half an hour or more. In pretend play, each child plays a particular role (bus driver, passenger, police officer) but they all function together to pursue ideas on their theme. Or, with simple games, children cooperate to follow rules so that they are interacting together in one connected event.

Select a group of preschool children engaged in cooperative play. Write down exactly what happens here.

_____

_____

_____

_____

Your Field Advisor will verify that these observations are completed.

Types of children's play
- **solitary play** (one child playing alone)
- **parallel play** (two children playing side-by-side)
- **cooperative play** (two or more children playing together)

Children can learn to be friendly and cooperative in your program at the same time you are respecting these age-appropriate types of play. Although many of the toys and activities that programs tend to provide encourage cooperative play, all three types of play should be available to children.

Sometimes a child involved in isolated or parallel play needs to have you to protect her or his right not to be interfered with. You may need to resist the temptation to encourage children to play together or share toys and materials.

Joshua is pouring water into and out of the containers at the water table. Riley comes over and starts taking over all the containers. You move in. "Riley, come with me to the other sink. I'll get you some containers of your own to use."

Two children are in the dress-up area, both preparing separate meals with separate menus for separate pretend families. You watch quietly, without encouraging the children to share. You only offer assistance if either child needs something.

There are plenty of opportunities to foster cooperative play as a way to help children build skills in making friends. But remember to balance them with opportunities for children to be at the center of their own world.

Making friends and getting along. **One of our long-term goals for children is to help them become friendly and cooperative. Yet developmentally, it takes a long time for children to be able to put others' needs ahead of their own. Don't always insist that they do. But when the opportunity arises, model cooperative behavior for them as a way to resolve disputes.**

"I can see that both Marilena and Robrett want to play with the wagon. You are both tugging on the handle. What can you do to both use the wagon at the same time? Well, Marilena could pull while you ride, and then you pull while she rides. Or you could both get in and I'll pull!"

Also remember to catch children behaving appropriately! Let them know that you notice their growing skills.

"Shannon, that was so generous of you to share your paint smock with Akua. We'll have to look some more to find hers."

"Si, nosotros podemos mirar el libro juntos. What good friends you are, Carlos and Craig. You are always thinking up fun things to do together."

Children will learn to compromise and share freely as they mature, when they are given enough positive experiences and lots of reinforcement.

Support shy and aggressive children

New children in a program will generally be more reserved. Most newcomers take a few days to really settle in.

Some children just are naturally less outgoing than others, even when they have been in the group a long time.

And of course, other children are so aggressive that they are not appealing as friends. How do you support these children's social and emotional development?

Shy children. Shyness can result from one or a combination of factors. Some children seem to be shy because their parents are. Others are just less socially or intellectually mature for their age. Some are shy only in certain situations and more outgoing in others. We may also interpret certain cultural behaviors as shyness—some children may look down or pause before answering a question, for example. Unfamiliarity with other children's language may also make it difficult for children to interact easily with others. Before you become concerned that a

Techniques for working with shy children

- Teach shy children strategies for joining and leaving groups: ask a question, volunteer, create a new role that fits into the theme.
- Read books together about how other shy children deal with their shyness.
- Help shy children relax. Use their home language whenever possible.
- Keep your daily routines as predictable as possible.
- Never frighten shy children by coming up from behind them.
- Pair a shy child with a younger or more popular playmate.
- Be loving but don't create too much dependence.
- Encourage children's sense of humor.
- Keep groups small.
- Assist children with personal grooming skills.
- Be positive about the shy child's behavior.

Note: Adapted from "The Shy Child" by A. Honig, *Young Children*, May 1987, 42(4), 53–64. Copyright © 1987 by National Association for the Education of Young Children. Reprinted with permission.

child is shy, talk with the parents, learn all you can about the culture, and observe the child in many situations.

You can help shy children feel more comfortable in a group program by using all of the positive guidance techniques we have already discussed and by following Alice Honig's recommendations (outlined in the box on page 242).

Children who are out of control. Sometimes a child engages in actions are dangerous and disrespectful to other people: running wildly, yelling, biting, hitting, pushing, kicking, spitting, calling names, using offensive language, and throwing tantrums, for example.

How do you handle explosive episodes?

First, maintain your own control, regardless of what the children are doing. **Never allow yourself to act like a child.** Remember, we want to show children how to behave by acting the way we want children to act. That is why we never hit, bite back, spank, or otherwise lash out at a child.

While maintaining your control, you try to figure out what went wrong. You stop the aggressive child from hurting anyone (you and the aggressive child included). You remain calm and you use words, "I cannot allow you to hit. Hitting hurts. We don't hurt our friends."

Focus your attention first on the injured child, if there are any, and console him or her. Remember, all the children who are in the vicinity are watching what happens. During the entire episode, children are learning that you will protect them from others and help them control themselves.

As for the aggressor, you may need to physically restrain and leave the room with her or him until the child calms down. Do so gently and in a way that helps the child feel secure.

When the child has regained self-control and is able to talk coherently, you can begin to use your listening skills. You make it possible for children to retain their dignity, to trust you to be strong when they are out of control.

Sometimes children's behavior will make you angry. You may want to scream and take out your frustration on the child. But you are an adult and a professional early childhood educator. You have better ways to help children learn to control themselves. Your goal is always to look at the future and give children the opportunity to learn self-control in a positive way.

What are some techniques you use to calm yourself down so you can use professional techniques to help children regain their self-control when they are acting up?

(What would you do if a child spit in your face?)

_____

_____

_____

_____

Be sure to think carefully because you will be asked to share your ideas with your Seminar group—everyone is searching for ways to stay calm.

Manage superhero play

This type of play poses a dilemma for many adults because it often results in dangerously aggressive play among children. Is it appropriate for children to imitate superheroes? Do superheroes just reinforce stereotypes? What are children really learning in this type of play? Why is it so popular?

Not surprisingly, this is not a topic about which early childhood professionals agree. Some argue that superhero fantasy play is overwhelming for young children because until children are about age 6 they do not always know what is real and what is pretend. They point out the negative behaviors associated with so many superheroes—violence, guns, and antisocial actions.

Others contend that superhero play—when it is well supervised—can help children feel a sense of power in a safe setting. They note that children can even handle fearful characters because the behaviors of the superhero are so limited by the role. Some superheroes even have admirable qualities—courage, honesty, fairness, and compassion. And of course, as with all pretend play, children can learn to get along with each other, develop their vocabularies, solve problems, and find ways to cooperate through superhero play. If you support this position, turn to good literature in order to locate some superheroes. Classic stories like Johnny Appleseed, Paul Bunyan, and Pecos Bill can be read and acted out to provide children superhero play.

Because of its popularity on television and among commercial toys, it's unrealistic not to

Make superhero play manageable

- Help children recognize human characteristics of superheroes.
- Discuss real heroes and heroines.
- Talk about the pretend world of acting.
- Limit the place and time for superhero play.
- Explore related concepts—bats, space travel.
- Help children develop goals for superheroes—figure out a plan for a rescue mission or treasure hunt, for example.
- Help children de-escalate rough-and-tumble play. Provide a safety zone for those who do not wish to participate.
- Make it clear that aggression is unacceptable.
- Give children control over their lives in other areas.
- Praise children's attempts at mastery.

Note: Adapted from "Living with He-Man: Managing Superhero Fantasy Play" by M. J. Kostelnik, A. P. Whiren, and L. C. Stein, *Young Children*, May 1986, *41*(4), 7. Copyright © 1986 by National Association for the Education of Young Children. Reprinted by permission.

expect some superhero play in most programs for young children. There are ways that you can make such play more manageable. Some of these techniques, suggested by three experienced educators, seem to strike a balance between both positions.

Look at the ideas on page 244 on how to make superhero play more manageable. Decide for yourself whether you believe superhero play can be managed in a positive way with your group.

If you decide to include superhero play and help children control it, record an incident of this type of play. Write a paragraph about what happened here:

_____

_____

_____

_____

What problems did you encounter when you tried to make superhero play more productive? What techniques did you use to resolve them?

_____

_____

_____

If you decide not to include superhero play, write a paragraph explaining why.

_____

_____

_____

_____

_____

Discuss your ideas and experiences with your Advisor. Then save your notes to share with others in your CDA Seminar.

Encourage pride in sexual identity

Frilly pink dresses and lace for baby girls. Baseball suits, race cars, and trucks for baby boys. Just look at the greeting cards or clothing for new babies! Long after women have made great strides towards equality, sexism still permeates our society. In fact, many people don't even know how to interact with a baby if they don't know its sex.

No wonder, then, that children learn what is expected of them as a boy or a girl—behaviors, attitudes, aspirations—from a very young age and from every person they meet and every experience they have. But if girls learn to be weak and act helpless, and boys learn to be powerful, emotionless, and in control, some of what they learn may limit their thinking about how to live their lives.

Although the options are decidedly broader for both men and women than they were just a few years ago, many teachers are dismayed to find that most boys are more aggressive, play more with blocks, and like to ride tricycles at great speeds. Many girls, on the other hand, still enjoy playing with dolls, dressing up, and making cakes in the sandbox. What are you to do?

It is not an easy task to help children be comfortable with who they are as a boy or girl and what that means in their lives. Many parents have very strong feelings about how they want their children to think and behave based on which sex they are: Girls grow up to marry and raise families while boys work, for example. Some ethnic groups are adamant about the differences between what proper behavior is for each sex.

This clearly is an area that requires working together with parents — or you may find yourself contradicting childrearing beliefs without even knowing it. It is always important to take into account parents' desires for their own children and to balance those with your broader professional responsibility to guide children toward the ability to function well in the real world.

If the two views disagree, sometimes you can only compromise by agreeing to have one set of expectations in your program while the parents have another set at home. You may already be doing this with some discipline techniques, and this may be another area in which you and parents agree to disagree.

Because one of your long-term goals is to help children feel good about who they are, understanding what it means to be a boy or a girl is

an important part of that. You have seen how shared bathrooms enable children to appreciate similarities and differences in their bodies. Your comments and observations are an excellent way to help children feel proud of who they are and to learn more about their bodies.

"You are a girl. Your body is special. When you grow up you will be able to have a baby. You have special parts inside where a baby can grow, just the way you grew inside your mother."

"Boys have penises and girls have vaginas. Penises are outside boys' bodies and vaginas are inside girls' bodies. Both of your bodies have special places. And both of you also have arms, and eyes, and belly buttons!"

You also support children's self-esteem in other ways related to the fact that they are a boy or a girl.

"Christopher, you are such a good cook. You got the carrots so clean and then you cut them in sticks. Your friends will enjoy them so much. You are a boy who can be proud of his work."

"One of our most productive block builders has done it again. Angelica has built a really complicated apartment building. Maybe someday she will be an architect."

Interestingly, although children know very early which sex they are, it will not be until they reach the elementary school years that they come to realize that is what they will **always** be. Some girls, especially those who have been overprotected or who have been referred to as tomboys, may even say they want to be boys when they grow up! And some boys may wish they were girls, perhaps so they could have a baby.

You will need to listen for children's signs of wanting to be the other sex, and gently explain that becoming a boy (or a girl) is not possible.

"Jessica, you will always be a girl. Girls can be carpenters, too, when they grow up."

"You really wish you could be a girl so you could be a Mommy. Well, Brian, you will always be a boy. But you can grow up to be a Daddy and take good care of your children, too."

You have many other excellent ways to help children understand that boys and girls alike can do many things. Be especially careful about which children's books you choose to make sure that they do not portray sexist roles. There are many fine book selections that portray children and adults in a variety of roles. Joe Lasker's *Mothers Can Do Anything* is a fine example.

Similarly the posters and pictures you choose should show men and women, boys and girls, in a diversity of jobs. Stand firm that in your program girls can wear hard hats and drive trucks, and boys can put on aprons and play with dolls in pretend play. Point out how strong and capable children of both sexes are.

You may feel uncomfortable with some of these ideas yourself. **List some issues here**

that concern you about the development of children's sexual identities, or note any disagreements about sex roles you have had with parents.

_____

_____

_____

_____

You will be able to discuss how you can resolve these questions when you talk with your Field Advisor.

Using the criteria in "Ten Quick Ways to Analyze Children's Books for Racism and Sexism" (page 177), select five good children's picture books that portray boys, girls, men, and women in roles that support development of children's sexual identity. List those books here and add the list to your Professional Resource File.

_____

_____

_____

_____

Introduce these books to the children in your care if you have not already done so. Your Field Advisor will discuss the reasons for your selections with you.

Cope with fears

Monsters. The dark. Dogs. A friend's Halloween mask. Thunder. Children may be frightened of so many things. Some fears seem logical; others don't. But understanding development helps us know what to do to help children cope with their fears.

We have already seen how, during one stage of infancy, many children are afraid of strangers — or even people they see fairly often.

Other fears may also be explained mostly by understanding child development. During the infant and toddler years, children still rely a lot on the surface appearances of things and often think that objects have life.

Anika (22 months) was watching her parents to get ready for a Halloween party. She seemed to enjoy it until Daddy put on his mask. Her face puckered up and she turned away, even when Daddy tried to reassure her by saying, "Anika, it's still me. There's nothing to be afraid of."

Brett (30 months) was playing happily outdoors when the family child care provider began to drag the hose out to fill the wading pool. The hose snaked from its pile across the grass, and Brett went running away.

Nicholas (age 1) arrived earlier than usual at his family child care provider's home. She was still putting on her makeup and didn't have her glasses on. He refused to go to her and looked very puzzled.

Preschool children are also generally afraid of other categories of things: monsters, the dark, or animals. Sometimes they are afraid because they have seen others be afraid. Sometimes they have had a frightening experience themselves — watching too many scary movies or being lost in the store. And sometimes they are just afraid for reasons we adults cannot comprehend.

Write down some of the things that infants and toddlers you have known seem afraid of:

What are some common fears you have seen in preschool children?

Most fears will disappear with time, as children develop a better cognitive understanding that people and things stay the same regardless of their outward appearance and that objects are not really alive.

In the meantime, you can help children cope with their fears by taking their fears seriously and reassuring children that we will keep them safe. Children need our calm explanations, even though they may not yet be quite ready to fully understand them.

It's not enough, however, to tell children, as Anika's father did, "There's nothing to be afraid of." For there is indeed something to be afraid of or the child would not have reacted in fear! Instead, acknowledge the child's fear in the language most comfortable for the child: "I can see this mask really scared you." Try to change the situation: "Here, let me take it off." Then reassure the child: "See, it's Daddy underneath. I just put on this silly mask for Halloween. I'm sorry it scared you."

Obviously, masked parties (Halloween, Mardi Gras) are not a good idea for most young children. Even some kindergarten children have trouble dealing with masks. If you celebrate these or similar events, stick to simple costumes and a touch of makeup. Meanwhile, play "Peek-A-Boo," "Hide and Seek," and other games that help children figure out how the world works.

Pretend play is a marvelous way to help children deal with their fears. With a few carefully selected and nonthreatening props, they can play out the situations you know are scary for them. Let the children choose the play for themselves so they can feel in control of the situation. Most children can work through their fears by playing them out and channeling their aggression in safe ways during play with themes such as visits to the doctor or scary movies.

Reading books may help children see how others have coped with similar fears. One favorite is *Milk and Cookies* (Asch, 1982) about a fire-breathing dragon in the basement. Ask your librarian to help you find others related to the fears the children in your group have.

Children who are afraid of animals or other specific things may be helped by gradually introducing smaller, quieter replicas of the same item. For instance, you might help a child who is afraid of cats by doing several related things that gradually help the child adjust to more intense experiences over a period of time: put a cat puzzle together, look at pictures and books with cats, pet a stuffed animal that looks like a cat, take a walk through the neighborhood to look for cats, and perhaps finally actually touch one of the furry creatures. Never rush a child, and be sure to stop if the child indicates either with words or behavior that the experience is frightening.

Sometimes a lighthearted approach works.

Four-year-old Tracy was afraid of sleeping in her own room. Her parents tried a night light. That didn't help. They tried sitting with her while she fell asleep, but she would wake up when they left.

Finally, in frustration, her parents talked with her teacher about what might be the problem. Tracy's teacher suggested they talk with her about why she was having difficulty sleeping in her room. They did, and learned she was afraid a bad witch lived under her bed. The Tooth Fairy had visited her older sister and apparently this idea was translated into a bad witch for Tracy.

That night a few minutes before bedtime, Mommy and Tracy went to her room. Mommy bent over to look under the bed. "OK, witch," she said in a gruff voice. "It's time to get out of Tracy's room. She wants to sleep.

SCAT!" Mommy playfully chased the invisible witch out the window. Together, she and Tracy waved goodbye.

Your listening skills are essential when you talk with children about what they fear. Questions such as "And then what do you think would happen?" or "What would you do if . . .?" may help children figure out how to deal with the problem themselves. As always, try to stay away from questions that have just a yes or no answer, and use the child's home language.

Fears in general are another area in which you need to work closely with parents. Your support and their parents' understanding will help children feel protected. Together, you can help eliminate much of the stress of growing up.

You support families dealing with life's stressful events

Children's lives are filled not only with developmental challenges, but also with stressful events—some major and others minor. Let's look at how you support children and families as they deal with some of life's stressful events: children's new brothers and sisters; divorce, separation, and blended families; moving; disabilities; illness and hospitalization; death; and child abuse.

In all these situations, your primary goal will be to reduce stress as much as possible. At the same time, you will keep in mind children's long-term development, rather than applying a bandage approach.

As a professional, parents will often look to you for advice on these topics. Be prepared to give an informed response and know when to refer them to more expert help.

Prepare for new babies

When a new child enters a family, everything changes. An only child is no longer an only. The youngest child is now somewhere in the middle. And parents must adjust their time, resources, and energy to the new size of their family. What can you do to help parents make this experience a positive one for their young children?

Young children are still developing their sense of time. Because 7 or 8 months away is really much too long a time for them to grasp, you probably recommend that parents wait a little bit to inform their other children about the new baby.

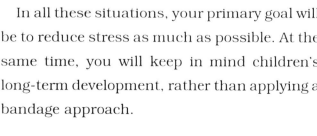

However, once their mother's body starts to change, and preparations for the arrival begin, children can and should be informed about the good news and included in the joyful changes. Adults' positive and sensitive attitudes help children feel accepted and involved in their growing family.

Many children become more interested in taking care of baby dolls when they learn a new brother or sister is on the way. Others have fun sort-

Helping children and their families cope with stress using children's books

Separation causes great stress in children. Some separations may seem insignificant to adults but are real fears in children: going to bed (leaving the family circle); getting lost in a store; having a babysitter; going to school for the first time; staying overnight with family or friends; moving or changing schools; parents going on a trip (business or pleasure); child's illness or loved one's illness, particularly hospitalization; differences from peer group (shy, thin, fat, tall, short, rich, poor); a parent incarcerated; a parent in the armed service; divorce, abandonment, separation and the most stressful of all, fear of death (the child's own or a loved one's).

Children must be reassured that they will always be cared for. They are afraid they will be alone. Children are affected by the worries of the parents, especially if the parents act differently. Children need proper preparation for the separations listed above in order to minimize the stresses. Communication is extremely important and the ability to discharge their fears with a caring adult, such as a teacher, helps children to cope. Often the use of children's literature elicits discussion from even shy students because they can see that other children and/or animal characters have the same problems; the way those characters cope may give the children ideas for managing their own stress. It may, according to Fassler (1978), help them to see that they have already solved some of the problems the book characters have, and this gives the children a sense of power.

A few good children's books dealing with stress are listed below:

Bedtime: *Goodnight Moon, There's a Nightmare in My Closet*

Constancy: *Runaway Bunny*

Staying over: *Ira Sleeps Over*

Business trip: *Friday Night Is Papa Night*

Illness: *I Want Mama*

Divorce/Separation: *A Father Like That, I'm Not Going Without a Father, My Father Lives in a Downtown Hotel*

Death: *Freddie the Leaf; The Dead Bird; The Two of Them; My Grandpa Died Today; Sam, Bangs and Moonshine; Annie and the Old One; Bridge to Terabithia*

ing through their toys, selecting those they have outgrown and putting them aside for baby. If a new baby means a change in sleeping arrangements for a young child, discuss these changes in terms of their growing up.

All during this process, children need to feel involved, to see how much they are growing up, and to feel that their needs are being met with respect. You can do this by talking about how wonderful it is to be a big brother or sister. Or point out how much children have grown since they were babies. Perhaps a mother is willing to bring her older baby in to bathe or diaper—children can see how lovingly these routines are done. Build enthusiasm for babies!

There are many good books for young children that can help them understand how babies grow in special places inside their mothers. Find some and list two or three of your favorites here and in your Professional Resource File so you can recommend them the next time a parent asks. If possible, read them with your group:

Just before the baby's arrival, remind parents to tell children, in simple, clear terms, what arrangements have been made for their care while mother is away. How frightening to wake up some morning and find a strange person there instead of your parents!

Once baby comes home, young children can contribute to the baby's care in developmentally appropriate ways. They can sing lullabies, bring a diaper or clean shirt, fold laundry, or listen for the baby to wake up—even toddlers feel so grown up when they have some responsibility.

On the other hand, children's own needs also must be met. And this is where your daily interactions can play such a big part. You can listen to children's concerns. You can make sure there are plenty of baby-related items in the housekeeping area. Your support, at a time when parents may feel overwhelmed, can be a major factor in giving families a good start together.

Preschool children who already have babies in their families may be a big booster for new siblings because they are so eager to share their experiences. In fact, children who do not have a baby may begin to encourage their parents to have one because their friends have a baby brother or sister to love.

When these positive steps are taken, children are much less likely to feel jealous or left out. Occasionally, despite everything all of you do, some children will find it difficult to accept their changed place in the family. You can use your observations and knowledge of child development to know when to recommend parents or children to experts who can counsel them through such situations.

With most children, becoming a brother or sister is a wonderful event. You and their parents can work together to set a positive, loving atmosphere for the entire family.

What are some ways that you have found to be particularly effective in helping young children enjoy becoming new brothers or sisters?

Support separating, divorced, and blended families

Much as we wish it weren't true, marriages are not always successful. And after two parents no longer choose to live together, it is very difficult for them to keep their children's needs in perspective at a time when they are dealing with their emotions and deep disappointment in their own lives. Likewise, when parents find a new partner, it is sometimes difficult to make sure children still feel welcome and included in the new family.

Regardless of the situation—separation, divorce, or remarriage—forming a new family is a stressful time for everyone. Your strength and support can make it possible for the children to deal with these traumatic events in ways that reduce stress and contribute to their long-term development.

Children often blame things that go wrong on themselves. Knowing that, you and the parents need to make it clear to the children that they are in no way responsible for a family break-up. Tell them that the divorce is an adult problem, and that you will still all work together to take good care of the children. Children must be told again and again in the language that is most familiar to them that they are still loved and secure, even if mother and father no longer love each other.

Once in a while, parents handle arrangements for custody and visitation with only a few disagreements. Children are given the information they need to feel secure about where they will live, who will take care of them, and where they will go during the day.

But sometimes a friendly separation is not possible. Children must be told in a kind way that only mommy, or only daddy, will be taking care of the family from now on. They need to know how often, or even if, they will have any contact with their other parent. Covering up the truth or even lying will destroy trust between parents and children—and never will children need to trust a parent more than at a time like this.

Similarly, when a parent is looking for and then finds a new partner, children may feel left out unless both partners make a concerted effort to continue to consider children's needs and feelings as well as their own. They need to know their parents still love them.

Children need to be included early in any new relationship. They should meet potential step-brothers or sisters long before the wedding day. And of course, throughout the relationship, the parent must make a special effort to do things just with the children and without the partner.

In a remarriage, the stepparent may bring other children into the family. Children need to know where they will live, which room is theirs, and whether they can keep all their favorite toys or the family pet.

Even the youngest children deserve to know about arrangements like these that affect them. Urge parents to be sensitive to children's concerns throughout the breaking up or re-forming of a family.

As an early childhood teacher, your primary role will be to listen and understand the child's strong feelings, to lend some stability when everything seems to be changing, and to help children come to terms with what has happened through no fault of her or his own. Young children may need lots of cuddling and individual attention. They may need time to take out their anger in acceptable ways: pounding clay, hammering nails, throwing pillows.

Most children benefit from knowing that other children have faced similar situations and have resolved them in a positive way. Many fine children's books deal with separation, divorce, and families formed by remarriage. Others focus on the wide variation in the types of families.

Find at least three good children's picture books about separation, divorce, remarriage, or blended families. List the titles on the right and in your Professional Resource File.

Sometimes children who have been through similar experiences can be a great support to their friends.

Sheryl, almost age 5, had never known her father, but had been part of a large extended family of aunts, uncles, cousins, and grandparents. When her mother decided to marry, Sheryl was understandably not enthusiastic. Her mother planned a big birthday party, in part to help Sheryl see that her needs would continue to be met in her new family.

Just before the party, Sheryl spent a day with Julie. Julie's mother had recently remarried. Julie explained how great it was to have two dads. She told about how thrilled she was to have a beautiful flower girl dress for the wedding.

Before the day was out, Sheryl couldn't wait for her mother to get married.

Children can be very resilient about new situations when their needs and feelings are handled with care and sensitivity. You can help maintain stability in children lives if you

- **keep your expectations consistent**—do not condone misbehavior just because children are facing a difficult transition. On the other hand, be understanding if the child's behavior temporarily regresses.
- **give children the solitude or extra atten-**

tion they may be missing at home—some time alone with you or on your lap can work wonders.

- **give children many opportunities to feel successful and in control of other aspects of their lives**—compliment children for their efforts, offer choices children can handle, make your program a pleasant place to be.

- **encourage dramatic play or other appropriate activities for children to work through strong feelings**—children may want to rip paper, draw pictures of their family, or dance vigorously.

- **avoid taking sides with parents**—keep your commitment instead to the child's well-being—you may be the only one who does so for a time.

- **don't let your own opinions about divorce affect your behavior**—you must act professionally regardless of your personal feelings.

Some other adjustments in your program routines may be required. When you schedule parent conferences, you may need to plan two for some children. If you prepare Father's Day, Mother's Day, or other holiday gifts, again, two gifts may be needed—one for the parent and one for the stepparent or grandparent. Make a special effort to include parents and stepparents in any events such as parent meetings, fundraisers, and other group gatherings.

You may also have some legal obligations concerning who will pick the child up and when. To protect everyone involved, it is essential that you have a signed form with the names of all people authorized to pick the child up. Don't depend on the child's word. Ask that parents inform you immediately if any court order or other legal action could affect these important arrangements. Do not get caught in the middle of a child custody fight. Get legal advice if you are in a difficult situation.

If either parents or their children seem unable to make positive strides in resolving their personal problems, you may need to suggest they consult the director of your program who can refer them to an appropriate professional. If you are a family child care provider, you may need to recommend they obtain counseling.

Help children and families who are moving

Moving may accompany changes in family make up. Families may also move for job changes and other reasons. Whether children are moving far away or just around the corner, this can be an upsetting time for everyone.

Children may worry what will happen to their beloved possessions or their pet, or whether they will see their friends again.

Parents may be preoccupied with packing and financial arrangements, or with how they will be able to adjust to a new location. What can you do to help children and families?

Moving away. Just as with every other event in life, children need to feel respected and secure when they are moving. They need time to prepare themselves. They need information about how they will be affected. And they need to be reassured that they are loved. When possible, they need to feel included in the family's plans.

Parents should be encouraged to tell their children at a reasonable time in advance what is happening. Perhaps someone has a new job in a new city. Or the family wants to find an apartment that is more convenient and has more play space. Remind the parents to reassure their children that all of you will take care of them before, during, and after the move.

Most young children are primarily concerned about their space, their toys, and their pets when they move. Ask parents to take their children with them to their new home before they move if at all possible. (Be sure parents explain that the furniture and toys will come later, so children don't think they will sleep in an empty room!) Read some books together about other children who have moved.

To involve children in moving and getting settled, give them a choice of bedrooms or a choice of paint colors, if possible. Preschoolers may have some suggestions for where they would like their bed or toy shelf. Take pictures of the old house. Exchange addresses with friends.

Suggest that parents pack children's favorite toys last and unpack them first. Children could even paste or draw pictures on the boxes so they will know what's inside. Encourage parents to get the children's sleeping arrangements settled before working on the rest of the home. Chil-

dren won't mind sitting on the floor to eat on paper plates!

If the child is leaving your program, do something special to help the children keep in touch. Perhaps a book of snapshots or a collection of friends' artwork will be treasured. Be sure the other children in your group know a week or so in advance that one of their friends is leaving so they have time to adjust as well. Remind parents to visit the child's new program before the first day of enrollment. Take the child along to meet the new caregiver, and if possible go together on the first day and stay to observe and be there if the child needs support.

Postcards, letters, or even phone calls can be exchanged after the child moves—all are excellent ways to keep in touch. Contact the child's new teacher to further add to the sense of continuity for the child.

What other ideas do you have to ease the transition when children move?

_____

_____

_____

_____

Children who leave your group. Infants become toddlers, toddlers become preschoolers, and preschoolers move on to kindergarten. As teachers, we have said goodbye to many children over the years. It never gets any easier.

Just as you do when a child moves away, you

want to help children and their parents say goodbye to you. Although you don't want to extend the goodbye too long, a month in advance is not too soon for older preschoolers. Even infants and toddlers need at least a week or two to get used to the idea of being in another classroom or with another family child care provider.

You can be a great help to parents in keeping children in contact with one another. They will need the phone numbers and mailing addresses for their children's friends. Make sure it is OK with parents before you give out the information. As we have seen, these friendships can be quite close even during the toddler years.

Let families know how much the children have grown while they have been with you and that you will miss them. Your observation diary will provide some excellent personal examples to use. If you weighed or measured children early in the year, repeat it at the end.

"I remember when you first came to our family child care program. You were just 14 months old and you barely could walk then. Now you can run, and jump, and ride a two-wheeler. You have grown up so much in just 4 years. And now you are going to begin kindergarten. Please stop by and visit us once in a while. We will miss you."

Remember, you and the children's parents are setting an example for children about how to say goodbye. Rather than avoid the pain, find positive ways to say goodbye and keep in touch. An excellent children's book that offers good ideas for adults as well is *My Teacher Said Good-Bye Today* (Osborne, 1987).

Perhaps a picnic once a year for your program's alumni is appropriate. Or a potluck dinner would give the children who were together in a family child care program a chance to renew friendships. Letters, photos, and drawings can be exchanged all year long.

Strategies to help children adjust to moving

- Acknowledge that preschoolers are affected by moving. Keep them informed and involved. Be patient and understanding.

- Be flexible. Give children time to observe before they are expected to participate.

- Be alert and sensitive to verbal and nonverbal expressions of feelings. Treat newcomers warmly and courteously.

- Provide continuity. Emphasize similarities between the new and old environments.

- Promote peer interaction. Have the new child arrive a few minutes early so others join the newcomer.

- Use children's literature to show how others cope with moving.

Note: From "When Children Move," by M. R. Jalongo, *Young Children*, September 1985, *40*(6), 54. Copyright © 1985 by National Association for the Education of Young Children. Reprinted with permission.

What ideas do you have to help children say goodbye to you?

All through their lives children will be saying goodbye. Start them off with some good strategies to deal with these stressful times. You will probably find the suggestions by Mary Renck Jalongo on page 257 useful in helping children adjust.

Assist with disabling injuries

We have already talked in general about working on a daily basis with children with disabilities, and you know how to locate resources for their families. We have also discussed bias and stereotypes about disabilities and you know how to eliminate them from your environment. But sometimes, families and children experience sudden disabling injuries and require additional support from you.

Families may understandably be stressed when first facing a family member's disabling condition. Assistance from a medical provider or specialist will most likely be required.

Helping a child learn to adapt and accept a sudden parent or sibling disability will require some special forms of support, much like other family crises. Specialists are best suited to make recommendations to you.

However, if the situation is one where the disability affects a child enrolled in your program, you will base your strategies on principles of good early childhood practice.

In a good classroom, you already have books

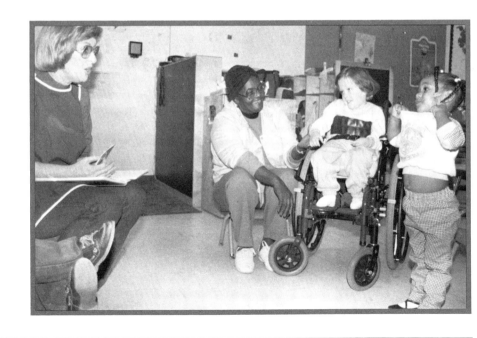

One of your goals with disabled children will be to adapt to each child's needs by making changes in the environment. Remember, you want all children to participate as fully, and as independently, as possible in your activities.

about and pictures of people who have different abilities. You may have dolls or puppets with a range of physical attributes. The dramatic play props include equipment such as glasses or crutches.

Children will feel comfortable enough to ask questions and express their concerns about people's abilities. You always treat children with respect and expect them to treat others that way. So most of your preparations for a child's re-enrollment (or a new child's enrollment) are already part of your daily interactions with children.

When a child who has been disabled is about to be enrolled, you need to talk to toddlers and preschoolers so they will be prepared in a way that is sensitive to everyone's concerns. Puppets or dolls with different abilities often work well when giving an explanation. For example, you might say something like this:

"Tomorrow, Nicholas will join our group. Remember how he likes to play with blocks and to ride tricycles? Nicholas was in an accident. Many doctors and nurses have helped him get better. You may notice that some of his skin looks and feels rougher than yours. That is where he was burned in his accident. We are so glad Nicholas will be here to play with us again. What can we do to help him feel welcome?"

Or, in the case of a child who has a disability from birth, you might explain the child's physical differences in this way.

"We are so glad that Marina will be in our class tomorrow. She loves to paint and play ball. Marina was born with very short arms. Our arms keep growing, but hers grow more slowly. That won't happen to your arms. Marina likes to do things by herself, just like you do. It will be fun to have Marina as a new friend."

Older preschoolers may have more questions once the new child arrives and they see the extent or particulars of their disability. Answer questions as truthfully but reassuringly as possible.

"Yes, Nicholas has many scars on his skin. He was burned in an unusual accident. We all are very careful here to make sure everyone is safe."

"You are worried that your arms might get short or stop growing. That won't happen. Marina's arms were this way even before she was born."

Keep your explanations brief, respectful, and use words children will understand. Never make children—the special needs or regular needs child—feel guilty or uncomfortable.

If the child with a disability is not used to being around others who are so curious, you may also need to explain why the children have so many questions.

"These boys and girls have never met someone quite like you. You are very special. They are curious and want to get to know you better. We all like to learn more about each other so we can be good friends."

One of your goals with disabled children will be to adapt to each child's needs by making changes in the environment. Remember, you want all children to participate as fully, and as independently, as possible in your activities. You may need to lower or raise a table, widen spaces between furniture, install ramps, or learn to sign. If you need some ideas about how to adapt your program, talk with the child's parents or other member of the treatment team.

Because you are so in tune to needs of the children in your group, you may find that other children want to be overly helpful to those with disabilities. A few words to them may help them see how important it is for each child to be as independent as possible.

"Patrick is trying so hard to put his shoes on by himself. You feel so grown up when you put your own shoes on. Soon Patrick will have practiced a lot and he will be able to do it as easily as you do."

Parents of disabled children are learning to cope with additional challenges each day. As their child's teacher, you can provide them an additional support. Listen to their concerns and help them find appropriate solutions to any problems.

Sometimes they will have difficult questions. If you do not feel qualified, be sure to refer parents to your program director or another professional with more training in special education or medicine. You will discuss this more in your CDA Seminar.

What ideas do you have to create a classroom climate where children with disabling conditions can thrive along with the other children?

Share your suggestions with your CDA Advisor.

Prepare for illness and hospitalization

Children's illnesses that require hospitalization come in three major forms: some are emergencies, some are scheduled procedures with an almost certain recovery, and others are long-term fights for life. In all three situations, as a professional you will be called upon to support children and their parents. Your role will be to help eliminate as much stress as possible and to find constructive ways to deal with difficulties.

None of us can ever be prepared for an emergency. However, both before and after an emergency trip to a hospital, we can give children a sense of security that they will be well taken care of.

Play is the primary vehicle for teaching young children, as we have seen many times already. We need to provide a wide variety of props for children to act out medical care experiences: ambulances, stethoscopes, surgical masks, and prescription pads are essential in a good early childhood program. Children's ideas about medical care often come out through play and in their artwork.

Children's books are another excellent way to broaden their understanding about the people and equipment in a hospital. *The Hospital Book* (Howe, 1981) takes children on an excellent tour with pictures and clear descriptions. Be sure to present information in the languages with which children are most comfortable.

A brief trip to a doctor's office or hospital might also be arranged for a small group of children. Such a trip would need to be well organized to ensure that children are not frightened and that the staff and patients in the facility are not disrupted.

Children who are scheduled to enter the hospital should certainly have a visit beforehand. Some hospitals even have special tours for children. If possible, parents should be encouraged to use a hospital that supports their presence, night and day, and that has a staff who use the family's language. Hospitals have strange smells, strange people, always have the lights on, and are filled with unusual noises. No wonder children are so frightened without someone close to them right there.

Call your local hospital(s) and write their policies regarding these issues:

Having a group of young children visit on a field trip:

Orientation for children scheduled to enter the hospital:

Rooming in for parents:

If you have a choice, which hospital seems most sensitive to children's emotional needs for security and trust? Make a copy of their policies for your Professional Resource File.

Hospital name:

On rare occasions, a child in your care may be terminally ill. Before you talk with the children about how very ill the child is, you need to resolve your own feelings. Only then will you be able to respond appropriately to children's anger or fear.

Talk with the parents and perhaps the medical care provider to better understand the illness and how to help the child and family. Medical opinion remains divided on whether children themselves should be told, but most experiences seem to indicate the child has some intuitive sense about impending death even if the adults are not forthright.

Use the information you have to make a wise decision about how much to tell the other children in the group. As always, your role is to help alleviate stress and not to create more.

Teach children about death

"Bang! Bang! You're dead," shouts a child on the playground. The victim drops to the ground and lies still for an instant. Then she gets up and begins chasing the criminal.

If only life were so simple: Someone who is killed in one movie soon appears again in another. Cartoon characters never die regardless of how many bombs are dropped on them or how many cliffs they fall from.

On the other hand, children's lives are often touched by real death—of a beloved pet, a grandparent, a neighbor, or even a close family member. They find a dead butterfly. They see a pile of motionless fur in the road. How confusing it must be when the dead animal or person doesn't leap up!

There are many reasons to have animals in the programs for young children, because children can learn so much: They can take responsibility for their care. Children can see first hand different animal's nesting habits, sleeping, and eating patterns. An animal's unfortu-nate death can be yet another vehicle to support children's learning and their emotional growth.

Through their real experiences with animals and people, children start to learn what death really means. They see that the dead one can no longer see, hear, feel, move, or breathe—and never will again. Children are curious about death. You can support their interest by caring for and studying animals, alive and dead.

The next step is not nearly so easy. Only when children have an understanding of what death means physically can they begin to deal with the emotional aspects of death. Children will ask whether they will die. Or whether their parents will die. How do you deal with such a difficult topic?

Erna Furman's ideas seem especially rooted in what we know about how young children develop and are extremely sensitive to the feelings of people as well. These recommendations are based on her work. They are primarily for older preschool children, as younger children cannot yet comprehend the finality of death.

You can deal with death best when you know what children are thinking and what their parents believe is the best approach. Some families choose to ignore the topic, others exhibit wishful thinking, some rely solely on religious explanations, and still others try to help children understand reality without overwhelming them.

Once you know the family's approach, you can then try to help parents understand that children are still developing a sense of time, that abstract concepts such as heaven are not yet meaningful to young children, and that children do have strong feelings about death. If it is a parent or sibling who has died, your support will be even more essential.

It would be dishonest to respond to the question "Will I (or you) die?" with "No" because eventually everyone dies. On the other hand, you cannot respond with a simple "Yes," or the child may believe it could happen instantly.

Instead, we should respond in a manner that tells the truth but also puts it positively in the context of time.

"Well, we will all die someday. But before then, you probably will grow up, and have a fine job, and love your wife and children, and even become a grandparent!"

Part of our role as teachers is to help children learn how to deal with strong feelings such as anger, sadness, and disappointment. We have already discussed appropriate' ways to help children build their own strengths in these areas.

At the same time, we don't want children's strong feelings to be dulled so that they feel no pain in emotionally difficult situations. If a child did not react strongly to a death, we would be even more worried about her or his development. What if children didn't care if their cat died? Or if they seemed indifferent to someone's suffering?

You probably have already been asked by at least one parent about whether their children should be told of a grandparent's death, for example, or should attend the funeral. Let's see what the best way is to handle such situations, based on what we know about children's long-term emotional development.

You want children to talk with you, to trust you, to feel secure. Surely these goals are never more important than when you help a child face the loss of an pet or person. So you do want children to know the cause of death and to help them deal with their anger and sadness.

Children are curious about why things die. While you surely would not provide gory details, you might explain an animal's death like this.

"Brownie was a wonderful guinea pig for our class. He lived a long life and made many children happy. But his body was wearing out, because guinea pigs don't live as long as people do. His heart finally stopped beating and he died."

Be sure to answer children's questions about why someone died in as forthright a manner but as simply as possible. One of the best books about the topic is *When People Die* (Bernstein, 1977).

Dealing with the feelings about death is difficult. You may say something such as this:

"I am so sorry to learn of your grandfather's death, Tara. You and he shared so many good times together. It may be hard for you to talk about it right now, but I know you may want to remember some of your happy times with him. You can come to me whenever you would like to talk about him."

One way people come to terms with sadness, to ease the transition between life and death, is to have a funeral. Children often request funerals for dead pets.

Della was almost 5. Her 10-year-old goldfish was floating on the top of its aquarium. She found a box for it and asked her parents if it could be buried in the back yard. Fish was placed on a tissue and the box was closed. The family walked solemnly to the grave site, which was marked by a large rock. The hole was dug, the box placed in it, and earth gently pushed over the top. Della carefully perched the rock atop the grave. Her parents had tears in their eyes—Fish had been with them a long time before Della was born.

Della paused for a second, then skipped off merrily, asking, "Can we go buy my new shoes now?"

Weeks later, though, she still talked about Fish, and frequently went to the backyard to look at his grave.

Simple funerals such as this one are certainly appropriate for young children. Sometimes children want to sing their favorite songs. It is not unusual to hear "B-I-N-G-O" or "The Farmer in the Dell" at a pet's funeral.

Before deciding to take a young child to a formal funeral, however, encourage parents to think about what type of service it is and whether the parents feel comfortable with it, who will be available to comfort the child, and whether the parents feel the experience would be sensitive to the child's needs.

Long, emotional services would tax a young child beyond her or his limits. If the parents resent the child's presence (perhaps not wanting to demonstrate their emotions in front of the child) or feel that an open casket could upset the child, it might be better to make other arrangements.

However, if the service and events are not going to be emotionally upsetting but rather supportive of the family, young children probably should be invited to attend. Families need to join together in sharing their grief for and memories of loved ones. They can be a source of strength to each other and give children a real sense of belonging.

If children are excluded from the funeral, they may feel left out, especially if the person was someone very important to them. One child had the measles and still was upset that she was unable to go to her beloved great-grandmother's funeral. She was the only child she knew who even had a great-grandmother.

If the parents decide the child will not attend, be sure they make arrangements for the child's care appropriate to the child's feelings—a trip to an amusement park would not be a constructive way to help the child deal with the death.

Everyone in the family will be searching for ways to come to terms with the death long after the funeral. No one can rush the mourning process. On the other hand, if a child or parent seems stuck and unable to get on with life, or if the death was of a parent or sibling, you may need to refer the family for counseling.

Some of you may have strong beliefs—religious, cultural, or personal—that determine your thinking about how to handle death with young children. What are some of those beliefs that seem to conflict with what you know about child development and good early childhood practice? (Fill in your answer on the next page.)

List here any conflicts or questions you have about helping children cope with death.

Discuss them with your CDA Field Advisor.

Recognize signs of abuse

We talked briefly about your obligation to report potential child abuse in Unit 3. It may be your skill at detecting the signs of child abuse—physical, sexual, or emotional—that will bring the child safety and protection.

As a teacher, you see children almost every day. You are therefore in a good position to notice any changes in a child's behavior or physical condition. You also are very aware of how the parents treat their children and what stresses the family might be under.

You have a professional, legal, and ethical responsibility to report any **suspected** harm or potential risk of harm to a child.

Reporting your suspicions does not mean accusing or reporting the abuser. *It means reporting any signs on or about the child that may have been caused by abuse:* suspicious marks that could not have been caused by accident for example, or a child's report of abuse. Remember, your job is not to make accusations, nor to determine the guilt or innocence of anyone who might be involved. **You will discuss at length in your CDA Seminar the reporting procedures in your community.**

You need to plan now how you will work with a family should a child in your group be abused. Most teachers find themselves in a state of shock or feel numb when something like this happens. If you have a plan to follow you can let it guide you.

Much of how you deal with the abuse of the child will depend on the circumstances. If the abuser is someone you know—a member of the family—for example, and/or the abuse has been going on for some time, the situation may be very difficult for you to deal with personally. You may feel guilty that you did not recognize that the child was being abused. You may be very angry that someone you know and trusted could take advantage of a child for whom you care so much. You may well feel emotionally overwhelmed yourself.

Abuse by a stranger may be equally chilling. You may wish you had done more to help children say "NO" to strangers. You may find

Indicators of possible child abuse

Child

- bruises or wounds in various stages of healing
- injuries on two or more planes [sides] of the body
- injuries reported to be caused by falling but which do not include hands, knees, or forehead
- oval, immersion [in hot liquid], doughnut-shaped, or imprint [hot iron or cigarette] burns
- reluctance to leave school [or child care program]
- inappropriate dress for the weather
- discomfort when sitting
- sophisticated sexual knowledge or play
- radical behavior changes or regressive behavior
- child withdraws or watches adults
- child seems to expect abuse
- revealing discussion, stories, or drawings

Adult

- unrealistic expectations for child
- reliance on child to meet [adult] social or emotional needs
- lack of basic childrearing knowledge or skills
- substance abuse

Stress

- positive or negative changes—moving, new baby, unemployment, divorce

Note: From "Child Abuse and Neglect," by B. J. Meddin and A. L. Rosen, *Young Children*, May 1986, *41*(4), 28. Copyright © 1986 by National Association for the Education of Young Children. Reprinted with permission.

yourself suspecting every stranger who walks past your outdoor play area. You may keep saying, "If only I had . . . ."

In addition, if criminal charges have been filed against a family member, you may have some legal obligations, especially in terms of who is authorized to pick the child up. If a stranger was involved, parents may demand additional security measures for their children when they go on field trips or play outdoors, for example.

Regardless of the situation, you will probably react with shock and disbelief, with horror and disgust, and with anguish for the child who is so dear to you. Despite your feelings, you must be in control as a professional.

Before you are confronted with a child abuse situation, find out where to get support in your community to help you, the family, and the child deal with the problem. Many localities have a child abuse hot line, a family counseling center, or a child welfare agency with staff to assist families.

Write the name of the counseling/child welfare agency and the phone number here and on your phone emergency list. Then you can find it easily if you ever need it. Add the agency name and phone number to your Professional Resource File.

_____

_____

_____

_____

As a teacher, your first responsibility must be to the child. Confidentiality about the case is an absolute must. In a center program, only your supervisor needs to know because of any possible legal consequences.

When the child returns to your group, you will need to continue to offer your support by giving more individual attention, or allowing the child time alone, or listening about the child's confusion.

On the other hand, you will not support the child's long-term development if you are over-protective or otherwise play favorites at the expense of the other children. You want the child to have time to deal with the situation but you also want the child to resume the usual activities in life as they are appropriate.

Some children's books deal with child abuse. An especially good one for older preschool children is *My Body Is Private* (Girard, 1984). **Select one or two especially good books and**

list the titles here. Then you can obtain them without searching should you need to use them. If a child is abused, you will need to make a decision about whether to read the books to the whole group, to just the child involved, or to recommend them to the parents to read at home.

_____

_____

_____

_____

Discuss your selections with your CDA Field Advisor.

Although your efforts and those of the counselors involved will be directed toward helping the child return to a more secure life, you will at times be frustrated. Court proceedings can sometimes drag on for months. Children may have to relive their experiences before one or more juries or judges. Again, you can be a great support to the child during this harrowing time.

You may even be called to testify, perhaps to verify that the child is capable (or not capable) of taking the stand, is truthful, or to report on any observed changes in the child's behavior after the incident. If you become involved in this aspect of such a case, you must obtain legal advice immediately.

Most parents will rely on your support as well. Few family incidents are as upsetting as having a child abused. Your strength can help the family weather this storm. But your support alone is not enough. Almost without exception, abused children and their families need additional professional counseling. Work together with your program director, a social worker, psychiatrist, or other trained professional to help the family rebuild its strengths.

This is an excellent time to put all you have just learned into action. Refer back to your brief descriptive sketches that you did in Unit 3 for each child in your group. Right now you are especially in tune with children's social and emotional strengths and needs.

Look through your notes for any patterns that might give you clues about children who need additional support in their socioemotional development. List those children here, and begin to make a plan to work with them and their parents to help children build on their strengths and overcome their weaknesses.

CHILD'S NAME _____

Socioemotional concerns _____

_____

Support strategies _____

_____

_____

_____

CHILD'S NAME _____

Socioemotional concerns _____

_____

Support strategies _____

_____

_____

_____

Discuss your plans with your CDA Field Advisor.

You have reached the end of the self-study portion of one of the most difficult parts of your CDA training. Why is social and emotional development such a difficult topic? Because so many people have so many different discipline methods. Because so many of us had parents who were not aware of how important our feelings were. And because so many of us had teachers who weren't aware of the role of culture in development. We can't always rely on our own experiences to make us good teachers!

We must all continue to improve how we teach by making changes in what we do. These changes might not always feel comfortable at first, but by using child development-based approaches to teaching, you will feel good about yourself, and children's long-term development will benefit.

You have much of the basic information you need to start to improve your teaching strategies. Mark your progress by checking the box in your CDA Progress Record for this Unit.

Then continue to use this more child development-based approach to teaching. And for the rest of your career, keep learning more about children's social and emotional development. Researchers are always finding new, more effective ways to guide children's development. Keep up with your profession by reading and attending workshops or classes.

By the time you complete your CDA Professional Preparation Program, you will have a solid background in how to foster children's social and emotional growth. Much of what you will have learned also applies when you work to advance their physical and intellectual competence. We will now focus on those two aspects of children's development.

Resources for more information

Anti-bias curriculum [Videotape—30 min.]. Available from Toys 'n Things Press, 450 N. Syndicate, Suite 5, St. Paul, MN 55104-4125. 800-423-8309.

Asch, F. (1982). *Milk and cookies.* New York: Parents Magazine Press.

Benham, H., & Derman-Sparks, L. (1990, November/December). Understanding diversity. *PreK Today, 5*(3), 44.

Bernstein, J.E., & Gullo, S.V. (1977). *When people die.* New York: Dutton.

Bookfinder: When kids need books (4th ed.). Circle Pines, MN: American Guidance, 1989.

Burger, M. L. H. (1991, March). The teacher's role in helping children and their families deal with stress. *ACEI Exchange, 59*(4), 1.

Derman-Sparks, L. (1987). *What is anti-bias curriculum?* Unpublished manuscript.

Derman-Sparks, L., & the A.B.C. Task Force. (1989). *Anti-bias curriculum: Tools for empowering young children.* Washington, DC: National Association for the Education of Young Children.

Derman-Sparks, L., Higa, C.T., & Sparks, B. (1980). Children, race and racism: How race awareness develops. *Council on Interracial Books for Children Bulletin, 11*(3 & 4), 3–15.

Easing the transition from preschool to kindergarten: A guide for early childhood teachers and administrators. Washington, DC: Head Start Bureau, 1987.

Faber, A., & Mazleish, E. (1982). *How to talk so kids will listen and listen so kids will talk.* New York: Avon.

Fassler, J. (1978). *Helping children cope.* New York: Free Press Division, Macmillan.

Frelease, Jim. (1989). *New read-aloud handbook.* New York: Penguin.

Froschl, M., Colon, L., Rubin, E., & Sprung, B. (1984). Annotated bibliography: Resources for creating an inclusive classroom environment. In *Including all of us: An early childhood curriculum about disability.* New York: Educational Equity Concepts., Inc.

Froschl, M., Colon, L., Rubin, E., & Sprung, B. (1984). Checklist for an inclusive environment. In *Including all of us: An early childhood curriculum about disability.* New York: Educational Equity Concepts., Inc.

Froschl, M., Colon, L., Rubin, E., & Sprung, B. (1984). *Including all of us: An early childhood curriculum about disability.* New York: Educational Equity Concepts., Inc.

Froschl, M., & Sprung, B. (1983). Providing an anti-handicappist early childhood environment. *Interracial Books for Children Bulletin, 14*(7–8), 21–23.

Furman, E. (1978, May). Helping children cope with death. *Young Children, 33*(4), 25–32.

Gillespie, J. T., & Naden, C. J. *Best books for children* (constantly revised). New York: Bowker.

Girard, L.W. (1984). *My body is private.* Niles, IL: Whitman.

Gold, B., & Trumbo, N. (Co-producers). *Krista.* [Video-tape—23 min.]. Available from Child & Family Services, 626 North Coronado, Los Angeles, CA 90026. 213-413-0777.

Greenspan, S., & Greenspan, N.T. (1985). *First feelings.* New York: Penguin.

Hearne, Betsy. (1981). *Choosing books for children.* New York: Delacorte.

"Helping children learn self-control: A guide to discipline." Washington, DC: National Association for the Education of Young Children, 1986.

Helping children love themselves and others: A professional handbook for family day care. Washington, DC: The Children's Foundation, 1990.

Helping children love themselves and others: A resource guide to equity materials. Washington, DC: The Children's Foundation, 1990.

Honig, A. (1985). "Love and learn: Discipline for young children." Washington, DC: National Association for the Education of Young Children.

Honig, A. (1987, May). Research in review: The shy child. *Young Children, 42*(4), 53–64.

Howe, J. (1981) *The hospital book.* New York: Crown.

Jalongo, M.R. (1985, September). When young children move. *Young Children, 40*(6), 51–57.

Kirchner, A. B. (1985). *Basic beginnings: A handbook of learning games and activities for young children.* New York: Acropolis.

Kostelnik, M.J., Whiren, A.P., & Stein, L.C. (1986, May). Living with He-Man: Managing superhero fantasy play. *Young Children, 41*(4), 3–9.

Lasker, J. (1976). *Mothers can do anything.* Chicago: Whitman.

Leipzig, J. (1986). Fostering prosocial development in infants and toddlers. In D.P. Wolf (Ed.), *Connecting: Friendship in the lives of young children and their teachers.* Redmond, WA: Exchange Press.

Lima, C. W., & Lima, J. A. (1990). *A to zoo: Subject access to children's books,* (3rd ed.). New York: Bowker.

Lionni, L. (1968). *Swimmy.* New York: Pantheon.

McAfee, O.D. (1985, September). Research report. Circle time: Getting past Two Little Pumpkins. *Young Children, 40*(6), 24–29.

McCracken, J.B. (1986). "So many goodbyes: Ways to ease the transition between home and groups for young children." Washington, DC: National Association for the Education of Young Children.

McCracken, J.B. (Ed.). (1986). *Reducing stress in young children's lives.* Washington, DC: National Association for the Education of Young Children.

Meddin, B.J., & Rosen, A.L. (1986, May). Child abuse and neglect: Prevention and reporting. *Young Children, 41*(4), 26–30.

Mitchell, G. (1982). *A very practical guide to discipline with young children.* Marshfield, MA: Telshare.

Morris, L., Sather, G., & Scull, S. (Eds.). (1986). *Extracting learning styles from social/cultural diversity: A study of five American minorities.* Norman, OK: Southwest Teacher Corps Network.

Neugebauer, B. (1987). *Alike and different: Exploring our humanity with young children.* Redmond, WA: Exchange Press.

Osborne, J. (1987). *My teacher said good-bye today.* P.O. Box 971, Brookline, MA 02146: Emijo Pubs.

Pellowski, A. (1987). *Storytelling handbook.* New York: Macmillan.

Process for implementing bilingual/multicultural programs [Videotape-Head Start Information Series]. College Park, MD: Institute for Child Study, College of Education, University of Maryland, 1986.

Rogers, F. (1985). *Going to day care.* New York: Putnam.

Roopnarine, J.L., & Honig, A.S. (1985, September). Research in review: The unpopular child. *Young Children, 40*(6), 59–64.

Schiller, P., & Bermudez, A. B. (1988). Working with non-English-speaking children. *Texas Child Care Quarterly, 12*(3), 3–8.

Smith, C.A., & Davis, D.E. (1976, September). Teaching children non-sense. *Young Children, 31*(6), 438–447.

Sprung, B. (1975). *Non-sexist education for young children: A practical guide.* New York: Citation.

Stone, J.G. (1978). *A guide to discipline* (rev. ed.). Washington, DC: National Association for the Education of Young Children.

Swick, K.J. (Ed.). (1987). *Multicultural learning in early childhood education.* Little Rock, AR: Southern Association on Children Under Six.

Timberlake, P. (1990, April). Let's cancel graduation! It's inappropriate for young children. *Dimensions, 18*(3), 10–12.

Veach, D.M. (1977, May). Choice with responsibility. *Young Children, 32*(4), 22–25.

Wolf, D.P. (Ed.). (1986). *Connecting: Friendship in the lives of young children and their teachers.* Redmond, WA: Exchange Press.

5

Steps to advance children's physical and intellectual competence

 T THIS POINT in your CDA Early Childhood Studies, you are familiar with how children develop: You know what it takes to set up a safe, healthy environment that invites learning through play. You know how important it is to interact with children in positive ways.

But you may still be asking yourself the question: "What do the children **DO** all day?"

In this unit we will combine all of what you have learned so far with many more specific, appropriate teaching strategies. Then you will be better prepared to promote children's socioemotional, physical, and cognitive development through play—you can plan what children do all day.

We will start by looking at what you want children to learn. Then we will focus on how children learn and what you need to do to be a great teacher of young children.

Part 1

What do you want children to learn?

Pretend for a moment that Graham, Jerrod, and Maya are three children in your program. Think about some typical events that might happen.

"Wow! Look at that! The paint doesn't stick to where I colored. It only shows on the paper," exclaims Graham, a preschooler who has just discovered the wonders of crayon resist.

Jerrod, 13 months old, stands at the bottom of the 3-step climber with a slide. He lifts his leg and finally gets his knee on the step. He pulls up his other leg and perches his foot on the step. Then balancing carefully and holding on to the railings, he lifts himself and stands on the first step. He beams, wiggles his bottom in delight at his success, and begins to tackle the next step. He's on his way to the top!

Maya, a toddler, finds a basket of large wooden beads and shoestrings. She puts the basket on the floor, plunks down next to it, and picks a bright red bead and a pink shoelace.

First she tries to poke the end with the knot in it through the hole. But nothing happens. She looks around.

Her teacher is watching nearby. "What else could you try to get the lace through the bead?" she asks

Maya. Maya tries another bead, but the knotted end still doesn't go through.

Then she grabs another shoestring, this time from the other end, and pokes it through the blue bead. Soon she has three beads on her string, and asks her teacher to "Make a necklace." Her teacher ties the beads loosely around her neck.

If the parents of these children asked you what they were learning, how would you respond? Would you say, "Oh, Graham is just doing art," or "Jerrod is just playing," or "Maya just loves to dress up"?

Any of these answers are OK, but they are incomplete. They are only part of the picture of what these children are really doing.

Sure, Graham was doing art. But he was also

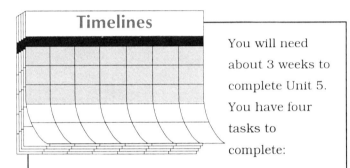

Timelines

You will need about 3 weeks to complete Unit 5. You have four tasks to complete:

1 Prepare for conference with your Field Advisor to discuss five topics (goals for children's learning, planning physical activities, helping children communicate, promoting exploration and discovery, and planning curriculum themes).

2 Complete three assignments (identify appropriate materials and activities, plan a specific activity area, and develop a sample weekly plan) and two entries for the Professional Resource File.

3 Complete four assignments for Seminar (build a collection of songs, examine pros and cons of using food in art activities, observe children's thinking, and think about ways to help children become more responsible citizens).

4 View the accompanying videotape using the Viewer's Guide.

Word list

Closed-ended question—Question that has one right answer.

Large muscle—When children use their arms, legs, backs, and torsos. Generally is play that requires big movements.

Open-ended question—Question that could have many different answers (these questions often begin with why or how or what do you think would happen if . . . ?).

Rote—Memorizing facts.

Small muscle—When children use their fingers and hands. Generally is play that requires fine coordination.

Transition—Times when children are finishing one activity and moving on to the next one.

figuring out some of the basic principles of physics—that wax and water do not mix—and experiencing how much fun it can be to learn. He used his hands and fingers to draw and paint. And he was making his own discoveries. His self-esteem was bolstered, and he was eager to share his accomplishments with others.

Jerrod was indeed playing and at the same time figuring out how to make his legs work together to climb steps. But he was also solving the problem of how to get to the top of the slide by himself. And he was thrilled to do be able to do it!

Maya was discovering how to string beads skillfully and she used what she made to decorate her body. But she also was picking up some new vocabulary *(through)*. She found, through trial and error, what really worked to get the string through the beads and she solved her problem herself—that's science in action. She is learning to ask for, and receive, help when she needs it.

Some of what these children learned did contribute to their physical growth. Some was related to their intellectual abilities. Some of it strengthened them as people. *As you can see, most learning doesn't fit into the neat little categories of either physical, cognitive, or socioemotional growth—because in nearly every learning situation each area of development is involved. They all overlap.*

Children learn many different things from what seem like such insignificant happenings—you only need to know what to look for and how to guide what happens.

What are we looking for when children learn?

Long-term dreams for children's physical and intellectual development

Parents and teachers want children to

- **develop** strong, well-coordinated bodies;
- **use** words, art, and music to communicate with others;
- **make** sense out of the world;
- **recognize** real problems and figure out solutions to them;
- **think** critically and logically, ask questions that lead to more questions; and
- **lead** well-balanced, productive lives.

Being a teacher means giving a great deal of thought to what you want children to learn in your program.

In Unit 4, we listed some dreams for social and emotional growth that parents and teachers share for children now and all during their youth: to feel good about themselves, to be competent, eager to learn, in control of themselves, friendly, to appreciate their uniqueness, to be secure, independent, and trusting.

Now let's add to that list with some specific dreams for children's long-term physical and intellectual development. These are some of the other goals you probably share with parents:

- **develop** strong, well- coordinated bodies;
- **use** words, music, and art to communicate with others;
- **make** sense out of the world;
- **recognize** real problems and figure out solutions to them;

- **think** critically and logically, ask questions that lead to more questions; **and probably most of all**
- **lead** well-balanced, productive lives.

-
-
-
-

Please add any other broad goals that you, your program, or the parents have for children. Think carefully about your own specific program and the specific cultural groups and families in it. If your program has written goals, get a copy. Your Field Advisor will discuss them with you.

Your challenge is to work toward all these goals in developmentally appropriate ways. Let's see how to do that.

Part 2

How do children learn—and how do you teach?

Let's picture two imaginary programs based on two very different ideas about how children learn: the "School for Tots" and the "Children's Learning Center." Few toddler or preschool programs in a center or family child care home are exactly like these examples. But most are more like one or the other. Try to imagine how it would feel to be a child, or a teacher, in these programs.

"School for tots"

The room is decorated with a border around the top of the walls. The teacher hand-made or purchased these materials for the border: pictures of words beginning with each letter of the alphabet, numbers from 1 to 20, examples of 10 colors, and 5 shapes.

All children sit quietly at large tables or their own desks for most of the day. The teacher talks to the entire group most of the time. Children raise their hands when they want to speak.

Children work on workbooks or other projects assigned by the teacher. They all do the same thing at the same time. If they finish early, they may choose a coloring book or worksheet. The teacher marks any errors on their work in red ink.

Flashcards and rote are used to teach numbers and the alphabet. Children rush to be the first to get the correct answer.

Teachers drill children learning English as a second language using flashcards to memorize vocabulary in English.

The teacher does science experiments while the children watch. The teacher asks questions to get children to memorize facts. There is only one right answer.

Twice a week, children copy a model for art. Every project is supposed to be as perfect as the teacher's. Messy projects (finger painting, sand, water) are avoided. One day a week for 30 minutes, children sing songs chosen by the teacher.

The teacher gets out what children are to use and gives instructions on how to use it. The teacher puts things away after each project while the children wait to be told what to do next.

The teacher strictly enforces rules: no talking, no running, no hitting, no lying, no talking back.

Gold stars are awarded for good performance. Children are punished with timeouts or loss of outdoor play time.

Children get to play outdoors for half an hour after lunch. They get to watch TV in the late afternoon. They often stand and wait in line.

The teacher's main goal is to get children ready for kindergarten.

"Children's learning center"

Children's scribbling/writing and artwork are hung at their eye level. Spellings are mostly invented by the children. Children write in the language that is most comfortable for them. Artwork is unique to each child.

Children move about freely, talking with each other as they play. They sit on the floor, at a table, or stand, depending on comfort and convenience. Children learn at their own pace and in their own style. The room hums with activity. The teacher moves among activities, talking with each child, observing, offering support, suggesting new ideas, assisting as needed, asking open-ended questions occasionally.

Teachers use the child's first language for new concepts and experiences throughout the day and talk with children in second language at a level a little above the level the child uses, in context, fostering bilingualism.

Children choose activities and materials they want to work with. Sometimes special projects are offered and the number of children who can participate is limited, but everyone who wants to participate eventually gets a chance. Children return items to their proper places when they are finished.

Real objects from many cultures — tools, blocks, food and utensils for cooking, accessories for water and sand play, animals to tend to, plants to care for, dress-up clothes, pretend play props, children's picture books, toys, aids used by people with disabilities, puzzles, games — are neatly arranged on low shelves.

Art materials are available to use in creative ways. Messy activities such as finger painting are encouraged. Easels are always available. The emphasis is always on the fun of doing, not the end result.

Children help set their own rules for friendly behavior: We walk indoors. We use words when we don't agree. We cooperate with each other.

Children are always eager to play and pursue their projects. When they have disagreements, they work out solutions by talking to each other. Sometimes the teacher guides them to figure out their own solutions.

Most of the day is reserved for play, some indoors and some outdoors. Routines and transitions such as toileting, meals, and moving to another activity are treated as learning times. The schedule is flexible but it gives the day a sense of order and continuity.

The teacher's main goal is to help children become fun-loving, well-rounded, self-motivated, people who control their own behavior.

How would you feel as a child or teacher in the "School for tots?"

. . . in the "Children's learning center?"

Which one of these groups seems more like your program?

By this point in your Professional Preparation Program, you should feel uncomfortable with some of the teaching methods used at the "School for tots." Perhaps you noticed that much of what happens in that program is not developmentally appropriate. Maybe you were surprised that teachers would still use such outdated forms of discipline. In fact, the "School for tots" is filled with examples of things that professional early childhood educators **never** do because we believe that our long-term goals for children would probably not be reached in such a program.

On the other hand, most of us remember being taught in elementary school like the teacher at "School for tots" and sometimes, even when we **know** there are better ways to teach younger children, we fall back on how we were taught.

We were drilled until we memorized our multiplication tables. We read about strange people who lived in other times and other places. We did as our teachers told us. We

Children's bodies develop when children are healthy and when they have lots of opportunities to use their large and small muscles in a wide variety of developmentally appropriate ways.

How do young children learn most effectively?

We used to think young children learned best when they

- listened to and watched adults
- memorized facts
- thought about abstract ideas
- followed directions
- had their mistakes corrected
- practiced tasks selected by others
- sat quietly at desks

Now we know young children learn best when they

- actively **participate**
- work at their **own pace and in their own style**
- talk with each other
- use **real, authentic objects**
- **build on their own experiences**
- follow their **natural curiosity**
- **experiment** to find solutions to their own real problems
- **choose** what they want to do
- **PLAY**

braced ourselves for papers to be returned covered with red marks. We sat quietly (most of the time). Everything seemed *so far away* from our lives and experiences! But, as you learn more about how young children learn, you will see why different teaching methods are more appropriate.

The "Children's learning center" example is filled with ideas about how to foster children's learning in positive, child-oriented ways. Teaching in this way gives children a good start toward reaching our long-term goals for them.

Fortunately, many teachers of children 5 and younger have always used these teaching methods. For at least the last century or so, teachers in nursery schools, kindergartens, and child study centers all over the world kept children's long-term development in mind—they saw first-hand how children really learned best.

New insights about children's learning have led to some modifications, of course, but the teaching strategies pictured in the "Children's learning center" and recommended throughout this CDA curriculum are indeed time-tested.

These techniques work in real classrooms with real children—researchers, teachers, and parents have seen it happen.

Are you beginning to see just how very different teaching is with young children? You set up a rich environment. The children choose what to do. You are there to encourage and support their efforts.

If you see yourself as being even a little bit like the teacher at "School for tots," check those areas that are most like you:

_____ teacher decorates room/provides models for art projects or does projects for children

_____ teacher directs activities/children sit quietly

_____ uses workbooks/worksheets/coloring books/dittoes/flashcards

_____ teacher sets rules/rewards/punishments

_____ rules tell children what **not to do**

_____ schedule is rigidly followed/little time for play

_____ emphasis is on rote learning

_____ goals for children are for the immediate or near future

The areas you checked are the ones where you will need to work hardest to examine and change as you complete your CDA.

Talk to your Field Advisor about your reactions to the "School for tots" and "Children's learning center" examples. Go over the checklist of items which are most like you.

If you want to read more, start with some of the resources listed at the end of this unit. **Ask your Field Advisor to help you select some additional reading.** Also, remember to use the public library as a source of books and other resources to assist you in your teaching.

Now, on to what children do all day. And how you teach.

You enable children to develop strong, well-coordinated bodies

Children's bodies develop when children are healthy and when they have lots of opportunities to use their large and small muscles in a wide variety of developmentally appropriate ways. How then, do you enable children to develop strong, well-coordinated bodies?

Play outdoors frequently

Even in the coldest of climates, children need to go outdoors every day for at least a few minutes. Children should be dressed properly of course, but since the fresh air is vital to their health, spend as much time as you can outdoors. Give children things to do while they're out. Older children can help carry tables and materials. Puzzles, blocks, paints, water play, dress-up clothes—everything can go out. Never restrict yourself to just "recess" or typical playground equipment outdoors. Meals and snacks always taste better on picnics. Read a story on a blanket under a tree. Think of every activity you do inside as a potential outdoor activity.

What activities have you never done outdoors?

_____

_____

_____

_____

_____

Choose something from the list and as soon as possible, take it outside. Watch how children use the activity differently outdoors.

Balance active (large muscle) and quiet (small muscle) play

Children need lots of play time each day—in fact, most of their day should be spent in play. During this play time, children are free to choose what they want to do indoors and outdoors.

You provide the time, equipment, and activities that enable children to use their bodies, muscles, and brains in a variety of ways. For example, sometimes a toddler will want to use a table toy such as a puzzle or interlocking blocks. Other times that same toddler will want to jump around on the mats and cushions. Give them both choices.

Trust children. Children **will** choose something that is a good match for their development—if you have provided a wide range of activities and materials suitable for the children's development.

And of course, you adapt activities and materials for any children who have special needs.

Perhaps a paintbrush will need to be attached to an arm or a brace. Maybe you need knob puzzles with a large number of pieces for a preschooler who has difficulty picking up small items. Do whatever is necessary to enable the disabled child to be as independent and feel as secure as possible.

Sometimes children have been ill, or overprotected, or find an activity too difficult, or were injured doing something similar. You don't push or force children to participate. You want children to feel competent and successful. You watch as their muscle development unfolds and provide activities that are a good match for what they can do and what they soon will be able to do.

Young infants. For the first few months, infants' large muscles are developing at a rapid pace and their fine motor coordination also begins. Infants need space to kick, to roll over, to drop things, to bounce, to crawl, to balance themselves, to walk, to dance. They need spoons to grasp and chunks of food to pick up.

Eleven-month-old Brooke has discovered the wonderful taste and feel of cereal bits. Feeding herself is exciting. She crawls over to the cupboard and jabbers. As soon as her family child care provider gets out the box, Brooke begins to pop the cereal into her mouth.

Newborns sometimes are comforted by being wrapped tightly, but soon they find out how glorious it feels to kick their legs and wave their arms. Safely attach bells to their wrists or ankles and see how delighted babies are to make music. Happily play a baby's favorite game of dropping and picking things up—plastic measuring cups, keys, or toys. You can probably think of other safe ways to give young babies a feeling that what they do can make a difference in their environment.

As babies grow more mobile, you give them safe places to move about. Some areas are carpeted. You provide cushions to climb on and cardboard boxes to climb in. Empty diaper boxes make great wagons for pulling babies. They love to play "Pat-A-Cake" and ride the horse (your bouncing leg). Pounding benches, drums, and a small basin of water to splash in are wonderful for growing arms. Finger foods enable children to begin to feed themselves as their small muscles and budding teeth begin to work for them.

You would not give an infant small beads or tiny plastic blocks. Why? Because infants put everything in their mouths and they could choke. Nor can you expect infants to draw with markers, turn the thin paper pages of a book, do finger plays, or feed themselves with a spoon. Keep your expectations reasonable.

List some appropriate large- and small-muscle toys and household objects that should be available for infants to choose from every day:

Discuss your list with your CDA Field Advisor.

Older infants and toddlers. Toddlers' large muscles are still developing, but they are also beginning to coordinate their hands and fingers with more skill.

Infants put everything in their mouths!

Emilia is engrossed with the clay dough. She takes a large hunk from the covered can, kneads the clay with her hands for a long time, and then plops it on the table. She rolls it by pushing hard with her arms, then picks off tiny chunks and lines them up carefully. "Look, I made cookies!" she exclaims to no one in particular. Then she picks up her cookies and pokes them one at a time back into her ball.

So you provide toddlers with lots of places to run and climb; fairly low places to jump from; music for dancing; smaller items to fit together

Toddlers are developing finer muscle control and enjoy playing with objects that they can put together and take apart.

and take apart; sand and water to pour, carry, and sift; items to balance and dump and fit pieces together; things to push or pull; and the chance to feed themselves with spoons.

Ramps and steps with play areas below can provide hours of fun for toddlers. Slides, low bikes to pedal, wagons to pull, small shopping carts or lawn mowers to push — all are great fun. Open grassy areas give them space to run. Give a toddler a bucket of water, a 3-inch paintbrush, and a wooden fence or the side of a building—and they have a ball! Much of the typical toddler's day is spent in large-muscle activities, so both your indoor and outdoor play areas should center around these types of activities and equipment.

Toddlers also are developing finer muscle control. Puzzles with knobs make it easy for them to remove and replace the pieces. They like fitting things into containers and then dumping them all out again: Try a plastic ice cream container filled with screw-type jar lids — the clatter is delightful!

Large pieces of blank paper work well for scribbling and drawing with wide markers or fat crayons. At first, children will make random marks or move the crayon back and forth across the page just for the fun of it. Clay is wonderful to roll and squish, as Emilia has discovered. Usually toddlers prefer to work on the floor or to stand at a small table for these activities.

Appealing books for toddlers have sturdy paper pages and bright pictures. More and more book publishers are paying attention to the needs of the younger child. "Board" books (so named because their pages are made out of cardboard) are available with colorful, bright illustrations of familiar objects. Some new ones on the market include books on colors, shapes, and letters. Action songs—"The Wheels on the Bus," "Johnnie Hammers with One Hammer," and a simple version of the "Hokey-Pokey"—are always hits. Toddlers love to put their hand into a mystery bag or box and try to guess what they feel with their fingers. Dress-up clothes have large buttons, snaps, or zippers so children can fasten them themselves and for others. Get large cardboard blocks (or make some from empty milk cartons). Begin with some basic shapes in unit and table blocks. Find items toddlers can fit together, such as clean plastic bottles with their lids or egg cartons and colorful plastic eggs (with surprises inside the eggs).

Mealtimes will be messy, but young toddlers can begin to feed themselves with increasing skill—and they certainly won't learn unless you give them the chance to practice. Likewise, learning to use the toilet may result in a few accidents. That's part of life. Enlist children's help to clean up.

On the other hand, you do not expect toddlers to write with a pencil, to color between the lines, to use water colors, to build with tiny plastic blocks, to draw on small sheets of paper, to make realistic looking art products, or to feed themselves thin soups. Why? Because toddlers hands and fingers are not yet ready for such difficult tasks. Nor are their minds ready to deal with abstract paper-and-crayon tasks imposed on them. Match your expectations to their development.

All young children are much more interested in the **doing** rather than in coming up with an end product. Doing is real learning.

List here some good activities that are always available for toddlers' muscle development. Remember to balance active and quiet play.

Review these with your CDA Field Advisor.

Preschool children. By the age of 3 or 3½, children's legs and arms are becoming quite well coordinated. They can use low riding vehicles with pedals easily and are ready to drive around increasingly difficult obstacle courses. Preschoolers can climb and swing their bodies in the air. They want to learn how to do forward rolls and other more complicated things with their bodies.

Shou-min chooses to paint at the easel almost every day. He gets his smock from the hook and asks a friend to button it in back for him. He makes sure there are at least four colors and four 1-inch brushes in the tray. Then he uses tiny strokes with the side of the brush to make intricate designs. Some days he will use broad strokes as well. Once in a while, he paints over everything and crumples up the paper. On other days, he puts his name on a corner of the paper and hangs it to dry.

Preschoolers also love to run and chase (play "Follow the Leader;" "Duck, Duck, Goose;" or tag), to stand at the top of the high slide, to play catch—be sure to include different types of games from around the world. At this age, cooperation in physical activities is far more important than competition.

Building becomes much more intricate during these years. Preschoolers plan and carry out elaborate ideas with blocks. They need lots of unit blocks in many different shapes. Large hollow blocks are wonderful if your budget will allow them. Smaller building blocks—such as interlocking plastic blocks, wooden logs, and

Potential contributions of blocks for early childhood curriculum*

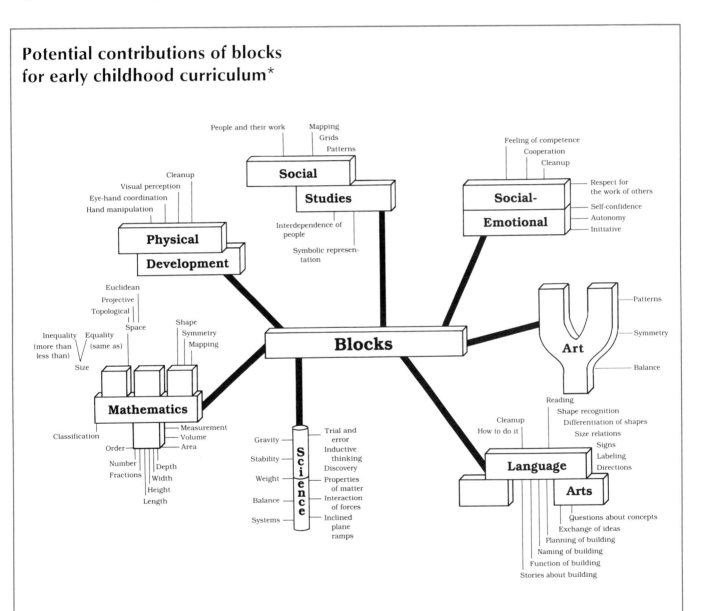

*Adapted from Charlotte and Milton Brody. *The Block Book* (1st ed.) (1974) edited by Elisabeth S. Hirsch. National Association for the Education of Young Children, 1834 Connecticut Avenue, N.W., Washington, DC 20009.

Fine motor coordination improves greatly during the preschool years. Preschoolers can work puzzles with more and more pieces.

stick-together pieces — add yet another dimension for building with small muscles.

Hardwood unit blocks are a superb investment. They last for generations. Best of all, they have **unlimited potential for learning** in nearly every area of children's development: physical, socioemotional, math, science, social studies, art, and language arts, for example. Pat Hutchins' book, *Changes, Changes*, if read to preschoolers, can change their imagination play with blocks.

Fine motor coordination improves greatly during the preschool years. Every few months, 4-year-olds can work puzzles with more and more pieces. Wooden or rubber ones are the sturdiest for hard use in programs, but chil-

dren also enjoy ones you make. Cut up cereal boxes or paste pictures on cardboard and cut them up. Older preschoolers can even make their own puzzles like this.

Woodworking, weaving, sewing, and other fine motor skills begin to appeal to children during these early years. The equipment and materials should always be selected to assure that children can do these projects successfully and safely: Real carpentry tools, large yarn needles, soft woods such as pine for easy hammering and sawing, thick yarn or open-weave fabrics such as burlap or nylon net for sewing — and guidance in how to use all these things properly.

The process of doing these types of activities is far more important than the product — never make children feel they have to make something. Sawing a small board or pasting some yarn on fabric may be all the child is interested in doing. Respect that choice.

Pretend play consumes a great deal of the day for many preschoolers. Props should represent diverse jobs and cultures, so children can try out many different roles. They can use their bodies, hands, and fingers as they play: Buttons can be smaller, children may be ready to tie bows on shoes or aprons, bandages need to be wrapped carefully around those who pretend to be injured. How much they can do by themselves!

Preschoolers also are increasingly interested in identifying and making letters or numbers (with finer markers, regular crayons, or pens). They may want to make signs or write their

Although preschoolers can do a lot with their muscles, there are many so-called educational activities that are really *not* developmentally appropriate:

- Preschoolers should never be expected to form letters and numbers perfectly when they write them. Just encourage children to write the best they can and commend them for their efforts.

- Coloring books, tracing, and drawing with stencils make children feel like failures when their own drawings don't look like the patterns. Give them the materials and see how much more interesting the results are when children use their imaginations.

- Don't make a sample of any art for children to copy, or expect them to paste or assemble shapes that an adult has cut out for them. You can spend hours cutting things out, and the children will finish pasting all those pieces in 3 minutes. Why not let the children do their own cutting? And while children can try (if they want) to cut on the lines they draw, don't expect perfection every time.

- Jumping rope and riding two-wheel bicycles call for an incredible amount of balance and coordination of arm and leg muscles, so most preschoolers find it too difficult. Team sports with lots of rules, such as baseball, football, or soccer, are beyond preschoolers' physical and social skills. Bring out the balls and let children make up their own games or just plain exercise!

names on their artwork. Drawings and clay sculptures, for example, start to look more realistic, but most preschoolers are still far more interested in what they are doing than what the final product looks like.

Preschoolers love to cut and paste and glue all kinds of things together—discards such as fabric scraps, leaves, packing chips, bits of yarn, pictures children cut out of old magazines or catalogs are some of the best art materials available.

List several developmentally appropriate muscle development activities and materials that should be offered every day for preschoolers:

_____

_____

_____

_____

Your CDA Field Advisor will want to see your list.

Develop children's senses

The whole world awaits children through their senses—hearing, smell, taste, sight, and touch. Right from birth, we can support the development of—but be careful not to overstimulate—children's senses. If you know or work with children who have limitations such as vision or hearing difficulties, you truly can appreciate just what an important learning tool our senses are.

Hearing. Children's ears open the door to spoken language and to music. Infants are responsive to sound before they are born. They recognize their mother's voice within days. You will want to talk and sing with infants, using their home language as much as possible. Even if you are slightly off key, they will love the sound of your voice.

Play pleasing music from several cultures to acquaint them with a variety of sounds and beats. Within the first few months, infants begin to hear and repeat things that are funny—

they can blow "raspberries" (make a sputtering kiss), create strange noises, and imitate squeak toys.

Continue to introduce more wonderful things to hear throughout the early years. Choose real musical instruments that sound pleasing and that children can play with the skills they have. If they're making music together in a band, give each child a chance to play every instrument as they seem interested.

Preschoolers might enjoy spooky sounds on a record at Halloween or any other time of year. One game young children enjoy is to guess what made a familiar sound—a door closing, the Jack-in-the -Box popping up, or a friend's voice. Keep the game brief and the children involved in making the sounds.

Language is a joy for all ages. Talk gently to babies during diapering. Use many different ways to express ideas—elaborate on your own language. Speak and sing in the preferred languages of the child's family, including signing or cueing for those who are hearing impaired. Use short poems about topics that intrigue children, including some that don't rhyme. Tell stories with a flannel board or puppets, making sure the characters are diverse.

Read books to just two or three children so it is an intimate experience for everyone. Use lots of expression when you read and make sure children can see the pictures. Let children retell the story into a tape recorder and then listen to themselves. Read from books written in languages other than English, or ask parents to translate some favorites for you. Your local

When you read books to children, make sure they can see the pictures.

librarian is a tremendous resource for you to check for finding all sorts of books and materials.

Remember to use language a little more advanced than the children's, particularly when working with children learning a second language. Children benefit from hearing language varieties and complexities well before they can use them themselves.

Children rarely listen with only their ears—their whole bodies seem to want to respond to music and words. Action songs and moving or dancing to music are marvelous for young children. Make sure the words are appropriate, just as you choose children's books that do not stereotype others.

Listening to the teacher's voice is not the only important listening children do. **Children need to talk with each other as they play.** An appropriate classroom is one that buzzes with busy children's voices. Children learn from each other and from expressing themselves with words. Adults should never dominate children's conversations during play.

List some appropriate activities that you offer every day for children to choose to hear.

_____

_____

_____

_____

_____

_____

_____

Talk with your CDA Field Advisor about your choices.

Children are sure to have a more nutritious diet if they can choose from a wide variety of foods.

Smell. Whether the reaction is "Yuck!" or "Now I'm hungry," children learn with their noses. Rather than making up artificial experiences in which children guess what the smell is, try to keep your nose out for everyday smells in real life. Alert the children to the wonders of smell.

"Ummm. How wonderful the freshly cut grass smells! Who can smell the grass?"

"It's almost time for lunch. You know how I know?"

A preschooler points to her nose and shakes her head.

"What do you think we are having?"

"Black beans with rice!"

"Oh, my, we forgot to clean Cocoa Butter's cage yesterday. Who can figure out how I can tell we need to clean it now?"

How much there is to discover about our bodies and the world with our noses!

What was the last smell you talked about with the children in your group? How did they react?

_____

_____

_____

_____

_____

_____

Taste. Since babies will try to put everything into their mouths, your biggest worry will be to make sure they don't taste anything that is unsafe. Wood chips were considered a real delicacy by a 1-year-old boy! Make sure everything they can get to is safe for small mouths.

Children are sure to have a more nutritious diet if they can choose from a wide variety of foods. And the more things they taste, the more likely they will

appreciate many foods. Without being overbearing about it, encourage children to enjoy tasting many different foods.

Every day in a full-day program, you serve at least two snacks and one meal. One snack is always served in a part-day program. You certainly don't need made-up tasting experiences when you already have so many perfect built-in opportunities!

Casually talk about how things taste, what foods taste similar to others, and other topics as you prepare and eat the food. Don't turn the snack or meal into a lesson about the color of the broccoli or the shape of the orange. Just comment on how crunchy, or salty, or sticky something tastes — or wait for children to create a natural learning opportunity.

A 26-month-old, a 3-year-old, and a 5-year-old are eating their morning snack at their family child care provider's home.

The youngest child has never eaten apples with peanut butter. The two older children urge her on.

"Come on, Ashley. Look, you like peanut butter, right? You eat it on crackers all the time. Isn't that yummy? Well, on an apple, it's wetter. Your teeth don't stick together so much."

The 3-year-old gives the recipe. "Take the knife. Take the peanut butter. Smear it on the apple? See?"

Ashley agrees to try just a taste on a very thin slice. She shakes her head. "I want a cracker now," she requests.

Your attitude is the most important factor here. Tastes are just waiting for each of us to discover them. But everyone likes different things.

What new tastes do you want to introduce to the children in your group? How will you do that? What happened when you did? Write your ideas here.

_____

_____

_____

_____

Sight. Most mothers knew better, but some experts used to claim that babies couldn't see much when they were born. Can you imagine?!

You don't want to bombard young babies or overwhelm them, but you do want them to have some interesting things to look at because they can't move around yet. Hang a mobile above the crib and another over the changing table. Be sure to choose or make mobiles that have a interesting view from the baby's viewpoint!

Hang some colorful or high-contrast pictures next to the changing table or play yard or at floor level. Put a mirror in the play yard or along the floor so babies can see themselves. Move babies about frequently so they can watch you and the other children. Choose cardboard books with bold, bright drawings and prop them within view.

Toddlers and preschoolers love colors. Use color when you decorate. Maybe a colorful parachute can be hung above a crawling space. Children's cubbies could be color coded. Keep the tempera paints at the easel fresh (so children can mix them if they want). Offer many colors of construction paper. Make sure crayons and markers have a variety of colors.

Children will learn the names of colors as they use them in their art projects, as they get dressed, and as they notice color used in many ways in real life. Too often, parents and teachers expect children to learn their colors by rote.

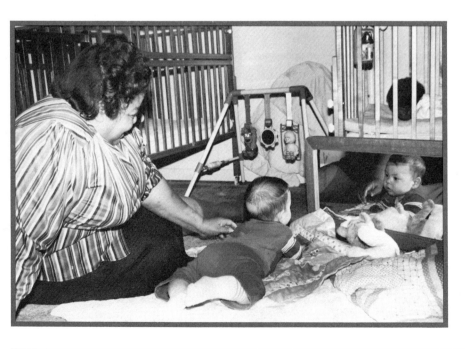

Put a mirror in the play yard or along the floor so babies can see themselves.

Steps to advance children's physical and intellectual competence

But there are so many natural opportunities to use color that it is completely unnecessary to teach colors in lessons. Here are just a few of the ways color can be a part of your daily conversations with children.

"Who wants to wear the yellow apron?"

"We have three different cups for our juice. Verde, azul, rojo. Which color would you like?"

"You look so grown up in your new lavender dress, Laura."

"Today there is a special art activity for anyone who is interested. We have some gorgeous green paper, some sticky paste, and some red and white tissue paper. Who would like to start at the art table? We have space for four children at a time."

Simple children's games often rely on color recognition. Children will catch on fast to the names of colors if they want to play a board game such as "Color Lotto" with their friends.

There are many more things to see than just color, too. Every day, children can be helped to be more aware of the world around them.

Yesterday, you took a group of four toddlers down the street to visit a construction site. Later, you ask the children to choose an activity a lot like something they saw on their visit.
One child begins to work with blocks.
Another drives trucks while wearing a hard hat.
A third digs in the sand table.
A fourth asks for help to write a story. "We saw people making a new place. It was noisy." She dictates the words and you write them down. Then she draws a picture with lots of blue (most of the noisy machines were blue).

Children can learn so much through their eyes. Field trips provide new things to see. They should be planned often, well organized, and appropriate for the children's ages and interests (short and not too far away, for example).
You can provide many related but **real**

Through their bodies, children grow and learn.

experiences, before and after the trip, to help children make sense of what they see. You may need to read a book, or show pictures, or talk about what they might see (or hear or touch or smell). A thank you note from the children (either one they dictate or their drawings of what they saw, for example) is always appreciated.

What are some of the most interesting things happening in your program's neighborhood?

_____

_____

_____

_____

Sometime within the next week, take the children on a walking trip to see one of these things. What are some preparation and follow-up activities that will help make the experience more meaningful to the children?

_____

_____

_____

_____

Talk with your Advisor about what happened.

Touch. Scratchy whiskers, soft baby skin, warm toast, smooth velvet, juicy peaches — **real** things are waiting for children to feel them! Rather than teaching children with abstract things like pictures of these objects, make sure the materials in your room have a variety of hard/soft, cool/warm, rough/smooth textures. Children will naturally experience these in their play.

Then, when a child announces, "Mrs. Duvall, these crackers have little bumps on them," you will be prepared. What would you say?

_____

_____

What new textures can you add to your teaching environment?

_____

_____

_____

_____

Through their bodies, children grow and learn. In all the examples and ideas just discussed, did you recognize the beginnings of school subjects such as science, social studies, reading, and mathematics? Children are learning about these ideas through active, sensory experiences in **meaningful, integrated** ways, rather than as isolated, unrelated, teacher-structured activities.

All through this section, we have found how children's physical development overlaps with their intellectual and socioemotional development. We have talked about how to involve children in active learning with real objects at their own level. We have seen how you can help them build on their experiences to learn even more by relying on their natural curiosity. *This is how you teach and how children begin their long journey toward making the most of their lives now and in the future.*

Before we move on, **really think** about these principles and how any activity, no matter what it is, can contribute to all areas of children's development at once. Look at the following chart about woodworking. Then using another activity area, think about your learning goals for children in each area of development.

Goals for children's learning through woodworking

Cognitive

1. To develop relationship thinking: cause and effect; relatedness of things, feelings, activities; classification.

2. To understand number concepts through concrete use of counting, one-to-one correspondence, awareness of simple shapes, comparison of size, experience with metric measure in three dimensions.

3. To know and use wood and tools with purpose and satisfaction.

4. To experience joy in discovery, in active learning, in striving to find out information children need for their own purposes.

5. To increase communication skills through talking about woodworking and tools, reading directions or labels.

6. To solve problems through divergent thinking and planning creatively with three-dimensional wood constructs.

Physical

1. To develop and coordinate large and small muscle, delight in movement and rhythm, feel competent in motor control and skill achievement.

2. To master physical woodworking skills: measuring, hammering, sawing, planing, filing, finishing.

3. To expand sense through smells, textures, and sounds of woodworking.

Goals for children's learning through woodworking, continued

Emotional

1. To build strong, positive feelings about self.
2. To foster ability to meet new situations well.
3. To learn to sustain interest and overcome frustration successfully.
4. To become open and sensitive to feelings in self and others.
5. To expand intuitive learning through self-directed creativity such as feeling and testing hunches about performance of wood, tools, co-workers.
6. To [enjoy] satisfying firsthand experience with wood and tools.

Social

1. To cooperate with others.
2. To learn to grasp and follow rules for the safety of others as well as for oneself.
3. To accept differences among children with understanding and compassion.
4. To achieve satisfying friendships.
5. To sense responsibility to the group and status gained from this.
6. To experience joy in . . . group accomplishment.
7. To achieve a deeply felt awareness that authority and group structure can promote individual fulfillment.

These goals are guidelines along which children may venture in their own way and at their own pace.

Note: Adapted from *Woodworking for Young Children* (p. 2–3) by P. Skeen, A. P. Garner, and S. Cartwright, 1984, Washington, DC: National Association for the Education of Young Children. Copyright © 1984 by National Association for the Education of Young Children. Reprinted by permission.

Now, on page 296, choose another activity area and try to identify three learning goals for children in each area of development. Discuss your ideas with your Field Advisor.

Goals for children's learning through _____

Cognitive

1. _____

2. _____

3. _____

Physical

1. _____

2. _____

3. _____

Emotional

1. _____

2. _____

3. _____

Social

1. _____

2. _____

3. _____

The next long-term goal is to enable children to communicate. Let's see what activities and materials lead children to improve their skills in this area.

You enable children to use words, music, and art to communicate with others

The very youngest babies communicate by crying. As they grow older, they smile and look at you in the eye. Next they use gestures, and before you know it, they are talking. Soon they will be reading and writing.

All through human civilization, language is used to communicate. Literature, plays, poetry, finger plays, conversation, nursery rhymes—all are language. Sometimes what we want to get across is best expressed not through words alone, but through music or art. Parents and teachers help children become more fully human by using all of these tools to communicate their thoughts and feelings.

Strengthen children's use of spoken language

Before we look at specifics about how to promote children's language, look back at the developmental milestones chart in Unit 2. Refresh your memory about what communicative and expressive behaviors are typical for children at different ages—they change so fast during the first few years.

Also remember that children develop at their own pace and in their own style. Look at your daily diary for the children in your care—or at your summarized notes in Unit 3 for each child. You can probably pick out which children seem especially verbal, which ones are intent listeners, and who uses lots of nonverbal communication.

You use all of this information to figure out

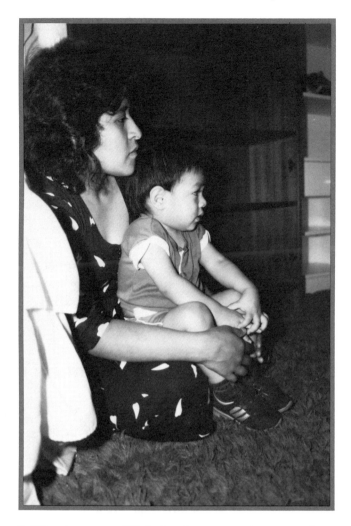

Building language skills in two languages at once requires specific strategies. Your goal is to strengthen children's ability to continue to be bilingual.

what to expect for each child and to decide on the best ways to facilitate each child's learning. The strategies we suggest here for helping children learn language should all be incorporated into your daily activities as naturally as possible.

Teach more than one language. Many of the principles of good practice discussed in early childhood education and throughout *Essen-*

tials apply to children who speak only one language—the same language of the society in general. But you are well aware that, although English is the official language of this country, many families speak other languages at home and within their neighborhoods and communities. When more than one language is an issue in your program, it is important to understand how to use those principles as well as some additional ones.

We have already talked about how important to children's social and emotional development it is to foster development in their own family's culture and to respect parents' choice about what language they want to use to communicate with their children. This consideration is also important *from a language development standpoint*, because building language skills in two languages at once requires some specific strategies.

Following are some suggestions of teaching strategies that support language development in children of non-English-speaking families.

Working with non-English Speaking children

by Pam Schiller and Andrea B. Bermudez

. . . . While most English-speaking children continue to use the same language and learning styles when they enter child care or school, limited English proficient (LEP) children often experience an abrupt change. Therefore, it is important that caregivers . . . assist LEP children in making this transition.

These four items are a base for work with LEP children.

- Oral and written language proficiency in English as a second language cannot be attained unless the child's first language is strengthened.

- Involving parents in the learning experience of LEP children is necessary to establish continuity between home and school.

- Self-concept in children is the key to success in learning. However, what makes up a positive self-concept for children may vary from culture to culture.

- Learning, motivational, and problem-solving styles are different among cultures and different within cultures.

Oral and written language proficiency

Preschool children have great imagination, and they explore ideas by reaching out physically as well as verbally. As a result, language development goes hand in hand with creativity and intellectual ability.

At the same time they are expanding their native language, LEP children are faced with learning a new language, English. This challenge can be overwhelming unless children are allowed to experience activities in the language that is comfortable. A good way for children to use both languages is to introduce English gradually and not assume that an all-English classroom will happen overnight.

Besides contributing to creativity and intellectual ability, the comfortable language can promote a child's social development during the preschool years. Caregivers recognize that 2-year-olds who bite or hit or behave in other unacceptable ways are probably frustrated because they cannot use language to express their thoughts and emotions. This frustration also occurs in older preschool children who are acquiring a new language and may lead to unacceptable behavior from them, too.

The caregiver's role is to change obstacles into opportunities. Assume, for example, that two children are building a ranch house in the block center, and a third child with LEP comes over and starts playing with blocks on the floor. The two children get angry and demand that he stop. Unable to ask why the children are angry, he kicks the blocks and starts to leave. An observant caregiver will take the third child by the hand and explain that the blocks on the shelf are available for playing, and suggest that he build a corral for horses.

Involving parents

Any successful preschool program will have a high level of cooperation and communication between center and family. This is particularly true for non-English-speaking families.

Despite the best intentions, the majority of school programs . . . have difficulty incorporating parent expectations for their children's schooling. It takes a sensitive caregiver to recognize, for example, that a certain Hispanic child never asks questions or speaks up because his parents value respect for authority and view questions as rude interruptions. Or that a Vietnamese child is reluctant to use her native language because her parents believe their children should speak only English in school. . . .

Balancing individual needs and capabilities with the goals of parent involvement is a delicate task. Parents of language minority children usually cannot communicate in the language of the center and, in many cases, do not understand their rights and responsibilities in the education of their children. Where possible, for example, the center might ask a volunteer translator to interpret for non-English-speaking parents at parent meetings and children's programs.

In many families, the parents are working full time. After-work opportunities for conferences and other activities are essential if working parents are to get involved.

Self-concept variations

Self-expression is a critical aspect of self-esteem. This makes language a focal point in the development of self-concept in all groups.

Children's abilities to express themselves are strongly related to . . . cooperation, sharing, respect for others, and similar behaviors. Their prosocial behavior, in turn, is strongly related to positive self-esteem.

In order for LEP children to gain confidence

socially, they must be able to interact with others in a language with which they feel comfortable and in command. A sensitive caregiver will allow LEP children to communicate in their own way during social interaction with other children. . . .

Independent play and outdoor play offer excellent opportunities for children to interact with each other in the comfortable language. A caregiver must give verbal as well as non-verbal support to LEP children in both languages. . . .

Learning, motivational, and problem-solving styles

Cognitive behavior involves the ability to use prior knowledge to solve new problems. It is a child's attempt to make sense of the world.

Cognitive development for LEP children is basically the same as for children who only speak one language. Because language and cognitive development are closely linked, LEP children must have an opportunity to express their thoughts in the language that is comfortable for them. For example, when describing the events in a story a caregiver has just finished, LEP children need opportunities to discuss the events in both languages. Children do not organize thoughts in the same way across cultures, so what LEP children may select as important may not agree with the caregiver's . . . .

Challenging children is essential to motivation. Children who feel that caregivers' expectations are low or too simple will often fail to strive. On the other hand, if expectations are too high, children stop trying.

Children feel successful if they use their first language in their cognitive achievements and social interactions. As children begin to use the English language, caregivers should focus on ideas expressed rather than on language choice. For example, if Carmen says, "I have hungry," caregivers should reward the effort rather than correct her use of grammar or pronunciation.

In addition, to promote prosocial development, caregivers should encourage children to communicate in the best way they can. Discouraging the use of the comfortable language can limit a child's prosocial development and hinder self-confidence. . . .

Note: Condensed from *Texas Child Care Quarterly*, Winter 1988, 12(3), 3–8. Copyright ©1988 by Texas Department of Human Services. Reprinted with permission.

There are a number of different views about which strategies are best, and with experience, you will select among them the ones that are most appropriate for you and your particular group of families. In general, however, you should start by understanding that in order to adapt your teaching strategies to match children's experiences, you must learn to distinguish between children who are **monolingual** and children who are **bilingual**.

The ALERTA program—Strategies for language teaching and learning

For acquisition of a second language by monolingual speakers

1. Work on those concepts children already know in their first language.
2. Introduce a limited amount of new vocabulary at one time.
3. Imbed new vocabulary in a natural context.
4. Use "action" activities.
5. Use objects familiar to the children.
6. Allow children to manipulate and explore the objects.
7. Provide opportunities for natural repetition. Do **not** use drill.
8. Use songs and games as frequently as possible.

Further development of a second language in bilingual children

1. Plan stimulating activities.
2. Provide many opportunities for children to speak.
3. Introduce new concepts in the dominant language.
4. Imbed new vocabulary in a natural context.
5. Use open-ended questions as much as possible.
6. Use concrete objects in the activities.
7. Allow children to manipulate and explore the objects.
8. Provide opportunities for natural repetition. Do **not** use drill.
9. Use songs and games as frequently as possible.
10. Listen **carefully** for gaps in language and for stages in language learning.

Note: From *ALERTA: A Multicultural, Bilingual Approach to Teaching Young Children* (p. 210) by L. R. Williams and Y. De Gaetano, 1985, Menlo Park, CA:Addison-Wesley Publishing Company, Inc. Copyright © 1985 by Addison Welsey. Reprinted by permission.

Monolingual children speak only one language, but you want them to learn a second. Young children are quite capable of learning a second language easily, and they do it much the same way they learned their first one. They spend time listening—a few weeks or even 4 to 6 months—then begin to use one- or two-word sentences Some children will suddenly stop speaking their first language. Concerned parents may be astonished that their child refuses to speak to them except in English. "English! Read to me in English . . . I don't hear Spanish!"

This may cause family stress, so be open to discussing this issue with parents. Assure them that you provide plenty of reinforcements for the use of both languages at school, and that this resistance is natural and will soon pass. Be sure you make children feel comfortable in the program and convey an acceptance of a child's attempts at speaking the new language. Concentrate on what they are trying to say, rather than the way they say it. Speak naturally. Use one language at a time and use it in the context of first hand experiences. Have fun with languages!

Bilingual children have the ability to speak or at least understand two languages, and you want to build their skills in both. The level of development in the second language will vary from child to child and your observations will be important in deciding what to emphasize with each individual child. Remember, children often understand more complex language than they use—challenge growth by speaking to the child at a more advanced, but appropriate, level of difficulty. Talk, sing songs, and provide learning materials in both languages. Routinely incorporate both languages into daily routines. Encourage children to use either language to express themselves. Provide resources to parents to help them understand the cognitive benefits that bilingual children have over their monolingual counterparts. Your goal is to strengthen their ability to continue to be bilingual!

Spark conversations. All children learn to talk and appreciate the function and beauty of language when they take part in everyday conversations.

"Good morning, DaRoyce. It's so good to see you this morning. When you have your things put away, please find something you would like to play with."

"I already know," the 3-year-old smiles. "I want to play in the water."

"You always enjoy that, don't you?" says Mr. Castillo. "Garrett and Melinda are already at the water table."

"We need more bottles," DaRoyce points out as he joins the group.

"Who would like to help me get some more plastic bottles for the water table?" asks their teacher. All three children volunteer to help carry them.

As they walk to the closet, Melinda comments, "Let's get that blue one with the funny lid."

"Yeah, and the one with the top cut off. To pour," adds Garrett."

"Let's paste," Nicole says to her friend 5-year-old Shailee.

They eagerly go to the

art area. Shailee searches through the labeled boxes on the shelf. "Here it is. Let's paste with these bea-u-ti-ful ribbons."

"OK. And here are some sequins we could add, too," suggests Nicole.

"Y hojas secas," adds Shailee.

"We can make a wonderful picture. What color of paper do you want to paste on, Shailee?" asks Nicole as she reaches on the shelf for a blue sheet for herself.

"Thara, it's time for a clean diaper. Let's go change you. Christopher just got a fresh diaper, and now it's your turn. Here we go!" Patricia, the community volunteer, picks up 9-month-old Thara.

"Would you like to talk on this little telephone while we change you? That's it, wrap your fingers around it tightly so it doesn't drop. Here's your clean diaper, and here are your wipes."

Thara holds the toy phone near the top of her head—she's getting the idea! Patricia picks up on her motions. "Ringgg. Ringgg. Hello, Thara. It's Patricia calling."

"Aaammm," replies Thara.

"Now we are taking off your soiled diaper. Into the trash it goes. What have you been doing this morning?"

Thara responds with, "Dadada. Bbbbaa."

"Oh, you've been looking in the mirror and making funny faces. You and Preston were trying on some hats."

"MMMM," smiles Thara.

"And then you played the drums. BOOM, BOOM, BOOM—here comes the marching band."

Gabriel, almost 3, arrives with four pussy willow sticks in his hand. The children crowd around him, eager to feel the softness.

Quietly, their teacher begins one of her favorite poems:

I know a little pussy
Her coat is silver gray
She lives down in the meadow
Not very far away.

She'll always be a pussy,
She'll never be a cat,
For she's a pussy willow.
Now what do you think of that?

The children immediately calm down. Later, several ask for cotton balls so they can make their own

Talk **with** children, not *at* them.

pussy willows. They talk about the soft cotton and the hard sticks, and about cats, and about their favorite songs, while they work. Some of the children ask their teacher to write the poem on their artwork.

SPONTANEOUS. That's what most language with young children should be. Just fun conversation as they play together, as you go about your daily routines with them such as diapering or eating together, and as you pick up on their interests. Talk **with**, not *at* children. Mostly **listen**. With all children, use the kind of language you want them to use. And make sure they talk with each other.

Children need lots of time to choose what they want to play with, to talk with each other, to tell you what they need, to ask questions, to talk about feelings, to do finger plays, to say nursery rhymes, to play games with words, **and a little time** to listen attentively to adults.

While they talk and play, alone or with each other, you move about the room or playground. Sometimes you sit on the floor or grass. You are always available and you step in when children are in danger of hurting themselves or others. You set up the environment and the children use it to learn.

Sometimes, as you walk through the areas where children are playing, *you don't say anything* because you don't want to interfere and are not needed. You observe what is happening and make written or mental notes on children's development or ideas for future activities. You see many children talking together.

Sometimes, when it seems just right, *you comment briefly on what is happening* — being

sure not to interrupt the activity. You might say, "That's really hard to get those shapes in the right holes. You keep trying and trying, and then one fits!" And then you watch the child work or listen as the child talks.

You might expand on something a child said or did, adding new or different words to express the same idea. "Baby. Yes, that's baby Rachel. She is Jonathan's sister." Or you could repeat a child's statement, but in a second language. "Nuestra planta necesita más agua. Yes, our plant needs more water."

Sometimes you might give the child a chance to hear an idea expressed more appropriately.

You hear a child say, "He don't pick it up."

You reply, "You've noticed, he *didn't* pick up the car. He left it on the floor where we could step on it. What should we say to him about the car?"

If you change a child's use of words by directly saying, "Don't say *don't*. That's not right. You should say *didn't*," you make the child feel incompetent. Instead, just gently repeat whatever you think is a better word usage.

Children will begin to see how language styles change depending on the situation. For example, the language of the Black community or a dialect of Spanish may be expected at home and in the neighborhood, but standard English usages may be expected in elementary school. Children can easily learn both styles without feeling that one is correct and the other incorrect.

Sometimes you ask questions to help children take their ideas a step further. If children seem to be playing rather aimlessly in the housekeeping area, you might comment, "You are so busy in the kitchen. What are you cooking?" to help lend some direction to their play.

Sometimes you help children solve problems. "What other ways have you tried?" or "How can we find out?" or "Why do you think it's not working?" If children ask, "What letter does Dad begin with?" you respond with a brief introduction to the relationships between sounds and letters, "D — D — Dad. Dad begins with a D."

In many instances, **YOU DON'T TELL, YOU LISTEN.** You encourage children to use their own language to figure things out for themselves or to express themselves in creative and clear ways. Your questions lead children to think up their own ideas.

And of course, *you always speak in ways that give children an appropriate model.* You never use baby talk. Your goal is to help children want to express themselves freely in language — one or more. It takes a long time to learn all the rules. They'll learn the accepted usage in their community when they hear it often.

Build vocabularies with real experiences. Word games — making up silly or rhyming words, for example — can be lots of fun for preschoolers. Older infants are always asking *"Dat?"* ("What's that?").

Toddlers want to know *why?* Preschoolers try to figure out *how?* Perhaps a child has learned a new game or song that is part of a grandparent's heritage. It may be in another language. Ask the child to help you teach it to the other children, or invite a relative to assist both of you.

Pick up on children's cues and use what you know about language development to broaden children's vocabularies and experiences. Take advantage of every *teachable moment* — they happen all day long every day when you know what to look for:

The children find a fuzzy worm on the playground. You ask, "How can we find out what kind of worm it is and whether it will become a butterfly?"

Or a child starts to hum an unfamiliar tune. When you mention it, the child says his aunt is visiting from Japan and she taught him a song.

Or, when you ask, "What is the best way to fix the greens that Lanette's mother brought?" several children offer suggestions.

Your **curriculum really is what happens** because you and your schedule are flexible and can make the best of every situation. Some things you plan, others happen on the spur of the moment. But you don't want to miss any great opportunities for learning.

If you have not already done so, start now to collect your favorite finger plays and word games to use with children. List three of your favorites here:

_____

_____

_____

You might want to keep these on file cards, in

a notebook, or in an accordion file. Try to add at least one new word game or finger play to your collection each week. Don't limit yourself just to English. Use these creative and expressive forms of language frequently and informally with your children.

Recall at least one _teachable moment_ with words that happened within the last week. What did you do to help the children get the most from the experience?

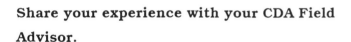

Share your experience with your CDA Field Advisor.

Strengthen children's use of written language

In addition to spoken words, children encounter written words. The first word of real interest is usually their own name—labels on clothes, lunches, or backpacks. Toddlers begin to recognize the first letter and then later all the letters, especially if more than one child's name begins with the same letter. Preschoolers learn each other's names after a few weeks of seeing them on their artwork and cubbies.

Children also see signs in the classroom that help them know what a play area is for and how

Children who have lots of experience with books during their preschool years are more successful when they learn how to read and write in elementary school.

many children can fit in it comfortably: "Discovery Area: Space for 3 children." Children will soon want to know: What are the words? How many are _three?_

Soon they want to make a label for their castle. Or write a list of things to take on a field trip. As you measure windows for new curtains, they ask you what the numbers on the yardstick mean.

Written words and numbers are everywhere they look and when children are ready, you are ready to help them make connections between written and spoken words.

Use books. People of all ages love to read and hear stories. Young children love books—even babies. Just watch their faces when you read!

What do children learn when they have lots of experiences with books? According to one expert, infants, toddlers, and preschoolers. . . learn

- how books work,
- that print should make sense,
- that print and speech are related in a specific way,
- that book language differs from speech, and
- that books are enjoyable.

(Schickedanz, 1986, pp. 38–39)

Children naturally absorb these things every day as they handle books and as you read with them. There is no question that **children who have lots of experience with books during their preschool years are more successful when they learn how to read and write in elementary school.**

When you plan your learning environment, the book area should invite children to enter. Provide a carpet to sit on, some pillows, a child-sized rocker, and maybe some pictures of children reading books.

Low, open shelves are always the best way to display any items—children can easily see what their choices are and can return the book when they are finished. Book covers should always face the children. For babies, you might stand books on the floor. One teacher found a discarded greeting card display stand to hold books. Of course, commercial book racks are also available, but unless you have a generous budget, your money is better spent on books themselves.

Be sure to include a variety of types of books so each child can find something appealing. In order to build up their own collections, some teachers suggest that parents donate a book in the child's name instead of sending trinkets for birthday parties at the center or family child care home.

Choose books that meet the criteria we discussed in Unit 3. Books should always portray positive, authentic images of all people. Illustrations should be pleasing to look at so children learn to appreciate art as well as literature. Choose simple, bright, uncluttered picture books with themes that convey the messages and ideas we want children to learn: how to be friends, the world is a diverse and interesting place to live, constructive ways to deal with difficulties, information about how things work.

Go to the book area often as you move about during the day. Sit on the floor to chat or read. Children are always attracted to places where interesting things are happening.

What can you do to make your book area cozy and inviting?

_____

_____

_____

_____

Books for infants

Infant's books should have fat cardboard pages with rounded edges or be made of plastic or fabric because infants will chew on them. Prop books up so nonmobile children can see the bright pictures.

Once children can sit by themselves, they can safely hold books and begin to try to turn the pages—these are early physical development and reading skills!

How to read stories to babies

- Get the baby's attention. ("Oh, look!")
- Ask the baby a labeling question. ("What's that?")
- Wait for the baby to answer, or if necessary, provide or elaborate upon the answer. ("Yes, that's a monkey, isn't it?")
- Provide feedback. ("Well, it is brown like a dog, but that's a monkey. Monkeys have *long* tails.")

Note: From *More Than the ABCs: The Early Stages of Reading and Writing* (p. 34) by J. Schickedanz, 1986, Washington, DC: National Association for the Education of Young Children. Copyright © 1986 by National Association for the Education of Young Children. Reprinted by permission.

Books for toddlers

Toddlers especially enjoy simple stories about things that happen to them (toilet learning, going to the doctor) and about animals. They are curious about *why* things happen. Pictures hold their attention as well as the words.

They love books that repeat the same words or rhyme. They are beginning to understand that events happen in order. And they can begin to take care of books in responsible ways: turn pages gently, keep the pages clean, return books to the shelf when finished.

Read to groups of two or three children and don't be embarrassed to use different voices for each character! Really enjoy reading and make it a fun time for the children.

Books for preschoolers

By this age, if children have been read to often, they have learned a great deal about books. They are ready for stories with plots— real and pretend. They can find adventure, surprise, silly words, and scary situations (with reassuring endings) between a book's covers.

If you pause during a familiar story, they can fill in a word or a sentence. Or stop a new book just as the action gets exciting and ask the children: "Now what do you think will happen?" Or pause before you turn a page to heighten the suspense.

Preschoolers may become interested in "Where does it say that?" Show children the words they are interested in with your finger, reading each word as you go.

And remember, although preschoolers can sit longer for a lively or enchanting story, it's still a good idea to keep the group small.

Books are best when they are read to small, cozy groups. Children can sit on the floor or in your lap. For a larger group, you sit on a chair so children can see all the pictures and hear your voice.

Children should always be active participants, not just passive listeners when you read together. Make each book come alive! Roar with the lions! Laugh heartily! Whisper to build suspense. Encourage children to play out what happens.

Ask questions that make children think about the story—not to recall specific facts. Ask questions that begin with *why*, or *how*. Or have children think up different ways the story could have ended. Talk about how the book made children feel and why. Maybe a child will want to retell the story using the flannel board or translate it to their home language. Enjoy the adventure of every book with young children through spontaneous conversations.

Building a good collection of books for your program might take a little time. Books are expensive, and while paperbacks are more affordable, they won't withstand the wear of lots of young hands turning their pages. You might want to buy some of the best children's literature and supplement the selection from the library.

Libraries, too, very often have outreach programs. These vary and can usually be tailored to the needs of your center or family day care home. Librarians might make a site visit and do a story program to your class; they might speak to the parents about appropriate reading and what might be used with a given age of children; they might offer to train the teachers in storytelling and give some insight on some techniques for using puppets and flannel boards to accompany storytelling.

Use your daily diary notes to decide what book topics might be of interest to your children. List them here and check out some books on those topics from the library on your next trip.

What changes can you make in your program to ensure that *each day* children get to know books in ways that spark their interest in people, places, things, and most of all learning to read themselves?

Discuss your ideas with your CDA Field Advisor.

Set up a writing area. As children become familiar with words written by others, they are eager to learn to write themselves. Their early attempts may look like scribbles—but those scribbles are **SO** important to the children's over-all development. Sometimes children will call their marks "writing," sometimes they call them "drawings." At this early age, there may not be much difference between the two. *What's important is that they are learning to make connections about verbal and nonverbal ways to communicate.* Value these early attempts to use symbols—children have done it themselves.

When children begin to see the relationship between spoken language and print, they are eager to write shopping lists, train tickets, traffic signs, names on artwork, and on and on!

Many older toddlers or preschoolers ask to make their own books or to write their own stories. They may want to draw the pictures—you may need to write down the story they dictate. This is called an experience story, because it is based on the child's experience, even if it is an imaginary one. Some 5-year-olds might even want to try to write their own experience stories, using a typewriter or computer if one is available. When children write or dictate experience stories, they choose words that are powerful for them—capture each one!

While you will want to include writing materials at least in the pretend play area (to write lists or make signs or write prescriptions, for example) and in the art area, you may want to set up a special writing area as well.

Set up a small table and a chair or two in the writing area, and add some posters to make the space look appealing. Visit the area often yourself and be sure to be available whenever children have questions or need help with their writing.

You might even help a child make a personal dictionary, perhaps on index cards, of words that the child uses often, or of words in both of the languages being learned. Sometimes children appreciate a list of how to make each letter of the alphabet.

Every area in your program should be open to children by choice—never treat writing, or any other learning activity, as an assignment. When

What items do you need for a writing area?

- Pencils (thick lead for 3- and 4-year-olds, thinner leads with erasers for 5-year-olds).
- Watercolor markers with thin tips.
- Plain paper.
- Envelopes (ask parents to save their junk mail).

You can even pack everything in a box or suitcase for children to take home with them overnight. Other writing supplies such as chalk, colored paper, scissors, or paste are easy to get from the art area and can be added to the writing area if children use them frequently.

children are interested in figuring out how print works, they will get involved.

Provide children with good models of print. Print neatly yourself. Use capital letters for the first letters of names, and lower-case letters when they are appropriate. As you write, and if the child seems interested, talk about the sounds some of the letters make. Make your own writing accurate—check your spellings if you are unsure.

Encourage children to use *invented spelling*—children write down the letters they hear in the word. You'll be amazed how easy it is to read, and rest assured they will learn to spell properly when they are older. Just enjoy what the children write. As their muscles and minds mature, they will be able to write in ways that are more legible. For now, you want to keep children's interest and self-confidence at a peak.

Fill children's lives with print. When children are surrounded by language and print, they see how it is used and it begins to become familiar. You don't expect young children to learn to read, but you do expect them to feel comfortable with words—ideas and feelings—both spoken and written, in one or more languages.

One important factor in nurturing eager readers is for them to see others reading. Encourage parents to read to their children and to read to themselves for pleasure. Let children see them reading books, magazines, cereal boxes, recipes, instruction manuals, grocery lists, and coupons.

Print should be a real, everyday feature in your program—not just ABC letters on their plates or sneakers!

Print should be a **real, everyday** feature in your program—not just ABC letters on their plates or sneakers!

Instead, look for real uses of print. Labels on boxes and cans . . . directions for how to put something together . . . a chart or simple schedule . . . Maybe you play the piano or autoharp with music in front of you . . . you use the telephone book or the parent list to look up a number . . . you make a list of children who want to use an activity area that is temporarily full . . . you write a grocery or other list of supplies you need . . . you write children's names on their artwork. Help children see how print is used in everything they do.

Remember to expose children to print in various languages. Empty food containers with labels in different languages is one way. Books, magazines, and newspapers are another. When you label things—artwork, areas of the room, or materials—use two languages with a different color for each. The children will eventually ask questions and begin to see how words are written in different languages.

Take a look at the kinds of print that children encounter every day in your program. Make a list of the opportunities you see.

Can you think of new materials or activities to add? List some ideas here.

Keep the activities appropriate. You may have noticed that we haven't used the terms *reading readiness* or *pre-reading skills*. Why? Because reading is not something children do all of a sudden. There is no magical moment when they are "ready" to read or write.

All **real** experiences contribute to children's speaking, reading, and writing skills because they build a foundation of things to talk, and read, and write about. Children learn about language and reading *gradually*.

Therefore, early childhood professionals describe everything we have just talked about as **children's early reading skills**. You are not teaching children to read. You are giving them the foundation of experiences—and the inspiration—to **want** to learn to read.

- Alphabet blocks,
- rubber stamp letters,
- magnetic letters,
- charts of letters,
- alphabet lotto games,
- the ABC song, and
- other so-called readiness materials and activities . . .

. . . We have neglected to mention these kinds of things. Why?

Because they only make sense after children have had lots of experiences with real things and with words in the context of the things they do every day. You may want to include just a few of these items for more mature preschoolers, but none are necessary for children to be well prepared for later reading or for writing.

Infants, toddlers, and young preschool children benefit even less from such abstract materials, so think carefully about purchasing such items for them.

We hope by now it is also clear that we think the activities listed below are unnecessary and inappropriate for young children.

- flashcards
- worksheets
- workbooks
- phonics lessons
- drills

These won't help children reach any of our long-term goals and in fact **can easily turn children off, rather than on, to reading.** Don't take the risk! Make reading really fun and useful.

Parents may ask you about teaching their child to read, or may even pressure you to begin teaching formal phonics. Be prepared to respond with a professional answer about the values of a print-rich environment. Parents can best help their children learn to read by providing listening and word experiences. Singing, talking, reciting rhymes, and reading aloud provide the foundation a child needs to learn to read when he is ready.

Think about these points. Does your program share this view? Discuss this issue with the other staff in your classroom. If they have a different view of reading readiness, describe some developmentally appropriate ways you are learning to invite children to become readers. Tell your Advisor about your progress!

Let's now see how children's music and art can be used to build even further upon their ability to communicate.

Children enjoy the sound of music

SPONTANEOUS. Talking with children is best when it is spontaneous and a natural part of the day. And so is music. Don't wait until 10:15 on Wednesday to sing "The Eentsy Weentsy Spider." If it's raining, sing! If a child brings in some new maracas sent by a relative in Mexico, don't put off playing them until music time. Or if a child brings in a Michael Jackson record—put it on and dance!

What is the best part about music with young children? They love it. And they could care less whether you can carry a tune, or play an instrument, or read music, or even keep on time with the beat. Just enjoy yourselves.

Sing and sing and sing. Sing a lullaby to babies as they fall asleep. . . . When something great happens—a child has just become a new sister or brother—break out in a joyous version of "If You're Happy. . ." When you have spaghetti for lunch, start or finish with "On Top of Spaghetti."

Don't be shy! Stand up, move around, and sing!

A soothing voice can calm a restless baby. A lively version of a favorite song can prolong a playful mood. Songs with motions are fun even when the children can't yet duplicate them all. Most babies like the Bzzzzz and the surprise ending of "I'm Bringing Home a Baby Bumble Bee."

I'm bringing home a baby bumble bee.
(hands cupped and move back and forth)

Won't my Mama be so proud of me?
(big smile)

'Cause I'm bringing home a baby bumble bee.
(hands cupped)

Bzzzzzz!
(finger wiggles through air)

Oooh! It stung me!
(then playfully pokes child)

If you want to teach children a new song, use a recording if you are embarrassed to sing it yourself. Sometimes you can use pictures to help children remember the order of the words.

Lots of times parents are eager to come in to sing with the children and teach some folk songs or songs that reflect their language or heritage. Invite them often to sing in their first language.

Choose songs with lots of action so the children are involved—that's how they learn. "The Wheels on the Bus" is an all-time favorite, and children can add or translate their own verses easily.

Make up songs, too. Children's names with five letters fit nicely in "B-I-N-G-O." Create your own tune and/or words to respond to events with children:

Kelsey is a toddler who always wears dresses, even though you have urged her parents to dress her in play clothes so she can be more active.

Finally one day, when all of her friends are jumping from the third step of the climbing structure, Kelsey feels brave. She stands on the bottom step and bends her knees several times. She holds tightly to the railing. She looks around. And SHE JUMPS!

You greet her great accomplishment by singing joyfully (to the tune of "Old MacDonald"), "Kelsey leaped from the bot-tom step, E-I-E-I-O."

She quickly climbs up and jumps again.

When children first begin to sing, they will probably be off key. Encourage them to try to match the sounds, but do not expect them to really carry a tune until the age of 3 or so. Keep the number of notes to a minimum and if possible stick to fairly low tones (the notes from middle C to the A above it are best). Children's voices are not as high as we sometimes think they are.

Build up your own memorized collection of songs by going to workshops or checking out books and records from the children's section of your library. **When you join your CDA Seminar you can exchange favorite songs with the other participants.**

Teach yourself a new song during the next week. Write the title here.

_____

_____

As soon as you know it well, sing it with your children.

If you can play the piano, or want to learn the guitar or autoharp, these are all excellent instruments to use to accompany children's singing. A drum provides a nice rhythm background for songs. But don't worry if all you have is your voice and the children's.

Whenever possible, have children stand while they sing. Sitting on the floor or in chairs is fine sometimes. Just remember, children need to move while they sing—did you ever see a professional singer sit to perform?

A word of caution. . .

The words to some well-known songs, such as "Ten Little Indians" or "There Was An Old Lady" are demeaning to people. Always check out the words of songs to make sure they meet the same criteria as the books and other learning materials you select. Look for songs that celebrate our diverse heritages!

Find two songs from the culture(s) of the children in your group and two songs from other cultures that you can introduce to your children. Ask parents for their recommendations. List them here and add the music and words to your Professional Resource File.

_____

_____

_____

Groove to the tunes. Young children love to respond to music. Play recordings of a variety of types of music—show tunes, classical, 50s, ethnic, folk, country, contemporary—and watch children's reactions.

Most of the time, children will want to move to the music they hear. They can dance (although some parents may not want their children to participate for religious reasons) or move in other creative ways.

Always offer children a choice of another activity when others do creative movement activities. Children should never feel forced or even gently prodded into doing something that makes them uncomfortable.

Be sure you know how to expect children to be able to move based on their development and any disabilities. Babies might just wave their arms or kick their legs. Toddlers may rock back and forth, twist their whole bodies, or stamp their feet. The "Hokey-Pokey" for toddlers usually goes, "Put your whole body in" so they can follow the directions.

Preschoolers may enjoy more intricate body movements and may want to try dancing with scarves or capes. But young children never lose their interest in songs with lots of motion. Such songs keep children involved during transitions between activities or if a short wait is unavoidable.

Always allow children to think up their own responses to music rather than demonstrating how to be elephants or how to dance like a butterfly, for example. See how many different ways children can express themselves to the sound of music. How boring if they all do the same thing!

Sometimes children will be entranced enough by music to sit quietly to listen to a recording, but don't expect this very often or for very long. Great classics such as "Peter and the Wolf" or portions of "The Nutcracker" are lovely and usually hold their attention. Ask them to listen for something specific or to imagine what is happening.

Live performances can appeal to very young children if the music and setting is right—the performer chooses short pieces, is expressive, and is receptive to children's questions and even requests to try out the instrument. Check with parents—there are probably several who play an instrument, and perhaps some of those instruments are played primarily in other cultures.

Even if you or the visiting performers only took piano lessons as a child, you will seem accomplished to young children. Make sure any guests know to expect young children to get up and move around while they perform.

Making their own music is also a good experience for children learning to communicate.

We have already talked about how to select good, **real** musical instruments that are age appropriate. Slowly build up an orchestra of good instruments that children can play: drums, bells, triangles, wood blocks, tambourines, maracas, rhythm sticks, sandpaper blocks, stick bells, cymbals.

List two new musical experiences for listening and movement that you can introduce to your children—try out different types of music, or, using different versions of old favorites, try out different ways to move.

Tell your CDA Advisor what happened when you tried out your ideas.

Children learn through art

Creating through art is one of the learning experiences through the early years that fosters development in all areas at once. We have seen how children use their arm, hand, and finger muscles in increasingly controlled ways to paint, roll and shape clay, draw, cut, paste, weave, sew . . . the list seems endless. And we have discussed how to encourage and accept individual forms of creative expression to promote social and emotional development.

But in addition to these, children's involvement in creative expression through art—in all its various forms—fosters the intellectual development. As they manipulate materials according to their own ideas, **they actually make and change the world**. This is the most powerful form of human intellectual capability!

Since you have learned to observe children carefully, you are already aware that children can get intensely involved in the creative process of art—they finger paint with intensity (and get paint all over their arms and faces), they carefully select just the right materials to paste on their collage, they mix colors with delight! But children will only be this involved in expressing themselves creatively—and get the most from their experience—if you remember these four important points:

- **What children are doing**, not what they are making, **is the most important thing.** In art, as with all other early childhood activities, the **process** is far more important than any end product. Children need lots of time to see what happens when they do different things with the materials, to test out their

Children learn through art

Physical/perceptual development

Sensitivity to touch

Sight discrimination

Spatial awareness

Body awareness

Eye-hand coordination

Laterality and directionality

Shape, size, color discrimination

Figure-ground orientation

Part-whole discrimination

Fine motor control

Technical skills

Cognitive development

Clarify and elaborate meaning

Relate information and ideas

Put events in sequence

Understand cause and effect

Solve problems

Make decisions

Generalize

Communicate ideas nonverbally

Socioemotional development

Trust

Identity/individuality

Autonomy/independence

Express and deal positively with
    emotions

Extend flexibility

Appreciate beauty

Appreciate and value others' ideas
    and work

Share

Cooperate

Take turns (delay gratification)

Adapt to group needs/interests

Resolve interpersonal conflicts

Acquire interests for leisure time

Note: Adapted from *Art: Basic for Young Children* (p. 108) by L. Lasky and R. Mukerji, 1980, Washington, DC: National Association for the Education of Young Children. Copyright © 1980 National Association for the Education of Young Children. Reprinted by permission.

own ideas, and to mess with the paste or paint or clay. Children need to get messy — they're washable! As they near elementary school age, children naturally become more interested in making a product.

- Keep your expectations appropriate for children's motor skills and cognitive abilities. Not until the end of the preschool years will children's creations begin to resemble what adults think things look like. **Children's art won't necessarily look like anything recognizable, and that's the way it should be**.

That's why it is inappropriate to give children models of objects to copy. For example, a teacher who didn't know better might give preschoolers a toilet paper roll to cover with brown paper, three packing chips to paint green and paste on the roll to look like three frogs on a log, and expect them to duplicate it. With a lot of prodding from the teacher they might be able to make one like the teacher's, but so what?

Children usually have much better ideas of what to do with these art materials, and besides, they may not have the skills to coordinate all those pieces.

Individuality is much more interesting than uniformity. So put out the toilet paper rolls, the brown paper, the packing chips, the green paint, and some paste and see what exciting ideas children come up with on their own.

- Similarly, **children's art should be their own creation.** If they can't do it themselves, it is not an appropriate activity. You don't

Children's art should be their own creation. Give them the raw materials and let them figure out what they want to do with them.

Remember that children's creative art is very personal to them. Respect children's unique creations and you respect children as well!

need to practice cutting and pasting—so don't do it for the children. Let each child use the materials in her or his own unique way. Don't waste your time making a clay bowl for them to copy. **Give children the raw materials** and let them figure out what they want to do with them.

If you have always given children models to copy, the next time you are tempted to do so, just put out the materials and see what wonderful things children can do on their own. If they protest because they are used to being told what to do, just say, "This time, I want you to use your imagination. See what each of you can make with your own ideas."

Children will need some time to get used to your new approach to teaching!

- Art isn't something that happens at 3 p.m. on Thursdays, or any other "art time." **Every time is art time, indoors or outdoors.**

Provide materials. When children arrive in the morning, and throughout the day, they should be able to choose from a wide array of tempting and appropriate creative art materials:

- 18- x 24-inch sheets of plain paper manila paper, white drawing paper, newsprint
- construction paper in many colors and colored tissue paper
- watercolor markers with broad and narrow tips, fat crayons (for older infants and toddlers), regular crayons (for preschoolers)
- blunt-end scissors and paste and/or white glue
- easel, tempera paint (add a few soap flakes so any drips will wash up easily), 1-inch brushes, smocks, newspaper or shower curtain to put under the easel; or make a table easel with a cut-off cardboard box
- modeling dough (make your own to save money)
- collage materials—anything safe: fabric, yarn, packing chips, leaves, buttons, yogurt lids, meat trays, egg cartons, magazines to cut up, paper towel rolls, boxes, paper plates, paper bags
- woodworking—real tools, soft wood (requires close supervision), nails, glue

Each day you will probably also want to offer one or more special art activities for those who are interested. Additional materials will be needed for these occasions:

- finger paints and smooth paper
- sponges for printing
- oil crayons (Craypas)   *continued on page 320*

- chalk
- for older children only: water colors, charcoal, dyes, colored pencils, papier-mâché or sawdust, weaving and sewing supplies

Many teachers also use food as art materials for projects, such as stringing large macaroni, printing with potatoes, or finger painting with pudding. Other teachers object, since many children in this country and in the world do not have enough to eat. They do not feel comfortable destroying food when it could be used instead to nourish people! This is one of the many ethical decisions you will face as an early childhood educator.

How do you feel about using food as an art material?

_____

_____

_____

_____

Just wait—you're in for a lively discussion in your CDA Seminar.

While children are working in areas around the room, you are walking about, talking with them in ways that support their development. Remember, children's creative art is very personal to them. Treat it with respect. Instead of asking, "What is it?" comment on something about one or more elements of their art: color, line, shape, space, and design.

"You have used so many different colors!"

"Look how those lines go back and forth."

"Los pedacitos de papel son difíciles de agarrar. Teeny bits of paper are hard to hold."

"You really worked a long time to create your special project, didn't you?"

"What would you like to tell me about your art?"

Given openings such as these, children will not feel threatened or criticized about their art. They may tell you, "This is the firetruck that came to our apartment last night," and describe in vivid detail just what happened. Or they may say "red," or "That's fire," or just give you a big smile for being interested in what they did. That's the beauty of working with young children—you rarely know what to expect!

All children's art is beautiful in their eyes. Rather than make a value judgment about the art, concentrate on the child's effort instead. Children will fell good because your response supports their work, their vocabularies will expend, and they will learn more about their own creative abilities. Respect their unique creations—and you respect children as well!

Introduce new techniques. Most of the time, children can figure out what to do with materials by themselves. Children watch each other and get lots of new ideas. Sometimes, though, you may need to demonstrate a technique for children—for safety's sake, or because the materials are completely unfamiliar to them. Here's an example of how to give some simple directions on how to get started, without limiting the creative use of materials.

You have set up a low, sturdy woodworking bench where the noise will not disturb others. First, you want these young preschool children to learn how to use a hammer. You have three light claw hammers, some roofing nails, and three 12-inch squares of 2-inch thick white pine (some old tree stumps are even better if you can get them).

"Today we will start a new activity," you announce enthusiastically when you gather the group on the carpet to plan for the day.

"The hammers and nails!" one child calls out excitedly.

"Yes, we have a woodworking bench, three hammers, nails, and wood. Each of you can learn how to use the hammers. We will add more tools when you show you can use the hammers safely and well. While some children are hammering, the rest can play in other places. There are some new puzzles on one table, and we have added some hard hats and nail aprons in the pretend play area. Please go to the area of your choice now."

Six children want to hammer. "We only have space for three children. Who would like to volunteer to hammer in a few minutes when the first three children are finished?" You write down the names of the three volunteers and ask them to find something else to work on while they wait.

You pick up a hammer and hold it toward the back of the handle. "This is where you hold the hammer. Here is a hammer for each of you. Show me how you hold the hammer."

"Please move your hand toward the back of the handle a little more. That way your nails will go in straighter," you point out to one child.

"Excellent! You will all soon be fine carpenters. Now

we need some nails and wood and we are all set . . . . Spread out so each of you has room to work safely . . . . Choose the nail you would like to hammer. Who knows which end of the nail you hit with the hammer?"

"This flat end," shows one child.

"So which end goes into the wood?" you ask playfully.

"The pokey end, silly" giggles another.

The children hold their nails and begin pounding gently to get them started. You make sure each child holds the hammer properly. You stay with the children to help them figure out how to hammer. Each child who finishes is asked to tell the next child on the list that she or he can have a turn.

Each new material may need a little explanation so that children can see how to use it to best advantage. Be patient. It takes a long time for children to master scissors, for example, because their muscles are still growing.

You can probably see now why it is not appropriate to just put out scissors and paper with lines drawn on it so children can practice cutting, for example. Instead, put out scissors, paste, old magazines, construction paper, and let children figure out what they want to do. Maybe they will cut, maybe they will tear the paper. When materials like these are offered every day, children will eventually get all the practice they need while they pursue activities that appeal to them.

New techniques can also be introduced by real artists. Invite artists—potters, painters, printmakers, weavers—to visit you, or ask if you and the children can come watch them at work. Sometimes local museums or art groups sponsor special events just for children. Ask artists to share their ideas with children, or to talk about the culture in which the technique was first developed.

You can offer children similar materials if they are interested in trying some of the techniques used, but never ask them to try to make a similar painting or piece. That would be far beyond what young children could successfully accomplish.

Use all of these real art experiences as a way to heighten children's appreciation for beauty and the elements of design. And open up new ways for them to express their own ideas and to experiment with different ways of doing things.

What art materials would make a good addition to your supply?

_____

_____

_____

_____

What new techniques could you introduce to the children in your group?

_____

_____

_____

_____

Choose three creative activities (one each for toddlers, threes, and fours) to include in your Professional Resource File. List all the materials needed and how you expect children to use them.

Language, music, art—how much each of these curriculum areas fosters growth in every area of children's development! Every really good activity for young children touches on their socioemotional, physical, and cognitive development. Let's turn now to look at how children think and try to make sense out of the world as they go about their daily activities.

You enable children to use their curiosity to make sense out of the world

Young children are constantly trying to solve problems and figure things out. But children don't see or understand things the same way older children or adults do. After all, we have years of experience with things and people. Haven't you ever said, "If only I knew then what I know now!"? We picked up what we know gradually. Children are still discovering ways to figure it all out.

Three 4-year-olds want to play color bingo. They make three piles of markers with the same number in each pile. Lynn takes the pile that is all spread out "because it has the most."

Your toddlers are stacking cardboard bricks. The first

one in the stack is on its side. The pile topples over. The children start to rebuild again without changing the bottom block.

You and a baby are playing with a favorite rattle. You hide the rattle under a diaper. The child immediately turns to pick up another toy. Why didn't the baby just lift up the diaper?

You probably have hundreds of examples of how children see the world differently than we do—children do say and do the darnedest things. Sometimes their ideas give us a good chuckle.

Of course, now that you are becoming a professional early childhood educator, you are more than just amused by happenings like these. In fact, you will use the information you gather about how children's thinking changes as they mature to decide how to teach—to enable children to learn through activities by matching what you do to children's levels of development.

Thanks to the careful observation and research of some great scientists like Jean Piaget, we know that the typical ways children think and reason change at different ages. Just as they are egocentric in their social and emotional interactions, their cognitive functioning is also egocentric—their logic and ability to organize information are limited by what they see from their own point of view.

You will learn more about these changes in your CDA Seminar. But for now, return to the

Children learn when they touch, smell, work, watch others, pretend, imitate, try out, and experiment with real things.

chart of developmental milestones in Unit 2 and review the material in the sections, "children become aware of the world" and "children solve problems and use tools."

These characteristics will help you choose materials and plan appropriate activities to build on what you know about children's thinking. Three of the long-term goals for children's cognitive development overlap so much that we are going to consider them all at one time:

. . . **make sense of the world**

. . . **recognize real problems and figure out solutions to them**

. . . **think critically and logically, ask questions that lead to more questions**

Of course, we don't expect children to go off to kindergarten or first grade having mastered all of these goals! Some of **us** are still trying to make sense of the world! But a good early childhood program can give children the **confidence and the experience to begin to develop sound thinking skills.**

How, then, do you help children make sense of the world, figure out solutions to problems, and ask good questions? You put everything together that we have discussed so far.

Encourage discovery

Children are naturally curious. They are active learners. Children are self-motivated. They have their own personal ways of learning—but all children use their language, their senses, their bodies, and their minds. They are eager to dig in and their learning is messy and noisy!

So give them a wealth of **real materials**, an abundance of **appropriate activities**, lots of **choice and freedom** to move around, some **friends**, and **your observant eye and ear**. These things stimulate their thinking.

Children learn when they touch, smell, work, watch others, pretend, imitate, try out, and experiment with real things. Those real things don't need to be fancy "educational toys." Children also learn a lot from everyday items and even things that seem useless.

Geraldine has an apple tree in the back yard. Some of the apples are filled with worms. When she encourages the preschool children to pick up the apples, they are fascinated! They spend a long time just handling the apples and watching the worms crawl in and out.

Then she provides each child with a blunt knife and suggests that they carve a face or some other design in the apple. Some children want to do more than one.

"What do you think will happen if we let these apples sit on the shelf for a few days?" she asks as they finish.

Children offer several ideas—"Bugs will eat them." "They will get all yucky and brown." "We can take them home." "Nothing." "They'll get to be applesauce and we can eat it."

Geraldine writes each child's name on a paper towel, the children put their apples on the towel, and each day they check what is happening to their apples.

Events like this and the time and space for them to happen are an important part of the early childhood classroom. Of course, they can happen anytime or anywhere, provided you are open to them. But you might also want to set aside a special learning area that invites this type of exploration: The Discovery Area.

When children bring in seaweed, or some

coffee beans, or an old clock, feature them in the Discovery Area. You add other things that children are curious about or that fit in with your curriculum's theme for a week or two: a hearing aid, coins from several different countries, gardening tools, a Navajo blanket, or a

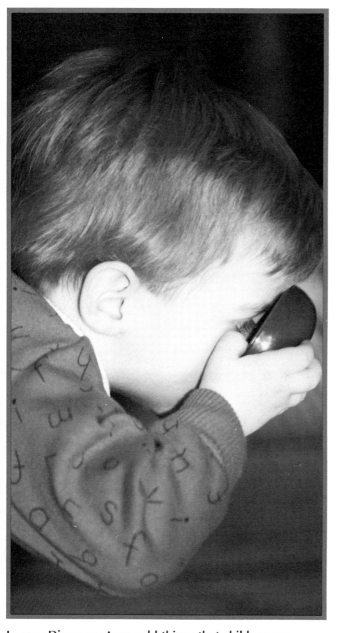

In your Discovery Area, add things that children are curious about or that fit in with your curriculum's theme for a week or two.

children's book/tape set in another language, or some corncobs, or shells.

If the theme is seeds, you might want to include some snow peas, peanuts or walnuts, and a nutcracker.

If you are talking about chickens, you will want feathers, eggs, and bones. Some of the permanent items in the Discovery Area will help children explore their world: magnifying glass, tape measure, scale, small containers, paper bags. These are the tools that scientists, engineers, mathematicians, and researchers of all ages use.

In the Discovery Area and all over the playroom, children will sort . . . compare . . . match . . . measure . . . weigh . . . use trial and error . . . count . . . solve problems . . . figure out how things work . . . touch . . . see what happens when they drop or roll something . . . try to fit things together . . . squeeze . . . shake . . . learn from their mistakes . . . smell . . . dig . . . saw . . . pour . . . estimate . . . put things in order . . . children will never run out of things to do!

Discovery and exploration involve a lot of activities that seem like math and science — and they are! But most things in a good early childhood program are math — and science — and language — and physical skills all wrapped into one! Children see how useful numbers are, for example, when they need to measure the flour to bake bread. They see how things change as they watch the yeast make the bread rise. They see the value of reading when they try to follow the recipe! And they know how strong their muscles are when they knead the dough! The world begins to make sense!

Most lunch and snack menus for young children contain at least one item that even toddlers could help fix. Children can help write lists, shop, scrub fruits or vegetables, stir soups, break up chunks of lettuce for tacos, pour juices, put their own sauce and toppings on their pizza—think about all the steps involved and see whether one or two children at least might participate. Tailor the tasks to the age and skills of the children.

When possible, take your group to the store to shop. There is so much to learn—how to choose the best produce, reading labels in one or two languages, checking out, paying for the food. A grocery store in the dramatic play area will surely be a big hit. Children can bring in empty food boxes from home and set up a cash register with play money. They're in business!

When you prepare foods with young children, be sure to really let the children do it. If you jump in and interfere, they will soon lose interest and won't have the opportunity to learn or practice a skill either. Who cares if the fruit chunks aren't all a uniform size, or if the meat is in funny shapes?

If you are responsible for very many children, you will probably want to break up into smaller groups. It is impossible for everyone to take part if there are more than four or five preschoolers working on one project. Two or three toddlers are more than enough.

If you are a family child care provider, you have the advantage with cooking—you have everything you need at your fingertips! If you work in a center, you may need to bring in an electric skillet or small oven, pans, or utensils, for example. Local regulations about what appliances you may use in the classroom vary, so be sure you check them first.

Be sure safety rules are established with the children and all of you have washed your hands thoroughly before you begin. Use plastic knives or table knives for children to cut with.

Real skills learned with **real** food are far more valuable than asking children to cut out food pictures and paste them on a paper plate! Always think **real** when you plan activities for children.

With everything children do in a good program, they **think**. So you set up a schedule that gives children lots of time to think—to play alone and together—to choose what they want to do and how they want to do it. You modify the materials or furnishings so those children with handicaps can be as involved as possible, too. And you are flexible, so that if something comes up during the day (and it always does) you can take advantage of the teachable moment.

Catch teachable moments

All day, as you move from activity to activity, you look for teachable moments that you can use to further children's thinking. Let's see how you can capitalize on some everyday occurrences.

Fourteen-month-old Daren is struggling with the stacking toy. The largest ring just won't fit because the smallest one is already on top.

"You have tried and tried to get that red ring on, but

it won't go. What seems to be the problem?" asks his family child care provider, Ms. Patel.

Daren looks underneath the green ring, his hair touching the floor. Then he dumps the ring from the spindle and smiles. "Bat," he announces.

"Now your spindle has no rings. Which one will you put on next?"

Daren was learning elementary physics — that two things won't fit in the same space at the same time.

But his teacher did not dump the ring off and show him how to make the red ring go on. She put his problem into words because he was just beginning to use language. She pointed out how persistent he had been and used words to talk about what he was doing.

Lots of trying to make sense of things, ordering, looking, trial and error, fitting together, and problem solving going on here! Science, math, language, physical development — all in 1 short minute!

Two toddlers are playing in the sand. "Let's do a birthday party!"

Their Head Start teacher, Mr. Rinaldi, hears the suggestion and walks closer.

"We need cupcakes," announces Michelle as she looks in his direction.

"Cupcakes usually have milk in them. Do you need a gallon of milk?" Mr. Rinaldi asks.

"Cupcakes are good with milk," Shanada replies.

"Who would like to help carry a bucket of milk for cupcakes?" their teacher asks. Both children volunteer, and they go to the storage shed to get the bucket. The three fill the bucket, and the two girls carry it back to the sandbox.

These toddlers chose a theme, decided what they needed to carry it out, and knew who to ask for help.

Their teacher was aware that their play was just beginning and knew that water adds so much to children's play with sand. He enabled them to expand their play and gave them a chance to cooperate by carrying the heavy gallon bucket of water.

The children were indeed making sense of their world, weighing, digging, pouring, recognizing a problem, and thinking about what they wanted to do!

A 4-year-old has found a long flashlight in the Discovery Area. He turns it on and watches it dance on the ceiling. Then he takes the batteries out. When he puts them back in, the flashlight doesn't work. He dumps the batteries on the floor, puts them back in, and still it doesn't work. In fact, now they jiggle around inside.

Mrs. Arias has been watching Colin's progress. She catches his eye. It looks questioning, so she walks over to the Discovery Area.

"What's the problem, Colin?" she says in a friendly voice.

"The flashlight doesn't work," he responds simply.

"Show me how it doesn't work," Mrs. Arias suggests.

"Well, see, I took this end off. Then I dumped out the batteries. I put them back in, and then it didn't work. So I dumped them here on the floor — oops! There's a battery under the shelf! No wonder it didn't work!"

Colin puts his batteries back, pushes the button — no light. "Oh no, it still doesn't work," he says with disappointment.

Mrs. Arias asks, "What do you think could be wrong?"

"Well, it is broken."

"Probably not, and if it worked today the bulb probably isn't the problem, either. Sometimes they wear out, too. What do you think it could be?"

Colin is silent. He dumps out the batteries one more time and studies each one carefully.

"Which end did you put in first, Colin?" his teacher asks.

"Does it matter?"

"Let's find out."

Those were long examples! But then, children need a long time to figure things out and Colin is still working on his problem! Mrs. Arias found out what he knew, saw that he needed a clue before he got discouraged, and offered it — he probably will have a working flashlight in a flash. And how well he will know that batteries have two ends and that it matters how they are stacked. No picture, no words, could ever substitute for this simple experience.

These are the kinds of everyday, simple, real activities that mean the most for children's learning. These are teachable moments. And your support can make the difference in just how much children learn. What do you do?

- You **observe** what is happening. Sometimes you don't need to do anything—you already did your part by putting out the item. Children can take it from there.

- You **describe** what is happening. Just the facts, just the facts. Sometimes a simple statement will help children notice what their problem is so they can go on to the next step in solving it.

- You **ask thought-provoking questions in the child's home language**—questions that have lots of possible answers are called open-ended questions. How . . . ? Why . . . ? What . . . ? What if . . . ? When . . . ? Where . . . ? Ask questions so children can think up a possible solution. Help them wonder. Give them a chance to talk about their ideas.

  Avoid closed-ended questions—those that have only one right answer or that can be answered with a simple yes or no. And don't answer children's questions for them until they have given the problem their best shot at a solution!

- You **encourage children to ask questions** about what they are doing. As they ask questions, they will think through their own answers. Lots of times two or more children will discuss what they are doing, and figure

Make the most of teachable moments

Children learn best in everyday, simple, real activities. Use one or more of these techniques to extend their learning:

- Observe what is happening.
- Describe what is happening.
- Ask thought-provoking questions in children's home language.
- Encourage children to ask questions.
- Let children come up with solutions and try the ideas themselves.
- Join in the play.

out what they need on their own. Children in the block corner frequently help each other out when a block is too long or a ramp is too steep.

Sometimes, of course, children just need an answer to their questions. "Where is the . . ?" "How do you spell . . . ?" "Is this good wood for sawing?" "What do rabbits eat?"

And if you don't know the answer, say so. "What an excellent question that is. I wonder what foods are good for rabbits. Where could we find an answer to that question?" Opportunities such as these are great for helping children learn about libraries, telephones, and how to do research.

- You **let children come up with solutions and try the ideas themselves.** Yes, even when you know something won't work. Especially when you know something won't work — children learn from trial and error. They learn from their mistakes. If it is safe, let them proceed uninterrupted.

Brandon and Rahsaan are helping prepare the toddler snack. They have cut up banana chunks and put them and the crackers on three small trays. Now they need to carry them to the tables.

Rahsaan takes one tray and places it on the closest table.

Brandon takes another tray and puts his on the same table.

The other toddlers begin to arrive for snack just as Rahsaan gets the last tray.

"Hey, this table doesn't have any food," points out Kimeon.

Rahsaan takes his tray to that table. One table still has no tray.

"Where is our snack?" asks Essence, who is always ready to eat. She looks around. "No fair, that table has two, and we don't have any."

Brandon takes one of the trays to the last table.

Children can learn so much from each other and by experiencing the consequences of their own actions! Their teacher didn't need to say a word. Eventually, Brandon and Rahsaan will learn a mathematical principle called *one-to-one correspondence* — one tray for each table.

- Sometimes you **join in their play**. "You need an ambulance driver and they are all out? Well, sure, I can drive the ambulance. Where is the person who is hurt?" You don't dominate or control the play, but rather take your cues from the children. And gracefully exit from the play as soon as you make your ambulance run.

Catch a teachable moment tomorrow. Practice using open-ended questions in place of closed-ended ones. Write what happened here.

_____

_____

_____

_____

_____

Discuss what happened with your Advisor.

These techniques sound a little bit like the listening you learned earlier. They are very similar — once you know how children learn and what you want them to learn, the same teaching techniques and activities come up over and over again in different ways. All of children's learning is so interrelated.

Let's move on now to our next long-term goal for children. Like all the others, it draws on ideas and techniques we have already talked about.

You enable children to lead well-balanced, productive lives

Life is meant to be lived to its fullest. Children are in your group for many waking hours every day. Everything you have learned through your experience and in this CDA material can be applied as you create an atmosphere and environment to support young children's growth toward happy and fulfilled lives as adults.

Children are learning how their bodies work,

how to communicate, how to think, and how to act responsibly. You already know the importance of children's self-esteem and why they must feel good about themselves. You know that children need to learn self-help skills and to feel independent. Part of feeling grown up is accepting responsibility — age-appropriate responsibility, of course.

We have talked about how children pick up prejudices and stereotypes from the people who are important to them — and in contrast, how they learn ways to treat other people with respect.

Likewise, children pick up a sense of responsible connectedness to a larger world outside their own families and absorb values about other more global issues such as pollution, hunger, waste/conservation, change, war/peace.

Children need to learn respect for our natural resources. They should learn to respect the human universe and to participate in keeping it

Children respect people.

safe, healthy, and fair for all living things. They learn this respect everyday—for things and each other—primarily from what you and their parents do and say, the kinds of activities you offer, how you make decisions, and the responsibilities children begin to assume.

- **Children respect people.** You expect children to take good care of themselves. Children treat their friends and families with respect. Children use words to work out problems. Diversity is a natural part of their everyday experience, so they are not threatened or uncomfortable with different ideas, skin colors, languages, or clothes. Children learn to speak up when they see that something is unfair or hurts feelings. These are small beginnings toward a more peaceful world.

- **Children respect nature and its resources.** Your example and attitude can make all the difference. Food is to be eaten, not wasted. You work to preserve animal life. Even if you are afraid of snakes or bugs, you are always curious and in control of yourself. You turn off the water or the lights when they are not in use. You use public transportation or walk with the children whenever possible, rather than driving in the car. Children will soon follow your example, and as a result more resources will be available for all of us and future generations to enjoy.

- **Children accept responsibility.** Right from babyhood, children can make choices and take responsibility for things that affect them.

Babies can decide what kind of cereal to eat, which toys to play with, and whether to climb to the top of the mountain of cushions or not. They can use a sponge to wipe off the tray of their high chair or a napkin to dab at their face. They learn to be kind to other children. And to pet the cat or dog gently.

Toddlers put their toys back when they are finished. They wipe up spills with a sponge. They can help make small repairs—sanding a rough block, taping a torn page, tightening a nut on the tricycle. They can turn off the water after they wash their hands.

Preschoolers can handle even more responsibility. Sharing toys and playing cooperatively. Coordinating their efforts to cook a holiday feast. They can keep the playground free of trash. And remind each other in the car to buckle up when it's time to go home.

What else can you think of to help children grow up to be more responsible citizens?

_____

_____

_____

_____

_____

What global issues in society do you care most about? Think about these and be ready to discuss your ideas with the other CDA Candidates in your Seminar.

Children appreciate beauty.

- **Children appreciate beauty.** Beauty is everywhere, not just in art or music. Beauty is the smell of hot vegetable soup on a cold winter day. Beauty is the hand of a close friend or a warm smile. Beauty is the sun glittering on water or a tall building. Beauty is the shade of a tree on a hot summer day. Beauty is a peaceful feeling of quiet after working hard on the playground. Beauty is the feel of silk, or bark, or the bricks of the sidewalk. Beauty is all around if we just take the time to appreciate it.

You make your environment appealing and reflective of children's cultural diversity.

You create a restful background on which to tastefully exhibit children's artwork, artifacts from around the world, items from nature, and a few fine art pieces.

You arrange shelves neatly with labels and/or pictures so children know where everything goes. Store extra toys and supplies in a closet or cupboard. Place plants, cut flowers, or dried arrangements where children can touch and smell them.

Let the air be filled with children's laughter and many languages. You play music that is in good taste at a comfortable sound level. Some quiet music at naptime can create a restful feeling even for adults.

You clean pet cages or aquariums often. Open the windows and shades every day to let fresh breezes and natural light stream in.

Select books, posters, and pictures that are pleasing to the eye. You avoid clutter, large quantities of dark or glaring colors, "cute" cartoon drawings. So many items intended for children are ugly and harsh. Strive for moderation.

Outdoors, you listen for birds or the leaves rustling in the wind. You use a variety of materials—sand, wood chips, grass, trees for playground design. You paint equipment to blend in with the environment rather than stand out like a sore thumb. You plant a garden that the children can watch. You keep the area free of litter.

Beauty is everywhere. It is not expensive.

Experience it everyday with your group of children.

List some ways that you can help children appreciate beauty in your environment.

_____

_____

_____

_____

Start to make your improvements immediately.

Children's development in all areas is enhanced through ordinary play.

To be a great teacher of young children, you need imagination and creativity . . . joy . . . curiosity . . . a sense of humor . . . boundless energy . . . a listening ear . . . a warm heart . . . enthusiasm—and the desire to learn along with the children.

You won't find these in any catalog and none of them costs a penny. But they are priceless qualities that you bring with you every day when you walk in the door, or when the children walk in your door. Use them wisely.

What are appropriate curriculum themes?

We have said over and over, curriculum is what happens . . . By now, you know this means that children's development in all areas is enhanced through ordinary play, which is enriched and made meaningful by the way you select and organize the space and activities in it.

When you plan what will happen each day, you always want to add some variety to make each day something to look forward to.

Many teachers, however, like to provide variety by highlighting one or more special activities. Children are still given lots of choice about what to do, but the choices vary from one day to the next.

Some teachers also like to choose a theme to give their daily activities some direction. It is

	Morning	**Afternoon**
Monday	Sharing about the weekend	Purple clay dough
Tuesday	Shop for fruit	Introduce tambourines
Wednesday	Make fruit salad for lunch	Draw with Craypas
Thursday	Finger-paint	Bug hunt
Friday	Obstacle course	Puppets

For example, you might plan these special activities for 1 week. Children are free to participate in these or to select from the array of other interesting things that are always available.

easy to get carried away with a theme, though, so you need to be careful to balance it with the many daily activities that children always love to do.

For instance, if children are especially excited about dinosaurs, you might want to hang up a few dinosaur pictures, put out a few dinosaurs to play with in the sand, and display some dinosaur books.

Or perhaps you could find some fossils, or some dinosaur rubber stamps, or cookie cutters to use with clay, or a couple of dinosaur puzzles. And maybe you could find a computer game with dinosaurs, or word cards in the writing area, or a card game of dinosaurs.

But you don't want all of these. It can be dreadfully boring for you and monotonous for the children as well if they have no relief from dinosaurs for every activity for a whole week. Enough is enough.

Keeping in mind, then, the need to balance the special themes with regular activities, here

are some more themes and ideas for teaching that are appropriate and interesting for young children.

We have left space with each one so you can add your own appropriate ideas. Add other themes that you can think of, too.

You use appropriate infant themes

We are growing. Show baby pictures to help children see how much they have changed, look at hair and other body parts in mirrors, play with dolls, talk about how much children can do.

What we eat. Try new foods with a sense of adventure, visit a grocery store, walk through a garden, smell foods as they cook, wash fruits and vegetables.

People we love. Exhibit pictures of families—not just parents but aunts, uncles, cousins, grandparents; talk about how friends treat each other; sing songs in many languages; invite relatives to visit and cuddle with the children; read stories about all kinds of families.

Animals. Watch fish swim, pet furry animals, sniff a wet dog, play guessing games about which animal makes the noise, imitate animal sounds.

What happens. Roll different kinds of balls (fabric, rubber, textured, smooth), pour water, slide down the slide, pick flowers, play instruments, send a small vehicle down a ramp.

We move our bodies. Move and sing to music from many cultures, climb a mountain of cushions, crawl through an obstacle course, ride vehicles, roll in the grass.

You use appropriate toddler themes

How big we are. Compare what infants can do with what toddlers can do (baby pictures/real children), weigh and/or measure each child once a month and chart their growth.

Food comes from animals. Watch a cow being milked, make ice milk, have a picnic with chicken hot dogs, visit a poultry farm, make books of pictures on how many ways you can eat eggs.

Where animals live. Tour a farm, read books or see movies about animal's natural habitats, watch an ant hill, walk through the woods and look for tracks and sounds, use animal puppets, set up a barn with animals.

Where we live. Visit children's homes or have them bring in pictures, talk about similarities and differences, walk through the neighborhood to look at where people live, watch a building being erected (visit every week, not just once), introduce carpentry skills.

At the beach. Play in sand and water with beach toys, collect shells or other debris, play with rubber sea animals, let water sit out and evaporate—what is left?, pretend to spend a day at the beach in the middle of the winter.

What we can smell. Ask children to bring in something they like to smell, play guessing games with smells, look at each other's noses, cook lots of ethnic dishes.

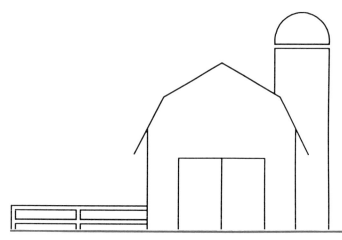

How things feel. Collect fabric scraps for children to paste or make into books, give each child a small bag to fill with treasures on a walk, touch a Braille book.

Harvest time. Shell corn, feed birds, collect and paste colored leaves, plan and cook a harvest feast, talk about things children are thankful for, how families celebrate harvests.

Weather. Put a thermometer on the playground and watch how it changes, watch the clouds, fly kites in the wind, provide dress-up clothes for each season.

Trucks, trains, and busses. Ride a bus or train, read *Freight Train*, watch and listen to a train go by, find different kinds of trucks— what is in them?, visit the fire station, listen for engine sounds.

You use appropriate preschool themes

All the themes for toddlers are appropriate, but with more ideas and activities to expand children's thinking even further beyond their own families and cultures.

People have different jobs. Provide props for pretend play from a variety of types of jobs, talk about what parents do, visit many different job sites.

People are the same and different. Make charts of hair color or eye color, feel different hair and skin textures, watch authentic movies about food and shelter and dress in other cultures, eat with utensils from other cultures, let children try out a wheelchair or glasses.

Dinosaurs. Compare dinosaur sizes to other more familiar things (elephants, trees); examine bones from chickens, cows, or pigs.

Where clothes come from. Watch a sheep being sheared or a weaver at work, grow cotton, paste cotton balls, feel the smoothness of silk, compare leather with vinyl, sew with yarn and burlap, visit a seamstress or tailor, add some new dress-up clothes.

Milk and dairy products. Visit a dairy farm, prepare milk shakes and write down children's original recipes, compare tastes and textures of cheeses, make a barn with a cardboard box.

How plants grow. Plant a garden, collect different seeds from food you eat, care for plants.

Money. Compare coins from many countries, set up a lemonade stand or tricycle wash, obtain a popular advertised item and decide whether it really performs like the commercial says it does, write "checks," set up a post office or grocery store with a cash register.

Time. Talk about birthdays and ages, find different kinds of clocks, compare to see whether older always means taller, bake bread.

Water. Freeze it, let it evaporate, make steam, pour and measure it, add food coloring, swim, raise fish.

There are hundreds of other topics that interest children—just listen every day and pick up on their ideas and questions.

WELL . . . now that you have seen all the videos and completed the exercises in these first five units, you have most of the basic tools you need to implement daily activities with the children in your care.

But you are not finished—for in order to pull EVERYTHING together to plan for your children you must establish positive working relations with their parents. We'll cover this in the next unit.

Meanwhile, to practice what you have learned so far, complete the following exercise of working out a weekly plan and be prepared to discuss it in detail with your Field Advisor.

Weekly plan

Curriculum theme _____

Special events _____

	MON.	TUES.	WED.	THURS.	FRI.
Self-directed activities					
Teacher-directed activities					
Special materials needed					
Arrangements to make					
Special focus for individual children (modifications)					

At last! You have put everything you know together to come up with an honest-to-goodness plan for teaching. It has taken a long time to get to this point, and you have worked hard on your CDA.

Turn to your CDA progress record and make a BIG check for having finished the self-study portion of Unit 5. Pause to take a deep breath, and then come back to finish Unit 6.

Resources for more information

Alaskan style: Starting in their first language. [Videotape]. Juneau: Alaska State Department of Education, 1990.

Bredekamp, S. (Ed.). (1987). *Developmentally appropriate practice in early childhood programs serving children from birth through age 8*. Washington, DC: National Association for the Education of Young Children.

Bowman, B. (1989). Educating language-minority children. *ERIC Digest* (No. EDO-PS-90-1). Urbana, IL: ERIC Clearinghouse on Elementary and Early Childhood Education.

Brown, J.F. (Ed.). (1982). *Curriculum planning for young children*. Washington, DC: National Association for the Education of Young Children.

Cataldo, C.Z. (1983). *Infant & toddler programs: A guide to very early childhood education*. Reading, MA: Addison-Wesley.

Crews, D. (1978). *Freight train*. New York: Greenwillow.

Elkind, C. (1986, May). Formal education and early childhood education: An essential difference. *Phi Delta Kappan*, 631–636.

Feeney, S., & Moravcik, E. (1987, September). A thing of beauty: Aesthetic development in young children. *Young Children, 42*(6), 6–15.

Gonzalez-Mena, J., & Eyer, D.W. (1980). *Infancy and caregiving*. Palo Alto, CA: Mayfield.

Haines, B.J.E., & Gerber, L.L. (1984). *Leading young children to music* (2nd ed.). Columbus, OH: Merrill.

Hendrick, J. (1986). *Total learning: Curriculum for the young child* (2nd ed.). Columbus, OH: Merrill.

Hill, D. (1979). *Mud, sand, and water*. Washington, DC: National Association for the Education of Young Children.

Hirsch, E.S. (Ed.). (1984). *The block book* (rev. ed.). Washington, DC: National Association for the Education of Young Children.

Holt, B. G. (1977). *Science with young children*. Washington, DC: National Association for the Education of Young Children.

Hutchins, P. (1971). *Changes, changes*. New York: Macmillan.

Hunsaker, D. (1990). *Alaskan style: Starting in their first language*. [Teacher's guide]. Juneau: Alaska State Department of Education.

Kamii, C., & Katz, L. (1979, May). Physics in early childhood education: A Piagetian approach. *Young Children, 34*(4), 4–9.

Katz, L., & Chard, S. (1989). *Engaging the minds of young children: The project approach*. Norwood, NJ: Ablex.

Lamme, L.L. (1985). *Growing up reading: Sharing with your children the joys of reading*. Washington, DC: Acropolis.

Lasky, L., & Mukerji, R. (1980). *Art: Basic for young children.* Washington, DC: National Association for the Education of Young Children.

McCracken, J.B. "More than 1, 2, 3 – The real basics of mathematics." Washington, DC: National Association for the Education of Young Children.

Schickedanz, J. (1986). *More than the ABCs: The early stages of reading and writing.* Washington, DC: National Association for the Education of Young Children.

Shure, M.B., & Spivack, G. (1978). *Problem-solving techniques in childrearing.* San Francisco: Jossey-Bass.

Skeen, P., Garner, A.P., & Cartwright, S. (1984). *Woodworking for young children.* Washington, DC: National Association for the Education of Young Children.

Spodek, B. (1985). *Teaching in the early years* (3rd ed.). Englewood Cliffs, NJ: Prentice-Hall.

Sprung, B., Froschl, M., & Campbell, P.B. (1985). *What will happen if . . . Young children and the scientific method.* New York: Educational Equity Concepts, Inc.

Taylor, B.B. (1978). *Making thoughts become: A handbook for teachers and adults.* New York: Children's Art Carnival.

Williams, C.K., & Kamii, C. (1986, November). How do children learn by handling objects? *Young Children,* 42(1), 23–26.

Williams, L. R., & De Gaetano, Y. (1985). *ALERTA: A multicultural, bilingual approach to teaching young children.* Menlo Park, CA: Addison-Wesley Publishing Co., Inc.

Zavitkovsky, D., Baker, K.R., Berlfein, J.R., & Almy, M. (1986). *Listen to the children.* Washington, DC: National Association for the Education of Young Children.

6

Keys to establish productive relationships with families

IN EARLY CHILDHOOD EDUCATION you always work with parents as partners to foster children's development. Together, you will assess children's needs, plan their experiences, and make decisions that influence how your program unfolds from day to day, month to month, and year to year. Your ability to develop effective relationships with parents is so important that parents' opinions of your work will be weighed in the final decision about your competence as a CDA!

As an early childhood educator, you play a very special role in the lives of families. Most of you see the children's parents daily, sometimes twice a day. You will celebrate happy occasions with families and cry with them at difficult times. Programs for young children enable parents to continue their education or to earn a living. You not only teach children—parents look to you, an experienced and trained professional, for ideas about how to be a good parent. You support parents in the challenging task of childrearing.

In this unit you will build upon your own experiences and learn new strategies to establish positive, productive relationships with families.

Programs usually have policies describing what the program must do for parents, and what is expected of parents. To begin this unit, review your own program's policies that affect your work with families: enrollment, arrival and departure procedures, conferences, screening, visits, and resource referral guidelines for example.

These policies sometimes are written in lengthy form, such as the Head Start Performance Standards. There may be a brief

> We will use the terms *parents* and *families* to mean those people who are primarily responsible for the children in your care, whoever they are—parents, stepparents, grandparents, cousins, guardians, foster families, or other household members.

program brochure, handbook, or even a simple typed sheet. Put a copy of all the policies for your program regarding parents in your Professional Resource File.

Part 1

How do you get off to a good start?

You make good first impressions

Although your involvement in the enrollment of children will vary depending on whether you are in a large group program or providing family child care, you need to be aware of the process to start off on the right foot to build and maintain a professional relationship with parents.

If you are a family child care provider, every time you pick up the phone you could be welcoming a prospective parent. In a center, you may first meet a potential family when they visit your classroom. Regardless of when or how you meet, both of you need some time to get to know each other before a decision about the child's enrollment can be made.

During these first conversations, family members are asking themselves, "Is this the kind of person we want to care for our child?" You are asking, "Is my program a good match for **this** child and family?"

Don't dismiss the importance of these first impressions and early reactions to you and your program. You are establishing the foundation for a long, close, professional relationship. Both you and the families want to make the right decision for the children.

Start off in a professional manner by being

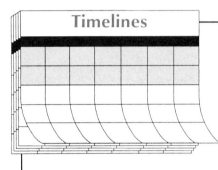
Timelines

This is the final unit to be completed during the self-study phase of your CDA Professional Preparation Program.

You will need about 2 weeks to finish these tasks:

1 Prepare for conference with your Field Advisor to discuss three topics (get off to a good start with new families, collaboration each day, and effective ways to exchange information).

2 Complete three assignments (observe a parent conference, plan a parent meeting, and complete two home visits) and one entry for the Professional Resource File.

3 Complete three assignments for Seminar (explore ways to involve parents, refine skills in conducting parent conferences, and resolve typical dilemmas that arise between parents and teachers).

4 View the accompanying videotape using the Viewer's Guide.

5 Distribute and collect the CDA Parent Questionnaire.

friendly and explaining the highlights of your program on the phone or in person. Then either you (if you are a family child care provider) or your program administrator will mail, or give, the parents a copy of your program's written policies.

These policies cover basics about such things as enrollment qualifications, fees, holidays/vacations, illness, emergency procedures, discipline, and educational philosophy. When these policies are in writing, you greatly reduce the chances for conflicts about these issues later—and you probably already know from experience that disagreements do arise. So much is at stake.

Encourage parents to visit your program at least once before they decide to enroll their child. Welcome the family warmly and with respect. Show them where their child would spend the day, including the playground, and the sleeping areas. Tell parents your expectations about working with them. Ask them about theirs.

Invite them to watch what happens and how the children are treated. You might want to give them a copy of one of these inexpensive brochures to help them make a good decision: "Finding the Best Care for Your Infant or Toddler" (NAEYC), or "How To Choose a Good Early Childhood Program" (NAEYC), or the "Child Care Checklist" (NBCDI). (See Unit 1 for contact addresses for these national early childhood associations.) Encourage the family to ask questions and share their concerns about what is important to them.

During the visit, your guest parents will want to talk with you (and perhaps your program director) about what happens in a good program for young children. You or your director will explain how your program is sensitive to families from different cultures or who speak a second language. All of you want to be comfortable that your program is a good match for the child and family.

You observe business and legal responsibilities

Business is the order of the day when a new child enrolls. Make sure contracts and emergency procedures are signed, deposits and fees paid, health forms complete, and all other paperwork is complete **before** the child's first day.

Your program provides families with a clear written statement about your responsibilities—and theirs—so that all of you know exactly what your roles are. Why? Because accidents do happen and misunderstandings arise.

For example, rather than wait until it is too late, clarify at the beginning who is responsible for children, especially during the critical times of arrival and departure. Put your policy in writing for every parent. Then, if a parent forgets the child's lunch in the car and rushes back to get it, there will be no question about who is responsible—you or the parent—in the event of an accident.

On page 346 is a list of some program and parent responsibilities in early childhood settings. Add other responsibilities to these lists

The program's responsibilities

- To meet all federal, state, local, and program requirements for health, safety, nutrition, staffing patterns, program, emergencies, illness, and other matters.

- To release child only to those people designated in writing by the custodial parent or guardian.

- To administer medicine only when authorized in writing by the parent or guardian.

- To plan an appropriate program for each child, taking into account language, culture, age, differing abilities, and all other pertinent factors.

- To communicate with parents in the language most comfortable for them.

- To keep records of budgets, income, expenses, licenses, permits, insurance, and other business information.

- To obtain parent permission whenever the child leaves the program premises during contract hours with staff (such as on field trips).

- To maintain confidential records of children's development and progress, and to make these records available to parents upon request and only to others (another program or school, for example) if authorized in writing by the parents.

- To report any suspected indicators of child abuse.

- To establish other policies where needed and apply them uniformly among staff, children, and parents. For example, policies about exclusion due to illness and about who is responsible for the child when the parent is present.

- To request parent permission and involvement when possible for developmental screening, photographs, and other similar activities.

- To discuss with parents the program's goals and objectives for children's development and negotiate openly any areas of discomfort or parental concern.

The parents' responsibilities

- To be involved with the staff in setting the program's direction and daily experiences by volunteering or serving on policy boards, for example.

- To agree in advance and in writing to follow all program policies.

- To pay deposits and established fees for child care services as stated in the program's policies.

- To provide any information about a child or the family that may affect decisions about the child's development.

- To discuss any areas of concern with the appropriate staff member(s).

that fit your program. **Check to see that these responsibilities are covered in writing for your program. If they are not, talk with your CDA Field Advisor about ways you can work together to have them added.**

If you are a family child care provider, you can begin immediately to make changes.

You work with parents on the child's first day

Advance planning is needed to get ready for a family's first day. You put the child's name on a cubby and cot or crib. Add the child's name to the sign-in list. Put the family's name on the parent bulletin board. Make a cheery welcome sign using the family's preferred language. If the children in the group are old enough, ask those who are interested to help you. Plan a familiar snack. Little touches can mean a lot toward helping a child and family feel really welcome.

Parents may react in many different ways to leaving their child. Every family is different.

Discuss in advance with parents what you expect on the first day. For example, make sure parents know to bring diapers, an extra change of clothes, bedding, a bag lunch, or other items.

Agree upon how long the parent will stay with the child and how the parent can help ease the separation for herself or himself as well as the child, knowing that the time may need to be extended or shortened depending on how it goes.

When the child and parent(s) arrive, warmly greet them. We already talked in Unit 4 about how to help children handle separation, so let's think now about how to help **parents** deal with their child's first day.

Parents may react in many different ways to leaving their child. Every family is different. Some adults may find it very difficult to leave. Others will know just when to say "Goodbye" or "¡Hasta luego!" to their child. Still others would prefer to rush out the door and not deal with their own, or their child's, feelings about this major change in their lives.

All parents will benefit from your support and understanding during what may be for them a difficult time—even if they treat it casually. You set the tone by being calm and friendly, welcoming parent and child alike. You will briefly want to suggest what the parent is expected to do, "You may hang your coat here and get a cup of coffee if you like. Here's a grown-up chair if you would like to sit where you can see what the children are doing. Then Nichole will know just where to find you."

Then turn your attention toward helping the

child be comfortable. As we said in Unit 4: call the child by name, walk to the child's cubby together, show her or him where the bathroom is and explain any procedures for using it. Perhaps arrange for another child who is fluent in the new child's language to act as a guide, and serve a snack or lunch with foods common to the child's culture or personal preferences.

During those first few hours especially (depending upon the child's age, personality, and previous group experience), the child may have more or less difficulty getting used to the new people and surroundings. Watch carefully and take any steps necessary to make the child, and the parent, increasingly feel a part of your program. You may want to talk informally with the parent about signs you see that the child is beginning to feel a part of the group. Or you may suggest that the parent feel free to read a story to the children who are gathering with her in the book corner.

Parents of very young children, or of those who are enrolled in a group for the first time, may want to stay one full day, and then gradually decrease the number of hours over the next week or two.

Some parents do not have the luxury of that much time and some children do not need to return to their "home base" as often as others. Talk with the family about the best arrangements for everyone involved. Saying goodbye is not easy, but it is not in the best interest of child or family to prolong it unnecessarily, either.

If a parent must leave a clinging child in tears, be sure to take a minute later in the day to call the parent and offer reassurance that the child is indeed feeling more comfortable in the group. (And let the parent know that it is OK for her or him to call.) Then at the end of the day, again describe how well the child settled into the day.

How can you improve your ability to help parents and children say goodbye to each other?

Ask the parents in your program how they felt about their first days and whether they have some suggestions for making enrollment work better.

Part 2

How do you work together each day?

Every day is a golden opportunity for you to learn more about the children and their families.

- Your enthusiastic greeting in the child's home language . . . makes everyone feel welcome.
- Your insistence that children and parents say goodbye when they separate . . . builds trust within the family.
- Your sharing about events in the child's day . . . provides continuity between home and program.
- The program's respect for parents' concerns and ideas . . . enables them to feel valued as people and reaffirms their child care choice.
- Your willingness to have families visit at any time . . . reassures them that their children are being well cared for.
- The staff's encouragement for parents to be involved in your program . . . builds support for your partnership on behalf of children.
- Your model of how to treat children . . . provides an example that most families will begin to follow. And most of all—
- The spirit of working together when planning all that happens in your program . . . creates an atmosphere of joint responsibility for the child.

All these close contacts happen for the most part in just the few short minutes each day that you have with families. So let's look at how to use that valuable time to build solid, productive relationships with families.

> **Be partners with parents each day**
> - **Greet** families enthusiastically
> - **Share** events in the child's day
> - **Respect** parents' concerns and ideas
> - **Welcome** parents as visitors
> - **Encourage** parent involvement
> - **Exchange** appropriate childrearing techniques
> - **Clarify** legal responsibilities

You share important information

Each day, you and the parents will need to exchange information about important events that occurred since you saw each other last. Take just a few seconds when the child arrives and again when the parent returns to fill each other in on what is happening with the child. Most providers prefer to do this in casual conversation with parents.

"Good morning, Marie. How are things with Elyse today?" Gwen asks.

"Elyse didn't sleep very well last night. She seemed especially hungry this morning. Maybe she is in a growth spurt."

"That could be. She's growing up so fast. We'll see how she does with food and naps today and let you know when you pick her up."

Parents of infants need to know how much and when their child ate, how many bowel movements she or he had that day, and when the child took naps. You might want to use a chart like this to keep track of this information and then tuck it in the child's bag when it is almost time to go home. Translate the chart into all the languages spoken by families in your program.

Daily Infant Record

Child _____ Day _____

Bottles at _____ a.m. _____ p.m.

Solid food _____

Naps at _____ a.m. _____ p.m.

Bowel movements _____

Supplies needed _____

Interesting things that happened _____

_____

_____

_____

Most information about toddlers and preschool children can be shared as you talk with parents. It usually takes just a few well-spent seconds of your day.

A mother arrives one morning brimming with pride. "Oh, Diane, Ayuko is so proud of the finger painting she did yesterday. We hung it up near the stairway at home so all of us can enjoy it."

"She had the best time making it, too," confirms Diane. "She just couldn't wait for it to dry so she could put it in her cubby to take home. She must be thrilled to see it hanging in a place where you all can see it."

If you work in a large program with many staff members, written notes between each other may be essential. If staff change between arrival and pick-up time, work out a system that is easy to use and yet allows everyone to feel well-informed about the children. The system should work for both parents and staff.

If parents don't have the time to spend in even a few moments of casual conversation, you might want to arrange a time when you can call them to talk a bit about how their child's day has been. Or if parents are nearly always in a hurry, jot down a quick note about the day's events and pin it to the child's backpack. You can find a way to share information, even if it is only briefly.

Sometimes, in addition to individual information about health, projects, and activities, you want to share general information with all parents. Perhaps you are planning a field trip, or a child has just gotten chicken pox, or a parent cooked a family recipe with a group in the program and it made a big hit.

Written forms are best for this kind of information, just to be sure everyone has been given all the details. You can use brief memos, letters, or even newsletters, depending upon the resources and staff available to help get them ready. **Always, always**, use the primary language of the parents for all written communications.

Be sure to keep a copy of all your notices to parents—many of them can be used when the situation arises again.

What ways do you use to communicate with parents?

Each family is different from every other. Culture, income level, aspirations, and religious beliefs all play a part in determining how parents raise their children.

How can you increase everyday communication?

Ask your Field Advisor for other suggestions.

You discuss major issues openly

Each family is different from every other. Some are outgoing and talkative while others are quiet and reserved. Some like lots of space while others thrive on intimacy. Some are compulsively neat while others are more casual about maintaining order. Some value cooperation while others build a strong sense of individual responsibility. Some extend their roots to friends and relatives while others may be just one parent and child.

Culture, income level, aspirations, and religious beliefs all play a part in determining how parents raise their children. Because families are so different you will want to make sure—right from the beginning—that your program is a good match for the parents and children. And for as long as the child is enrolled, you want to continue to keep the dialogue open, so that the good match can be maintained.

New issues arise as children grow and changes will probably need to continue as you work with parents to reach agreeable solutions on issues such as

- how and when to respond to a baby's cries,
- how to introduce new foods/utensils,
- ways to support the child's growing independence,
- the best method for toilet learning,
- appropriate discipline techniques,
- dealing with separation anxiety,
- why children need to spend a lot of time playing,
- how to prepare a child for kindergarten, and
- the role of child's first language in her or his development.

Parents' values and feelings should always be discussed openly and treated with respect, even when you disagree. Your listening skills are very helpful in working out a solution. You may need to set aside a special conference time if an issue seems to hold the potential for disagreement.

Many times you can adapt what you do to include parents' preferences in your program so that families feel more comfortable.

I can see how a long afternoon nap for Rachel means she doesn't want to go to bed at night. But she also seems too cranky at the center when she doesn't get her nap. If she stays up late, that takes away from the little time you and your husband have together each evening. Instead of letting her sleep for 2 hours, perhaps we could waken her after an hour and a half so she will be more ready to sleep at bedtime. Would you like to try this for a week or so and see whether she gets enough sleep that way?"

When parents learn more about how children grow and learn, they may be willing to be more flexible in their ideas, too. For instance, sometimes parents do not know that children will learn English better if they are firmly rooted in their first language. You may have to help them understand that children who speak their first language *and* English will have a real sense of competence. And by reinforcing their language and culture, their child builds pride and positive self-concept.

You can provide reading material designed for parents (you already have collected some in your PRF). Brochures and pamphlets are available from NAEYC, NBCDI, NAFDC, and other groups, as well as from libraries and pediatrician offices. The Public Health Service too has brochures on many child development topics. Start to collect some whenever you see them. They'll come in handy as you encounter issues with different families. One especially good and timely brochure based on a topic we've talked about so much in *Essentials* is "Teaching Young Children to Resist Bias: What Parents Can Do" (NAEYC). You should find it helpful in convincing parents about more effective ways to prepare their children for successful living.

Your approach should be to negotiate with parents when areas of disagreement arise. **Listen** to their views and share your own. Try to reach an agreement that you both can live with.

Encourage impromptu visits. Parents should *always* be welcome in your program.

Positive changes can take place in a good program. This exchange is between a teacher who believes in integration and a parent who does not.

At the height of the civil rights demonstrations, a parent said to me, "You and me ain't never going to agree about niggers, Mrs. West. But I do know that you love my boy, so you won't teach him nothing that will hurt him." Having already established positive relations with the child and his parents, I could then explain that their son was growing up in a world that would be different from the world they had known, that the school was trying to prepare him to function in that world.

In the most extreme cases, it may become necessary to say that parents have the right to teach their values to their children, but the school has the obligation to prepare children to function in a broader society. (West, 1987)

Sometimes you will have to make a hard professional decision, however, about what is in the child's best interests. Sometimes parents will ask you to do something that makes you uncomfortable:

"Why do you spend so much money on juice? Jeremy just loves Kool-Aid at home."

They may even ask the impossible:

"I have to work until 10 tonight. Could you take Kristi home with you?"

Or the unethical:

"Just spank him if he doesn't listen. Then when he gets home we'll get out the belt to make sure he has learned his lesson."

When situations like these happen, you must always make your decision based on what is best for the child. How would you respond to these dilemmas?

Junk food

A parent's last-minute overtime

Spanking

Most likely, you phrased your position in ways that didn't put down the parents. Here are some responses to think about:

"The children do love sugary drinks, don't they? But we prefer to buy the most nutrition for the money. Juice is so much healthier for the children."

"I'm really sorry but after a long day here I wouldn't have the energy to take good care of Kristi. Here is a list of emergency caregivers who might be able to help you out. Please give us a call so we will know who is picking her up."

"I'm afraid we could never do that. If you remember in our program policies, our philosophy is never to hit children and never to let them hit anyone else. Instead, we use words to figure out how to solve problems. We have found that children learn to control their own behavior much better with this type of discipline. Would you like to think about this for a while and then meet to discuss discipline ideas?"

When you are respectful, understanding, honest, fair, and ethical, you can work **together** with parents to resolve most problems in a harmonious manner.

At times, you may have to agree to disagree.

And sometimes, you may even recommend that the parents find another program that is more compatible with their ideas. We will talk more about the ethics of providing high quality care in the Seminar.

What issues have come up where you and parents disagree? What techniques have you used to resolve them in a harmonious way?

_____

_____

_____

_____

Talk with your CDA Advisor about what you have done.

You encourage impromptu visits

Parents should always be welcome in your program. There should be no exceptions. If you provide appropriate activities, you have nothing to hide. Don't leave yourself open to criticism or accusations—keep your door open to parents. If parents don't seem eager to visit, encourage them to do so, even if they can only stay a few extra minutes at one end of the day or the other.

You find meaningful ways to involve parents

What do we mean by parent involvement? Parents already lead busy lives. Involving them in meaningful ways takes careful thought. Keep your expectations reasonable and gently urge parents gradually to become more involved as they feel comfortable and see how much it means to them and to their children to be an **active partner** in their child's education.

Programs such as Head Start and co-ops started a trend long ago of parent involvement. In these programs, parents are decisionmakers, staff, and volunteers. These parents—who first get involved in education through early childhood programs—stay involved with their child's school throughout their children's elementary and later years as well. Your efforts to involve parents will pay off far beyond today and tomorrow!

In order to encourage parents to become involved, you must make them feel a real part of what happens with their child. Each parent can make a different contribution: Some may have time to spend with the children during the day. Others can help out by doing things in the evening or on weekends. Some will be eager to serve on policy boards or the board of directors for the program, making policy, financial, and other major decisions about the program. Parents can be involved at the center, in your home, or at their own homes!

Some families will feel honored to be asked to participate while others will feel intimidated at first. Some are willing to contribute time and skills, some have materials to donate, and some can give financial gifts to benefit the program.

Whatever parents do, their efforts will add to the continuity between home and program. Only then will children feel as if they truly belong in both their homes and your care.

Your role is to match each parent with a comfortable type and level of involvement in your early childhood program. Here are some ideas about things parents can do. Other early childhood educators have used these techniques to encourage parents to share their cultural experiences and talents with all of the children. Add your own ideas to this list.

Involve parents in your program

Time in the program

Read books with a small group

Cook a family recipe together

Accompany the group and/or drive on a field trip (perhaps to the parent's work or neighborhood)

Sing with the children

Teach children a dance or art technique

Write down children's experience stories

Eat lunch with the children

Breast-feed their infant during lunch break

Talk with children

Assist with screening children for possible disabilities

Help out with filing, typing, or other business duties

Answer telephones

Contribute to curriculum planning meetings

Time at home or after work

Mix new supplies of clay dough

Make minor repairs to equipment

Build toy shelves

Write down a favorite recipe or words to a song

Locate music, clothing, everyday objects, or a work of art from their own culture

Save "beautiful junk" such as toilet paper and paper towel rolls, plastic bags (for dirty clothes), meat trays, egg cartons, packing chips

Read books children bring home with them

Hang up children's artwork

Talk with children about their day

Help prepare for a special event (harvest feast, school picnic)

Write/edit a program newsletter

Assist with fund-raising activities

Serve on parent policy/advisory board

Parents often have great ideas about how to improve the program, but they may prefer to be asked first. You need to make sure that parents always feel free to make suggestions, attend staff planning meetings, or raise questions about what you do with children all day.

Perhaps a parent notices frequent traffic jams on the playground and has in mind a few simple changes to eliminate it. Other parents may have suggestions for menus that are more nutritious or offer greater variety.

Parents can help shape the curriculum in many ways. Children often ask parents questions—and some of those questions could lead to new curriculum areas to explore. Encourage parents to share with you interests their children have expressed.

Perhaps a parent has a special skill (such as speaking a foreign language, carpentry, sewing, art) or knows a lot about a subject of interest to young children (insects, gardening, how shoes or other familiar products are made). With these parents, plan several activities and experiences for children to introduce and build upon the parent's involvement.

Parents often see new angles on how to arrange play areas, know about interesting places to visit on field trips, or see minor problems that you may have overlooked because you've grown so familiar with the program. When parents participate in board meetings or in staff meetings on a regular basis, they will feel more comfortable in offering ideas and solutions. Stay alert to hearing about ways to improve your program for children and parents.

You and the parents of the children in your care are truly partners in your efforts to raise happy, healthy, well-adjusted children. When you work together to share ideas and work through problems, you, the parents, and the children will all benefit.

You and the parents of the children in your care are truly partners in your efforts to raise happy, healthy, well-adjusted children.

How do you enlist parent participation in your program?

Looking at the list of things parents can do in the program, what could you do to involve parents more fully?

You will exchange ideas about parents involvement with others in your CDA seminar.

You strengthen parenting skills

Teachers and parents change with experience. We all start out as rookies. At first, most of us are baffled and a little overwhelmed by the responsibility and time and work involved.

Once we begin to see how successful our efforts have been—the child seems healthy and happy—our confidence is bolstered. As a professional, you have the advantage of your experience and CDA Professional Preparation Program. But new parents usually don't have any training, and especially in the beginning, mothers and fathers alike are looking for ideas about how to parent.

You play a key, but often very subtle, role in shaping parenting skills. You set an example for parents to pick up. How you treat children every day can slowly but surely begin to make a difference in how parents treat their children.

You play a key, but often very subtle, role in shaping parenting skills. How you treat children every day can slowly but surely begin to make a difference in how parents treat their children.

You listen and observe how parents act with their children. Some parents apply all the principles professionals know. Others may not be aware of the long-term consequences of their actions. So, when the parent seems to be open to a different way, you can offer a new or different idea in a nonthreatening, uncritical way. For example, if a parent is having a difficult time with discipline, you might purposefully demonstrate a positive technique with another child while that parent is present.

You support their positive efforts to be good parents in both indirect and direct ways:

"One of these days soon we would love to have you stay with us for a few minutes to watch Amy. Ever since she started to wear play clothes she has been trying so many new things—she paints with a smock, builds with the blocks, and seems to have such a marvelous time on the playground. She is learning to control her muscles so well now that she is more comfortable."

"Lauren, don't forget to say '¡Adios!' to Dad. He will be busy at work all day, and I bet a good hug will make his day a lot better."

"What a thoughtful idea to put those notes in Kirk's lunch box. He looks forward to lunch every day. He usually talks about his wonderful family while he eats."

A resource shelf can contain parenting books, brochures, and videos on topics of great interest. Encourage parents to take materials home. You are always happy to discuss any questions and listen to parents' concerns. Put those listening skills into practice every day—you never know

what might be troubling parents or children.

You can also help parents improve their own skills by building ties with other parents.

Connecting families can be fostered if you provide a space for parents to chat together when they arrive or leave. A parent lounge area, if possible, is a nice idea. If space is limited, you might set up a message board so parents can share ideas and build networks with other families. This is the place to post a thought-provoking newspaper or magazine article. Tack up a brochure or notice about a community service or event and see what happens.

Encourage parents to put up business cards or service notices so they can share their skills with each other. Promote self-sufficiency and bolster confidence!

Your example of positive, appropriate ways to treat children may be the most long-lasting effect of your work as a CDA. Make every minute count.

Go to your local library and look through the parent books and videos that are available. List several titles that would be of special interest to parents in your group.

_____

_____

_____

_____

_____

For parents. . .

Set up a parent message board if you do not already have one. Where is the most visible place? What are some good ideas to get it started? How will you encourage parents to contribute?

How can you encourage parents to make use of the resources in your program and community?

Discuss everything you are doing to make sure parents play a more active role in your program with your CDA Field Advisor.

Part 3

How do you effectively exchange information?

In addition to daily contact, you also need to set aside some time when you and the parents can talk a little more about their children and parenting in general—or any other topic of special interest to the parent such as job interviews, nutrition, moving, or home budgets.

Parent conferences, parent meetings, home visits, and even telephone calls give you and the parents an opportunity to focus on the children or family needs.

Good early childhood programs can also offer another important service to families by helping to identify any possible disabilities. In most cases, the sooner any problems are found and something is done about them, the more likely they are to be resolved. When disabilities are discovered early, children can lead more productive lives. Parents should always be involved in any developmental screening.

Exchange information with parents during
- conferences
- meetings
- home visits
- telephone calls
- screening
- arrival and departure times

In all of these more formal contacts, as well as those that are informal, you keep any information you learn about the family in strict confidence (except suspected child abuse). You are a professional and must not allow yourself to make private information a public matter.

You hold parent conferences

Most parent conferences provide regular checkpoints for you (and any other staff involved) and the parents to share information and plan for their children. Conferences should be held whenever they seem like a good idea—at least twice a year—and preferably more often for infants and toddlers because they change so quickly. Occasionally, you will need to schedule a special conference to discuss a problem.

Make arrangements

You demonstrate respect for parents when you schedule conferences at their convenience. Many parents cannot take off work except in an emergency. Evenings and weekends may be the best times. If transportation or child care are problems, make your plans accordingly.

Be sure your time will not be interrupted and the setting will be comfortable. Create a warm, informal setting where you can be alone without distractions.

If you use a classroom for conferences and have to sit on child-sized chairs, make sure ALL of you sit on child-sized chairs so you don't tower above the parents. Better yet, sit around a table. Sitting behind a desk or in an office will not create a friendly atmosphere of working together.

Include parents with custody as well as the noncustodial parent whenever possible (two conferences may be necessary). Perhaps an interpreter will be needed if you do not speak a common language. Careful planning is essential for an effective conference!

Set up a mutually agreeable time and place for all participants, then follow up with a note to remind the parents. You might also suggest some things they could be thinking about that they might want to discuss with you.

Prepare a written agenda for yourself in advance. Use your daily diary to pull out your major points and questions for discussion. Look for lots of examples of the child's social, emotional, cognitive, and physical development.

On the day of the conference, you might want to make a quick friendly phone call to tell the parent how much you are looking forward to talking with them about their child. You could provide a pot of coffee so parents can serve themselves. Perhaps the children could fix a snack for their parents.

Generate discussions

Just as with all other interactions with parents and children, you will listen **at least** as much as you will talk. All of you want to get to know each other better so you can continue to keep the child's best interests in mind. A cheerful, positive atmosphere will help parents feel more comfortable, too.

You will probably start with a few friendly

comments to make the family feel welcome. Be sure to indicate that the parents should feel free to ask questions at any time. Then move into a brief, upbeat discussion of some positive examples of the child's experiences.

A conference is a time to look both back and forward. Together with the parents you see just how much progress the child has made. Save artwork—it's an excellent way to demonstrate the child's progress. Point out changes that show the parents just how much their child is growing. Ask parents which changes they have noticed at home. Share your insights about the child.

If the child has any type of problem, indicate what behaviors have led to your concern. Again, ask whether parents have observed similar difficulties at home and how they handle them there. Together, work out a plan to help the child, or discuss setting up a screening or counseling session, depending on the nature of the difficulty.

Avoid using labels (aggressive, destructive, learning disabled, slow, or retarded, for example) but instead concentrate on concrete examples of the child's behavior.

If things are going well for the child, talk about ideas each of you have for the future: activities, trips, enrollment in elementary school. Making these plans together will reaffirm your joint efforts with the family.

Always close on a positive, friendly note. Say how pleased you are to work with the family to provide good experiences for the child. Thank the parents for coming and bid them goodbye.

Developing skills in conducting parent conferences takes lots of experience. Start by observing during one. Ask permission to do so. Your CDA Advisor will help arrange it if you need assistance. When you observe, listen and watch. Fill in this information:

What did the teacher do to help the parent relax?

What positive examples of the child's behavior were reported?

What questions did the teacher ask the parent?

What information did the parent share?

_____

_____

_____

_____

_____

_____

What examples of children's work were shared?

_____

_____

_____

_____

_____

_____

_____

_____

What plans were agreed upon for the future?

_____

_____

_____

_____

_____

_____

_____

You will discuss this experience during your CDA Seminar.

You hold parent meetings

Many larger programs have regular or special parent meetings. These can serve a variety of purposes: to share information, to build parenting skills, to do specific activities together.

A number of parents have had unpleasant experiences with schools and may be reluctant to join in these groups. Some have complications with time, language, travel arrangements, or child care.

Use your own judgment about whether meetings will be successful with the parents of children in your group. If you think they will be well accepted, ask parents to suggest topics or speakers. These are some ideas that have worked well in other programs. Add to this list any topics you might like to consider for parent meetings:

- discipline
- bedtime
- allergies
- meal planning/nutrition
- gift ideas for children
- children's books
- early reading skills
- sick child care
- getting ready for kindergarten
- TV and movies
- holidays
- budgeting
- family recreation activities
- baby sitters
- home play activities

_____

_____

_____

Think about your conference with parents as time to discuss *with* not talk *to* or talk *at*

Plan your group meetings in much the same way you do the individual conferences to increase your chances for good participation. You may need to locate a community room in a library or church to accommodate the size of your group. Your classroom or living room may simply not be big enough! Adult furniture is almost a must if you expect to sit longer than 15 minutes or so.

Arrange for healthy refreshments, get any keys needed to get in or lock up, and make sure you know where to turn on the lights and how to close the building for the evening. You may need to make child care arrangements for a wide age range of children, including your own. Be sure you determine in advance how this person will be paid. Arrange for someone to answer the phone so you won't be interrupted.

Parents who speak English as a second language or do not speak English need translation. Participating in a large group setting is difficult for many adults; it becomes doubly difficult if you don't fully understand what's going on. If need be, arrange for a translator, either to sit next to one or two parents, or to translate

collectively for a group of parents. Headphones are used in some meetings to not lose time stopping for the translations. Parents may have other strategies.

Give lots of enthusiastic publicity at least a week ahead of time and talk with parents about the event as well. Make sure parents have a clear set of directions to the meeting site and know what time the meeting will start.

During the meeting, make parents feel welcome and keep them involved in the action. Any speakers or films should take just a few minutes, leaving lots of time for discussion and questions. People of all ages learn best when they are part of the action. A lively meeting will lead to more lively meetings!

Someone is sure to suggest that a parent meeting include some entertainment by the children. As we have discussed, performances in front of an audience, even their own parents, are not appropriate for young children. Instead, suggest that you all sing songs together or eat snacks the children have prepared.

If you feel a group meeting with parents would be of interest to the families in your program, work with your CDA Field Advisor, director, assistant, other staff, or parents to plan what you will do. If at all possible, ask to conduct a meeting yourself. Jot down your ideas here.

Topic/speaker

Time and place _____

_____

_____

_____

Meeting plan _____

_____

_____

_____

_____

After you have conducted the meeting, write what happened here. What was successful?

_____

_____

_____

_____

_____

_____

What could be improved another time?

_____

_____

_____

_____

_____

_____

Discuss your experience with your CDA Field Advisor and/or program director.

You make home visits

Since the very beginning of early childhood education, home visits have been a part of many programs—either where the teacher spends an hour or so just visiting a child and family at home, or where the teacher conducts a formal parent conference at the child's home.

Today some parents and teachers are reluctant to have home visits. These visits may seem like an invasion of privacy or an intrusion on the family. Others still welcome them as a way to further cement the continuity between program and school. Think very carefully about whether a home visit would be appropriate for the parents in your program.

Often, the children benefit the most from such a visit. They are nearly always delighted to show their teacher where they sleep, to introduce their grandmother, or to share some other favorite part of their home.

If you decide to make home visits, arrange them well in advance and make it clear what your agenda is: You want to spend a few minutes getting to know the parent and child in their own comfortable surroundings, away from the busy program. Reassure parents that no special arrangements are needed except for them and the child to be there.

Think of all the ways in which you can help parents feel comfortable with this visit: your professional but casual manner, how you dress, where you sit, how long you stay, how you will handle any language or custom differences. Try to adapt to the family's individual style so that all of you will feel comfortable.

Select two families in your group who might be receptive to home visits. Ask if you could arrange a visit soon. Write your plans here and carry them out. Then write a brief summary of what happened and discuss it with your Field Advisor.

Family _____   Family _____

Plan _____   Plan _____

_____   _____

_____   _____

_____   _____

What happened _____   What happened _____

_____   _____

_____   _____

_____   _____

_____   _____

You use the telephone

The telephone is a marvelous way to deal quickly with questions or minor concerns. Use it often. On the other hand, respect parents' time at work—if receiving phone calls is a problem, leave a message and ask the parent to return the call during a break.

Similarly, encourage parents to call you if they would like to discuss something that will take a few minutes. Let them know when good times are for calls (naptime, for example).

If you are a family child care provider or work in a small program, an answering machine can be a real asset. Whenever you need time to devote to the children, just turn on the machine. Of course, you will want to check for messages often and return calls promptly so parents don't feel they have lost touch with you and their children.

Part 4

What do you when you encounter difficulties?

Whenever people work together as closely as you and parents do, and whenever the issue involved is someone as dear as a child, there are bound to be times when there is conflict. Rather than wait for an argument to erupt, or an issue to get blown out of proportion, prepare yourself now so you will be ready to use a positive approach to deal with the problem.

We have seen how putting program policies in writing can help head off disagreements about fees, illness, and even teaching methods. You also know the steps involved for reporting

5 Cs of parent relations

COMMON SENSE

CONSISTENCY

COMMUNICATION

CARING

CONFIDENTIALITY

Note: From *Opening your door to children: How to start a family day care program* (p. 15) by K. Modigliani, M. Reiff, and S. Jones, 1987, Washington, DC: National Association for the Education of Young Children. Copyright © 1987 authors. Reprinted by permission.

suspected child abuse, whether it is physical or emotional. And you are prepared to communicate with parents in their preferred language, either by learning it yourself or using an interpreter.

Of course, sometimes family difficulties go beyond the issue of child care. In Unit 4, we discussed helping families deal with life's stressful events. Your support of families is especially critical during difficult times, so you want to constantly polish your skills so you can put them into practice at a moment's notice.

Each family has its own style of living and strategies for coping with difficulties it must face. Some families have tremendous resources and seem to be able to solve any problem that comes their way. Other families have few resources and from time to time may need or rely on you or your program administrators for help.

Try to understand each family's circumstances. Financial problems can cause a great deal of stress. Perhaps the parents had a difficult childhood. Racism may affect their lives. Is the family's home language one that is rarely spoken in your community? Are the parents under pressure at work? Do other children in the family require most of the family's emotional or physical resources? Most often, many different factors have led to the family's current state.

When the difficulties are minor, you can use your listening skills and resources to help the parents make progress. However, a great deal of specialized training is needed to help families directly deal with major difficulties. In those cases, consult with your director or other trusted professional about recommending a specialist – a family therapist, financial planner, or other community resource. Then the family can begin to solve the problem with your support as the child care provider.

You can help families move in directions that will enable them to have more productive lives. Think about any families that you believe might benefit from professional assistance. Consult with your Advisor about how to find two or three appropriate referrals. Ask your Advisor for guidance on how you can present your recommendations to the families in tactful, respectful ways.

You recognize parents' mixed emotions about child care

Professional child care is a relatively new idea in our country. The American ideal used to be (and may still be for some) that mother stayed home to raise the children. For most families, this is no longer an option, and for many it never was.

Even so, most parents are never sure they have made the right decision. Some "experts" have the opinion that child care, especially for infants, is harmful to children.

Grandparents may also be critical about "baby sitters" raising the next generation. Parents may worry about giving their children "quality" time. They may feel guilty that they are doing all they can for their children.

You need to be aware of these mixed feelings. Some parents will have them more than others.

Generally, if the parents are happy in their work or training program, and are confident they have chosen high quality child care for their children, they are content with their decisions.

Families who are less happy with their work or who don't really like their child care arrangements usually worry the most about whether they have done the right thing for their children.

First of all, you need to be aware that **appropriate** programs for young children are not harmful and indeed, as you might expect, do promote children's healthy development. So when you do a professional job, you – and children's parents – can rest assured that children will thrive in your care.

With your understanding and patience, parents will eventually begin to see just how much high quality child care supports their entire family. You supplement, not replace, the family's childrearing responsibilities. Together, you want the best for young children.

How do you help families accept that they have made a good decision about the care of their child?

You acknowledge competitive feelings about the child

Sometimes parents worry that their child will love the caregiver best. They may feel threatened when their children don't want to go home at night or when the teacher hugs and kisses their child each morning. It may be a shock when a child calls Mother by the teacher's name, or vice versa.

Infants usually become attached to their parents, and especially their mother or the other most important person in their lives, very early in their lives. They seem to sense that Mom is special.

Occasionally, this early attachment does not happen, even if the mother is the primary caregiver. In these rare instances, someone skilled in working with infant/parent relationships is needed to help the family develop more emotional closeness.

Ties between children and parents in most families are very strong, however. As a professional, your role is to build upon these ties with both your actions and your attitudes. Ideas about how to do this have been woven throughout this entire book.

For example, you support children's development within their own cultural context and encourage bilingual children to express themselves in the language of their choice. You encourage parent involvement and readily share children's successes.

You may have other ways to help parents feel you are a partner, not a competitor. List what you do to help parents know that your role as a teacher is different, but complementary to, their role as parents.

Ties between children and parents in most families are very strong. As a professional, your role is to build upon these ties with both your actions and your attitudes.

Part 5

What are parents' opinions about your work?

By the time you have all these kinds of contact with parents, they should know you well and you should know them well. Their opinions about your work with their children is valuable in helping you know how effective you are.

During your final evaluation for the CDA Credential, you will survey parents using the Council's CDA Parent Questionnaire. This questionnaire provides parents an opportunity to express their views of your competence. The information that parents provide is used by the Council to determine whether you have acquired the skills necessary to become a CDA.

We recommend that you use the Parent Questionnaire at this point in your studies to get a picture of what parents think about your work. You can use the information to help identify your strengths and weaknesses and to help you improve your practice with children and families. **Your CDA Field Advisor will assist you with distributing and collecting the questionnaires, and will discuss the results with you during a conference.**

Look at the items on the sample questionnaire that follows. What do you think parents will say about your contact with them and their children? Do you think every parent can an-

swer "YES" to every question? What areas will you need to improve before your final evaluation as a CDA?

CDA Parent Questionnaire
Cuestionario CDA Para Padres

CDA Candidate's Name _____

Nombre del Candidato/a CDA _____

<table>
<tr><td>

For each statement, circle the answer you think
  is best.

YES = CDA Candidate does this

NO = CDA Candidate does not do this

N/A = Do not know or does not apply

</td><td>

Haga un circulo alrededor de cada considera
  como la más.

SI = La Candidata CDA lo hace

NO = La Candidata no hace esto

N/A = Ud. no sabe o no es pertinente

</td></tr>
</table>

The CDA Candidate
El Candidato/a CDA

YES   NO   N/A   1.   Reports accidents or any first aid given to my child.

SI   NO   N/A   1.   Reporta accidentes o primeros auxilios dados a mi niño.

YES   NO   N/A   2.   Requires my written permission to give any medication to my child.

SI   NO   N/A   2.   Requiere mi autorización por escrito para poder dar cualquier medicina a mi niño.

YES   NO   N/A   3.   Tells me about my child's eating, sleeping, and toileting/diapering.

SI   NO   N/A   3.   Me dice como mi niño come, si duerme, sobre sus hábitos en el uso del baño, o cambio de pañales.

YES   NO   N/A   4.   Follows feeding instructions for my infant or for my child with allergies.

SI   NO   N/A   4.   Sigue instrucciones para la alimentacion de mi bebé o la de mi niño que sufre de alergias.

YES   NO   N/A   5.   Allows my child to be picked up only by people I have named.

SI   NO   N/A   5.   Permite que a mi niño lo recojan sólo aquellas personas a quien yo he autorizado.

YES   NO   N/A   6.   Reports to me about my child's play and learning.

SI   NO   N/A   6.   Me mantiene informado/a sobre el juego y el aprendizaje de mi niño.

YES   NO   N/A   7.   Organizes toys and play materials so my child can reach them easily.

SI   NO   N/A   7.   Organiza los juguetes y materiales de juego de manera que mi niño pueda alcanzarlos fácilmente.

YES   NO   N/A   8.   Provides a place for my child to store his or her own things and makes sure I can find the things I need to bring home.

SI   NO   N/A   8.   Provee un lugar para que mi niño pueda guardar sus pertenencias y se asegura de que yo pueda encontrar todas las cosas que necesito llevar a casa.

YES   NO   N/A   9.   Has enough toys and materials so children do not fight over popular toys.

SI   NO   N/A   9.   Tiene juguetes y materiales en número suficiente para evitar que los niños peleen por los juguetes más populares.

YES   NO   N/A   10.   Takes my child outdoors to play every day, except in bad weather.

SI   NO   N/A   10.   Lleva a mi niño a jugar afuera todos los días excepto cuando el tiempo esta muy malo.

YES   NO   N/A   11.   Talks with my child frequently.

SI   NO   N/A   11.   Habla frecuentemente con mi niño.

YES   NO   N/A   12.   Listens with interest when my child talks and encourages my child to talk.

SI   NO   N/A   12.   Escucha con interés cuando mi niño habla y lo anima a hablar.

YES   NO   N/A   13.   Helps my child learn to control his or her own behavior without spanking or other harsh punishment.

SI   NO   N/A   13.   Ayuda a mi niño a controlar su propio comportamiento, sin pegarle o sin usar castigos duros.

YES   NO   N/A   14.   Reads to my child often.

SI   NO   N/A   14.   Le lee a mi niño, con mucha frecuencia.

YES   NO   N/A   15.   Provides many music, art, block and pretend activities that my child can do in his or her own way.

SI   NO   N/A   15.   Provee muchas actividades de música, arte, bloques, actividades de pretender que mi niño puede hacer a su manera.

YES   NO   N/A   16.   Helps my child feel proud of what he or she can do.

SI   NO   N/A   16.   Ayuda a mi niño a sentirse orgulloso de lo que él puede hacer.

YES   NO   N/A   17.   Encourages children to enjoy getting along with each other.

SI   NO   N/A   17.   Alienta a los niños el disfrute de llevarse bien entre ellos.

YES   NO   N/A   18.   Gives me the feeling that she is truly interested in my child and me.

SI   NO   N/A   18.   Me hace sentir que ella/él esta verdaderamente interesada/o en mi niño y en mí.

YES   NO   N/A   19.   Is pleasant and friendly with me.

SI   NO   N/A   19.   Es agradable y amistosa/o conmigo.

YES   NO   N/A   20.   Is available to discuss my concerns.

SI   NO   N/A   20.   Esta disponible para hablar conmigo sobre mis preocupaciones.

YES   NO   N/A   21.   Asks me for ideas to use with my child, including activity ideas.

SI   NO   N/A   21.   Me pide ideas para usarlas con mi niño, incluyendo ideas sobre actividades.

YES   NO   N/A   22.   Asks me what I think is important in raising my child.

SI   NO   N/A   22.   Me pregunta sobre lo que yo pienso que es importante en la crianza de mi niño.

YES   NO   N/A   23.   Talks with me about any fears my child has.

SI   NO   N/A   23.   Me habla sobre cualquier temor o temores que tenga mi niño.

YES   NO   N/A   24.   Maintains confidentiality; does not freely discuss my child or family in the presence of others.

SI   NO   N/A   24.   Es reservada/o, mantiene informacion confidencial; no habla sobre mi niño o mi familia en la presencia de otras personas.

YES   NO   N/A   25.   Encourages me to visit at any time.

SI   NO   N/A   25.   Me alienta a visitar en cualquier momento.

YES	NO	N/A	26.	Lets me know of parent meetings and other ways I can become involved in the program.

SI	NO	N/A	26.	*Me hace saber cuando hay reuniones de Padres y me informa sobras otras maneras de involucrarme en el programa.*

YES	NO	N/A	27.	Schedules conferences at times that are convenient to me.

SI	NO	N/A	27.	*Señala fechas para reunirnos, en días y horas que me son convenientes.*

Indicate language(s) you use at home_____. Language(s) you prefer Candidate to use with your child_____.

Indique el idioma/s que usted habla en su casa _____. Idioma/s que ud. prefiere que la Candidata hable a su niño_____.

Please write your opinion about this Candidate's work with your child:

Por favor escriba lo que usted opina sobre el trabajo de esta Candidata/o con usted y con su niño:

What happens next?

You will be notified by the Council of the meeting dates and location of your CDA Seminar. These group sessions will build upon your knowledge and skills in early childhood education and prepare you to complete the Early Childhood Studies Review. After the Seminar ends, you and your Field Advisor will work together to complete the last two units in Essentials (which are bound under a separate cover). If you have any questions, review the information in the introduction to this guide (pages xiii–xvi) or call the Council on the Candidate Connection Hotline—**800-424-4310.**

You are now ready to share and build upon your experiences with other CDA Candidates in a group Seminar. This second phase of your CDA credentialing process is sure to be an exciting one!

Check that you have completed Unit 6 on your CDA progress record and then get ready for thought-provoking group experiences yourself!

Resources for more information

Ada, A. (1978). *Set one—Learning begins at home; Set two—Our language, our culture, ourselves; Set three—From home to school; Set four—Parent-school relationships.* [Film series]. Parent's Magazine Films, Inc.

Berger, E.H. (1981). *Parents as partners in education: The school and home working together.* St. Louis: Mosby.

Bjorklund, G., & Burger, C. (1987, January). Making conferences work for parents, teachers, and children. *Young Children, 42*(2), 26–31.

Brazelton, T.B. (1984). Cementing family relationships. In L.L. Dittmann (Ed.), *The infants we care for* (pp. 9–20). Washington, DC: National Association for the Education of Young Children.

"The childcare checklist." Washington, DC: National Black Child Development Institute, 1990.

Dittmann, L.L. (1985). "Finding the best care for your infant or toddler." Washington, DC: National Association for the Education of Young Children.

Dodge, D.T., & Phinney, J. (1990). *A parent's guide to early childhood education.* Washington, DC: Teaching Strategies. Available from Gryphon House, Inc., P.O. Box 275, Mt. Rainier, MD 20712.

Greenberg, P. (Ed.). (1989). *Beginner's bibliography—1989.* Washington, DC: National Association for the Education of Young Children. (1991 edition forthcoming. Updated every 2 years.)

Greenman, J. (1990). *My kind of place: Identifying quality child care for infants and toddlers* [Videotape]. Minneapolis, MN: Greater Minneapolis Day Care Association.

Honig, A.S. (1979). *Parent involvement in early childhood education.* Washington, DC: National Association for the Education of Young Children.

"How to choose a good early childhood program." Washington, DC: National Association for the Education of Young Children, 1974.

Lyons, P., Robbins, A., & Smith, A. (1983). *Involving parents: A handbook for participation in schools.* Ypsilanti, MI: High/Scope.

Modigliani, K, Reiff, M., & Jones, S. (1987). *Opening your door to children: How to start a family day care program.* Washington, DC: National Association for the Education of Young Children.

Neugebauer, B. (Ed.). (1987). *Alike and different: Exploring our humanity with young children.* Redmond, WA: Exchange Press.

Powell, D.R. (1986, May). Research in review. Parent education and support programs. *Young Children, 41*(3), 47–53.

Readdick, C.A., Golbeck, S.L., Klein, E.L., & Cartwright, C.A. (1984, July). The child-parent-teacher conference: A setting for child development. *Young Children, 39*(5), 67–73.

Riley, S.S. (1984). *How to generate values in young children.* Washington, DC: National Association for the Education of Young Children.

Stone, J.G. (1987). *Teacher-parent relationships.* Washington, DC: National Association for the Education of Young Children.

"Teaching young children to resist bias: What parents can do." Washington, DC: National Association for the Education of Young Children, 1989.

West, B. (1987). Children are caught—between home and school, culture and school. In Neugebauer, B. (Ed.), *Alike and different: Exploring our humanity with young children* (pp. 124–134). Redmond, WA: Exchange Press.

7

Putting it all together as an early childhood professional working with preschoolers

WHAT A LONG WAY you have come since you first started your CDA Professional Preparation Program! You have worked hard on your own. You have met many other CDA Candidates in your Seminar group. You probably have had a few exciting moments of discovery along the way when you saw how things fit together. You undoubtedly disagreed with a few ideas. You even may have felt that the struggle was not worth it, as you spent your weekends and evenings completing assignments and putting together your Professional Resource File. But now your CDA Credential will soon become reality.

You are almost at the end of one phase, and at the beginning of an even more difficult one in your work life. You are about to be recognized as an early childhood professional. You will be faced with problems to solve every day in this field. You will have to make decisions that affect the lives of children, par-

ents, or your colleagues. You may be faced with the need to take action on behalf of children, parents, or early childhood educators you don't even know.

And you are probably aware of just how much more there is to learn about how young children develop. Our field, like young children themselves, is constantly changing and growing. After you have earned your CDA, you will enter the early childhood profession and will be qualified for a responsible, professional position. In order to make progress on your career path, you must keep on building your skills through continuing education and through collaboration with your early childhood co-workers.

Will you accept the challenge? Where do you go from here?

This unit and the next are to be completed during the third and final phase of your CDA Professional Preparation Program. You will continue to apply what you have learned as you build your CDA Professional Resource File and work with your Field Advisor to complete these last units.

As you prepare to demonstrate your competency as a teacher of young children, you will complete these tasks:

1. Work through all of the activities in Unit 7, with your Field Advisor's support.

2. Collaborate with your Field Advisor to distribute the Parent Opinion Questionnaire to all the parents of children in your group.

3. Complete your CDA Professional Resource File.

4. Be obseved by your Field Advisor as you demonstrate your skills with children in a classroom setting.

5. Take part in the final assessment, at which time the Council Rep will interview you, review your Professional Resource File, and submit materials about you to the Council for Early Childhood Professional Recognition.

Part 1

Putting together all that you have learned

To be able to put everything together to create a high-quality program means using all the teaching strategies you know to foster development in children. Doing this will take yet another skill area: working as a member of an early childhood team.

Lots of **adults** are involved in programs for young children: families, licensing personnel, teaching assistants, staff (cooks, bus drivers), volunteers, community service people, consultants, medical personnel, substitutes, provider networks, supervisors, other teachers, neighbors. All of you must work as a team to provide the best possible care for children in your community. How can you do that?

Establish cooperative relationships

We have already talked about how to work with families: you both share information and plan together, you treat each other with respect, and you listen more than you talk. You use informal conversations, notes or letters, conferences, meetings, telephone calls, newsletters, and a variety of other ways to keep in touch with families. You are always pleasant, courteous, and tactful. You try to understand their point of view and keep their needs in mind. You are open to suggestions and are always trying to improve yourself.

As a professional early childhood educator, you will use these same skills when you collaborate with all the other people involved in your program. Whether you work in a large Head Start program, a medium-sized center in a nationwide chain, or in a small local child care center, your work puts you in touch with many other people. You are part of a team of professionals. And you are expected to conduct yourself in a professional way.

Whenever these other people are together with you and the children, you are showing children how adults get along with each other. When people respect each other, the day goes much more smoothly, too.

A new substitute is working with you today. She was called at the last minute and arrives after some of the children. You welcome her to the program, give her a statement of your program's philosophy and a quick summary of the activities for the children, and briefly outline what you expect her to do during the morning. "We're so glad you are here today. I will introduce you to each of the children. They can wear their name tags today if you would like.

Please help me walk around the room as the children play. We'll show interest in what they are doing, talk informally, ask questions to make them think, and offer assistance if we see the need. Around 9:30, I'll show you how to fix snack."

Helping volunteers, substitutes, and visitors feel welcome and comfortable requires some advance organization on the part of the staff person supervising the classroom. These are just a few of the things you must remember to prepare in advance so that the day can go as smoothly as possible:

• **Have a copy of your program's expectations for children—the program rules and the daily schedule—written out for the newcomer to read.** These guidelines will help ensure that methods are consistent and promote positive behaviors. This system eliminates surprises for children and adults, too. Make sure any questions the visitor might have are answered as soon as possible throughout the day.

• **Write out your plans for the day, and explain how you expect the volunteer or substitute to assist you with each activity.** If the person is new to work with young children, you may need to explain some basic principles about this kind of teaching. For example:

Fingerpainting at about 10 a.m.
Supplies: Place these supplies on the art table (supplies are in the cupboard above the sink): Orange, yellow and black fingerpaints; enough large sheets of fingerpaint paper for each child in the group.
Supervision: Three or four children may fingerpaint at a time. Ask them to help each other snap on their smocks and roll up their sleeves. Children may use their hands and arms to paint. They may choose any or all of the three colors, and can work as long as needed to finish. After washing and hanging up their smock, they can ask someone else in the group to take their place in the art area. Encourage casual conversation and experimentation. Remember, the fun children have is more important than whatever

the results are.

Things to talk about: Talk with children about what they are doing. Ask them to think about how the paint feels on their hands. You might suggest words such as cool, slippery, slimy, wet, gushy, mushy — make up a word or two. Point out how different techniques make different marks on the paper as the children use them: One finger makes a thin line, the side of the hand can erase everything. If children make a design and then cover it up, do not express disappointment or criticize, but rather focus on what the child is doing. If the paper gets too wet and tears, offer another sheet if the child wants to continue.

• Introduce the children and visitor by name. Some children may want to introduce themselves. Explain to each child who the person is and why she or he is there. If a teacher is ill, tell the children. If the visitor will be doing some testing, briefly explain the process. If you are being observed, say what the observer is looking for. Use name tags if your visitor prefers.

• Observe the person as she or he works with the children. Throughout the day, comment on how things are going. "You've been such a help to notice just where to be to give the children a boost. I'm so glad you're here today." Jot down any topics that need to be discussed later.

Many early childhood programs have support staff such as nutritionists, social workers, bus drivers, office staff, and janitors. To make sure they feel like a real part of your program's team, exchange information with them on a regular basis . . . about individual children's preferences or moods . . . about program plans . . .

when you'll need something special, for example. Encourage children to draw pictures or write letters for the staff who are responsible for special efforts.

With the nutritionist/cook: "In two weeks, on Wednesday, the 23rd, we have a field trip planned to the vegetable farm. We'll be needing bag lunches for the children that day. Think about what foods might travel well, and then we'll talk about how to organize our lunch plans at the end of this week."

With the cleaning staff: "I know that this has been a busy week for you. We brought in all those colorful leaves and then pasted them. Making applesauce really created quite a sticky mess, didn't it? We do try to have the children clean up after themselves, but are so glad you can handle the really big jobs for us. We really appreciate having a clean space to play every morning."

With the driver: "Sharee has really been working hard to sit quietly in her seat lately. We've been talking about safety on the school bus. How has she been doing?"

Children often express their feelings through art.

Throughout the year, you may also work with other adults from outside the program. Sometimes they will support your efforts, sometimes they will be critical of what you do, and sometimes you will work together on behalf of a child or family who has requested information about a topic. Or sometimes a staff member within your program, such as your supervisor may offer a negative opinion of your work.

Teachers are put on the spot a lot, and it is hard sometimes to accept criticism. Ask for a private conference time when you both are unhurried and can calmly discuss areas of concern in a productive way.

Your director has finished her evaluation. You are nervous about the results, even though you have tried hard to do your best. Sure enough, you are rated low in one area: children need to be offered more choices throughout the day.

You are disappointed at the criticism but eager to find out just what you can work on to do better. "We are trying hard to do that. Can you give us some examples of what you mean to improve our program?"

Your director begins tactfully, "I can see you have a good start. But instead of giving children a choice between an art activity you have set up and a game led by your assistant, you might want to broaden their choices. Offer choices that are something the children can do on their own without an adult imposing so much structure on what happens."

You reply, "Oh, you mean like letting them choose which art materials or table toys they want to use?"

"Exactly. The children may take a while to adjust to thinking more for themselves, but you have a lot of great materials. Let them pursue their own interests. Try giving them a little more freedom to choose within the activity, as well as choosing the activity itself."

"It's really helpful to see what kind of choices you mean. I'll work to see how I can offer better choices for children."

What techniques have you developed to respond to criticisms or challenges in productive ways?

_____

_____

_____

_____

Children should benefit from your professionalism.

You probably also have encountered the need to build support for what you do within your neighborhood or community.

> Your child care program is located in a residential neighborhood. One person who is home all day has been stirring up the people on your street by complaining about all the noise from the playground area.
>
> A parent hears about the stew from a friend, and tells you what is happening. "Thank you for clueing us in to the problem. We'll need to think of some ways to become better friends with our neighbors."
>
> You come up with several ideas to try: Send a newsletter to everyone in the area, or have a noon picnic and invite neighbors, or issue invitations for people to visit the program, or ask the local paper to do a story on what a good program you have.
>
> Some of these ideas may not work, but the process has been started. You meet with two parents to try to figure out what to do.

In a situation like this it's very important for you to remain calm and "professional." This is true even if the accusations are false, or make you angry. The parents will pick up on your tone and attitude.

What ideas do you have to maintain good community relations with your program's neighbors?

As a professional, you may also be called upon to lend your expertise to discussions of issues beyond your own program.

> A condominium homeowner's association in your city has just ruled that their policy against home businesses will be enforced. This means no family child care in a nearby neighborhood. And already there is a shortage of good care in your community. Parents are dismayed.
>
> You ask for a few minutes at the next AEYC meeting to raise the issue with your colleagues. You form a committee that includes several parents and a city administrator. Your goal is to plan strategies to increase the availability of child care.

> A teacher brings in an "English Only" leaflet that is being circulated in your neighborhood. It calls for a petition to do away with all bilingual services in the community.
>
> You call a meeting with staff and parents to discuss a strategy. A parent suggests an "English Plus" leaflet supporting diversity. Staff and parents take various responsibilities to work on it.

Are you ready to handle these kinds of responsibilities? As a CDA, others will look up to you. You will be expected to work with lots of people. The future of children is in your hands.

Use community resources

All through your *Essentials* curriculum, you have tracked down resources:

- the phone number to report child abuse
- your county Extension Service for nutrition information
- field trip possibilities
- services to screen children for possible disabilities and to take appropriate action
- resources for parents
- translator services for the languages spoken at your center

Now is the time to become familiar with all the other resources in your community that can help you be more effective in your work with children. Here are just a few of the typical resource agencies that serve families. You can probably list more. Get together with your program director, or perhaps talk with your licensing representative, if you need help to find out what your community offers.

Begin a card file of resources such as these, that you can share with your colleagues and with parents. Then call each group and find out what services or materials they have to help you.

Red Cross
Easter Seal Society
Safety groups
Mental health clinics
Medical clinics
Food stamps
WIC programs
Financial planning
Gymnastics classes
Child care resource and referral
Cultural resource groups
Resale shops
Educational supply stores
Performing artists' groups
Food cooperatives
Library
Community based organizations

All of these resources can broaden your ability to support the needs of the families in your program—and your program itself! Many have brochures, information, even curriculum materials appropriate for parents and/or young children. Take advantage of what is available in your community through government agencies, volunteer groups, and citizen action coalitions. Unless you use these wonderful supplements, you, the children, and their families will miss out on a lot of marvelous opportunities. Expand your horizons today.

Allow children the freedom to choose some of their own activities.

And, do not forget your local library. It contains a vast amount of resource material!

Manage efficiently

You are well aware that not all of your time is spent with children. Regardless of the type of program you work in, you have other responsibilities as well. You manage space, materials, activities, records, and other adults every day.

Organize space and materials

We have already seen how important it is to arrange your teaching space to make the most of it. But remember, maintaining a safe, healthy learning environment means rearranging it occasionally. Because children grow and change, and new children enter your care, you will want to periodically look carefully at your room arrangement and make changes to keep it fresh and interesting. Rotate equipment and materials as children's skills improve. Rejuvenate the outdoor play area with a fresh supply of sand or a new set of containers for water play.

Each time new material is added or a new theme is introduced, you have to examine these materials for bias. It is easy to slip back into a routine of what was done before.

Storage areas need to be neatly arranged and cleaned occasionally so you know what you have and where to find it. Who knows what buried treasure is lurking in the back of your closet!

Thoughtful planning of the environment also means you keep track of supplies so they can be ordered before you run out. One busy day and you can suddenly be out of glue! And you certainly don't want the guinea pig to go hungry! Periodically check the first-aid kit to make sure it is well supplied.

You plan ahead, too, to decide which special materials you will need—pipe cleaners, tissue paper, foods for a cooking project. Perhaps you need parents to bring in paper bags or scraps of fabric. Give them a little advance notice so they can save things.

Take a look at the floor plan you developed in Unit 3 of *Essentials* (page 165). Now that you have many new ideas, complete the final design using the chart on page 165, or review the design you completed during Seminar. **Discuss your design with your Field Advisor.**

Plan ahead for daily activities

Long before you start a new theme, gather all the materials needed so you won't have to scramble for something at the last minute. Check with your library to make sure the book titles or films you want are available, and reserve them if possible. Contact community resource groups about materials or visitors and arrange dates well in advance. The curriculum in your program will set the framework for what daily activities the children will do. But being prepared for each day will require you to think ahead.

For instance, most field trips must be scheduled far in advance because there are so many details to arrange. You will need to visit the place yourself and talk with the people there about how they can best accommodate young children. Travel, emergency medical permissions, and other forms must be signed. Bus or car arrangements have to be made. Special preparations may be needed for children with disabling conditions. Volunteers to go with you must be contacted. Be sure to include some type of exercise or activity that helps prepare children for the trip. Money may need to be collected.

Arrange for special visitors by giving them enough notice. Be sure to talk with them, in person or by phone before their visit, about the children's interests and attention spans and clarify what you expect the visitor to do.

Plan ahead to stay late on days when an activity will require a lengthy clean up. Arrive early when preparations for the day require extra time.

You may also need to make arrangements for parent meetings—make sure refreshments are ready and supplies (napkins, coffee, and so forth) are provided, and arrange for translators and translation equipment as needed.

Allow time in your day to keep notes for future planning. Sit down at the end of each day and look at your activities planned for tomorrow—do you have everything you need?

Keep records

By now, you should have quite a large collection of observations of the children recorded in your daily diary. By building a record of how each child grows and learns, you can use the information to plan themes and activities, to point out to parents how much progress their children are making, and to help identify any potential disabilities. Don't stop just because you have finished your CDA!

Date records and have a folder for each child. Records of children can also help families when the child leaves your program. For bilingual programs, for example, records on the first language of the child and his or her usage and understanding of the second language will be critical to planning. Families may want you to share some of what you have learned about the child with their child's next teacher. Always ask the parents first—summaries of your observations should only be released to others **if the parents approve**. Obtain permission from parents in writing. Remember this is confidential information. They will usually be quite agreeable if you explain that this is one way you can work together to build a bridge between the two programs for their child.

In every program some written records are needed just to ensure children's welfare while they are present. Proper procedures to report illness or accidents should be established. Attendance records must be accurate, especially in the event of an emergency evacuation. All programs must keep up-to-date health records, emergency forms, and written policies.

Depending on the type of program you work in, you may or may not be responsible for keeping other types of records. Family child care providers, for example, must maintain records for licensing/registration and for taxes. Your program director or finance officer must prepare a budget, maintain a checking account, and obtain liability insurance coverage. Zoning records may be needed. You may participate in the Child Care Food Program or serve children whose care is subsidized or paid for by an agency, and all of these require some paperwork. If you have any assistants, you will need health and wage records for them as well. And you may need to advertise your program. Early childhood programs are indeed businesses!

All written records must be legible so others can read them, and should be organized and kept in a place where they can be located easily. If your program is bilingual, records may need to be kept in more than one language.

Add samples of 3 types of record keeping forms used in group care programs to your Professional Resource File. Include your program's accident report and emergency form:

1.

2.

3.

Communicate

Your ability to listen and respond appropriately—to children, parents, and others—keeps coming up in your professional studies. That's because listening is such a valuable tool in your everyday work. Sometimes people are subtle and sometimes they are pretty direct. But you **will** find out what people think about your work, what they need, and how you could improve what you do. Keep your eyes and ears open to clues that something needs to be changed or that you are really doing a good job. It's a mark of a professional to be able to make positive changes in response to constructive criticism.

Here are some typical examples of the subtle types of feedback you may get. What would you do in each of these situations?

1. A child gets wet and you discover there are no extra clothes in her cubby. As you look around, you see other cubbies with few or no extra clothes as well.

   What are these parents telling you?

What should you do about it?

_____

_____

_____

_____

2. You sent field trip permission slips for a neighborhood walk out 2 weeks ago, and you have only 3 of the 7 permissions you need.

Why have so few been returned?

_____

_____

_____

What should you do?

_____

_____

_____

3. Group time has been reduced to 10 minutes for your oldest children. About half of them sit quietly, but the other half listen only a minute or two, and then they begin to wander around.

Why are the children so restless?

_____

_____

_____

_____

What should you do?

_____

_____

_____

_____

4. In your newsletter, you ask parents to provide healthy snacks for birthday treats. The first three birthdays after your notice are all celebrated with cupcakes and Kool-Aid.

Why did parents ignore your request?

How can you get parents to plan more nutritious birthday snacks?

5. Three monolingual Spanish speaking parents in a row have asked to move their children from your group to the group of a monolingual English speaking teacher.

What do their actions tell you?

What information about language development of bilingual children would you share?

How could you present it?

6. Your director gets a phone call from the local TV station about qualifications of child care providers. They would like to interview her. She agrees, and suggests they use your room as the setting.

What does the director's choice mean?

What can you do to prepare your room?

Managing efficiently means being sensitive to these indicators of feedback and making adjustments accordingly.

Every day you will make hundreds of decisions—about how to interact with children, about what to say to a parent, about how to work more effectively with colleagues. The more resources you have at your fingertips, the more likely you are to make good decisions. The fieldwork and Seminar parts of your *Essentials* curriculum have covered the basic information you need to make sound judgments. How you use that information professionally requires discussion of one more topic— professionalism.

Part 2

You try to make good decisions

Throughout your *Essentials* curriculum you have picked up information to build on your teaching experience. You have seen ways to make good decisions about how you teach, how you work with other adults, and how you plan and organize your work. You will look back again and again at some parts of this material as you continue to extend your ability to work with the youngest of children in a professional way. There is so much to absorb—people have learned a lot about children over many years.

Making good decisions means always being

ethical. Members of NAEYC have developed a code of ethics, which you will find in Unit 1 of *Essentials*. You are expected to agree to abide by it as a CDA.

With this code to help, each of us in the field must work out our own thoughts on what kind of teaching behavior is truly professional. We'll offer some guidelines here to help you make ethical decisions. While there are no right answers, here are some ways to help you consider as many factors as possible before you decide what to do in a specific situation. **Presented on the following pages are several situations. Think about each of these situations and discuss them with your Field Advisor.**

Have a healthy attitude about your power

Young children are so helpless and dependent upon adults. They are with you for so many of their waking hours. Their parents depend on you to give children the best experiences possible during those impressionable early years. In addition, parents need reliable child care so they can earn a living or prepare to earn one.

It is easy to abuse this power, either with children or adults. Some teachers are tempted to use physical force because they are stronger than children. Some teachers are tempted to take advantage of children psychologically because they believe children learn to be obedient out of fear. Some teachers fail to prepare children to become good world citizens. And some teachers think they can get away with almost anything because the parents are so

desperate for affordable, convenient child care.

Think for a minute about how much power you have and use every day. You have the power to enable children to grow strong and competent—or to be weak and inept. You have the power to help children become kind and generous—or mean and stingy. You have the power to validate children's home language and culture or make them feel inferior to other people. You have the power to help children get along with each other—or to hate and fear people who are different from them. You have the power to provide high-quality care—or minimal custodial care. What is the ethical approach?

As a professional, you make a commitment never to take advantage of children or their parents—physically, emotionally, intellectually, or financially. You respect them as people and treat them accordingly. You use your power to build strengths and to help overcome weaknesses.

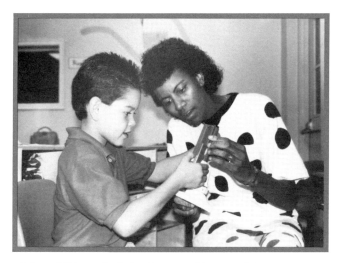

Giving children the help they need in a positive way enables them to be strong and competent.

How would you use your power in situations such as these? Jot down notes and discuss your responses with your Field Advisor.

1. A 4-year-old boy has been crying for 10 minutes. You have tried listening, hugging, and offering a favorite stuffed animal, all to no avail. *Do you scream at the boy and tell him to shut up, that big boys don't cry? Do you spank him and isolate him in the director's office?*

What is the professional thing to do?

2. Two young preschoolers are fighting in the sandbox. Before you can get there, one has thrown sand into the other's eyes. *Do you grab the child who threw the sand and drag her indoors to sit in the office? Do you tell both children to get out of the sandbox and that they may not play there for a week?*

What is the professional thing to do?

3. A new family has moved into your community. Their 5-year-old is hearing impaired. *Do you discourage the family when they inquire about enrollment? Do you accept the child but increase your fee because more effort is needed on your part?*

What is the professional thing to do?

Children will often look to you for reassurance and comfort. You have the power to do both.

4. An English speaking child announces she won't play with Marisol because she is stupid and can't talk. *Do you frown and tell the child she is wrong and you never want to hear her say anything like that again? Do you ignore the comment and act like you didn't hear it?*

What is the professional thing to do?

selves and others. You keep written records confidential. And you immediately report any possible abuse. Professionals do not announce what they have learned about a family to all the other teachers in the program, or to any other parents, or to their friends.

What do you do to stop yourself when you feel tempted to break a confidence about a family or a particular child in your program?

Keep confidences

During the course of your work, you will learn a great deal about families' personal lives. A parent may confide in you some upsetting details about a spouse. A child may blurt out, "Momma told me not to play with you because you are dumb." Parents may fill out financial forms so your program can qualify for financial reimbursement. Bruises on a Monday morning may lead you to suspect child abuse.

Whatever you hear or see as a CDA is privileged information. You are a professional, so you must take the appropriate steps to remedy the situation if there is a problem. Often you refer people to the appropriate community resources. You provide an accepting environment in which children feel good about them-

Parents trust you to keep information about them confidential. Parents have a right to privacy. Of course, you must balance that with the need to protect the child.

Protect children

You are legally and ethically responsible for the protection of all children in your care. Not just their safety, but their emotional well being, their physical development, their intellectual growth, and their social skills. You do not allow children to hurt themselves or each other. You do not allow any other adult to hurt children either. You show value for the way each child speaks and include their home language in the program. You are constantly alert for signs of any type of abuse. You base your decisions about what to do on the children's best interest.

Professional early childhood educators are constantly alert to conditions within the program to assure that children are protected in all these ways. For example, you quickly scan the outdoor play area every time you enter it for new hazards. You arrange for enough adult assistance on field trips so children are kept in small groups for easy supervision. You evaluate each new order of materials (or each donation) for safety and appropriateness. You always listen to and watch the children so you can promote cooperation and friendly behaviors. You are eager to learn more about what types of activities are most beneficial for preschool development, and you implement what you know.

Your role as a professional demands that you report suspected child abuse. Here are some examples of other situations that may arise, in which you will need to act as a protector for children.

Write down how you would handle each of these dilemmas, and then talk with your Field Advisor about your responses.

1. One child frequently hits and shoots pretend guns at the other children.

2. Often one of your 4-year-olds is listless all morning, then devours lunch and seems more lively in the afternoon.

3. The parents of a 3-year-old have purchased a kit with flashcards to teach their child to read. They are pressuring you to use it with all the children in the group.

Provide good quality care

There are many different types of programs for young children. You can adopt one of the models, or set up your own approach. Either way, as a professional you always provide developmentally appropriate activities, materials, and experiences for all the children. You know children learn best through their own self-directed play and manipulation of real objects. You want children to enjoy themselves and to pick up ideas and behaviors that they will keep throughout their lives. You provide good, safe care for children. To do less would be unethical.

One of the most difficult aspects of working with young children is to avoid the temptation to lapse back into your old ways of teaching and disciplining. Catch yourself before that happens.

There are still many commercial (and homemade) materials available that are not appropriate for young children. Some methods or materials are better used with older children. Parents may request worksheets for 4-year-olds, for example, and you now realize young children have better things to do.

You will need to put everything you know to work every day in making the right decisions about how to best foster the learning and development of young children.

Transitions from one activity to another also often prove to be difficult with a group of wiggly young children. The time between one activity and another may simply involve sitting and waiting . . . and waiting . . . and waiting. But now you know that's not an appropriate expectation. You know it's best to involve children in the transition to keep it smooth and not wasteful of anyone's time. Children can carry out the baskets of sand toys, for example. If you are waiting for another child to wash hands before lunch, do some fingerplays or sing songs with movements until everyone is ready. Keep children involved rather than waste their time.

Move about in small groups rather than herding children like cattle from place to place, or expect them to walk in a straight line with hands clasped behind their backs. If your schedule still isn't working to make transitions easier, revise it again with the long-term goals for children in mind. Remember, children are learning from everything they do!

You will be faced again and again with the need to make on-the-spot decisions about the best quality of care. It helps to think ahead about how you would handle problems that are sure to arise.

What would you do if . . .

. . . a young preschooler drew a beautiful picture with lots of colors, and then scribbled black all over the top of it?

. . . a child began spanking a doll in the housekeeping area?

. . . a 4½-year-old boy always enters a group of children like a bull in the china shop, demanding to be involved or destroying children's projects?

Discuss your responses with your Field Advisor, who can help you think about how to apply what you have learned about young children in dealing with these and similar incidents.

As a CDA, you will always strive to keep knowledgeable about the standards of the profession. You will need to know about other national voluntary self-evaluation systems designed to improve and recognize the quality of programs. Group programs can benefit greatly by going through these review processes, much as you are going through the CDA credentialing system.

If you feel your center is an excellent one, you may want to find out about getting it accredited through the National Academy of Early Childhood Programs. Call or write to NAEYC (see the list of national organizations on page 29, Unit 1) to request information about this system. Then talk with your program director about whether your program should take advantage of this excellent opportunity to be nationally recognized.

What else do you and other program staff do to constantly monitor whether you are providing good care for children?

What steps can you take to improve how your program's quality of care is assessed?

Respect parents' authority

Parents do have the ultimate authority to make decisions about their children— within legal limits of course. Every family and every cultural group stresses some values more than others, and then there are individual differences among families.

Parents may have standards of behavior for children at home that are not necessarily the same as those you have set in the program. Some families may live by a different code of morality than you accept. Parents may place a higher value on some things—wardrobe or financial status, for example—than you prefer.

We all know how important it is to respect differences, but sometimes it is difficult when you disagree with how parents are raising their children. Often, parents who have radically different ideas than you will probably not choose your program. At other times, however, they may have no choice but to enroll their children in your program. When that happens, you need to get to know each other well and work out a way to be as cooperative as possible. You must

make a concerted effort to learn all you can about the family and their way of life or beliefs. You may eventually agree to disagree. You will respect each other's differences—and agree that children will be expected to act differently at home and at school. That way, at least in your program, you can keep what you believe to be the child's best interests in mind.

Children also need to know that some differences between home and your program are acceptable and natural. A simple explanation that "Yes, you say grace before each meal at home. That is so important for your family. But here we wait until everyone is seated and then we begin to serve ourselves."

Without a doubt, as a CDA you will encounter some thorny value issues. Just remember there is more than one way to make things work for the benefit of the children. Be willing to listen and try new ideas.

As a professional, how would you deal with situations such as these?

1. Parents insist on dressing their 4-year-old boy in a white shirt almost every day, and they want to keep him clean.

2. A child clearly has not been bathed in many days — she has offensive body odor, her hair is tangled, and her fingernails are imbedded with dirt. The child is developing a rash.

4. Each morning, one parent stops at your sidewalk in front of the center, honks the horn, and then sends her child alone up to your door.

3. One 3-year-old boy has been biting other children. You know you should speak to the parents about it — but you also know that if you do they will probably beat the child.

Support diversity

As you have seen, all people are biased — we all think we are right and the best. And we all need to admit that we have those biases if we are to become good teachers. Your CDA Seminar experiences helped you see how these biases can affect your work.

Hard as it is, there is no room for favorites when you teach young children. Instead, you must do everything possible to help children feel good about themselves, their family, their heritage, their beliefs, their abilities, and their language — and to appreciate and respect those same characteristics in others.

We are helping to make it possible for children to become productive citizens of the world of today and tomorrow. The world is filled with many ethnic groups and people with varying capabilities who must get along with each other. Ultimately, our survival depends on peacefully resolving our differences and learning to live together. We all must accept and appreciate our wonderful diversity as human beings.

These are some ethical issues in this area that you may face. How would you deal with them?

1. Another teacher in your program always asks the older children to sit "Indian style."

2. You accept a child with HIV infection into your group. The other parents threaten to withdraw their children.

3. A child brings in a copy of *Little Black Sambo* or *The Five Chinese Brothers*.

4. Two White children say they are afraid that a Spanish-speaking child's "dirty color" will rub off on them if they hold hands.

Help protect consumers

Every state has different laws regarding programs for young children and qualifications for staff. You have already seen how important it is for good programs to be licensed or registered and for staff and providers to be well trained.

Sometimes, we forget that the purpose of the licensing and registration laws are for consumer protection. In fact, most regulations provide only a **minimum** form of protection — far less than in many other areas that we take for granted, such as driver's licenses or pet food standards, for example. Adhering to those laws is a must.

Regulations generally are designed to establish at least a floor for child-staff ratios, safety, staff qualifications, space, materials, and a variety of other important areas in programs for young children.

Your role as a professional is to protect children and families and advocate for what is in keeping with good practice. Above all, you should assure children's safety, health, and general well-being. All these while maintaining the ethical standards already discussed.

Here are some sticky consumer protection situations. What would you do?

1. The landlord has instructed that the heat must be set no higher that 62 degrees in the winter. The children and staff are too cold. Do you report your own program to the health department?

2. Your director doesn't count part-time children when reporting enrollment levels because "there are always some children out sick anyway."

Working with young children is demanding—of your energy, of your time, and of your conscience. Are you ready to become a professional? Are you prepared to take the most ethical action in sticky situations?

Taking time to listen to children is an important part of being a professional caregiver.

You keep learning

By now you probably have realized how much there is to learn about young children. Even if you have been working with young children for years, or are the parent of several, you have surely discovered that it is much more difficult to be a professional early childhood educator.

You are always learning from your experiences. The field is constantly changing, as we find out more about how children develop. This information affects how we teach. How can you keep up with the challenges to get better at what you love to do?

Improve yourself personally

All of us have things we would like to do better. These may include bad habits we want to break, or attitudes that have been questioned.

What are some of the areas you need to work on?

These are the areas you will want to begin to improve so you can be a better teacher. Perhaps you need to eat more healthy foods or you are always late.

Choose just one of the things you listed and write what steps you need to take to change your behavior.

You don't have to do it alone. Rely on the same community support groups to which you refer parents. Or talk with your supervisor, spouse, friend, or a respected colleague about how they can support your efforts. After you have made some progress in one area, select another and begin to work on it. As you make the most of your life, you can better help others make the most of theirs!

An ethical early childhood educator
- never abuses power with children or families
- keeps information confidential
- protects children's best interests
- provides good care
- respects parents and co-workers
- supports diversity
- favors consumer protection of programs
- improves personal habits
- keeps on learning
- advocates for children, families, and the profession

In Unit 1, you began networking by interviewing an early childhood professional in a job different from yours. You should continue to build this network by interviewing your CDA Field Advisor—you know each other well by now. Make a list of questions you would like to ask about what the distinctive issues are for a career working with preschoolers:

Learn more about your profession

How lucky you are to become a professional today. Just a few years ago there weren't many places you could turn to for information. Now nearly every community has an organized group of early childhood workers. Some of these groups are affiliates of NAEYC, NBCDI, SACUS, NHSA, or other large organizations. Some are state groups, and others are composed of active local people.

These professional networks are important. Most of you work alone or with just a few other professionals—and you never come in contact with the hundreds of thousands of other people who share the same commitment you do.

Now set up a time when the two of you can talk in general about the field for at least half an hour. Jot down what you learned here:

_____

_____

_____

_____

_____

_____

_____

_____

_____

The next task in building your network is to find the names of all the professional early childhood support groups in your area (a few national organizations are listed in Unit 1).

If you have not already done so, contact several groups to learn more about their activities. Then select one or two organizations that seem to be good matches for you. Attend their meetings (go with a co-worker or your CDA Field Advisor, if possible). **Join at least one.** If

there is no local chapter, consider starting one in your area. Be an active member! Volunteer!

Most of these groups publish newsletters, journals, books, videos, posters or other professional development materials. Ask for a sample copy of any regular periodicals that sound interesting. Which publications seem to be most useful to you? You might want to subscribe regularly to a journal or magazine. A few are listed here:

The Black Child Advocate
National Black Child Development Institute
1023 15th Street, NW, Suite 600
Washington, DC 20005
(202) 387-1281 (800) 423-3563

Childhood Education
Association for Childhood Education International
11141 Georgia Avenue, Suite 200
Wheaton, MD 20902
(301) 942-2443

Child Care Review
National Child Care Association
1029 Railroad Street
Conyers, GA 30207
(404) 922-8198 • (800) 543-7161

Day Care & Early Education
Human Sciences Press
233 Spring Street
New York, NY 10013
(212) 620-8000

Dimensions
Southern Association on Children under Six
P.O. Box 5403, Brady Station
Little Rock, AR 72215-5403
(501) 663-0353

Early Childhood Teacher
P. O. Box 6410
Duluth, MN 55806-9893
(218) 723-9215

Interracial Books for Children Bulletin
Council on Interracial Books for Children
1841 Broadway
New York City, NY 10023
(212) 757-5339

Nurturing News
187 Caselli Avenue
San Francisco, CA 94114
(415) 861-0847

NABE News
National Association of Bilingual Education
Union Center Plaza
810 First Street, N.E., 3rd Floor
Washington, DC 20002-4205
(202) 898-1829

National Head Start Association Journal
National Head Start Association
201 N. Union Street, Suite 320
Alexandria, VA 22314
(703) 739-0875

Newspatch: A Newsletter for the Early Intervention Practitioner
Creative Home Programs
P.O. Box 4869
Riverside, CA 92514

Pre-K Today
Scholastics, Inc.
411 Lafayette
New York, NY 10033
(212) 505-4900

Young Children
National Association for the Education
of Young Children
1509 16th Street, NW
Washington, DC 20036
(202) 232-8777 • (800) 424-2460

Find out whether any of these resources are available in your program or local library. If not, how can you include some of these items in your program budget? Order others as your personal budget permits.

Read! Read! Read! Or you will soon be left behind in your own profession. Become familiar with the "Resources for more information" found at the end of each unit of *Essentials*.

Workshops, conferences, and classes are marvelous ways to meet other people and learn more about how to care for groups of young children. Once you have completed your CDA, keep up with the field by regularly enrolling in a course or taking a workshop. Better yet, keep climbing that career ladder and continue to work on your college degree!

Children need opportunities to develop their language skills.

What topics would you like to learn more about?

Write up a plan to accomplish at least one of these goals. Find out where to go or what to read and continue to become even more professional. Then do it.

Becoming a professional also means contributing to the professional development of others. How do you share your new found knowledge with others?

These are just a few of the issues you will encounter as you continue to work with children. Your thinking about ethics will be constantly challenged. Are you prepared to meet those challenges and to act on behalf of young children?

Part 4

You act on behalf of young children

A teacher's work is never done. You already know that. And now we are going to suggest that you do even more. Just working with young children day-to-day is not enough. Thousands of children in our country and around the world are hungry, homeless, unhealthy, or have been harshly treated. Children are unable to defend themselves so we must take it upon ourselves to act in their behalf.

Stand up for good programs and services for children and families

You are now a committed early childhood professional. You have a responsibility to act in your local area, your state, nationally, and even on behalf of children in other countries you have never met. Here are some ways you can reach out, directly or indirectly, to improve the lives of children everywhere. **Add others to this list that you can think of or that you are already involved in.**

- Write letters to support stronger child care legislation, programs to strengthen families' self-sufficiency

- Become active in child advocacy groups

- Help parents become child advocates

- Read the Public Policy Report and the Washington Update in each issue of *Young Children*

- Vote in every election

- Speak up on behalf of developmentally appropriate practice: tell others, buy only appropriate materials, challenge others to learn more about how young children grow and learn

- Build an appreciation for diversity in the groups you are involved in: civic, church or synagogue, volunteer organizations, community service

- Volunteer for Week of the Young Child activities

- Support groups participating in the Worthy Wage Campaign

- Set up a network of supportive colleagues to phone for help

- Work with your school board or kindergarten teacher's association to ease the transition for children entering public school

- Advocate for appropriate services for children with disabling conditions

- _____

- _____

- _____

Don't wait another minute. If you are not taking an active role on behalf of all children and families, choose at least one activity from the list above and **get involved now!**

Advocate for your own profession

One of the most difficult issues facing us as early childhood educators is how to balance the need for affordable child care with our need to support ourselves. Salaries are low. Benefits are few or nonexistent. Most people still view our work as babysitting. But the rewards are so great that our ranks are swelling nevertheless!

Good programs for young children are especially expensive because so many staff are needed, so many materials are used, and so much space is required. We don't want to shortchange children. Nor do we want to settle for less than we deserve for our hard work and long hours doing one of the most important jobs on earth.

Remain committed to the entire profession. Don't isolate yourself only among workers who are like you. Keep learning about others --Head Start, private programs, church sponsored programs, family day care.

Don't fall into the old trap of "conquer and divide." Don't allow yourself or your program to be pitted against other programs serving children. That's where "listening" comes in. Support the efforts of early childhood professionals working in other communities as well.

What can you do to improve the quality of life for staff as well as families in programs for young children?

You will end this portion of your CDA Professional Preparation Program process by going back to where you began—by reaffirming your commitment to professional work with children. This statement first appeared in Unit 1. Now that you are nearly finished with your CDA—at last—this statement will probably have new meaning for you.

Children look for and often need your guidance to help them do the things they like to do.

Congratulations for taking on a very difficult task—enrolling in the CDA Professional Preparation Program. You can check the last box on your CDA Progress Record for your training. Your Professional Resource File is now, or soon will be, complete and you will take part in a final assessment. Our best wishes are with you during these final stages of meeting the requirements for your CDA Credential.

We welcome you as a professional early childhood educator. May your work be more rewarding than you ever dreamed possible and may you grow in your professional competencies each day. The world's children are counting on you.

Resources for more information

Accreditation criteria and procedures of the National Academy of Early Childhood Programs. Washington, DC: National Academy of Early Childhood Programs, National Association for the Education of Young Children, 1984.

Bredekamp, S. (1987). *Developmentally appropriate practice in early childhood programs serving children from birth through age 8,* (expanded ed.). Washington, DC: National Association for the Education of Young Children.

CDF Reports - The monthly newsletter of the Children's Defense Fund. Washington, DC: The Children's Defense Fund.

Celebrating early childhood teachers. [Videotape-22 min.]. Washington, DC: National Association for the Education of Young Children, 1987.

Katz, L. G., & Ward, E. H. (1978). *Ethical behavior in early childhood education.* Washington, DC: National Association for the Education of Young Children.

Kipnis, K. (1987, May). How to discuss professional ethics. *Young Children, 42*(4), 26-30.

NAEYC *position statement on licensing and other forms of regulation of early childhood programs in centers and family day care homes.* Washington, DC: National Association for the Education of Young Children, 1987.

NAEYC *position statement on quality, compensation, and affordability in early childhood programs.* Washington, DC: National Association for the Education of Young Children, 1987.

Pressma, D., & Emery, L. (1991). *Serving Children with HIV Infection in Child Day Care* -- a guide for center-based and family day care providers. Washington, DC: Child Welfare League of America, Inc.

Worthy Work, Worthless Wages. Oakland, CA: Child Care Employee Project, 1989.

Resources for bilingual programs

Ben Aeev, S. (1983) *Mechanisms by which childhood bilingualism affects understanding of language and cognitive structure.* In P. S. Horsnby, Bilingualism: Psychological, Social, and Educational Implications. New York: Academic Press.

Casasola, C. (1978). *Bilingual bicultural education: A manual for teacher trainers and trainees.* Editorial Justa Publication, Berkeley, CA.

Crawford, J. (1989). *Bilingual education: History, politics, theory and practice.* Crane Publishing Company, Inc., Trenton, NJ.

Fillmore, L. (1991, June). A question for early childhood programs: English first or families first? *Education Week.*

Fillmore, L. (1991, May). Report faults of preschool English for Language–Minority Children by Peter Schmidt. *Education Week.*

Fillmore, L. (1991). Language and cultural issues in early childhood education. In S. L. Kagan (ed.), *The 90th Year Book of the National Society for the Study of Education.*

Getting Involved Series (Spanish only) (1990). Washington, D.C.: Head Start Bureau, P.O. Box 1182.

Hakuta, K. (1986). *Mirror of language: the debate on bilingualism,* New York: Basic Book, Inc.

Porter, Rosalie Pedalino (1990). *Forked tongue: the politics of bilingual education.* New York: Basic Books, Inc.

Schon, I. (1991, May). Recent noteworthy books in Spanish for young children. *Young Children,* 46(4), 65.

Siegrist, D. (1976). *Language and bilingual education.* Multilingual, Multicultural Material Development Center, California State Polytechnic University, Pomona, CA.

U.S. Commission on Civil Rights (1975). *A better chance to learn.* Bilingual-Bicultural Education Clearinghouse Publication No. 51, Washington, D.C.

Williams, L. and Gaetano, Y. (1985). *Alerta.* Menlo Park, CA: Addison-Wesley Publishing Company.

8

Preparing for final assessment as a Child Development Associate

**ow**, at the conclusion of the CDA P_3, you should be prepared to complete your final assessment. The process will determine your ability to integrate the knowledge and skills developed in the Professional Preparation Program and to demonstrate your competence as a CDA working with young children and their families.

A specially trained Council Representative will be assigned by the national office to conduct an on-site visit to collect evidence of your competence working with young children and their families. The Council Rep will interview you, review the results of the Formal Observation and Parent Opinion Questionnaires, and examine your Professional Resource File. A summary of the results of this evidence will be forwarded to the Council office in Washington, D.C.

If you have successfully completed all phases of the CDA Professional Preparation Program, the Child Development Associate Credential will be awarded with an endorsement for center-based preschool programs.

Candidates working in bilingual settings and completing special additional requirements will be awarded the Bilingual Specialization.

Definition of a CDA

The Child Development Associate (CDA) is a person who is able to meet the specific needs of children and who, with parents and other adults, works to nurture children's physical, social, emotional, and intellectual growth in a child development framework. The CDA Credential is awarded to child care providers and home visitors who have demonstrated their skill in working with young children and their families by successfully completing the CDA assessment process.

Part 1

CDA Competency Standards

As a Candidate for the CDA Credential, you will be assessed based upon the CDA Competency Standards. These criteria are the national standards used to evaluate a caregiver's performance with children and families. The Competency Standards are divided into six **Competency Goals**, which are statements of a general purpose or goal for caregiver behavior. The six goals are defined in more detail in 13 **Functional Areas**, which describe the major tasks or functions that a caregiver must complete in order to carry out the competency goal. The national competency goals and functional area definitions are common to all child care settings whether in centers or family child care homes.

All of the evidence you collect to demonstrate your competence as a CDA will be judged by these standards.

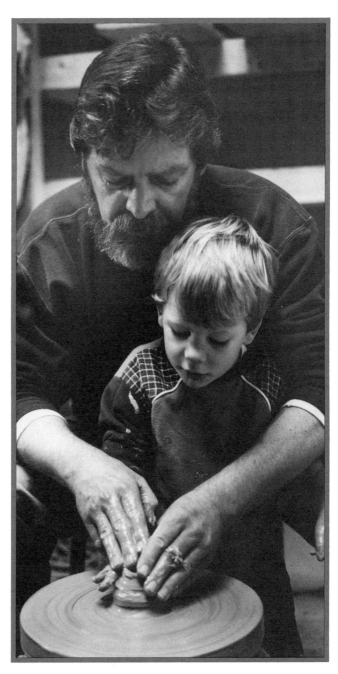

As you become more professional in your caregiver role, your ability to work with children will be enhanced.

"It has been a special privilege for me to have been given the opportunity to teach and to learn, to give and to receive friendship and to experience, again and again, the same joy that I felt on the day that I received my CDA."

CDA, 1990

CDA Competency Goals	Functional Areas	Definitions
I To establish and maintain a safe, healthy learning environment	1. Safe	Candidate provides a safe environment to prevent and reduce injuries.
	2. Healthy	Candidate promotes good health and nutrition and provides an environment that contributes to the prevention of illness.
	3. Learning Environment	Candidate uses space, relationships, materials, and routines as resources for constructing an interesting, secure, and enjoyable environment that encourages play, exploration, and learning.
II To advance physical and intellectual competence	4. Physical	Candidate provides a variety of equipment, activities, and opportunities to promote the physical development of children.
	5. Cognitive	Candidate provides activities and opportunities that encourage curiosity, exploration, and problem solving appropriate to the developmental levels and learning styles of children.
	6. Communi-cation	Candidate actively communicates with children and provides opportunities and support for children to understand, acquire, and use verbal and nonverbal means of communicating thoughts and feelings.
	7. Creative	Candidate provides opportunities that stimulate children to play with sound, rhythm, language, materials, space, and ideas in individual ways and to express their creative abilities.
III To support social and emotional development and provide positive guidance	8. Self	Candidate provides physical and emotional security for each child and helps each child to know, accept, and take pride in himself or herself and to develop a sense of independence.
	9. Social	Candidate helps each child feel accepted in the group, helps children learn to communicate and get along with others, and encourages feelings of empathy and mutual respect among children and adults.
	10. Guidance	Candidate provides a supportive environment in which children can begin to learn and practice appropriate and acceptable behaviors as individuals and as a group.
IV To establish positive and productive relationships with families	11. Families	Candidate maintains an open, friendly, and cooperative relationship with each child's family, encourages their involvement in the program, and supports the child's relationship with his or her family.
V To ensure a well-run, purposeful program responsive to participant needs	12. Program Management	Candidate is a manager who uses all available resources to ensure an effective operation. The Candidate is a competent organizer, planner, record keeper, communicator, and a cooperative co-worker.
VI To maintain a commitment to professionalism	13. Professiona-lism	Candidate makes decisions based on knowledge of early childhood theories and practices, promotes quality in child care services, and takes advantage of opportunities to improve competence, both for personal and professional growth and for the benefit of children and families.

Part 2

Documentation of Competence

Your final assessment as a CDA will involve a documentation of your competence. Five components make up the documentation:

> 1. *Early Childhood Studies Review*
> 2. *Professional Resource File*
> 3. *Formal Observation*
> 4. *Parent Opinion Questionnaires*
> 5. *Oral Interview*

As a Candidate enrolled in the CDA P$_3$, you have already completed one component of the assessment -- the Early Childhood Studies Review -- during your CDA Seminar. Now, you will complete the remaining components.

First, you will prepare to present evidence of your competence from the following (3) sources:

> 1. *Professional Resource File*
> 2. *Formal Observation by the Field Advisor*
> 3. *Parent Opinion Questionnaires*

Then, you will complete your Oral Interview during the Council Rep Verification Visit.

Professional Resource File

The Professional Resource File is a collection of materials that you will use as an early childhood professional in future work with young children and families. It is compiled for two purposes:

> 1. *It provides a picture of what information Candidates find valuable in their work as a basis for assessing competence as a CDA; and*
>
> 2. *It provides Candidates an important experience in locating resources and articulating their own view of the work in early childhood programs.*

The Professional Resource File is a working resource - one that should be USEFUL to you as a CDA during your career in early childhood education. The information it contains should serve as reference materials on a daily basis.

You have already collected most, if not all of the materials you need for your Professional Resource File and have drafted statements of competence for 5 of the 6 competency areas. Now it is time to revise and complete all three sections and arrange them in their final form.

Arrangement of the Resource File

The material in the Professional Resource File can be arranged in any one of many creative ways (e.g., bound in a notebook or contained inside file folders in a box). It should be professional looking and manageable in size. It should be organized and easy to add to or delete from. *There are no requirements about how it should look.* Whatever its physical form, the Professional Resource File should be portable — designed to be carried to and from a work site, on a home visit, or to a meeting — wherever early childhood professionals work.

Contents

The Professional Resource File has three major sections: (1) *Autobiography*; (2) *Statements of Competence*; and (3) *Resource Collection*.

1. <u>Autobiography</u>: Write a statement about yourself of about 300 words. In the first part tell who you are, and in the second part, tell what things about your life influenced your decision to work with young children. *If you wish, you may attach a formal resume of your education and work experiences.*

2. <u>Statements of Competence</u>: In your own words describe the things you do with children and families that demonstrate your ability to meet the specific needs of children in each of the following six (6) Competency Goal areas. The description in each area should be 200-500 words in length and should state your goals for children and give specific examples of what you do to achieve those goals. *For bilingual Candi-*

dates, statements must be specific to the goals of bilingual programs and the statements in three (3) Competency Goal areas must be written in Spanish.

Begin each section by writing out the Competency Goal Statement:

1. Establish and maintain a safe, healthy learning environment
2. Advance physical and intellectual competence
3. Support social and emotional development and provide positive guidance
4. Establish positive and productive relationships with families
5. Ensure a well-run, purposeful program responsive to participant needs
6. Maintain a commitment to professionalism

Remember, your statement for each Competency Goal should contain no more than 500 words. Of course, you cannot describe everything you do in such a limited space. Choose the most important goals you have for children and the best examples of practices that you feel represent your competence.

Write about your *current practice*, using examples of your work now (within the past 6 months). As you review the draft statements you wrote when you first started the CDA P_3, you may need to revise them based on changes in your beliefs and practices as you progressed through your study.

3. Resource Collection: There are seventeen (17) specific items to be included in the Resource Collection. Even though you have collected them as you worked through *Essentials* chapter by chapter, you should check them again for completeness. They should now be organized by Competency Goal areas and numbered so that each item can be located easily during the Council Representative verification visit. *For Bilingual Candidates, the resources used directly with children and families must be in two languages (Spanish/English).*

COMPETENCY GOAL I
To establish and maintain a safe, healthy learning environment

1. Name of agency and telephone number to report child abuse concerns.

2. A record of Red Cross or other agency first aid class certificate of completion. Certification must have been issued within the past 3 years.

3. Agency name(s) that supply information on nutrition for children (e.g., Cooperative Extension Service).

COMPETENCY GOAL II
To advance physical and intellectual competence

4. Four songs including two from other cultures. Include music, words, and any special instruction that may be needed.

5. Include three creative activities: one each for toddlers, 3's and 4's. List all materials and how you expect children to use them.

COMPETENCY GOAL III
To support social and emotional development and provide positive guidance

6. Titles, authors, publishers and copyright dates of 5 children's books that support development of gender identity by portraying males and females in diverse roles.

7. Titles, authors, publishers and copyright dates of 2 picture books that deal with the human reproductive process.

8. Titles, authors, publishers and copyright dates of 3 children's books that deal with separation, divorce, remarriage, or blended families.

9. Name of local hospital and its policies about group field trips, orientation for children scheduled for hospitalization, and parents' presence during children's inpatient stays.

10. Agency name and telephone number for making referrals to family counseling.

COMPETENCY GOAL IV

To establish positive and productive relationships with families

11. Policies for your program that specify what parents should do and what program does for parents.

COMPETENCY GOAL V

To ensure a well-run, purposeful program responsive to participant needs

12. Samples of 3 types of record keeping forms used in group care programs, including accident report and emergency form.

COMPETENCY GOAL VI

To maintain a commitment to professionalism

13. Name and contact information of agency that regulates child care centers and homes; copy of current regulations.

14. Brochure(s) and membership information from two or three national early childhood education associations.

15. Pamphlet(s) designed for parents about how children grow and learn. (No more than 5)

16. An observation tool for recording information about children's behavior. One copy should be blank; the other filled out with a sample observation of a child. (Anonymous)

17. Name and contact information of agencies in the community that provide resources for children with disabling conditions.

Formal Observation

A vital source of evidence of your skill is your actual hands-on work as primary caregiver with children and families. Documentation of these practices is collected through a formal observation.

You will be observed by your Field Advisor while you are working with young children in your field placement setting. This observation will be carried out exactly like your first formal observation conducted during Unit 6 of *Essentials* using the *CDA Observation Instrument.*

Your Field Advisor will arrange a time to conduct the observation. S/he may complete the formal observation in one visit or it may take several. Once the observation form is completed, it will be presented to the Council Representative during the verification visit. The instructions for your Field Advisor are included with the *CDA Observation Instrument.*

Keep in mind that the purpose of the observation is to rate your skill in the following specific performance areas. The items the Field Advisor will look for are listed on the next 2 pages.

In a bilingual setting, the Field Advisor will look for examples of your performance that show your skill in achieving bilingual development in children.

Candidate Performance Items to be Rated
by Field Advisor

Functional area 1: Safe

1.1 All toys and materials provided for use by children are safe.

1.2 Supervision is appropriate for developmental level of children.

1.3 Emergency procedures are well planned in advance and are well organized.

Functional area 2: Healthy

2.1 General hygiene practices are implemented consistently to cut down the spread of infectious disease.

2.2 Health maintenance habits in children are encouraged.

2.3 Diapering/toileting procedures are organized to maintain health.

2.4 Meals/snacks meet the developmental needs of children.

2.5 Pleasant and appropriate environment conducive to rest is provided daily.

Functional area 3: Learning environment

3.1 Well-arranged space is provided, which meets the developmental needs of children during routines and play.

3.2 A variety of developmentally-appropriate materials are made available.

3.3 Materials for play are well organized.

3.4 Schedule provided meets children's needs for routine and play.

Functional area 4: Physical

4.1 A variety of activities are offered which enable children to develop their large muscles.

4.2 A variety of activities are offered which enable children to develop their small muscles.

4.3 Program activities are adapted to meet individual needs and special needs of children with handicaps.

4.4 Opportunities are offered to help children develop their senses.

Functional area 5: Cognitive

5.1 A variety of age appropriate materials and activities which encourage curiosity, exploration, and problem solving are accessible to children throughout the day.

5.2 Interactions provide support for play, exploration, and learning.

5.3 Individual learning styles are recognized.

Functional area 6: Communication

6.1 Communication with each individual child is frequent.

6.2 Talk with children is developmentally appropriate.

6.3 Children are encouraged to talk.

6.4 Children's attempts to communicate are responded to positively.

6.5 A developmentally-appropriate, print-rich environment, in which children learn about books, literature, and writing, is provided.

Functional area 7: Creative

7.1 Individual expression and creativity are appreciated.

7.2 Many appropriate music experiences are available to children.

7.3 Art experiences are age appropriate and varied.

7.4 Dramatic play experiences, with a variety of age-appropriate props, are available.

7.5 Variety of age-appropriate block play opportunities are available.

Functional area 8: Self

8.1 Children are given the message that each is important, respected, and valued.

8.2 Individual children are helped to develop a sense of security.

8.3 Diapering/toileting procedures are developmentally appropriate and are organized to encourage self-help skills.

Functional area 9: Social

9.1 Each child is helped to feel accepted in the group.

9.2 Feelings of empathy and respect for others are encouraged.

9.3 Non-biased curriculum is used.

9.4 Children are encouraged to respect the environment.

Functional area 10: Guidance

10.1 Methods for avoiding problems are implemented.

10.2 Positive guidance techniques are used.

10.3 Guidance practices are related to knowledge of each child's personality and developmental level.

Functional area 11: Families

11.1 Various opportunities to appreciate children's families are part of the regular program.

11.2 Information about families' culture, religion, and childrearing practices is used in class room experiences.

11.3 Various opportunities are offered to help parents understand the development of their child and understand their child's point of view.

11.4 Resources are provided to help families meet their child's needs.

In addition, the Field Advisor will rate your performance in the two additional CDA functional areas where it may not be possible to actually observe your behavior during the formal observation. The Field Advisor may need to ask you some questions in order to complete her/his evidence of your skill in the following areas:

Functional area 12: Program management

Candidate manages by using all available resources to ensure an effective operation. Candidate is a competent organizer, planner, recordkeeper, communicator, and a cooperative co-worker.

Functional area 13: Professionalism

Candidate makes decisions based on knowledge of early childhood theories and practices, promotes quality child care services, and takes advantage of opportunities to improve competence, both for personal and professional growth and for the benefit of children and families. Candidate keeps abreast of regulatory, legislative, and workforce issues and how they affect the welfare of young children.

Good early childhood practices include encouraging children to work together and to respect each other's differences.

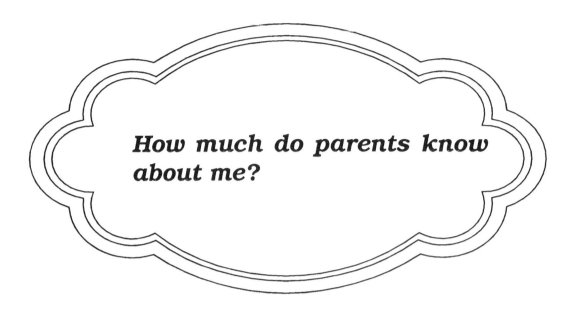

How much do parents know about me?

Parent Opinion Questionnaire

Parent perceptions about your skills and knowledge are extremely important in assessing whether you conduct yourself in a professional manner. Your Field Advisor will assist you in this process of gathering parent opinions. Each parent with a child in your care will be given an opportunity to complete a questionnaire. At least 75% of the questionnaires distributed must be completed. Your Field Advisor may have to make follow up telephone calls in order to get the questionnaires returned.

The questionnaires are confidential and you will not be able to read the parents' responses. The Field Advisor will collect the questionnaires and place them in a sealed envelope for you to present to the Council Representative. Instructions for distributing and collecting the responses to this questionnaire are included in the *Field Advisor's Guide*, along with the following cover letter and questionnaire.

Paying close attention to children reassures parents that you have their child's best interests at heart.

CDA PARENT OPINION QUESTIONNAIRE COVER LETTER

Dear Parents:

I am applying to be assessed for the Child Development Associate (CDA) Credential. The CDA Credential is awarded by the Council for Early Childhood Professional Recognition (Council), located in Washington, D.C. The Credential is awarded to competent caregivers and home visitors who have demonstrated their ability to meet the needs of children and parents on a daily basis.

The Council believes that parents have the right to know that the individuals caring for their children are competent. Therefore, parents have a very important role in the assessment of a person who wants to become a Child Development Associate. You can make an important contribution to a national effort to assure quality child care for young children by evaluating my work with your child and family.

As part of my assessment, I am required to collect the opinion of all parents who have children in my group. Therefore, I am asking you to fill out the questionnaire included with this letter. Your answers will be confidential. Please do not sign your name. Think about each question and answer it openly and honestly. Your specific comments at the end of the questionnaire will be very much appreciated.

I would be grateful if you would return your completed questionnaire to me in the enclosed envelope (**sealed**) by

————————————————— .

If you have any questions, please contact me at
————————————————————, or you may contact the Council hotline at 1-800-424-4310.

Thanks for your help.

Sincerely yours,

CDA Candidate

Queridos Padres:

Estoy solicitando ser evaluada/o para obtener mi Credencial de Asociada/o en el Desarrollo del Niño (CDA). Esta Credencial es otorgada por el Concillo ("Council") para el Reconocimiento Profesional de la Educación Infantil/Pre-escolar/Temprana, localizado en Washington, D.C. La credencial es otorgada a personas que demuestran ser capaces de satisfacer las necesidades específicas de los niños, y quienes trabajan con los padres para fomentar el progreso del niño.

El Concilio ("Council") cree firmemente que los padres/madres tienen el derecho de saber que los individuos a cargo del cuidado de sus niños son profesionales competentes, es por eso que los padres juegan un papel muy importante en la evaluación de una persona que desea convertirse en un Asociado en el Desarrollo del Niño (CDA). Usted podría contribuír grandemente a este esfuerzo nacional, de asegurar la calidad en el cuidado infantil/pre-escolar, evaluando mi trabajo con su niño/s y su familia.

Como parte de mi evaluación, tengo la responsabilidad de recolectar la opinióm de todos los padres de los niños en mi grupo. Por esta razón, le pido que llene el cuestinario adjunto a esta carta. Sus respuestas se mantendrán confidenciales. Por favor no escriba su nombre. Piense y responda a cada pregunta en forma libre y honesta. Sus comentarios específicos al final del cuestionario serán apreciados.

Le agradezco anticipadamente se sirva devolverme este cuestionario completo en un sobre **sellado**, antes del

————————————————— .

Si Ud. tiene alguna pregunta, por favor comuníquese conmigo al ————————————————, o Ud. puede llamar a la línea de ayuda del Concilio (*Council hotline*) al 1-800-424-4310.

Gracias por su apoyo.

Sinceramente,

Candidata/o CDA

CDA PARENT OPINION QUESTIONNAIRE
CUESTIONARIO CDA DE OPINION DE PADRES

CDA Candidate's Name _____

Nombre del Candidato/a CDA _____

For each statement, circle the answer you think is best.

Haga un circulo alrededor de cada respuesta que usted considera como la más correcta

YES = CDA Candidate does this
NO = CDA Candidate does not do this
N/A = Do not know or does not apply

SI = La Candidata CDA lo hace
NO = La Candidata no hace esto
N/A = Ud.no sabe o no es pertinente

The CDA Candidate/ El Candidato/a CDA:

YES NO N/A 1. Reports accidents or any first aid given to my child.
SI NO N/A 1. Reporta accidentes o primeros auxilios dados a mi niño.

YES NO N/A 2. Requires my written permission to give any medication to my child.
SI NO N/A 2. Requiere mi autorización por escrito para poder dar cualquier medicina a mi niño.

YES NO N/A 3. Tells me about my child's eating, sleeping, and toileting/diapering.
SI NO N/A 3. Me dice como mi niño come, si duerme, sobre sus hábitos en el uso del baño, o cambio de pañales.

YES NO N/A 4. Follows feeding instructions for my infant or for my child with allergies.
SI NO N/A 4. Sigue instrucciones para la alimentación de mi bebé o la de mi niño que sufre de alergias.

YES NO N/A 5. Allows my child to be picked up only by people I have named.
SI NO N/A 5. Permite que a mi niño lo recojan sólo aquellas personas a quienes yo he autorizado.

YES NO N/A 6. Reports to me about my child's play and learning.
SI NO N/A 6. Me mantiene informado/a sobre el juego y el aprendizaje de mi niño.

YES NO N/A 7. Organizes toys and play materials so my child can reach them easily.
SI NO N/A 7. Organiza los juguetes y materiales de juego de manera que mi niño pueda alcanzarlos facilmente.

YES NO N/A 8. Provides a place for my child to store his or her own things and makes sure I can find the things I need to bring home.
SI NO N/A 8. Provee un lugar para que mi niño pueda guardar sus pertenencias y se asegura de que yo pueda encontrar todas las cosas que necesito llevar a casa.

| YES | NO | N/A | 9. | Has enough toys and materials so children do not fight over popular toys. |
| SI | NO | N/A | 9. | *Tiene juguetes y materiales en número suficiente para evitar que los niños peleen por los juguetes más populares.* |

| YES | NO | N/A | 10. | Takes my child outdoors to play every day, except in bad weather. |
| SI | NO | N/A | 10. | *Lleva a mi niño a jugar afuera todos los días excepto cuando el tiempo esta muy malo.* |

| YES | NO | N/A | 11. | Talks with my child frequently. |
| SI | NO | N/A | 11. | *Habla frecuentemente con mi niño.* |

| YES | NO | N/A | 12. | Listens with interest when my child talks and encourages my child to talk. |
| SI | NO | N/A | 12. | *Escucha con interés cuando mi niño habla y lo anima a hablar.* |

| YES | NO | N/A | 13. | Helps my child learn to control his or her own behavior without spanking or other harsh punishment. |
| SI | NO | N/A | 13. | *Ayuda a mi niño a controlar su propio comportamiento, sin pegarle o sin usar castigos duros.* |

| YES | NO | N/A | 14. | Reads to my child often. |
| SI | NO | N/A | 14. | *Le lee a mi niño, con mucha frecuencia.* |

| YES | NO | N/A | 15. | Provides many music, art, block and pretend activities that my child can do in his or her own way. |
| SI | NO | N/A | 15. | *Provee muchas actividades de música, arte, bloques, actividades de pre tender, que mi niño puede hacer a su manera.* |

| YES | NO | N/A | 16. | Helps my child feel proud of what he or she can do. |
| SI | NO | N/A | 16. | *Ayuda a mi niño a sentirse orgulloso de lo que él puede hacer.* |

| YES | NO | N/A | 17. | Encourages children to enjoy getting along with each other. |
| SI | NO | N/A | 17. | *Anima a los niños el disfrute de llevarse bien entre ellos.* |

| YES | NO | N/A | 18. | Gives me the feeling that she is truly interested in my child and me. |
| SI | NO | N/A | 18. | *Me hace sentir que ella/él está verdaderamente interesada/o en mi niño y en mí.* |

| YES | NO | N/A | 19. | Is pleasant and friendly with me. |
| SI | NO | N/A | 19. | *Es agradable y amistosa/o conmigo.* |

| YES | NO | N/A | 20. | Is available to discuss my concerns. |
| SI | NO | N/A | 20. | *Esta disponible para hablar conmigo sobre mis preocupaciones.* |

| YES | NO | N/A | 21. | Asks me for ideas to use with my child, including activity ideas. |
| SI | NO | N/A | 21. | *Me pide ideas para usarlas con mi niño, incluyendo ideas sobre actividades.* |

YES	NO	N/A	22.	Asks me what I think is important in raising my child.
SI	*NO*	*N/A*	*22.*	*Me pregunta sobre lo que yo pienso que es importante en la crianza de mi niño.*

YES	NO	N/A	23.	Talks with me about any fears my child has.
SI	*NO*	*N/A*	*23.*	*Me habla sobre cualquier temor o temores que tenga mi niño.*

YES	NO	N/A	24.	Maintains confidentiality; does not freely discuss my child or family in the presence of others.
SI	*NO*	*N/A*	*24.*	*Es reservada/o, mantiene información confidencial; no habla sobre mi niño o mi familia en la presencia de otras personas.*

YES	NO	N/A	25.	Encourages me to visit at any time.
SI	NO	N/A	25.	*Me anima a visitar en cualquier momento.*

YES	NO	N/A	26.	Lets me know of parent meetings and other ways I can become involved in the program.
SI	*NO*	*N/A*	*26.*	*Me hace saber cuando hay reuniones de Padres y me informa sobre otras maneras de participar en el programa.*

YES	NO	N/A	27.	Schedules conferences at times that are convenient to me.
SI	*NO*	*N/A*	*27.*	*Señala fechas para reunirnos, en días y horas que me son convenientes.*

Indicate language(s) you use at home_____. Language(s) you prefer Candidate to use with your child_____.

Indique el idioma/s que usted habla en su casa_____. Idioma/s que ud. prefiere que la Candidata hable a su niño_____.

Please write your opinion about this Candidate's work with your child:
Por favor escriba lo que usted opina sobre el trabajo de esta Candidata/o con usted y con su niño:

Part 3

Verification Visit

Once you have completed your Professional Resource File, Formal Observation, and Parent Opinion Questionnaires, you are ready for the Verification Visit by the Council Representative.

Your Field Advisor will notify the Council that these materials are complete, and the Council Rep will telephone you to schedule a date for the Verification Visit.

You will need to provide a private place for the Council Rep to review your documents and conduct the interview. It is preferable to use space at the Center where you work. Be sure to get permission from the Program Director, and if you need help arranging a place, ask your Field Advisor to assist you.

Before the Council Rep arrives, prepare your documentation in the following way:

1. Put your Professional Resource File in final form. The Council Rep will check to see that all entries are complete and then return the File to you. *Make a xerox copy of your "Autobiography" and "Statements of Competence"* -- the Council Rep will mail these to the Council office in Washington, DC.

2. Get the completed CDA Observation Instrument from your Field Advisor. It should be in a sealed envelope for the Council Rep to mail to the Council.

3. Get the completed Parent Opinion Questionnaires from your Field Advisor. They should also be in a sealed envelope. The Council Rep will mail these to the Council.

As a caregiver, you play an important role in stimulating children's learning through creative play.

During the Verification Visit, the Council Rep will:

1. Check the "Autobiography" in the Professional Resource File and send one copy to the Council.

2. Check the "Statements of Competence" in the Professional Resource File and send the copies to the Council.

3. Check the Resource Collection in the Professional Resource File and return it to you.

4. Check the Parent Opinion Questionnaires and send them to the Council.

5. Check the Formal Observation and send it to the Council.

6. Conduct the Oral Interview.

Children's development is enhanced by their desire to perform some tasks independently.

Oral Interview

The Oral Interview provides an opportunity for you to show how the information you have learned would be applied in a variety of early childhood settings.

The interview consists of 10 structured situations and takes about 1 to 2 hours to administer. The situations will be specific to your endorsement as a preschool caregiver, and if you have chosen the bilingual specialization, specific to bilingual programs. Bilingual Candidates will be interviewed in the language of their choice.

For each situation, the Council Rep will show you a picture with a written description of the activity pictured. The Council Rep will read the description as you read along. Then s/he will pose a question and ask you to respond. As you respond, the Council Rep will listen, make notes and identify various aspects of your response. S/he may ask additional questions to help you give a clear and complete response. A sample interview question follows:

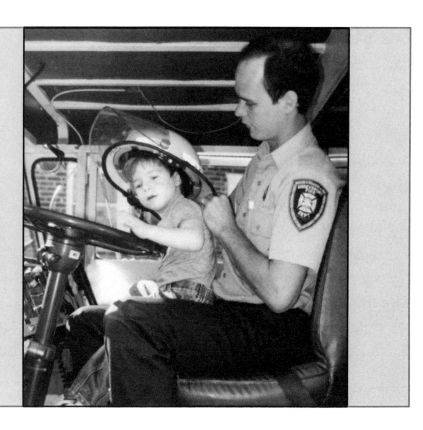

When the interview is finished, the Council Rep will score your responses and send the results to the Council.

After the Council receives the documentation of your competence, a committee will conduct a review and make a decision. If Credential award is recommended, the official Credential is sent to you, the new Child Development Associate. If the committee recommends more training, the Council will notify you and inform you of appeal procedures.

A CDA Credential is valid for 3 years from award, after which it may be renewed.

"Although earning the CDA Credential has been my most challenging effort to date, it has given me the greatest reward. Not only have I become more attuned to children's needs, I've also become more knowledgeable about taking care of their needs."

CDA, 1990

CONGRATULATIONS!

You have completed all the requirements for the CDA Professional Preparation Program and have been assessed as a CDA. In just a few weeks, you will receive notification from the Council of the decision about your Credential award.

There are over 50,000 CDAs across the country, the Commonwealth of Puerto Rico, and the U.S. territories of Guam and the Virgin Islands. You will join their ranks, as well as the ranks of the early childhood education profession.

The choice to work with young children and their families is one of the most important career decisions that one can make in our society. Best wishes for a rewarding and successful career ahead!

7

Putting it all together as an early childhood education professional working with infants and toddlers

WHAT A LONG WAY you have come since you first started your CDA Professional Preparation Program! You have worked hard on your own. You have met many other CDA Candidates in your Seminar group. You probably have had a few exciting moments of discovery along the way when you saw how things fit together. You undoubtedly disagreed with a few ideas. You even may have felt that the struggle was not worth it, as you spent your weekends and evenings completing assignments and putting together your Professional Resource File. But now your CDA Credential will soon become reality.

You are almost at the end of one phase, and at the beginning of an even more difficult one in your work life. You are about to be recognized as an early childhood professional. You will be faced with problems to solve every day in this field. You will have to make decisions that affect the lives of children, parents, or your col-leagues. You may be faced with the need to take action on behalf of children, parents, or early childhood educators you don't even know.

And you are probably aware of just how much more there is to learn about how young children develop. Our field, like young children themselves, is constantly changing and grow-ing. After you have earned your CDA, you will enter the early childhood profession and will be qualified for a reasonable, professional posi-tion. In order to make progress on your career path, you must keep on building your skills through continuing education and through col-laboration with your early childhood co-workers.

Will you accept the challenge? Where do you go from here?

This unit and the next are to be completed during the third and final phase of your CDA Professional Preparation Program. You will continue to apply what you have learned as you build your CDA Professional Resource File and work with your Field Advisor to complete these last units.

As you prepare to demonstrate your competency as a teacher of infants and toddlers, you will complete these tasks:

1. Work through all of the activities in Unit 7, with your Field Advisor's support.

2. Collaborate with your Field Advisor to distribute the Parent Opinion Questionnaire to all the parents of children in your group.

3. Complete your CDA Professional Resource File.

4. Be observed by your Field Advisor as you demonstrate your skills with infants and toddlers in a classroom setting.

5. Take part in the final assessment, at which time the Council Rep will interview you, review your Professional Resource File, and submit materials about you to the Council for Early Childhood Professional Recognition.

Part 1

Putting together all that you have learned

To be able to put everything together to create a high-quality program means using all the teaching strategies you know to foster development in children. Doing this will take yet another skill area: working as a member of an early childhood team.

Lots of **adults** are involved in programs for very young children: families, licensing personnel, teaching assistants, staff (cooks, bus drivers), volunteers, community service people, consultants, medical personnel, substitutes, provider networks, supervisors, other teachers, neighbors. All of you must work as a team to provide the best possible care for children in your community. How can you do that?

Establish cooperative relationships

We have already talked about how to work with families: you both share information and plan together, you treat each other with respect, and you listen more than you talk. You use informal conversations, notes or letters, conferences, meetings, telephone calls, newsletters, and a variety of other ways to keep in touch with families. You are always pleasant, courteous, and tactful. You try to understand their point of view and keep their needs in mind. You are open to suggestions and are always trying to improve yourself.

When you work with families of infants and toddlers, you probably sense that you are in a unique position. New parents are eager to learn more about their unfamiliar roles. At the same time, they may feel uncomfortable about leaving very young children in the care of another person, and they may feel quite guilty. Some parents might even see you as competition for their child's love. These feelings of guilt and competition often take the form of criticism. A parent who feels, "no one can take care of this child as well as I do," may have a new complaint or concern everyday. It is important for caregivers to understand why a parent like this complains so, and should help her get in touch with her real issue. It is very easy to become defensive when a parent is overly critical, and seemingly unappreciative of all your hard work. Your warmth, sensitivity, and understanding will be challenged as you work to help parents see how all of you can work together as partners to provide care for their youngest family members.

As a professional early childhood educator, you will use these same skills when you collaborate with all the other people involved in your program. Whether you work alone now or in the future as a family child care provider, in a large or small child care center, or in a drop-in program, your work puts you in touch with many other people. You are part of a team of professionals. And you are expected to conduct yourself in a professional way.

Your interaction with others will be an example to children of appropriate adult interaction. Cooperation in planning with other adults will assure a more appropriate and comprehensive program to meet the needs of very young children. A team approach to planning also lightens the load for all the players, and helps develop respect among people, assuring a more positive program.

A new substitute is working with you today. She was called at the last minute and arrives after some of the children. You welcome her to the program, give her a statement of your program's philosophy and a quick summary of the activities for the children, and briefly outline what you expect her to do during the morning. "We're so glad you are here today. I will introduce you to each of the children."

"Please sit with me on the floor as the children play. We'll talk informally with them, sing songs, read books, and offer assistance if we see the need. We'll change diapers when they're needed. Our rocking chairs are for reading, snuggling, and bottlefeeding. Around 9:30, I'll show you how to fix snack for the toddlers." Feel free to ask questions.

Helping volunteers, substitutes, and visitors feel welcome and comfortable requires some advance organization on your part. These are just a few of the things you must remember to prepare in advance so that the day can go as smoothly as possible:

• **Have the basics of how you work with infants and toddlers for the newcomer to read. Keep them simple.** These guidelines will help ensure that methods are consistent and promote positive behaviors. This system eliminates surprises for children and adults, too. Make sure any questions the visitor might have are answered as soon as possible throughout the day.

• **Write out your plans for the day, and explain how you expect the volunteer or substitute to assist you with each activity.** If the person is new in working with very young children, you may need to explain some basic principles about this kind of teaching:

> Dough clay for toddlers at about 10 a.m.:
>
> **Supplies:** Place these supplies on the low table (supplies are in the cupboard above the sink): large jar of dough clay, box of accessories for clay.
>
> **Supervision:** Three or four children may play at a time. Clay stays on the table. It may be rolled, pounded, squashed, and otherwise worked with their hands and fingers. Encourage casual conversation and experimentation. Please do not make a model for the children to copy. It is important for the children to be original. Remember, the fun children have is more important than whatever the results are.
>
> **Things to talk about:** Talk about what the children are doing. Children learn by doing. Ask children to think about how the clay feels on their hands. You might suggest words such as cool, soft, mushy—make up a word or two.
>
> **Clean up:** Return dough clay to container. Seal, so it stays moist. Rinse rollers and hammers in sink.

• **Introduce the children and visitor by name.** Explain to each child who the person is and why he or she is there. If a teacher is ill, tell the children. If the visitor will be doing some testing, briefly explain the process. If you are being observed, say what the observer is looking for. Use name tags if your visitor prefers.

• **Observe the person as she or he works with the children.** Throughout the day, comment on how things are going. "You've been such a help to notice just where to be when the babies needed a hug or to be distracted with a fingerplay. I'm so glad you're here today." Jot down any topics that need to be discussed later.

Many early childhood programs have support staff such as nutritionists, social workers, bus drivers, office staff, and janitors. To make sure they feel like a real part of your program's team, exchange information with them on a regular basis . . . about individual children's preferences or moods. . . about program plans . . . when you'll need something special, for example. Encourage children to do something special for the staff who are responsible for special efforts. Invite them to share a project with the children - a hand print, a smile, a wave, a game of patty cake, or peek a boo.

The extra interest of these special adults can add a great deal to the children's time in your program. There is a richness that comes from their diversity which extends the "home like" feeling of your program. It becomes a community of caring.

Throughout the year, you may also work with other adults from outside the program. Sometimes they will support your efforts, sometimes they will be critical of what you do, and sometimes you will work together on behalf of a child or family who has requested information about a topic. Or sometimes a staff member within your program, such as your supervisor may offer a negative opinion of your work.

Teachers are put on the spot a lot, and it is hard sometimes to accept criticism. Ask for a private conference time when you both are unhurried and can calmly discuss areas of concern in a productive way.

Your director has finished her evaluation. You are nervous about the results, even though you have tried hard to do your best. Sure enough, you are rated low in one area: the toddlers need to be offered more choices throughout the day.

You are disappointed at the criticism but eager to find out just what you can work on to do better. "We are trying hard to do that. Can you give us some examples of what you mean to improve our program?"

Your director begins tactfully, "I can see you have a good start. But instead of giving children a choice between an art activity you have set up or singing with your assistant, you might want to broaden their choices. Offer choices that are something the children can do on their own without an adult imposing so much structure on what happens."

You reply, "Oh, you mean like letting them choose which art materials they want to use?"

"Exactly. The children may take a while to adjust to thinking more for themselves, but you have a lot of great materials. Let them pursue their own interests. Try giving them a little more freedom to choose within the activity, as well as choosing the activity itself."

"It's really helpful to see what kind of choices you mean. I'll work to see how I can offer better choices for children."

What techniques have you developed to respond to criticisms or challenges in productive ways?

_____

_____

_____

_____

You probably also have encountered the need to build support for what you do within your neighborhood or community.

Your infant/toddler program is located in a residential neighborhood. One person who is home all day has been stirring up the people on your street by complaining about all the strollers on the sidewalk.

A parent hears about the stew from a friend, and tells you what is happening. "Thank you for clueing us in to the problem. We'll need to think of some ways to become better friends with our neighbors."

You come up with several ideas to try: Send a newsletter to everyone in the area, or have a noon picnic and invite neighbors, or issue invitations for people to visit the program, or ask the local paper to do a story on what a good program you have.

Some of these ideas may not work, but the process has been started. You meet with two parents to try to figure out what to do.

In a situation like this it's very important for you to remain calm and "professional." This is true even if the accusations are false, or make you angry. The parents will pick up on your tone and attitude.

What ideas do you have to maintain good community relations with your program's neighbors?

As a professional, you may also be called upon to lend your expertise to discussions of issues beyond your own program.

> A condominium homeowner's association in your city has just ruled that their policy against home businesses will be enforced. This means no family child care in a nearby neighborhood. And already there is a shortage of good care in your community. Parents are dismayed.
>
> You ask for a few minutes at the next AEYC meeting to raise the issue with your colleagues. You form a committee that includes several parents and a city administrator. Your goal is to plan strategies to increase the availability of child care.

> A teacher brings in an "English Only" leaflet that is being circulated in your neighborhood. It calls for a petition to do away with all bilingual services in the community.
>
> You call a meeting with staff and parents to discuss a strategy. A parent suggests an "English Plus" leaflet supporting diversity. Staff and parents take various responsibilities to work on it.

Are you ready to handle these kinds of responsibilities? As a CDA, others will look up to you. You will be expected to work with lots of people. The future of children is in your hands.

Use community resources

All through your *Essentials* curriculum, you have tracked down resources:

- the phone number to report child abuse
- your county Extension Service for nutrition information
- field trip possibilities
- services to screen children for possible disabilities and to take appropriate action
- resources for parents
- translator services for the languages spoken at your center

Now is the time to become familiar with all the other resources in your community that can help you be more effective in your work with infants and toddlers. Here are just a few of the typical resource agencies that serve families. You can probably list more. Get together with your program director, or perhaps talk with your licensing representative, if you need help to find out what your community offers.

Begin a card file of resources such as these, that you can share with your colleagues and with parents. Then call each group and find out what services or materials they have to help you.

Parenting programs

Red Cross

Easter Seal Society

Safety groups

Mental health clinics

Medical clinics

Food stamps

WIC programs

Financial planning

Gymnastics classes

Child care resource and referral

Cultural resource groups

Resale shops

Community based organizations

Performing artists' groups

Food cooperatives

Library

Children's programs 0-3

Children's book stores

Early and periodic screening programs for very young children

Any service organization that might contribute people or funds to your program

All of these resources can broaden your ability to support the needs of the families in your program—and your program itself! Many have brochures, information, even curriculum materials appropriate for parents and/or young children. Pay special attention to those designed for parents of infants - these may be more difficult for parents to find. Take advantage of what is available in your community through government agencies, volunteer groups, and citizen action coalitions. Unless you use these wonderful supplements, you, the children, and their families will miss out on a lot of marvelous opportunities. Expand your horizons today.

And, do not forget your local library. It contains a vast amount of resource material!

Manage efficiently

You are well aware that not all of your time is spent with children. Regardless of the type of program you work in, you have other responsibilities as well. You manage space, materials, activities, records, and other adults every day.

Organize space and materials

We have already seen how important it is to make the most of children's playing, eating, and sleeping spaces. But remember, maintaining a safe, healthy learning environment means rearranging it occasionally. Because children grow and change, and new children enter your care, you will want to periodically look carefully at your room arrangement and make changes to keep it fresh and interesting. Rotate equipment and materials as children's skills improve— and that can be once a week with infants and toddlers. Rejuvenate the diaper changing area with a new mobile or some bright new pictures at children's level.

Storage areas need to be neatly arranged and cleaned regularly so you know what you have and where to find it. Who knows what buried treasure is lurking in the back of your closet!

Thoughtful planning of the environment also means you keep track of supplies so they can be ordered before you run out. One hungry day and you can suddenly be out of formula! Have an ample selection of diapers and wipes, as well as hand lotion. Periodically check the first-aid kit to make sure it is well supplied and that parent emergency numbers are correct.

Plan ahead to decide which special materials you will need—tissue paper, foods for a cooking project. Perhaps you need parents to bring in milk cartons or scraps of fabric, empty cans for stacking, etc. Give them a little advance notice so they can save things.

Take a look at the floor plan you developed in Unit 3 of *Essentials* (page 165). Now that you have many new ideas, complete the final design using the chart on page 166 or review the design you completed during the Seminar. Make sure you have included spaces for young infants, mobile infants, and toddlers, or if you prefer, make a separate plan for each age group. **Discuss your design with your Field Advisor.**

Plan ahead for daily activities

Long before you start a new theme, gather all the materials needed so you won't have to scramble for something at the last minute. Check with your library to make sure the book titles or films you want are available, and reserve them if possible. Contact community resource groups about materials well in advance. Constantly teach yourself new fingerplays, chants and songs. Embrace all cultures.

The curriculum in your program will set the framework for what daily activities the children will do. But being prepared for each day will require you to think ahead.

For instance, most field trips must be scheduled far in advance because there are so many details to arrange. You will need to visit the place yourself and talk with the people there about how they can best accommodate very young children. Remember not all field trips are appropriate for toddlers and few for infants. Travel, emergency medical permissions, and other forms must be signed. Bus or car arrangements have to be made. Car seats need to be available for each child. Volunteers (enough for every child or two) to go with you must be contacted. Money may need to be collected.

Arrange for special visitors by giving them enough notice. Be sure to talk with them, in person or by phone before their visit, about the children's interests and attention spans and clarify what you expect the visitor to do. During certain periods of development, infants and toddlers are fearful of strangers. Keep this in mind when planning for visitors.

Plan ahead to spend additional time to prepare for an activity, or to clean up. At the end of the week be prepared to gather laundry and make time for additional cleaning.

You may also need to make arrangements for parent meetings—make sure refreshments are ready and supplies (napkins, coffee, and so forth) are provided.

Allow time in your day to keep notes for future planning. Sit down at the end of each day and decide on your activities planned for tomorrow—do you have everything you need?

Keep records

By now, you should have quite a large collection of observations of your infants and toddlers recorded in your daily diary. By building a record of how each child grows and learns, you can use the information to plan themes and activities, to point out to parents how much progress their children are making, and to help identify any potential disabilities. Don't stop just because you have finished your CDA!

Date records and have a folder for each child. Records of children can also help families when the child leaves your program. For bilingual programs, for example, records on the first language of the child and her usage and understanding of the second language will be critical to planning. Families may want you to share some of what you have learned about the child with their child's next teacher. Always ask the parents first—summaries of your observations should only be released to others **if the parents approve**. Obtain permission from parents in writing. Remember this is confidential information. They will usually be quite agreeable if you explain that this is one way you can work together to build a bridge between the two programs for their child.

In every program some written records are needed just to ensure children's welfare while they are present. Proper procedures to report illnesses or accidents should be established. Attendance records must be accurate, especially in the event of an emergency evacuation. All programs must keep up-to-date health records, emergency forms, and written policies.

Caregivers of infants and toddlers often like to fill out a brief report about the child's day, because such young children aren't likely to chat about their experiences as much as preschoolers do. For instance, you should report feeding times, body functions, and nap times to parents, so they'll have a better idea of what to expect for the remainder of the day, and to notice any changes in their child.

Depending on the type of program you work in, you may or may not be responsible for keeping other types of records. Family child care providers, for example, must maintain records for licensing/registration and for taxes. In centers, the director or finance officer must prepare a budget, maintain a checking account, and obtain liability insurance coverage. Zoning records may be needed. You may participate in the Child Care Food Program or serve children whose care is subsidized or paid for by an agency, and all of these require some paperwork. And you may need to advertise your program. Early childhood programs are indeed businesses!

All written records must be legible so others can read them, and should be organized and kept in a place where they can be located easily. If your program is bilingual, records may need to be kept in more than one language.

Add samples of three types of record keeping forms used in group care programs to your Professional Resource File. Include your program's accident report and emergency form:

1.

2.

3.

Communicate

Your ability to listen and respond appropriately—to children, parents, and others—keeps coming up in your professional studies. That's because listening is such a valuable tool in your everyday work. Sometimes people are subtle and sometimes they are pretty direct. But you will find out what people think about your work,

what they need, and how you could improve what you do. Keep your eyes and ears open to clues that something needs to be changed or that you are really doing a good job. It's a mark of a professional to be able to make positive changes in response to criticism.

Here are some typical examples of the subtle types of feedback you may get. What would you do in each of these situations?

1. A baby gets wet and you discover there are no extra clothes in her cubby. As you look around, you see other cubbies with few or no extra clothes as well.

   What are these parents telling you?

   What should you do about it?

2. A parent of a just enrolled 8-week-old seems very intense when she leaves her child each morning. At pick up each day she has complained about something in the program.

What should you do?

_____

_____

_____

3. Group time has been reduced to 5 minutes for your oldest toddlers. About half of them sit quietly, but the other half last only a minute or two, and then they begin to wander around.

Why are the children so restless?

_____

_____

_____

What should you do?

_____

_____

_____

_____

4. One parent constantly compares her child's development to another child in the program. She is usually critical of her child and sees her child as "slow."

What is she concerned about?

_____

_____

_____

How should you respond?

_____

_____

_____

5. In your newsletter, you ask parents to provide healthy snacks for birthday treats. The first three birthdays after your notice are all celebrated with cupcakes and Kool-Aid.

Why did parents ignore your request?

How can you get parents to plan more nutritious birthday snacks?

6. Three monolingual Spanish speaking parents in a row have asked to move their children from your group to the group of a monolingual English speaking teacher.

What do their actions tell you?

What information about language development of bilingual children would you share?

How could you present it?

7. Your director gets a phone call from the local TV station about qualifications of child care providers. They would like to interview her. She agrees, and suggests they use your infant room as the setting.

What does the director's choice mean?

What can you do to prepare your room?

Managing efficiently means being sensitive to these indicators of feedback and making adjustments accordingly.

Every day you will make hundreds of decisions—about how to interact with children, about what to say to a parent, about how to work more effectively with colleagues. The more resources you have at your fingertips, the more likely you are to make good decisions. The fieldwork and Seminar parts of your *Essentials* curriculum have covered the basic information you need to make sound judgments. How you use that information professionally requires discussion of one more topic—professionalism.

Part 2

You try to make good decisions

Throughout your *Essentials* curriculum you have picked up information to build on your experiences with infants and toddlers. You have seen ways to make good decisions about how you teach, how you work with other adults, and how you plan and organize your work. You will look back again and again at some parts of this material as you continue to extend your ability to work with the youngest of children in a professional way. There is so much to absorb—people have learned a lot about children over many years.

Making good decisions means always being ethical. Members of NAEYC have developed a code of ethics, which you will find in Unit 1 of *Essentials*. You are expected to work throughout your career to live up to this ethical code.

With this code to help, each of us in the field must work out our own thoughts on what kind of teaching behavior is truly professional. We'll offer some guidelines here to help you make ethical decisions. While there are no right answers, here are some ways to help you consider as many factors as possible before you decide what to do in a specific situation. **Presented on the following pages are several situations. Think about each of these situations and discuss them with your Field Advisor.**

Have a healthy attitude about your power

Infants and toddlers are so helpless and dependent upon adults. They are with you for so many of their waking hours. Their parents depend on you to give children the best experiences possible during those impressionable early years. In addition, parents need reliable child care so they can earn a living or prepare to earn one.

It is easy to abuse this power, either with children or adults. Some teachers are tempted to use physical force because they are stronger than children. Some teachers are tempted to take advantage of children psychologically because they believe children learn to be obedient out of fear. Some teachers fail to prepare children to become good world citizens. And some teachers think they can get away with almost anything because the parents are so desperate for affordable, convenient child care.

Think for a minute about how much power you have and use every day. You have the power to enable children to grow strong and competent—or to be sickly and quitters. You have the power to help children become kind and generous—or mean and stingy. You have the power to validate children's home language and culture -- or make them feel inferior to other people. You have the power to help children get along with each other—or to hate and fear people who are different from them. You have the power to provide high-quality care—or minimal custodial care. What is the ethical approach?

As a professional, you make a commitment never to take advantage of children or their parents—physically, emotionally, intellectually, or financially. You respect them as people and treat them accordingly. You use your power to build strengths and to help overcome weaknesses.

How would you use your power in situations such as these? Jot down notes and discuss your responses with your Field Advisor.

1. A 4-month-old has been crying for half an hour. You have tried a clean diaper, a bottle, rocking, a warmer blanket, and soothing music, all to no avail. *Do you scream at the baby and tell him to shut up, that big boys don't cry? Do you spank him and isolate him in his crib?*

What is the professional thing to do?

2. Two toddlers are fighting in the sandbox. Before you can get there, one has thrown sand into the other's eyes. *Do you grab the child who threw the sand and drag her indoors to sit in the office? Do you tell both children to get out of the sandbox and that they may not play there for a week?*

What is the professional thing to do?

_____

_____

_____

3. A new family has moved into your community. Their 9-month-old child is hearing impaired. *Do you discourage the family when they inquire about enrollment? Do you accept the child but increase your fee because more effort is needed on your part?*

What is the professional thing to do?

_____

_____

_____

Keep confidences

During the course of your work, you will learn a great deal about families' personal lives. A parent may confide in you some upsetting details about a spouse. A child may blurt out, "Dammit!" Parents may fill out financial forms so your program can qualify for financial reimbursement. Bruises on a Monday morning may lead you to suspect child abuse.

Whatever you hear or see as a CDA is privileged information. You are a professional, so you must take the appropriate steps to remedy the situation if there is a problem. Often you refer people to the appropriate community resources. You provide an accepting environment in which children feel good about themselves and others. You keep written records confidential. And you immediately report any possible abuse. Professionals do not announce what they have learned about a family to all the other teachers in the program, or to any other parents, or to their friends.

What do you do to stop yourself when you feel tempted to break a confidence about a family or a particular child in your program?

Parents trust you to keep information about them confidential. Parents have a right to privacy. Of course, you must balance that with the need to protect the child.

Protect children

You are legally and ethically responsible for the protection of all children in your care. Not just their safety, but their emotional well being, their physical development, their intellectual growth, and their social skills. You do not allow children to hurt themselves or each other. You do not allow any other adult to hurt children either. You show value for the way each child speaks and include their home language in the program. You are constantly alert for signs of any type of abuse. You base your decisions about what to do on the children's best interest.

Professional early childhood educators are constantly alert to conditions within the program to assure that children are protected in all these ways. For example, you quickly scan the outdoor play area every time you enter it for new hazards. You evaluate each new order of materials (or each donation) for safety and appropriateness. You keep up with the latest methods for diaper changing and sanitation of baby toys. You always listen to and watch the children so you can promote cooperation and friendly behaviors. You are eager to learn more about what types of activities are most beneficial for infant and toddler development, and you implement what you know.

Your role as a professional demands that you report suspected child abuse. Here are some examples of other situations that may arise, in which you will need to act as a protector for children.

Write down how you would handle each of these dilemmas, and then talk with your Field Advisor about your responses.

1. An older toddler frequently hits and shoots pretend guns at the other children.

2. Often one of your 1-year-olds is listless all morning, then devours lunch and seems more lively in the afternoon.

3. The parents of a 2-year-old have purchased a kit with flashcards to teach their child to read. They are pressuring you to use it with all the children in the group.

4. Grandmother and mother are pushing an 18-month-old boy to get toilet trained. Whenever he arrives in training pants and wets himself, he sobs so much that you have reason to believe he is being punished at home for his inability to stay dry.

Provide good quality care

There are different types of ways to design appropriate programs for infants and toddlers. You can adopt one of the models, or set up your own approach. Either way, as a professional you always provide developmentally appropriate activities, materials, and experiences for all the children. You know children learn best through their own self-directed play and manipulation of real objects. You want children to enjoy themselves and to pick up ideas and behaviors that they will keep throughout their lives. You provide good, safe care for children. To do less would be unethical.

One of the most difficult aspects of working with infants and toddlers is to avoid the temptation to lapse back into your old ways of teaching and disciplining. Catch yourself before that happens.

Maybe it's so easy for you to use baby talk. Or perhaps you want toddlers to sit quietly for 20 minutes to listen to your favorite music. A parent might expect an 18 month old to be toilet trained. Now you know why these are not appropriate methods or expectations.

There are still many commercial (and home-made) materials available that are not appropriate for babies and toddlers. Some are unsafe, some too advanced, and some just plain have little value for learning.

You will need to put everything you know to work every day in making the right decisions about how to best foster the learning and development of young children.

Transitions from one activity to another also often prove to be difficult with a group of young children, some of whom need to be carried. The time between one activity and another may simply involve sitting and waiting . . . and waiting . . . and waiting. But now you know that's not an appropriate expectation.

Remember, children are learning from everything they do!

You will be faced again and again with the need to make on-the-spot decisions about the best quality of care. It helps to think ahead about how you would handle problems that are sure to arise.

What would you do if . . .

...a toddler in your program consistently kisses other children on the cheek, then bites them?

. . . a toddler drew a beautiful picture with lots of colors, and then scribbled black all over the top of it?

. . . an 18-month-old began spanking a doll in the housekeeping area?

. . . for Halloween, the parent of an infant brings in popcorn and balloons to share with the group?

Discuss your responses with your Field Advisor, who can help you think about how to apply what you have learned about infants and toddlers in dealing with these and similar incidents.

As a CDA, you will always strive to keep knowledgeable about the standards of the profession. You will need to know about other national voluntary self-evaluation systems designed to improve and recognize the quality of programs. Group programs can benefit greatly by going through these review processes, much as you are going through the CDA credentialing system.

If you feel your center is an excellent one, you may want to find out about getting it accredited through the National Academy of Early Childhood Programs. Call or write to NAEYC (see the list of national organizations on page 29 - Unit 1 of *Essentials*) to request information about this system. Then talk with your program director about whether your program should take advantage of this excellent opportunity to be nationally recognized.

What else do you and other program staff do to constantly monitor whether you are providing good care for children?

What steps can you take to improve how your program's quality of care is assessed?

Respect parents' authority

Parents do have the ultimate authority to make decisions about their children—within legal limits of course. Every family and every cultural group stresses some values more than others, and then there are individual differences among families.

Parents may have standards of behavior for children at home that are not necessarily the same as those you have set in the program. Some families may live by a different code of morality than you accept. Parents may place a higher value on some things—wardrobe or financial status, for example—than you prefer.

We all know how important it is to respect differences, but sometimes it is difficult when you disagree with how parents are raising their children. Often, parents who have radically different ideas than you will probably not choose your program. At other times, however, they may have no choice but to enroll their children in your program. When that happens, you need to get to know each other well and work out a way to be as cooperative as possible. You must make a concerted effort to learn all you can about the family and their way of life or beliefs. You may eventually agree to disagree. You will respect each other's differences—and agree that children will be expected to act differently at home and at school. That way, at least in your program, you can keep what you believe to be the child's best interests in mind.

Children also need to know that some differences between home and your program are acceptable and natural. A simple explanation that "Yes, you say grace before each meal at home. That is so important for your family.

But here we wait until everyone is seated and then we begin to serve ourselves."

Without a doubt, as a CDA you will encounter some thorny value issues. Just remember there is more than one way to make things work for the benefit of the children. Be willing to listen and try new ideas.

As a professional, how would you deal with situations such as these?

1. Parents insist on dressing their 15-month-old girl in frilly dresses almost every day, and they want her to keep clean.

2. A child clearly has not been bathed in many days—she has offensive body odor, her hair is tangled, and her fingernails are imbedded with dirt. The child is developing a rash.

3. One 2½-year-old has been biting other children. You know you should speak to the parents about it—but you also know that if you do they will probably beat the child.

4. A child in your center has bitten several children. The parents are demanding the name of the biter.

> *"Becoming a CDA is fulfillment of a dream that once seemed out of reach"*
> *CDA, 1991*

5. A 10-month-old who is fairly new to your program usually cries when the parent leaves. The parent has asked that you get the child busy with something so the parent can sneak out without saying goodbye and the child won't cry.

Support diversity

As you have seen, all people are biased—we all think we are right and the best. And we all need to admit that we have those biases if we are to become good teachers. Your CDA Seminar experiences helped you see how these biases can affect your work.

Hard as it is, there is no room for favorites when you teach young children. Instead, you must do everything possible to help infants and toddlers feel good about themselves, their family, their heritage, their beliefs, their abilities, and their language—and to appreciate and respect those same characteristics in others.

Sensitivity to family values and concerns, even when different from your own, is also important. Culture plays a big role in how adults interact with infants and toddlers. Cultural differences about food, touching, dress, and general care are sometimes very strong in the first few years of life. These differences can enrich your program.

We are helping to make it possible for children to become productive citizens of the world of today and tomorrow. The world is filled with many ethnic groups and people with varying capabilities who must get along with each other. Ultimately, our survival depends on peacefully resolving our differences, and learning to live together. We all must accept and appreciate our wonderful diversity as human beings.

These are some ethical issues in this area that you may face. How would you deal with them?

1. You have just admitted a new infant and you are in a program that requires records on ethnic/racial background -- one parent is white, one black. A staff member using a strained voice says, "What is this kid anyway?"

2. You accept a baby with AIDS into your group. The other parents threaten to withdraw their children.

3. A child's parent brings in a copy of *Little Black Sambo* or *The Five Chinese Brothers*.

4. A group of 2-year-olds have a new classmate who is dark complected with lots of dark, black hair. The other children have fair skin. One child points and says to you, "He dirty." What do you do?

Regulations require early childhood programs to have adequate space and materials.

Help protect consumers

Every state has different laws regarding infant/toddler programs and qualifications for staff. You have already seen how important it is for good programs to be licensed or registered and for staff to be well trained.

Sometimes, we forget that the purpose of the licensing and registration laws are for consumer protection. In fact, most regulations provide only a **minimum** form of protection—far less than in many other areas that we take for granted, such as driver's licenses or pet food standards, for example. Adhering to those laws is a must.

Regulations generally are designed to establish at least a floor for child-staff ratios, safety, staff qualifications, space, materials, and a variety of other important areas in programs for young children.

Your role as a professional is to protect children and families and advocate for what is in keeping with good practice. Above all, you should assure children's safety, health, and general well-being. All these while maintaining the ethical standards already discussed.

Working with young children is demanding—of your energy, of your time, and of your conscience. Are you ready to become a professional? Are you prepared to take the most ethical action in sticky situations?

Here are some sticky consumer protection situations. What would you do?

1. The landlord has instructed that the heat must be set no higher than 62 degrees in the winter. The children and staff are too cold. Do you report your own program to the health department?

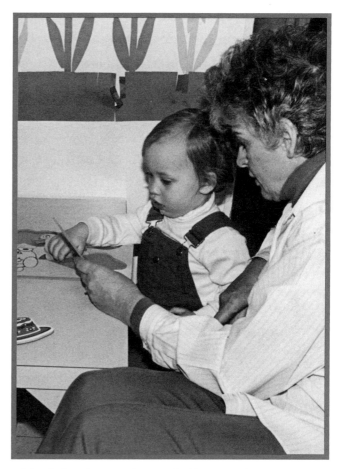

Giving help whenever it's needed is part of being a CDA.

2. Your director doesn't count part-time children when reporting enrollment levels because "there are always some children out sick anyway."

Part 3

You keep learning

By now you probably have realized how much there is to learn about infants and toddlers. Even if you have been working with young children for years, or are the parent of several, you have surely discovered that it is much more difficult to be a professional early childhood educator.

You are always learning from your experiences. The field is constantly changing, as we find out more about how children develop. This information affects how we teach. How can you keep up with the challenges to get better at what you love to do?

Improve yourself personally

All of us have things that we would like to do better. These may include bad habits we want to break, or attitudes that have been questioned.

What are some of the areas you need to work on?

These are the areas you will want to begin to improve so you can be a better teacher. Perhaps you need to eat more healthy foods or to get to work on time.

Choose just one of the things you listed and write what steps you need to take to change your behavior.

You don't have to do it alone. Rely on the same community support groups to which you refer parents. Or talk with your supervisor, spouse, friend, or a respected colleague about how they can support your efforts. After you have made some progress in one area, select another and begin to work on it. As you make the most of your life, you can better help others make the most of theirs!

An ethical early childhood educator

- never abuses power with children or families
- keeps information confidential
- protects children's best interests
- provides good care
- respects parents and co-workers
- supports diversity
- favors consumer protection of programs
- improves personal habits
- keeps on learning
- advocates for children, families, and the profession

Learn more about your profession

How lucky you are to become a professional today. Just a few years ago there weren't many places you could turn to for information. Now nearly every community has an organized group of early childhood workers. Some of these groups are affiliates of NAEYC, SACUS, NHSA, NBCDI, NAFDC or other large organizations. Some are state groups, and others are composed of active local people.

These professional networks are important. Most of you work alone or with just a few other professionals—and you never come in contact with the hundreds of thousands of other people who share the same commitment you do.

In Unit 1, you began networking by interviewing an early childhood professional in a **job different from yours. You should continue to build this network by interviewing your CDA Field Advisor—you know each other well by now. Make a list of questions you would like to ask about what the distinctive issues are for a career working with infants and toddlers:**

Now set up a time when the two of you can talk in general about the field for at least half an hour. Jot down what you learned here:

The next task in building your network is to find the names of all the professional early childhood support groups in your area (a few national organizations are listed in Unit 1).

If you have not already done so, contact several groups to learn more about their activities. Then select one or two organizations that seem to be good matches for you. Attend their meetings (go with a co-worker or your CDA Field Advisor, if possible). **Join at least one.** If there is no local chapter -- consider starting one in your area. Be an active member! Volunteer!

Most of these groups publish newsletters, journals, books, videos, posters or other professional development materials. Ask for a sample copy of any regular publications that sound interesting. Which publications seem to be most useful to you? You might want to subscribe regularly to a journal or magazine. A few are listed on the following page.

Always make sure that children's needs are taken care of.

The Black Child Advocate
National Black Child Development Institute
1023 15th Street, N.W., Suite 600
Washington, DC 20005
(202) 387-1281

Childhood Education
Association for Childhood Education
International
11141 Georgia Avenue, Suite 200
Wheaton, MD 20902
(301) 942-2443 • (800) 423-3563

Child Care Information Exchange and
Beginnings Books
P. O. Box 2890
Redmond, WA 98073-2890
(206) 882-1066

Day Care & Early Education
Human Sciences Press
233 Spring Street
New York, NY 10013
(212) 620-8000

Dimensions
Southern Association on Children under Six
P.O. Box 5403, Brady Station
Little Rock, AR 72215-5403
(501) 663-0353

Early Childhood Teacher
P. O. Box 6410
Duluth, MN 55806-9893
(218) 723-9215

Interracial Books for Children Bulletin
Council on Interracial Books for Children
1841 Broadway
New York City, NY 10023
(212) 757-5339

NHSA News
National Head Start Association
201 N. Union Street, Suite 320
Alexandria, VA 22314
(703) 739-0875

Nurturing News
187 Caselli Avenue
San Francisco, CA 94114
(415) 861-0847

Pre-K Today
Scholastics, Inc.
411 Lafayette
730 Broadway
New York, NY 10033
(212) 505-4900

Young Children
National Association for the Education of Young
Children
1509 16th Street, NW
Washington, DC 20036
(202) 232-8777 • (800) 424-2460

Zero to Three
National Center for Clinical Infant Programs
2000 14th Street North, Suite 380
Arlington, VA 22201
(703) 528-4300
Find out whether any of these resources are

available in your program or local library. If not, how can you include some of these items in your program budget? Order others as your personal budget permits.

Read! Read! Read! Or you will soon be left behind in your own profession. Become familiar with the "Resources for more information" found at the end of each unit of *Essentials*.

Workshops, conferences, and classes are marvelous ways to meet other people and learn more about how to care for groups of infants and toddlers. Once you have completed your CDA, keep up with the field by regularly enrolling in a course or taking a workshop. Better yet, keep climbing that career ladder and start to work on your college degree!

What topics would you like to learn more about?

Write up a plan to accomplish at least one of these goals. Find out where to go or what to read and continue to become even more professional. Then do it.

Becoming a professional also means contributing to the professional development of others. How do you share your newfound knowledge with others?

These are just a few of the issues you will encounter as you continue to work with children. Your thinking about ethics will be constantly challenged. Are you prepared to meet those challenges and to act on behalf of young children?

> *"Being a CDA has helped me to carefully evaluate my work with young children. Now that I feel confident about my work, my ability to meet each child at his/her level of need has been enhanced."*
> CDA, 1991

Part 4

You act on behalf of young children

A teacher's work is never done. You already know that. And now we are going to suggest that you do even more. Just working with infants and toddlers day-to-day is not enough. Thousands of children in our country and around the world are hungry, homeless, unhealthy, or have been harshly treated. Children are unable to defend themselves so we must take it upon ourselves to act in their behalf.

Stand up for good programs and services for children and families

You are now a committed early childhood professional. You have a responsibility to act in your local area, your state, nationally, and even on behalf of children in other countries you have never met. Here are some ways you can reach out, directly or indirectly, to improve the lives of children everywhere. **Add others to this list that you can think of or that you are already involved in.**

- Write letters to support stronger child care legislation, programs to strengthen families' self-sufficiency

- Become active in child advocacy groups

- Help parents become child advocates

- Read the Public Policy Report and the Washington Update in each issue of *Young Children*

- Vote in every election

- Speak up on behalf of developmentally appropriate practice: tell others, buy only appropriate materials, challenge others to learn more about how young children grow and learn

- Build an appreciation for diversity in the groups you are involved in: civic, church or synagogue, volunteer organizations, community service

- Volunteer for Week of the Young Child activities

- Support groups participating in the Worthy Wages Campaign

- Set up a network of supportive colleagues to phone for help

- Advocate for appropriate services for children with disabling conditions.

- _____

  _____

- _____

  _____

- _____

  _____

Don't wait another minute. If you are not taking an active role on behalf of all children and families, choose at least one activity from the list above and **get involved now!**

Advocate for your own profession

One of the most difficult issues facing us as early childhood educators is how to balance the need for affordable child care with our need to support ourselves. Salaries are low. Benefits are few or nonexistent. Most people still view our work as babysitting. But the rewards are so great that our ranks are swelling nevertheless!

Good programs for infants and toddlers are especially expensive because of the low ratio of children to staff. We don't want to shortchange children. Nor do we want to settle for less than we deserve for our hard work and long hours doing one of the most important jobs on earth.

Remain committed to the entire profession. Don't isolate yourself only among workers who are like you. Keep learning about others -- Head Start, private programs, church-sponsored programs, family day care.

Don't fall into the old trap of "conquer and divide." Don't allow yourself or your program to be pitted against other programs serving children. That's where "listening" comes in. Support the efforts of early childhood professionals working in other communities as well.

What can you do to improve the quality of life for staff as well as families in programs for young children?

You will end this portion of your CDA Professional Preparation Program process by going back to where you began—by reaffirming your commitment to professional work with children. This statement first appeared in Unit 1. Now that you are nearly finished with your CDA—at last—this statement will probably have new meaning for you.

Competent caregivers establish a relaxed mealtime routine that makes eating pleasant for each child.

Congratulations for taking on a very difficult task—enrolling in the CDA Professional Preparation Program. You can check the last box on your CDA Progress Record for your training. Your Professional Resource File is now, or soon will be, complete and you will take part in a final assessment. Our best wishes are with you during these final stages of meeting the requirements for your CDA Credential.

We welcome you as a professional early childhood educator. May your work be more rewarding than you ever dreamed possible and may you grow in your professional competencies each day. The world's children are counting on you.

Children want you to get involved in what they do.

Putting it all together as an early childhood professional working with infants and toddlers

Resources for more information

Accreditation criteria and procedures of the National Academy of Early Childhood Programs. Washington, DC: National Academy of Early Childhood Programs, National Association for the Education of Young Children, 1984.

Bredekamp, S. (1987). *Developmentally appropriate practice in early childhood programs serving children from birth through age 8.* Expanded ed. Washington, DC: National Association for the Education of Young Children.

CDF Reports - The monthly newsletter of the Children's Defense Fund. Washington, DC: The Children's Defense Fund.

Celebrating early childhood teachers [Videotape-22 min.]. Washington, DC: National Association for the Education of Young Children, 1987.

Katz, L. G., & Ward, E. H. (1978). *Ethical behavior in early childhood education.* Washington, DC: National Association for the Education of Young Children.

Kipnis, K. (1987, May). How to discuss professional ethics. *Young Children,* 42(4), 26-30.

NAEYC position statement on licensing and other forms of regulation of early childhood programs in centers and family day care homes. Washington, DC: National Association for the Education of Young Children, 1987.

NAEYC position statement on quality, compensation, and affordability in early childhood programs. Washington, DC: National Association for the Education of Young Children, 1987.

Pressma, D. & Emery L. (1991). *Serving Children with HIV Infection in Child Day Care* - A guide for center-based and family day care providers. Washington, DC: Child Welfare League of America, Inc.

Worthy Work, Worthless Wages. Oakland, CA: Child Care Employee Project, 1989.

Resources for bilingual programs

Casasola, C. (1978). *Bilingual-bicultural education: A manual for teacher trainers and trainees.* Editorial Justa Publication, Berkeley, CA.

Crawford, J. (1989). *Bilingual education: History, politics, theory and practice.* Crane Publishing Company, Inc., Trenton, NJ.

Fillmore, L. (1991, June). A question for early childhood programs: English first or families first? *Education Week.*

Fillmore, L. (1991). Language and cultural issues in early childhood education. In S. L. Kagan (ed.), *The 90th Year Book of the National Society for the Study of Education.*

Getting Involved Series (Spanish only) (1990). Washington, D.C.: Head Start Bureau, P.O. Box 1182.

Hakuta, K. (1986). *Mirror of language: The debate on bilingualism,* New York: Basic Book, Inc.

Porter, Rosalie Pedalino (1990). *Forked Tongue: The Politics of Bilingual Education.* New York: Basic Books, Inc.

Schon, I. (1991, May). Recent noteworthy books in Spanish for young children. *Young Children,* 46(4), 65.

Siegrist, D. (1976). *Language and bilingual education.* Multilingual, Multicultural Material Development Center, California State Polytechnical University, Pomona, CA.

U.S. Commission on Civil Rights (1975). *A better chance to learn.* Bilingual-Bicultural Education Clearinghouse Publication No. 51, Washington, D.C.

8

Preparing for final assessment as a Child Development Associate

Now, at the conclusion of the CDA P$_3$, you should be prepared to complete your final assessment. The process will determine your ability to integrate the knowledge and skills developed in the Professional Preparation Program and to demonstrate your competence as a CDA working with young children and their families.

A specially trained Council Representative will be assigned by the national office to conduct an on-site visit to collect evidence of your competence working with young children and their families. The Council Rep will interview you, review the results of the Parent Opinion Questionnaire and Formal Observation, and examine your Professional Resource File. A summary of the results of this evidence will be forwarded to the Council office in Washington, D.C.

If you have successfully completed all phases of the CDA Professional Preparation Program, the Child Development Associate Credential will be awarded with an endorsement for center-based infant/toddler programs. Candi-

dates working in bilingual settings and completing special additional requirements will be awarded also the Bilingual Specialization.

Definition of a CDA

The Child Development Associate (CDA) is a person who is able to meet the specific needs of children and who, with parents and other adults, works to nurture children's physical, social, emotional, and intellectual growth in a child development framework. The CDA Credential is awarded to child care providers and home visitors who have demonstrated their skill in working with young children and their families by successfully completing the CDA assessment process.

Part 1

CDA Competency Standards

As a Candidate for the CDA Credential, you will be assessed based upon the CDA Competency Standards. These criteria are the national standards used to evaluate a caregiver's performance with children and families. The Competency Standards are divided into six (6) **Competency Goals**, which are statements of a general purpose or goal for caregiver behavior. The six goals are defined in more detail in 13 **Functional Areas**, which describe the major tasks or functions that a caregiver must complete in order to carry out the competency goal. The national competency goals and functional area definitions are common to all child care settings whether in centers or family child care homes.

All of the evidence you collect to demonstrate your competence as a CDA will be judged by these standards.

Ensuring children's safety is one of your many functions as a CDA.

"It has been a special privilege for me to have been given the opportunity to teach and to learn, to give and to receive friendship and to experience, again and again, the same joy that I felt on the day that I received my CDA."

CDA, 1990

CDA Competency Goals	Functional Areas	Definitions
I To establish and maintain a safe, healthy learning environment	1. Safe	Candidate provides a safe environment to prevent and reduce injuries.
	2. Healthy	Candidate promotes good health and nutrition and provides an environment that contributes to the prevention of illness.
	3. Learning Environment	Candidate uses space, relationships, materials, and routines as resources for constructing an interesting, secure, and enjoyable environment that encourages play, exploration, and learning.
II To advance physical and intellectual competence	4. Physical	Candidate provides a variety of equipment, activities, and opportunities to promote the physical development of children.
	5. Cognitive	Candidate provides activities and opportunities that encourage curiosity, exploration, and problem solving appropriate to the developmental levels and learning styles of children.
	6. Communication	Candidate actively communicates with children and provides opportunities and support for children to understand, acquire, and use verbal and nonverbal means of communicating thoughts and feelings.
	7. Creative	Candidate provides opportunities that stimulate children to play with sound, rhythm, language, materials, space, and ideas in individual ways and to express their creative abilities.
III To support social and emotional development and provide positive guidance	8. Self	Candidate provides physical and emotional security for each child and helps each child to know, accept, and take pride in himself or herself and to develop a sense of independence.
	9. Social	Candidate helps each child feel accepted in the group, helps children learn to communicate and get along with others, and encourages feelings of empathy and mutual respect among children and adults.
	10. Guidance	Candidate provides a supportive environment in which children can begin to learn and practice appropriate and acceptable behaviors as individuals and as a group.
IV To establish positive and productive relationships with families	11. Families	Candidate maintains an open, friendly, and cooperative relationship with each child's family, encourages their involvement in the program, and supports the child's relationship with his or her family.
V To ensure a well-run, purposeful program responsive to participant needs	12. Program Management	Candidate is a manager who uses all available resources to ensure an effective operation. The Candidate is a competent organizer, planner, record keeper, communicator, and a cooperative co-worker.
VI To maintain a commitment to professionalism	13. Professionalism	Candidate makes decisions based on knowledge of early childhood theories and practices, promotes quality in child care services, and takes advantage of opportunities to improve competence, both for personal and professional growth and for the benefit of children and families.

Part 2

Documentation of competence

Your final assessment as a CDA will involve a documentation of your competence. Five components make up the documentation:

> 1. Early Childhood Studies Review
> 2. Professional Resource File
> 3. Formal Observation
> 4. Parent Opinion Questionniares
> 5. Oral Interview

As a Candidate enrolled in the CDA P_3, you have already completed one component of the assessment — the Early Childhood Studies Review — during your CDA Seminar. Now, you will complete the remaining components.

First, you will prepare to present evidence of your competence from the following three (3) sources:

> 1. Professional Resource File
> 2. Formal Observation by the Field Advisor
> 3. Parent Opinion Questionnaire

Then you will complete your Oral Interview during the Council Rep verification visit.

Professional Resource File

The Professional Resource File is a collection of materials that you will use as an early childhood professional in future work with young children and families. It is compiled for two purposes:

> 1. It provides a picture of what information Candidates find valuable in their work as a basis for assessing competence as a CDA; and
> 2. It provides Candidates an important experience in locating resources and articulating their own view of the work in early childhood programs.

The Professional Resource File is a working resource - one that should be USEFUL to you as a CDA during your career in early childhood education. The information it contains should serve as reference materials on a daily basis.

You have already collected most, if not all of the materials you need for your Professional Resource File and have drafted statements of competence for 5 of the 6 competency areas. Now it is time to revise and complete all three sections and arrange them in their final form.

Arrangement of the Resource File

The material in the Professional Resource File can be arranged in any one of many creative ways (e.g., bound in a notebook or contained inside file folders in a box). It should be professional looking and manageable in size. It should be organized and easy to add to or delete from. *There are no requirements about how it should look.* Whatever its physical form, the Professional Resource File should be portable — designed to be carried to and from a work site, on a home visit, or to a meeting — wherever early childhood professionals work.

Contents

The Professional Resource File has three major sections: (1) *Autobiography*; (2) *Statements of Competence*; and (3) *Resource Collection*.

(1) <u>Autobiography</u>: Write a statement about yourself of about 300 words. In the first part tell who you are, and in the second part, tell what things about your life influenced your decision to work with infants and toddlers. *If you wish, you may attach a formal resume of your education and work experiences.*

(2) <u>Statements of Competence</u>: In your own words describe the things you do with children and families that demonstrate your ability to meet the specific needs of young infants, mobile infants, and toddlers in each of the six (6) CDA Competency Goal areas. The description in each area should be about 200-500 words in length and should state your goals for children and give specific examples of what you do to achieve those goals. Give an example for children in each of the three infant/toddler subage groups — young infants, mobile infants, and toddlers. <u>OR</u>, you may write about a general activity with specific details about how the activity applies differently to each subage group. *For bilingual Candidates, statements must be specific to the goals of bilingual programs and the statements in three (3) Competency Goal areas must be written in Spanish.*

Begin each section by writing out the Competency Goal Statement:

---

1. Establish and maintain a safe, healthy learning environment
2. Advance physical and intellectual competence
3. Support social and emotional development and provide positive guidance
4. Establish positive and productive relationships with families
5. Ensure a well-run, purposeful program responsive to participant needs
6. Maintain a commitment to professionalism

Remember, your statement for each Competency Goal should contain no more than 200-500 words. Of course, you cannot describe everything you do in such a limited space. Choose the most important goals you have for children and the best examples of practices that you feel represent your competence.

Write about your *current practice*, using, whenever possible, examples of your work now (within the past 6 months). As you review the draft statements you wrote when you first started the CDA P$_3$, you may need to revise them based on changes in your beliefs and practices as you progressed through your study.

(3) <u>Resource Collection:</u> There are seventeen (17) specific items to be included in the Resource Collection. Even though you have collected them as you worked through *Essentials* chapter by chapter, you should check them again for completeness. For some items, little detail for infant/toddler Candidates was provided earlier in Essentials. More specific detail is provided below. They should now be organized by Competency Goal areas and numbered so that each item can be located easily during the Council Representative verification visit. *For Bilingual Candidates, the resources used directly with children and families must be in two languages—Spanish/English.*

COMPETENCY GOAL I
To establish and maintain a safe, healthy learning environment

1. Name of agency and telephone number to report child abuse concerns.

2. A record of Red Cross or other agency first aid class certificate of completion. Training must include first aid for children 0-3 years of age (e.g., CPR for infants and toddlers). Certification must have been issued within the past 3 years.

3. Agency name(s) that supply information on nutrition for children (e.g., Cooperative Extension Service).

COMPETENCY GOAL II
To advance physical and intellectual competence

4. Four songs, chants or fingerplays, including two from other cultures. Include music and words.

5. Nine (9) stimulating activities that promote physical, cognitive and creative development – three (3) for young infants, three (3) for mobile infants, and three (3) for toddlers. Describe the materials you use, the skills they encourage, and how you expect children to use them.

COMPETENCY GOAL III

To support social and emotional development and provide positive guidance

6. Titles, authors, publishers and copyright dates of 5 colorful and durable books for children under 3 that support development of gender identity by portraying males and females in diverse roles.

7. Titles, authors, publishers and copyright dates of 2 picture books that deal with everyday activities and routines.

8. Titles, authors, publishers and copyright dates of 3 books you would recommend for parents of children under 3 that deal with separation, divorce, remarriage, or blended families. The books may either be children's or adult's books.

9. Name of local hospital and its policies about group field trips, orientation for children scheduled for hospitalization, and parents' presence during children's inpatient stays.

10. Agency name and telephone number for making referrals to family counseling.

COMPETENCY GOAL IV

To establish positive and productive relationships
with families

11. Policies for your program that specify what parents should do and what program does for parents. Include strategies to maximize communication between caregiver and parent on informal as well as formal basis.

COMPETENCY GOAL V

To ensure a well-run, purposeful program
responsive to participant needs

12. Samples of 3 types of record keeping forms used in group care programs, including accident report and emergency form.

COMPETENCY GOAL VI

To maintain a commitment to professionalism

13. Name and contact information of agency that regulates child care centers and homes; copy of current regulations.

14. Brochure(s) and membership information from two or three national early childhood education associations.

15. Pamphlet(s) designed for parents about how children grow and learn. (No more than 5)

16. An observation tool for recording information about children's behavior. One copy should be blank; the other filled out with a sample observation of a child. (Anonymous)

17. Name and contact information of agencies in the community that provide resources for children under 3 years old with disabling conditions.

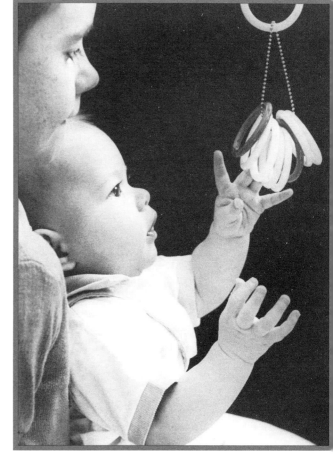

Nurturing children through various stages of development – that's what being a CDA is all about.

Formal Observation

A vital source of evidence of your skill is your actual hands-on work as primary caregiver with children and families. Documentation of these practices is collected through a formal observation.

You will be observed by your Field Advisor while you are working with young children in your field placement setting. This observation will be carried out exactly like your first formal observation conducted during Unit 6 of *Essentials* using the *CDA Observation Instrument*. However, since your Field Advisor must document your skill with young infants (birth - 8 months), mobile infants (9-17 months), and toddlers (18-36 months), it may be necessary for him/her to complete the observation/interaction requirement by *conducting a separate observation, in a classroom or group other than where you work on a daily basis*. Following the instructions on the Observation/Interaction Form, your Field Advisor will accompany you to a setting where you can spend a few hours interacting with children. The Field Advisor will record what s/he observes, and include it as part of the formal observation.

Your Field Advisor will arrange a time to conduct the observation(s). S/he may complete the formal observation in one visit or it may take several. Once the observation form is completed, it will be presented to the Council Representative during the verification visit. The instructions for your Field Advisor are included with the *CDA Observation Instrument*.

Keep in mind that the purpose of the observation is to rate your skill in the following specific performance areas. The items the Field Advisor will look for are listed on the next 2 pages.

In a bilingual setting, the Field Advisor will look for examples of your performance that show your skill in achieving bilingual development in children.

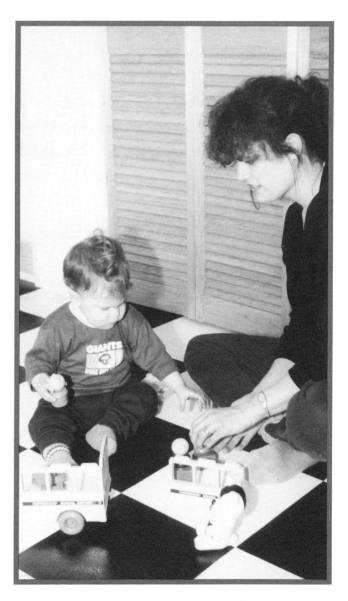

Observation of your hands-on work with children is a critical part of the credentialing process.

Candidate Performance Items to be rated by the Field Advisor

Functional area 1: Safe

1.1   All toys and materials provided for use by children are safe.

1.2   Supervision is appropriate for developmental level of children.

1.3   Emergency procedures are well planned in advance and are well organized.

Functional area 2: Healthy

2.1   General hygiene practices are implemented consistently to cut down the spread of infectious disease.

2.2   Health maintenance habits in children are encouraged.

2.3   Diapering/toileting procedures are organized to maintain health.

2.4   Meals/snacks meet the developmental needs of children.

2.5   Pleasant and appropriate environment conducive to rest is provided daily.

Functional area 3: Learning environment

3.1   Well-arranged space is provided, which meets the developmental needs of children during routines and play.

3.2   A variety of developmentally-appropriate materials are made available.

3.3   Materials for play are well organized.

3.4   Schedule provided meets children's needs for routine and play.

Functional area 4: Physical

4.1   A variety of activities are offered which enable children to develop their large muscles.

4.2   A variety of activities are offered which enable children to develop their small muscles.

4.3   Program activities are adapted to meet individual needs and special needs of children with handicaps.

4.4   Opportunities are offered to help children develop their senses.

Functional area 5: Cognitive

5.1   A variety of age appropriate materials and activities which encourage curiosity, exploration and problem solving are accessible to children throughout the day.

5.2   Interactions provide support for play, exploration, and learning.

5.3   Individual learning styles are recognized.

Functional area 6: Communication

6.1   Communication with each individual child is frequent.

6.2   Talk with children is developmentally appropriate.

6.3   Children are encouraged to talk.

6.4   Children's attempts to communicate are responded to positively.

6.5   A developmentally-appropriate, print-rich environment, in which children learn about books, literature, and writing, is provided.

Functional area 7: Creative

7.1   Individual expression and creativity are appreciated.

7.2   Many appropriate music experiences are available to children.

7.3   Art experiences are age appropriate and varied.

7.4   Dramatic play experiences, with a variety of age-appropriate props, are available.

7.5   Variety of age-appropriate block play opportunities are available.

Functional area 8: Self

8.1   Children are given the message that each is important, respected, and valued.

8.2   Individual children are helped to develop a sense of security.

8.3   Diapering/toileting procedures are developmentally appropriate and are organized to encourage self-help skills.

Functional area 9: Social

9.1   Each child is helped to feel accepted in the group.

9.2   Feelings of empathy and respect for others are encouraged.

9.3   Non-biased curriculum is used.

9.4   Children are encouraged to respect the environment.

Functional area 10: Guidance

10.1   Methods for avoiding problems are implemented.

10.2   Positive guidance techniques are used.

10.3   Guidance practices are related to knowledge of each child's personality and developmental level.

Functional area 11: Families

11.1 Various opportunities are offered to appreciate children's families are part of the regular program.

11.2 Information about families' culture, religion, and childrearing practices is used in classroom experiences.

11.3 Various opportunities are provided to help parents understand the development of their child and understand their child's point of view.

11.4 Resources are provided to help families meet their child's needs.

In addition, the Field Advisor will rate your performance in the two additional CDA functional areas where it may not be possible to actually observe your behavior during the formal observation. The Field Advisor may need to ask you some questions in order to complete her/his evidence of your skill in the following areas:

Functional area 12: Program management

Candidate manages by using all available resources to ensure an effective operation. Candidate is a competent organizer, planner, recordkeeper, communicator, and a cooperative co-worker.

Functional area 13: Professionalism

Candidate makes decisions based on knowledge of early childhood theories and practices, promotes quality child care services, and takes advantage of opportunities to improve competence, both for personal and professional growth and for the benefit of children and families. Candidate keeps abreast of current regulatory, legislative, and workforce issues and how they affect the welfare of young children.

Parent Opinion Questionnaire

Parent perceptions about your skills and knowledge are extremely important in assessing whether you conduct yourself in a professional manner. Your Field Advisor will assist you in this process of gathering parent opinion. Each parent with a child in your care will be given an opportunity to complete a questionnaire. At least 75% of the questionnaires distributed must be completed. Your Field Advisor may have to make follow-up telephone calls in order to get the questionnaires returned.

The questionnaires are confidential and you will not be able to read the parents' responses. The Field Advisor will collect the questionnaires and place them in a sealed envelope for you to present to the Council Representative. Instructions for distributing and collecting the responses to this questionnaire are included in the *Field Advisor's Guide*, along with the following cover letter and questionnaire:

By observing children interacting with each other you can learn more about each child.

CDA PARENT OPINION QUESTIONNAIRE COVER LETTER

Dear Parents:

I am applying to be assessed for the Child Development Associate (CDA) Credential. The CDA Credential is awarded by the Council for Early Childhood Professional Recognition (Council), located in Washington, D.C. The Credential is awarded to competent caregivers and home visitors who have demonstrated their ability to meet the needs of children and parents on a daily basis.

The Council believes that parents have the right to know that the individuals caring for their children are competent. Therefore, parents have a very important role in the assessment of a person who wants to become a Child Development Associate. You can make an important contribution to a national effort to assure quality child care for young children by evaluating my work with your child and family.

As part of my assessment, I am required to collect the opinion of all parents who have children in my group. Therefore, I am asking you to fill out the questionnaire included with this letter. Your answers will be confidential. Please do not sign your name. Think about each question and answer it openly and honestly. Your specific comments at the end of the questionnaire will be very much appreciated.

I would be grateful if you would return your completed questionnaire to me in the enclosed envelope (**sealed**) by

_____.

If you have any questions, please contact me at _____, or you may contact the Council hotline at 1-800-424-4310.

Thanks for your help.

Sincerely yours,

CDA Candidate

Queridos Padres:

Estoy solicitando ser evaluada/o para obtener mi Credencial de Asociada/o en el Desarrollo del Niño (CDA). Esta Credencial es otorgada por el Concillo ("*Council*") para el Reconocimiento Profesional de la Educación Infantil/Pre-escolar/Temprana, localizado en Washington, D.C. La credencial es otorgada a personas que demuestran ser capaces de satisfacer las necesidades específicas de los niños, y quienes trabajan con los padres para fomentar el progreso del niño.

El Concilio ("Council") cree firmemente que los padres/madres tienen el derecho de saber que los individuos a cargo del cuidado de sus niños son profesionales competentes, es por eso que los padres juegan un papel muy importante en la evaluación de una persona que desea convertirse en un Asociado en el Desarrollo del Niño (CDA). Usted podría contribuír grandemente a este esfuerzo nacional, de asegurar la calidad en el cuidado infantil/pre-escolar, evaluando mi trabajo con su niño/s y su familia.

Como parte de mi evaluación, tengo la responsabilidad de recolectar la opinióm de todos los padres de los niños en mi grupo. Por esta razón, le pido que llene el cuestinario adjunto a esta carta. Sus respuestas se mantendrán confidenciales. Por favor no escriba su nombre. Piense y responda a cada pregunta en forma libre y honesta. Sus comentarios específicos al final del cuestionario serán apreciados.

Le agradezco anticipadamente se sirva devolverme este cuestionario completo en un sobre **sellado**, antes del

_____.

Si Ud. tiene alguna pregunta, por favor comuníquese conmigo al _____ , o Ud. puede llamar a la línea de ayuda del Concilio (*Council hotline*) al 1-800-424-4310.

Gracias por su apoyo.

Sinceramente,

Candidata/o CDA

CDA PARENT OPINION QUESTIONNAIRE
CUESTIONARIO CDA DE OPINION DE PADRES

CDA Candidate's Name _____

Nombre del Candidato/a CDA _____

For each statement, circle the answer you think is best.

Haga un circulo alrededor de cada respuesta que usted considera como la más correcta

YES = CDA Candidate does this
NO = CDA Candidate does not do this
N/A = Do not know or does not apply

SI = La Candidata CDA lo hace
NO = La Candidata no hace esto
N/A = Ud. no sabe o no es pertinente

The CDA Candidate/ El Candidato/a CDA:

YES NO N/A 1. Reports accidents or any first aid given to my child.
SI NO N/A 1. Reporta accidentes o primeros auxilios dados a mi niño.

YES NO N/A 2. Requires my written permission to give any medication to my child.
SI NO N/A 2. Requiere mi autorización por escrito para poder dar cualquier medicina a mi niño.

YES NO N/A 3. Tells me about my child's eating, sleeping, and toileting/diapering.
SI NO N/A 3. Me dice como mi niño come, si duerme, sobre sus hábitos en el uso del baño, o cambio de pañales.

YES NO N/A 4. Follows feeding instructions for my infant or for my child with allergies.
SI NO N/A 4. Sigue instrucciones para la alimentación de mi bebé o la de mi niño que sufre de alergias.

YES NO N/A 5. Allows my child to be picked up only by people I have named.
SI NO N/A 5. Permite que a mi niño lo recojan sólo aquellas personas a quienes yo he autorizado.

YES NO N/A 6. Reports to me about my child's play and learning.
SI NO N/A 6. Me mantiene informado/a sobre el juego y el aprendizaje de mi niño.

YES NO N/A 7. Organizes toys and play materials so my child can reach them easily.
SI NO N/A 7. Organiza los juguetes y materiales de juego de manera que mi niño pueda alcanzarlos facilmente.

YES NO N/A 8. Provides a place for my child to store his or her own things and makes sure I can find the things I need to bring home.
SI NO N/A 8. Provee un lugar para que mi niño pueda guardar sus pertenencias y se asegura de que yo pueda encontrar todas las cosas que necesito llevar a casa.

YES	NO	N/A	9.	Has enough toys and materials so children do not fight over popular toys.
SI	*NO*	*N/A*	*9.*	*Tiene juguetes y materiales en número suficiente para evitar que los niños peleen por los juguetes más populares.*

YES	NO	N/A	10.	Takes my child outdoors to play every day, except in bad weather.
SI	*NO*	*N/A*	*10.*	*Lleva a mi niño a jugar afuera todos los días excepto cuando el tiempo esta muy malo.*

YES	NO	N/A	11.	Talks with my child frequently.
SI	*NO*	*N/A*	*11.*	*Habla frecuentemente con mi niño.*

YES	NO	N/A	12.	Listens with interest when my child talks and encourages my child to talk.
SI	*NO*	*N/A*	*12.*	*Escucha con interés cuando mi niño habla y lo anima a hablar.*

YES	NO	N/A	13.	Helps my child learn to control his or her own behavior without spanking or other harsh punishment.
SI	*NO*	*N/A*	*13.*	*Ayuda a mi niño a controlar su propio comportamiento, sin pegarle o sin usar castigos duros.*

YES	NO	N/A	14.	Reads to my child often.
SI	*NO*	*N/A*	*14.*	*Le lee a mi niño, con mucha frecuencia.*

YES	NO	N/A	15.	Provides many music, art, block and pretend activities that my child can do in his or her own way.
SI	*NO*	*N/A*	*15.*	*Provee muchas actividades de música, arte, bloques, actividades de pre tender, que mi niño puede hacer a su manera.*

YES	NO	N/A	16.	Helps my child feel proud of what he or she can do.
SI	*NO*	*N/A*	*16.*	*Ayuda a mi niño a sentirse orgulloso de lo que él puede hacer.*

YES	NO	N/A	17.	Encourages children to enjoy getting along with each other.
SI	*NO*	*N/A*	*17.*	*Anima a los niños el disfrute de llevarse bien entre ellos.*

YES	NO	N/A	18.	Gives me the feeling that she is truly interested in my child and me.
SI	*NO*	*N/A*	*18.*	*Me hace sentir que ella/él está verdaderamente interesada/o en mi niño y en mí.*

YES	NO	N/A	19.	Is pleasant and friendly with me.
SI	*NO*	*N/A*	*19.*	*Es agradable y amistosa/o conmigo.*

YES	NO	N/A	20.	Is available to discuss my concerns.
SI	*NO*	*N/A*	*20.*	*Esta disponible para hablar conmigo sobre mis preocupaciones.*

YES	NO	N/A	21.	Asks me for ideas to use with my child, including activity ideas.
SI	*NO*	*N/A*	*21.*	*Me pide ideas para usarlas con mi niño, incluyendo ideas sobre actividades.*

YES	NO	N/A	22.	Asks me what I think is important in raising my child.
SI	*NO*	*N/A*	*22.*	*Me pregunta sobre lo que yo pienso que es importante en la crianza de mi niño.*

YES	NO	N/A	23.	Talks with me about any fears my child has.
SI	*NO*	*N/A*	*23.*	*Me habla sobre cualquier temor o temores que tenga mi niño.*

YES	NO	N/A	24.	Maintains confidentiality; does not freely discuss my child or family in the presence of others.
SI	*NO*	*N/A*	*24.*	*Es reservada/o, mantiene información confidencial; no habla sobre mi niño o mi familia en la presencia de otras personas.*

YES	NO	N/A	25.	Encourages me to visit at any time.
SI	NO	N/A	25.	*Me anima a visitar en cualquier momento.*

YES	NO	N/A	26.	Lets me know of parent meetings and other ways I can become involved in the program.
SI	*NO*	*N/A*	*26.*	*Me hace saber cuando hay reuniones de Padres y me informa sobre otras maneras de participar en el programa.*

YES	NO	N/A	27.	Schedules conferences at times that are convenient to me.
SI	*NO*	*N/A*	*27.*	*Señala fechas para reunirnos, en días y horas que me son convenientes.*

Indicate language(s) you use at home_____. Language(s) you prefer Candidate to use with your child_____.

Indique el idioma/s que usted habla en su casa_____. Idioma/s que ud.prefiere que la Candidata hable a su niño_____.

Please write your opinion about this Candidate's work with your child:
Por favor escriba lo que usted opina sobre el trabajo de esta Candidata/o con usted y con su niño:

PART 3

Verification Visit

Once you have completed your Professional Resource File, Formal Observation, and Parent Opinion Questionnaires, you are ready for the Verification Visit by the Council Representative.

Your Field Advisor will notify the Council that these materials are complete, and the Council Rep will telephone you to schedule a date for the Verification Visit.

You will need to provide a private place for the Council Rep to review your documents and conduct the interview. It is preferable to use space at the Center where you work. Be sure to get permission from the Program Director, and if you need help arranging a place, ask your Field Advisor to assist you.

Before the Council Rep arrives, prepare your documentation in the following way:

1. Put your Professional Resource File in final form. The Council Rep will check to see that all entries are complete and then return the File to you. *Make a xerox copy of your "Autobiography" and "Statement of Competence"* -- the Council Rep will mail these to the Council office in Washington, D.C.

2. Get the completed *CDA Observation Instrument* and the *Supplemental Observation Form* from your Field Advisor. They should be in a sealed envelope for the Council Rep to mail to the Council.

3. Get the completed Parent Opinion Questionnaires from your Field Advisor. They should also be in a sealed envelope. The Council Rep will mail these to the Council.

"Nothing can replace the joy of being told by other child care professionals, 'congratulations, you're competent!' The excitement of having achieved what may have seemed unreachable instills in you a sense of pride.

When your competence is validated by experts in the field, it reinforces the idea that you are professional, too."

CDA, 1992

During the Verification Visit, the Council Rep will:

1. Check the "Autobiography" in the Professional Resource File and send one copy to the Council.

2. Check the "Statements of Competence" in the Professional Resource File and send the copies to the Council.

3. Check the Resource Collection in the Professional Resource File and return it to you.

4. Check the Parent Opinion Questionnaires and send them to the Council.

5. Check the Formal Observation and send it to the Council.

6. Check the Supplemental Observation Form(s), if required.

7. Conduct the Oral Interview.

Oral Interview

The Oral Interview provides an opportunity for you to show how the information you have learned would be applied in a variety of early childhood settings.

The interview consists of 10 structured situations and takes about 1 to 2 hours to administer. The situations will be specific to your endorsement as an infant/toddler caregiver, and if you have chosen the bilingual specialization, specific to bilingual programs. Bilingual Candidates will be interviewed on the language of their choice.

For each situation, the Council Rep will show you a picture with a written description of the activity pictured. The Council Rep will read the description as you read along. Then s/he will pose a question and ask you to respond. As you respond, the Council Rep will listen, make notes and identify various aspects of your response. S/he may ask additional questions to help you give a clear and complete response. A sample interview question follows:

"Having the CDA Credential is a testimony of my competence as an early child hood professional. Going through the credentialing process has helped me to grow both personally and professionally."

CDA, 1988

Peter is 3 months old and has just started child care two days ago. He has had trouble eating and sleeping at the center, and has been fussy in general. The caregiver arrives at the center late today, and seeing the child crying, checks for a wet diaper. He finds that it is dry. **What should the caregiver do next?**

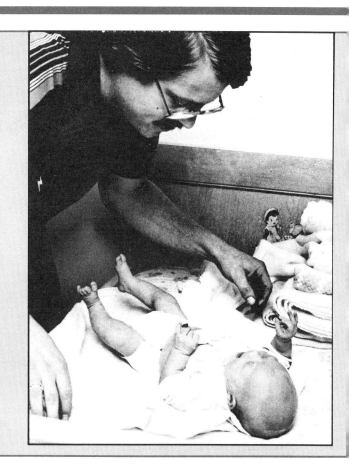

When the interview is finished, the Council Rep will score your responses and send the results to the Council.

After the Council receives the documentation of your competence, a committee will conduct a review and make a decision. If Credential award is recommended, the official Credential is sent to you, the new Child Development Associate. If the committee recommends more training, the Council will notify you and inform you of appeal procedures.

A CDA Credential is valid for 3 years from award date, after which it may be renewed.

"Every successful credential renews my zeal for the CDA process. Although I now function in a different capacity, I look forward to serving as a mentor/Advisor under the new process and to continuing my support of CDA."

CDA, 1990

CONGRATULATIONS!

You have completed all the requirements for the CDA Professional Preparation Program and have been assessed as a CDA. In just a few weeks, you will receive notification from the Council of the decision about your Credential award.

There are over 50,000 CDAs across the country, the Commonwealth of Puerto Rico, and the U.S. territories of Guam and the Virgin Islands. You will join their ranks, as well as the ranks of the early childhood education profession.

The choice to work with young children and their families is one of the most important career decisions that one can make in our society. Best wishes for a rewarding and successful career ahead!

Putting it all together as an early childhood professional providing family day care

HAT A LONG WAY you have come since you first started your CDA Professional Preparation Program! You have worked hard on your own. You have met many other CDA Candidates in your Seminar group. You probably have had a few exciting moments of discovery along the way when you saw how things fit together. You undoubtedly disagreed with a few ideas. You even may have felt that the struggle was not worth it, as you spent your weekends and evenings completing assignments and putting together your Professional Resource File. But now your CDA Credential will soon become reality.

You are almost at the end of one phase, and at the beginning of an even more difficult one in your work life. You are about to be recognized as an early childhood professional. You will be faced with problems to solve every day in this field. You will have to make decisions that affect the lives of children, par-

ents, or other child care professionals. You may be faced with the need to take action on behalf of children, parents, or early childhood educators you don't even know.

You are probably aware of just how much more there is to learn about how young children develop. Our field, like young children themselves, is constantly changing and growing. After you have earned your CDA, you will enter the early childhood profession and will be qualified for employment in a number of different positions including that of family day care provider. In order to make progress on your career path, you must continue to build your skills through continuing education and through collaboration with your early childhood colleagues.

Will you accept the challenge? Where do you go from here?

This unit and the next are to be completed during the third and final phase of your CDA Professional Preparation Program. You will continue to apply what you have learned as you build your CDA Professional Resource File and work with your Field Advisor to complete these last units.

As you prepare to demonstrate your competency as a teacher of young children, you will complete these tasks:

1. Work through all of the activities in Unit 7, with your Field Advisor's support.

2. Collaborate with your Field Advisor to distribute the Parent Opinion Questionnaire to all the parents of children in your group.

3. Complete your CDA Professional Resource File.

4. Be observed by your Field Advisor as you demonstrate your skills with children in a home setting.

5. Take part in the final assessment, at which time the Council Rep will interview you, review your Professional Resource File, and submit materials about you to the Council for Early Childhood Professional Recognition.

Part 1

Putting together all that you have learned

To be able to put everything together to create a high quality family day care program means using all the teaching strategies you know to foster development in children. Doing this will take yet another skill area: working as a member of an early childhood team.

Even if you work by yourself providing family day care in your home, lots of **adults** are involved: families, licensing personnel, volunteers, community service people, consultants, your substitutes, provider networks, neighbors. All of you must work as a team to provide the best possible care for children in your community. How can you do that?

Establish cooperative relationships

We have already talked about how to work with families: you both share information and plan together, you treat each other with respect, and you listen more than you talk. You use informal conversations, notes or letters, conferences, meetings, telephone calls, newsletters, and a variety of other ways to keep in touch with families. You are always pleasant, courteous, and tactful. You try to understand their point of view and keep their needs in mind. You are open to suggestions and are always trying to improve yourself.

As a professional early childhood educator, you will use these same skills when you collaborate with all the other people concerned about children. Your work puts you in touch with many other people. You are part of a team of professionals. And you are expected to conduct yourself in a professional way.

Whenever these other people are together with you and the children, for example, you are showing children how adults get along with each other. When people respect each other, the day goes much more smoothly, too.

A new substitute is working with you today so the children can get to know her better should you need her to fill in for you. You welcome her to the program, give her a quick summary of the activities for the children, and briefly outline what you expect her to do during the morning. "We're so glad you are here today. I will introduce you to each of the children."
"Please walk around with me as the children play. We'll show interest in what they are doing, talk informally, ask questions to make them think, and offer assistance if we see the need. Around 9:30, I'll show you how to fix snack." Feel free to ask questions.

Helping volunteers, substitutes, and visitors feel welcome and comfortable requires some advance organization on your part. These are just a few of the things you must remember to prepare in advance so that the day can go as smoothly as possible:

• **Have a copy of your expectations for children—the program rules and the daily schedule—written out for the newcomer to read.** These guidelines will help ensure that discipline is consistent and teaching strategies promote positive behaviors. This system eliminates surprises for children and adults, too. Make sure any questions the visitor might have are answered as soon as possible throughout the day.

• **Write out your plans for the day, and explain how you expect the volunteer or substitute to assist you with each activity.** If the person is new to the field of early childhood education, you may need to explain some basic principles about teaching young children. For example:

Fingerpainting at about 10 a.m.:
Supplies: Place these supplies on the kitchen table (supplies are in the cupboard above the sink): Orange, yellow, and black fingerpaints; enough large sheets of fingerpaint paper for each child in the group.
Supervision: Three children may fingerpaint at a time. Ask them to help each other snap on their smocks and roll up their sleeves. Children may use their hands and arms to paint. They may choose any or all of the three colors, and can work as long as needed for them to finish. After washing and hanging up their smocks, they can ask someone else to take their place. Encourage casual conversation and cooperation. Remember, the fun children have in doing this is more important than what the results are.
Things to talk about: Talk with children about what they are doing. Ask them to think about how the

paint feels on their hands. You might suggest words such as cool, slippery, slimy, wet, gushy, mushy—make up a word or two. Point out how different techniques make different marks on the paper as the children use them: One finger makes a thin line; the side of the hand can erase everything. If children make a design and then cover it up, do not express disappointment or criticize, but rather focus on what the child is doing. If the paper gets too wet and tears, offer another sheet if the child wants to continue.

• **Introduce the children and the visitor by name.** Some children may want to introduce themselves. Explain who the person is and why they are there. If the visitor will be doing some testing, briefly explain the process. If you are being observed, say what the observer is looking for, and direct the observer to a comfortable place with a good view. Use name tags if your visitor prefers.

• **Observe the person as she or he works with the children.** Throughout the day, comment on how things are going. "You've been such a help to notice just where to be to give children a boost. I'm so glad you're here today." Jot down any topics that need to be discussed later.

Most likely you handle all the responsibilities of a nutritionist, bus driver, office staff, and janitor. If you have someone helping you, make sure they feel like a real part of your program's team, exchange information with them on a regular basis . . . about individual children's preferences or moods . . . about program plans . . . when you'll need something special, for example. Encourage children to write let-ters (or draw pictures) to the person responsible.

Throughout the year, you may also work with other adults from outside the program, such as social workers or medical consultants. Sometimes they will support your efforts, sometimes they will be critical of what you do, and sometimes you will work together on behalf of a child or family who has requested information about a topic. Or sometimes a licensing worker may offer a negative opinion of your work.

Teachers are put on the spot a lot, and it is hard sometimes to accept criticism. Ask for a private conference time when you both are unhurried and can calmly discuss areas of concern in a productive way.

Your licensing worker has finished her evaluation. You are nervous about the results, even though you have tried hard to do your best. Sure enough, you are rated low in one area: children need to be offered more choices throughout the day.

You are disappointed at the criticism but eager to find out just what you can do better. "I am trying hard to do that. Can you give me some examples of what you mean to improve the program?"

Your licensing worker begins tactfully, "I can see you have a good start. But instead of giving children a choice between an art activity you have set up and a game with the school-age children, you might want to broaden their choices. Perhaps at least three choices would help. Make at least one of them something the children can do on their own without an adult or older child imposing so much structure on what happens." You reply, "Oh, you mean like letting them choose which art materials or table toys they want to use?"

Putting it all together as an early childhood professional providing family day care

"Exactly. The children may take a while to adjust to thinking more for themselves, but you have a lot of great materials. Let them pursue their own interests. Try giving them a little more freedom to choose within the activity, as well as choosing the activity itself."

"That's really helpful to see what kind of choices you mean. I'll work to see how I can offer better choices for children."

What techniques have you developed to respond to criticisms or challenges in productive ways?

You probably also have encountered the need to build support for what you do within your neighborhood or community.

Your family day care program is located in a residential neighborhood. One person who is home all day has been stirring up the people on your street by complaining about all the noise from the playground area.

A parent hears about the stew from a friend, and tells you what is happening. "Thank you for clueing us in to the problem. We'll need to think of some ways to become better friends with our neighbors." You come up with several ideas to try: Send a newsletter to everyone in the area; or have a noon picnic and invite neighbors; or issue invitations for people to visit the program; or ask the local paper to do a story on what a good program you have. Some of these ideas may not work, but the process has been started. You meet with two parents to try to figure out what to do.

In a situation like this, it's very important for you to remain calm and "professional." This is true even if the accusations are false, or make you angry. The parents will pick up on your tone and attitude.

What ideas do you have to maintain good community relations with your program's neighbors?

As a professional, you may also be called upon to lend your expertise to discussions of issues beyond your own program.

A condominium homeowner's association in your city has just ruled that their policy against home businesses will be enforced. This means no family day care in a nearby neighborhood. And already there is a shortage of good care in your community. Parents are dismayed.

You ask for a few minutes at the next AEYC meeting to raise the issue with your colleagues. You form a committee that includes several parents and a city administrator. Your goal is to plan strategies to increase the availability of child care.

A teacher brings in an "English Only" leaflet that is being circulated in your neighborhood. It calls for a petition to do away with all bilingual services in the community.

You call a meeting with parents to discuss a strategy. A parent suggests an "English Plus" leaflet supporting diversity. Parents take various responsibilities to work on it.

Are you ready to handle these kinds of responsibilities? As a CDA, others will look up to you. You will be expected to work with lots of people. The future of children is in your hands.

Use community resources

All through your *Essentials* curriculum, you have tracked down resources:

- the phone number to report child abuse
- your Extension Service for nutrition information
- field trip possibilities
- services to screen children for possible disabilities and take appropriate action
- resources for parents

Now is the time to become familiar with all the other resources in your community that can help you be more effective in your work with children. Here are just a few of the typical resource agencies that serve families. You can probably list more. If you need help to find out what your community offers, get together with your licensing representative.

Begin a card file of resources such as these, that you can share with your colleagues and with parents. Then call each group and find out what services or materials they have to help you.

Red Cross
Easter Seal Society
Safety groups
Mental health clinics
Medical clinics
Food stamps
WIC programs
Financial planning
Gymnastics classes
Child care resource and referral
Cultural resource groups
Resale shops
Educational supply stores
Performing artists' groups
Food cooperatives
Library
Community based organizations

All of these resources can broaden your ability to support the needs of the families in your program and your program itself! Many have brochures, information, even curriculum materials appropriate for parents and/or young children. Take advantage of what is available in your community through government agencies, volunteer groups, and citizen action coalitions. Unless you use these wonderful supplements, you, the children, and their families will miss out on a lot of marvelous opportunities. Expand your horizons today.

And, do not forget your local library. It contains a vast amount of resource material!

Manage efficiently

You are well aware that not all of your time is spent with children. You have other responsibilities as well. You manage space, materials, activities, records, and other adults every day.

Organize space and materials

We have already seen how important it is to arrange your shared home and teaching space to make the most of it. But remember, maintaining a safe, healthy learning environment means rearranging it occasionally. Because children grow and change, and as new children enter your care, you will want to periodically look carefully at your room arrangement and make changes to keep it fresh and interesting. Rotate equipment and materials as children's skills improve. Rejuvenate the outdoor play area with a fresh supply of sand or a new set of containers for water play.

Each time new material is added or a new theme is introduced, you have to examine these materials for bias. It is easy to slip back into a routine of what was done before.

Storage areas need to be neatly arranged and cleaned occasionally so you know what you have and where to find it. Who knows what buried treasure is lurking in the back of your closets!

Thoughtful planning of the environment also means you keep track of supplies so you can purchase them before you run out. One busy day and you can suddenly be out of glue! And you certainly don't want the guinea pig to go hungry! Periodically check the first aid kit to make sure it is well supplied.

You plan ahead, too, to decide which special materials you will need— pipe cleaners, tissue paper, foods. Perhaps you need parents to bring in paper bags or scraps of fabric. Give them a little advance notice so they can save things.

Take a look at the floor plan you developed in Unit 3 of *Essentials* (page 165). Now that you have many new ideas, complete the final design using the chart on page 165, or review the design you completed during the Seminar. **Discuss your design with your Field Advisor.**

Plan ahead for daily activities

Long before you start a new theme, gather all the materials needed so you won't have to scramble for something at the last minute. Check with your library to make sure the book titles or films you want are available, and reserve them if possible. Contact community resource groups about materials or visitors and arrange dates well in advance.

The curriculum in your family day care program will set the framework for what daily activities the children will do. But being prepared for each day will require you to think ahead.

For instance, most field trips must be scheduled uled far in advance because there are so many details to arrange. You will need to visit the place yourself and talk with the people there about how they can best accommodate young children. Travel, emergency medical permissions, and other forms must be signed. Bus or car arrangements have to be made. Special preparations may be needed for children with disabling conditions. Volunteers to go with you must be contacted. Money may need to be collected. Be sure to include some type of exercise or activity that helps prepare children for the trip.

Arrange for special visitors by giving them enough notice. Be sure to talk with them, in person or by phone before their visit, about the children's interests and attention spans and clarify what you expect the visitor to do.

Plan ahead to work late on days when an activity will require a lengthy clean up, or ask a family member to assist you. You may also need to plan early when preparation for an activity requires extra time.

You may also need to make arrangements for parent meetings—make sure refreshments are ready and supplies (napkins, coffee, and so forth) are provided.

Allow time in your day to keep notes for future planning. Sit down at the end of each day and look at your activities planned for tomor-row. Do you have everything you need?

Keep records

By now, you should have quite a large collection of observations of the children recorded in your daily diary. By building a record of how each child grows and learns, you can use the information to plan themes and activities, to point out to parents how much progress their children are making, and to help identify any potential disabilities. Don't stop just because you have finished your CDA!

Date records and have a folder for each child. Records of children can also help families when the child leaves your family day care program. For bilingual programs, for example, records on the first language of the child and his or her usage and understanding of the second language will be critical to planning. Families may want you to share some of what you have learned about the child with their child's next teacher. Always ask the parents first—summaries of your observations should only be released to others **if the parents approve**. Obtain permission from parents in writing. Remember this is confidential information. They will usually be quite agreeable if you explain that this is one way you can work together to build a bridge between the two programs for their child.

In every program, some written records are needed just to ensure children's welfare while they are present. When you set up your family day care program, you established proper procedures to report illnesses or accidents. Your attendance records must be accurate, especially in the event of an emergency evacuation. All programs must keep up-to-date health records, emergency forms, and written policies.

As a family day care provider, you must maintain records for licensing/registration and for taxes. You must prepare a budget, maintain a checking account, and obtain liability insurance coverage. Zoning records may be needed. You may participate in the Child Care Food Program or serve children whose care is subsidized or paid for by an agency, and all of these require some paperwork. If you have any assistants, you will need health and wage records for them as well. And you may need to advertise your program. Family day care is indeed a business!

All written records must be legible so others can read them, and should be organized and kept in a place where they can be located easily. If your program is bilingual, records may need to be kept in more than one language.

Children connect word meaning to experiences and familiar objects.

Add samples of 4 types of record keeping forms used in family day care programs to your Professional Resource File: 2 small business forms; such as bookkeeping, insurance, and taxes; 2 program operation forms, such as accident report and emergency form.

1.

2.

3.

4.

Communicate

Your ability to listen and respond appropriately—to children, parents, and others—keeps coming up in your professional studies. That's because listening is such a valuable tool in your everyday work. Sometimes people are subtle and sometimes they are pretty direct. But you **will** find out what people think about your work, what they need, and how you could improve what you do. Keep your eyes and ears pen to clues that something needs to be changed or that you are really doing a good job. It's a mark of a professional to be able to make positive changes in response to constructive criticism.

Here are some typical examples of the subtle types of feedback you may get. What would you do in each of these situations?

. A child gets wet and you discover there are no extra clothes in her tote bag. You see other tote bags with few or no extra clothes as well.

What are these parents telling you?

_____

_____

_____

_____

What should you do about it?

_____

_____

_____

2. You sent field trip permission slips home 2 weeks before the trip. Now it's 2 days away, and you have only 2 of the 5 permissions you need.

Why have so few been returned?

_____

_____

_____

_____

What should you do?

_____

_____

_____

_____

Allow children to communicate with each other.

3. You spend about 20 minutes a day reading books to your toddlers. One or two usually sit quietly, but the other half listen only a minute or two and then they begin to wander around.

Why are the children so restless?

What changes do you need to make in your toddler plans?

4. In your newsletter you ask parents to provide healthy snacks for birthday treats. The first birthday after your notice is celebrated with cupcakes and Kool-Aid.

Why did parents ignore your request?

How can you get parents to plan more nutritious birthday snacks?

Managing efficiently means being sensitive to these indicators of feedback and making adjustments accordingly.

Every day you will make hundreds of decisions about how to interact with children, about what to say to a parent, about how to work more effectively with neighbors and consultants. The more resources you have at your fingertips, the more likely you are to make good decisions. The fieldwork and Seminar parts of your *Essentials* curriculum have covered the basic information you need to make sound judgments. How you use that information professionally requires discussion of one more topic— professionalism.

Part 2

You try to make good decisions

Throughout your *Essentials* curriculum, you have picked up information to build on your teaching experience. You have seen ways to make good decisions about how you teach, how you work with other adults, and how you plan and organize your work. You will look back again and again at some parts of this material as you continue to extend your ability to teach in a professional way. There is so much to absorb—people have learned a lot about children over many years.

Making good decisions means always being ethical. Members of the NAEYC have developed a code of ethics which you will find in Unit 1 of *Essentials*. You are expected to agree to abide by it as a CDA.

With this code to help, each of us in the field must work out our own thoughts on what kind of teaching behavior is truly professional. We'll offer some guidelines here to help you make ethical decisions. While there are no right answers, here are some ways to help you consider as many factors as possible before you decide what to do in a specific situation. **Presented on the following pages are several situations. Think about each of these situations and discuss them with your Field Advisor.**

Have a healthy attitude about your power

Young children are so helpless and dependent upon adults. They are with you for so many of their waking hours. Their parents depend on you to give children the best experiences possible during those impressionable early years. In addition, parents need reliable child care so they can earn a living or prepare to earn one.

It is easy to abuse this power, either with children or adults. Some teachers are tempted to use physical force because they are stronger than children. Some teachers are tempted to take advantage of children psychologically because they believe children learn to be obedient out of fear. Some teachers fail to prepare children to become good world citizens. And some teachers think they can get away with almost anything because the parents are so desperate for affordable, convenient child care.

Think for a minute about how much power you have and use every day. You have the power to enable children to grow strong and competent or to be sickly and quitters. You have the power to help children become kind and generous-- or mean and stingy. You have the power to validate a child's home language and culture -- or make them feel inferior to other people. You have the power to help children get along with each other or to hate and fear people who are different from them. You have the power to provide high quality care or minimal custodial care. What is the ethical approach?

As a professional family day care provider, you make a commitment never to take advantage of children or their parents—physically, emotionally, intellectually, or financially. You respect them as people and treat them accordingly. You use your power to build strengths and to help overcome weaknesses.

How would you use your power in situations such as these? Jot down notes and discuss your responses with your Field Advisor.

1. A 6-month-old boy has been crying for half an hour. You have tried a clean diaper, a bottle, rocking, a warmer blanket, and soothing music, all to no avail. *Do you scream at the baby and tell him to shut up, that big boys don't cry? Do you spank him and isolate him in his crib?*

   What is the professional thing to do?

2. Two toddlers are fighting in the sandbox. Before you can get there, one has thrown sand into the other's eyes. *Do you grab the child who threw the sand and drag her indoors to sit in the corner of the living room? Do you tell both children to get out of the sandbox and that they may not play there for a week?*

   What is the professional thing to do?

3. A new family has moved into your community. Their first grader is hearing impaired and needs care before and after school. *Do you discourage the family when they inquire about enrollment? Do you accept the child but increase your fee because more effort is needed on your part?*

   What is the professional thing to do?

4. An English speaking child announces she won't play with Marisol because she is stupid and can't talk. *Do you frown and tell the child she is wrong and you never want to hear her say anything like that again? Do you ignore the comment and act like you didn't hear it?*

What is the professional thing to do?

_____

_____

_____

Keep confidences

During the course of your work, you will learn a great deal about families' personal lives. A parent may confide in you some upsetting details about a spouse. A child may blurt out that "Momma told me not to play with you because you are dumb." Parents may fill out financial forms so your program can qualify for financial reimbursement. Bruises on a Monday morning may lead you to suspect child abuse.

Whatever you hear or see as a CDA is privileged information. You are a professional, so you must take the appropriate steps to remedy the situation if there is a problem. Often you refer people to the appropriate community resources. You provide an accepting environment in which children feel good about themselves and others. You keep written records confidential. And you immediately report any possible abuse. Professionals do not announce what they have learned about a family to other family day care providers, to teachers in other programs, or to any other parents, or to their friends.

What do you do to stop yourself when you feel tempted to break a confidence about a family or particular child in your program?

_____

_____

_____

Parents trust you to keep information about them confidential. Parents have a right to privacy. Of course, you must balance that with the need to protect the child.

Protect children

You are legally and ethically responsible for the protection of all children in your care. Not just their safety, but their emotional well being, their physical development, their intellectual growth, and their social skills. You do not allow children to hurt themselves or each other. You do not allow any other adult to hurt children either. You show value for the way each child speaks and include their home language in the program. You are constantly alert for signs of any type of abuse. You base your decisions about what to do on the children's best interests.

Professional early childhood educators are constantly alert to conditions within their programs to assure that children are protected in all these ways. For example, you quickly scan the outdoor play area every time you enter it for new hazards. You arrange for enough adult assistance on field trips so children are kept in small groups for easy supervision. You evaluate each new order of materials (or each donation) for safety and appropriateness. You always listen to and watch the children so you can promote cooperation and friendly behaviors. You are eager to learn more about what types of activities are most beneficial for children's development, and you implement what you know.

Your role as a professional demands that you report suspected child abuse. Here are some examples of other situations that may arise in which you will need to act as a protector for children.

Write down how you would handle each of these dilemmas, and then talk with your Field Advisor about your responses.

1. One child frequently hits and shoots pretend guns at the other children.

2. Often one of your 4-year-olds is listless all morning, then devours lunch and seems more attentive in the afternoon.

3. The parents of a 3-year-old have purchased a kit with flashcards to teach their child to read. They are pressuring you to use it with all the children in your home.

Provide good quality care

There are many different types of programs for young children. You can adopt one of the models or set up your own approach. Either way, as a professional you always provide developmentally appropriate activities, materials, and experiences for all the children. You know children learn best through their own self-directed play and manipulation of real objects. You want children to enjoy themselves and to pick up ideas and behaviors that they will keep throughout their lives. You provide good, safe care for children. To do less would be unethical.

One of the most difficult aspects of working with young children is to avoid the temptation to lapse back into your old ways of teaching and disciplining. Especially in your own home, it is easy to find yourself falling back into the role of a parent, so you will need to catch yourself before that happens.

There are still many commercial (and home-made) materials available that are not appropriate for young children. Some methods or materials are better used with older children. Parents may request worksheets for 4-year-olds, for example, and you now realize young children have better things to do. You will need to put everything you know to work every day in making the right decisions about how to best foster the learning and development of young children.

Transitions from one activity to another also often prove to be difficult with a group of wiggly young children. The time between one activity and another may simply involve sitting and waiting . . . and waiting . . . and waiting. But now you know that's not an appropriate expectation. You know it's best to involve children in the transition to keep it smooth and not wasteful of anyone's time. Children can carry out the baskets of sand toys, for example. If you are waiting for another child to wash hands before lunch, do some finger plays or sing songs with movements until everyone is ready. Remember, children are learning from everything they do!

You will be faced again and again with the need to make on-the-spot decisions about the best quality of care. It helps to think ahead about how you would handle problems that are sure to arise.

What would you do if . . .

...a child drew a beautiful picture with lots of colors, and then scribbled black all over the top of it?

...a child began spanking a doll in the house-keeping area?

...a 4½-year-old boy always enters a group of children like a bull in the china shop, demanding to be involved or destroying children's projects?

Discuss your responses with your Field Advisor, who can help you think about how to apply what you have learned about young children in dealing with these and similar incidents.

As a CDA, you will always strive to keep knowledgeable about the standards of the profession. You will need to know about other national voluntary self-evaluation systems designed to improve and recognize the quality of programs. Group programs can benefit greatly by going through these review processes, much as you are going through the CDA credentialing system.

Contact the National Association for Family Day Care (refer to the National Organizations list on page 29) about the Family Day Care Home Accreditation System.

If you know about an excellent center, you may want to recommend that it become accredited through the National Academy of Early Childhood Programs. Call or write to the National Association for the Education of Young Children also listed on page 29 to request information about this system. Then talk with the program director about this excellent opportunity to be nationally recognized.

What else do you do to constantly monitor whether you are providing good care for children?

What steps can you take to improve how your program's quality of care is assessed?

_____

_____

_____

_____

Respect parents' authority

Parents do have the ultimate authority to make decisions about their children within legal limits of course. Every family and every cultural group stresses some values more than others, and then there are individual differences among families.

Parents may have standards of behavior for children at home that are not necessarily the same as those you have set in your program. Some families may live by a different code of morality than you accept. Parents may place a higher value on some things -- wardrobe or financial status, for example --than you prefer.

We all know how important it is to respect differences, but sometimes it is difficult when you disagree with how parents are raising their children. Often, parents who have radically different ideas than yours will probably not choose your family day care program. At other times, however, they may have no choice but to enroll their children in your program. When that happens, you need to get to know each other well and work out a way to be as cooperative as possible. You must make a concerted effort to learn all you can about the family and their way of life or beliefs. You may eventually agree to disagree. You will respect each other's differences and agree that children will be expected to act differently at their home and in your home. That way, at least in your program, you can keep what you believe to be the child's best interests in mind.

Children also need to know that some differences between their home and your program are acceptable and natural. A simple explanation that "Yes, you say grace before each meal at home. That is so important for your family. But here we wait until everyone is seated and then we begin to serve ourselves." Without a doubt, as a CDA you will encounter some thorny value issues. Just remember there is more than one way to make things work for the benefit of the children. Be willing to listen and try new ideas.

As a professional, how would you deal with situations such as these?

1. Parents insist on dressing their 4-year-old boy in a white shirt almost every day and they want to keep him clean.

_____

_____

_____

2. A child clearly has not been bathed in many days-- she has offensive body odor, her hair is tangled, and her fingernails are imbedded with dirt. The child is developing a rash.

3. One 3-year-old boy has been biting other children. You know you should speak to the parents about it-- but you also know that if you do they will probably beat the child.

4. Each morning, one parent stops at your sidewalk, honks the horn, and then sends her child alone up to your door.

Support diversity

As you have seen, all people are biased ---we all think we are right and the best. And we all need to admit that we have those biases if we are to become good teachers. Your CDA Seminar experiences helped you see how these biases can affect your work.

Hard as it is, there is no room for favorites when you teach young children. Instead, you must do everything possible to help children feel good about themselves, their family, their heritage, their beliefs, their abilities, and their language --and to appreciate and respect those same characteristics in others.

We are helping to make it possible for children to become productive citizens of the world of today and tomorrow. The world is filled with many ethnic groups and people with varying capabilities who must get along with each other. Ultimately, our survival depends on peacefully resolving our differences and learning to live together. We all must accept and appreciate our wonderful diversity as human beings.

These are some ethical issues in this area that you may face. How would you deal with them?

1. A neighbor who is a family day care provider always asks children to sit "Indian style."

_____

_____

_____

_____

2. You accept a child with AIDS into your group. The other parents threaten to withdraw their children.

_____

_____

_____

_____

3. A child brings in a copy of _Little Black Sambo_ or _The Five Chinese Brothers_.

_____

_____

_____

_____

4. Two White children say they are afraid that a Spanish-speaking child's "dirty color" will rub off on them if they hold hands while playing a game.

_____

_____

_____

Help protect consumers

Every state has different laws regarding programs for young children and qualifications for staff. You have already seen how important it is for good programs, family day care, and other group programs to be licensed or registered and for providers to be well trained.

Sometimes, we forget that the purpose of the licensing and registration laws are for consumer protection. In fact, most regulations provide only a **minimum** form of protection far less than in many other areas that we take for granted, such as driver's licenses or pet food standards, for example. Adhering to those laws is a must.

Regulations generally are designed to establish at least a floor for child-staff ratios, safety, staff qualifications, space, materials, and a variety of other important areas in programs for young children.

Your role as a professional is to protect children and families and advocate for what is in keeping with good practice. Above all, you should assure children's safety, health, and general well being. All these while maintaining the ethical standards already discussed.

Here are some sticky consumer protection situations. What would you do?

1. Your apartment's landlord keeps the heat very low in the winter. The children and you are too cold, and the temperature at floor level is 8 degrees lower than your state's family day care regulations permit. Do you report your landlord to the health department?

2. Another family day care provider in your network doesn't count part-time children when reporting enrollment levels because "there are always some children out sick anyway."

3. In your state, family day care registration is voluntary. If you register, you will have to report your income on your taxes. This means you may lose your rent subsidy.

Working with young children is demanding --of your energy, of your time, and of your conscience. Are you ready to become a professional? Are you prepared to take the most ethical action in sticky situations?

Part 3

You keep learning

By now you probably have realized how much there is to learn about young children. Even if you have been working with children for years, or are the parent of several, you have surely discovered that it is much more difficult to be a professional early childhood educator.

You are always learning from your experiences. The field is constantly changing as we find out more about how children develop. This information affects how we teach. How can you keep up with the challenges to get better at what you love to do?

Improve yourself personally

All of us have things we would like to do better. These may include bad habits we want to break, or attitudes that have been questioned.

What are some of the areas you need to work on?

These are the areas you will want to begin to improve so you can be a better family day care provider. Perhaps you need to eat more healthy foods or you are never dressed when the first child arrives in the morning.

Choose just one of the things you listed and write what steps you need to take to change your behavior.

You don't have to do it alone. Rely on the same community support groups to which you refer parents. Or talk with your licensing representative, spouse, friend, or a respected child care provider about how they can support your efforts. After you have made some progress in one area, select another and begin to work on it. As you make the most of your life, you can better help others make the most of theirs!

An ethical early childhood educator:

- never abuses power with children or families
- keeps information confidential
- protects children's best interests
- provides good care
- respects parents and co-workers
- supports diversity
- favors consumer protection of programs
- improves personal habits
- keeps on learning
- advocates for children, families, and the profession

In Unit 1, you began networking by interviewing an early childhood professional in a job different from yours. You should continue to build this network by interviewing your CDA Field Advisor. You know each other pretty well by now. Make a list of questions you would like to ask about what the distinctive issues are for a career working in family day care:

Learn more about your profession

How lucky you are to become a professional today. Just a few years ago there weren't many places you could turn to for information. Now nearly every community has an organized group of early childhood workers. Some of these groups are affiliates of NAEYC, NBCDI, SACUS, NHSA, or other large organizations. Some are state groups, and others are composed of active local people.

These professional networks are important. You probably work alone or with just a few other professionals and you never come in contact with the hundreds of thousands of other people who share the same commitment you do.

Now set up a time when the two of you can talk in general about the field for at least half an hour. Jot down what you learned here:

_____

_____

_____

_____

_____

_____

_____

_____

_____

The next task in building your network is to find the names of all the professional early childhood support groups in your area (a few national organizations are listed in Unit 1).

If you have not already done so, contact each group to learn more about their activities. Then select one or two organizations that seem to be good matches for you. Attend their meetings (go with another family day care provider or your CDA Advisor if possible). **Join at least one.** If there is no local chapter -- consider starting one in your area. Be an active member! Volunteer!

Most of these groups publish newsletters, journals, books, videos, posters or other professional development materials. Many magazines, books, and newsletters are available from other publishers as well. Ask for a sample copy of any regular periodicals that sound interesting. Which publications seem to be most useful to you? You might want to subscribe regularly to a journal or magazine. A few are listed here:

The Black Child Advocate

National Black Child Development Institute
1023 15th Street, N.W., Suite 600
Washington, DC 20005
(202) 387-1281

Childhood Education

Association for Childhood Education International
11141 Georgia Avenue, Suite 200
Wheaton, MD 20902
301-942-2443   800-423-3563

Child Care Information Exchange and Beginnings Books

P.O. Box 2890
Redmond, WA 98073-2890
206-883-9394

Day Care & Early Education

Human Sciences Press
233 Spring Street
New York, NY 10013
212-620-8000

Dimensions
Southern Association on Children Under Six
P.O. Box 5403, Brady Station
Little Rock, AR 72215-5403
501-663-0353

Early Childhood Teacher
P.O. Box 6410
Duluth, MN 55806-9893
(218) 723-9215

Family Day Care Bulletin
The Children's Foundation
725 Fifteenth Street, NW, Suite 505
Washington, DC 20005
202-347-3300

Interracial Books for Children Bulletin
Council on Interracial Books for Children
1841 Broadway
New York, NY 10023
(212) 757-5339

The New National Perspective
National Association for Family Day Care
1331A Pennsylvania Ave., NW, #348
Washington, DC 20004
(800) 359-3817

Newspatch: A Newsletter for the Early Intervention Practitioner
Creative Home Programs
P.O. Box 4869
Riverside, CA 92514

Nurturing News
187 Caselli Avenue
San Francisco, CA 94114
415-861-0847

Pre-K Today
Scholastic Inc.
411 Lafayette
New York, NY 10033
(212) 505-4900

Resources for Child Care
Newsletter for Family Day Care Providers
Rural Route 3, Box 8755
Union, ME 04862
(207) 785-5272

Texas Child Care
Texas Dept. of Human Srevices
4029 Capitol of Texas Highway S.
Suite 102
Austin, TX 78704
512-440-8555

Young Children
National Association for the Education of Young Children
1509 16th Street, NW
Washington, DC 20036
202-232-8777 800-424-2460

Join the group or subscribe to at least one publication so you can keep abreast of the latest happenings in early childhood.

Write or call for copies of brochures from early childhood publishers. Look through the lists of resources at the end of each unit for some names to contact. **Read through the offerings from these groups and select the books or other items that are of most interest to you. Write the titles here.**

_____

_____

_____

_____

Find out whether any of these resources are available in your family day care network office or local library. If not, how might you include some of these items in your program budget? Order others as your personal budget permits. Read! Read! Read! Or you will soon be left behind in your own profession. Become familiar with the "Resources for more information" found at the end of each unit of *Essentials*.

Workshops, conferences, and classes are marvelous ways to meet other people and learn more about how to teach young children. Once you have completed your CDA, keep up with the field by regularly enrolling in a course or taking a workshop. Better yet, keep climbing that career ladder and start to work on your college degree!

What topics would you like to learn more about?

_____

_____

_____

_____

Write up a plan to accomplish at least one of these goals. Find out where to go or what to read and continue to become even more professional. Then do it.

Becoming a professional also means contributing to the professional development of others. How do you share your newfound knowledge with others?

_____

_____

_____

These are just a few of the issues you will encounter as you continue to work with children. Your thinking about ethics will be constantly challenged. Are you prepared to meet those challenges and to act on behalf of young children?

Part 4

You act on behalf of young children

A family day care provider's work is never done. You already know that. And now we are going to suggest that you do even more. Just working with young children day-to-day is not enough. Thousands of children in our country and around the world are hungry, homeless, unhealthy, or have been harshly treated. Children are unable to defend themselves so we must take it upon ourselves to act in their behalf.

Stand up for good programs and services for children and families

You are now a committed early childhood professional. You have a responsibility to act in your local area, your state, nationally, and even on behalf of children you have never met in other countries. Here are some ways you can reach out, directly or indirectly, to improve the lives of children everywhere. **Add others to this list that you can think of or that you are already involved in.**

- Write letters to support stronger child care legislation, programs to strengthen families' self-sufficiency

- Become active in child advocacy groups

- Help parents become child advocates

- Read the Public Policy Report and the Washington Update in each issue of *Young Children*

- Vote in every election

- Speak up on behalf of developmentally appropriate practice: tell others, buy only appropriate materials, challenge others to learn more about how young children grow and learn

- Build an appreciation for diversity in the groups you are involved in: civic, church or synagogue, volunteer organizations, community service

- Volunteer for Week of the Young Child activities

- Support groups participating in the Worthy Wage Campaign

- Set up a network of supportive colleagues to phone for help

- Work with your school board or kindergarten teacher's association to ease the transition for children entering public school

- Advocate for appropriate services for children with disabling conditions

- _____

  _____

- _____

  _____

- _____

  _____

Don't wait another minute. If you are not taking an active role on behalf of all children and families, choose at least one activity from the list above and **get involved now!**

Advocate for your own profession

One of the most difficult issues facing us as early childhood educators is how to balance the need for affordable child care with our need to support ourselves. Salaries are low. Benefits are few or nonexistent. Most people still view our work as babysitting. But the rewards are so great that our ranks are swelling nevertheless! Good programs for young children are expensive because one person can only care for a small number of children, so many materials are used, and so much space is required. We don't want to shortchange children, nor do we want to settle for less than we deserve for our hard work and long hours doing one of the most important jobs on earth.

Get involved in Worthy Wage Day for child care providers. Remain committed to the entire profession. Don't isolate yourself only among workers who are like you. Keep learning about others -- Head Start, private programs, church sponsored programs.

Don't fall into the old trap of "conquer and divide." Don't allow yourself to be pitted against other programs serving children. That's where "listening" comes in. Support the efforts of early childhood professionals working in other communities as well.

What can you do to improve the quality of life for staff as well as families in programs for young children?

_____

_____

_____

You will end this portion of your CDA Professional Preparation Program process by going back to where you began by reaffirming your commitment to professional work with children. This statement first appeared in Unit 1. Now that you are nearly finished with your CDA—at last—this statement will probably have new meaning for you.

Family day care providers get involved with their children.

The National Association for the Education of Young Children
Statement of Commitment

As an individual who works with young children, I commit myself to furthering the values of early childhood education as they are reflected in the NAEYC Code of Ethical Conduct.

To the best of my ability I will:

- *Ensure that programs for young children are based on current knowledge of child development and early childhood education.*

- *Respect and support families in their task of nurturing children.*

- *Respect colleagues in early childhood education and support them in maintaining the NAEYC Code of Ethical Conduct.*

- *Serve as an advocate for children, their families, and their teachers in community and society.*

- *Maintain high standards of professional conduct.*

- *Recognize how personal values, opinions, and biases can affect professional judgment.*

- *Be open to new ideas and be willing to learn from the suggestions of others.*

- *Continue to learn, grow, and contribute as a professional.*

- *Honor the ideals and principles of the NAEYC Code of Ethical Conduct.*

Congratulations for taking on a very difficult task enrolling in the CDA Professional Preparation Program. You can check the last box on your CDA Progress Record for your training. Your Professional Resource File is now, or soon will be, complete and you will take part in a final assessment. Our best wishes are with you during these final stages of meeting the requirements for your CDA credential.

We welcome you as a professional early childhood educator. May your work be more rewarding than you ever dreamed possible and may you grow in your professional competencies each day. The world's children are counting on you.

Resources for more information

Accreditation criteria and procedures of the National Academy of Early Childhood Programs. Washington, DC: National Academy of Early Childhood Programs, National Association for the Education of Young Children, 1984.

Celebrating early childhood teachers [Video, 22 mins.]. Washington, DC: National Association for the Education of Young Children, 1987.

Alston, F.K. (1984). Caring for other people's children: A complete guide to family day care. Baltimore: University Park Press.

Bredekamp, S. (Ed.). (1987). Developmentally appropriate practice in early childhood programs serving children from birth through age 8 (expanded ed.). Washington, DC: National Association for the Education of Young Children.

CDA Reports - The monthly newsletter of the Children's Defense Fund. Washington, DC: The children's Defense Fund.

Garcia, R. (1985). Home centered care: Designing a family day care program— a guide for caregivers and parents. San Francisco: Children's Council of San Francisco.

Katz, L.G., & Ward, E.H. (1978). Ethical behavior in early childhood education. Washington, DC: National Association for the Education of Young Children.

Kipnis, K. (1987, May). How to discuss professional ethics. Young Children 42(4): 26-30.

Modigliani, K., Reiff, M., & Jones, S. (1987). Opening your door to children: How to start a family day care program. Washington, DC: National Association for the Education of Young Children.

NAEYC position statement on licensing and other forms of regulation of early childhood programs in centers and family day care homes. Washington, DC: National Association for the Education of Young Children, 1987.

NAEYC position statement on quality, compensation, and affordability in early childhood programs. Washington, DC: National Association for the Education of Young Children, 1987.

Pressma, D. & Emery, L. (1991). Serving Children with HIV Infection in Child Day Care -- a guide for center-based and family day care providers. Washington, DC: Child Welfare League of America, Inc.

The Partnership Guide: Strategies for Supporting Family Day Care in Your Community. New York: The National Family Day Care Project, National Council of Jewish Women, 1991.

Worthy work, worthless wages.Oakland, CA: Child Care Employee Project, 1989.

Resources for bilingual programs

Casasola, C. (1978). *Bilingual bicultural education: A manual for teacher trainers and trainees.* Editorial Justa Publication, Berkeley, CA.

Crawford, J. (1989). *Bilingual education: History, politics, theory and practice.* Crane Publishing Company, Inc., Trenton, NJ.

Fillmore, L. (1991, June). A question for early childhood programs: English first or families first? *Education Week.*

Fillmore, L. (1991, May). Report faults of preschool English for Language—Minority Children by Peter Schmidt. *Education Week.*

Fillmore, L. (1991). Language and cultural issues in early childhood education. In S. L. Kagan (ed.), *The 90th Year Book of the National Society for the Study and Education.*

Getting Involved Series (Spanish only) (1990). Washington, D.C.: Head Start Bureau, P.O. Box 1182.

Hakuta, K. (1986). *Mirror of language: the debate on bilingualism,* Basic Book, Inc.

Porter, Rosalie Pedalino (1990). *Forked tongue: the politics of bilingual education.* New York: Basic Books, Inc.

Schon, I. (1991, May). Recent noteworthy books in Spanish for young children. *Young Children,* 46(4), 65.

Siegrist, D. (1976). *Language and bilingual education.* Multilingual, Multicultural Materia Development Center, California State Polytechnic University, Pomona, CA.

U.S. Commission on Civil Rights (1975). *A better chance to learn.* Bilingual-Bicultural Education Clearinghouse Publication No. 51, Washington, D.C.

8

Preparing for final assessment as a Child Development Associate

Now, at the conclusion of the CDA P$_3$, you should be prepared to complete your final assessment. The process will determine your ability to integrate the knowledge and skills developed in the Professional Preparation Program and to demonstrate your competence as a CDA working with young children and their families.

A specially trained Council Representative will be assigned by the national office to conduct an on-site visit to collect evidence of your competence working with young children and their families. The Council Rep will interview you, review the results of the Formal Observation and Parent Opinion Questionnaires, and examine your Professional Resource File. A summary of the results of this evidence will be forwarded to the Council office in Washington, D.C.

If you have successfully completed all phases of the CDA Professional Preparation Program, the Child Development Associate Credential will be awarded with an endorsement for family day care programs.

Candidates working in bilingual settings and completing special additional requirements will be awarded also the Bilingual Specialization.

Definition of a CDA

The Child Development Associate (CDA) is a person who is able to meet the specific needs of children and who, with parents and other adults, works to nurture children's physical, social, emotional, and intellectual growth in a child development framework. The CDA Credential is awarded to child care providers and home visitors who have demonstrated their skill in working with young children and their families by successfully completing the CDA assessment process.

Part 1

CDA Competency Standards

As a Candidate for the CDA Credential, you will be assessed based upon the CDA Competency Standards. These criteria are the national standards used to evaluate a caregiver's performance with children and families. The Competency Standards are divided into six *Competency Goals*, which are statements of a general purpose or goal for caregiver behavior. The six goals are defined in more detail in 13 *Functional Areas*, which describe the major tasks or functions that a caregiver must complete in order to carry out the competency goal. The national competency goals and functional area definitions are common to all child care settings whether in centers or family child care homes.

All of the evidence you collect to demonstrate your competence as a CDA will be judged by these standards.

Children want and need to feel secure with you.

"It has been a special privilege for me to have been given the opportunity to teach and to learn, to give and to receive friendship and to experience, again and again, the same joy that I felt on the day that I received my CDA."

CDA 1990

CDA Competency Goals	Functional Areas	Definitions
I To establish and maintain a safe, healthy learning environment	1. Safe	Candidate provides a safe environment to prevent and reduce injuries.
	2. Healthy	Candidate promotes good health and nutrition and provides an environment that contributes to the prevention of illness.
	3. Learning Environment	Candidate uses space, relationships, materials, and routines as resources for constructing an interesting, secure, and enjoyable environment that encourages play, exploration, and learning.
II To advance physical and intellectual competence	4. Physical	Candidate provides a variety of equipment, activities, and opportunities to promote the physical development of children.
	5. Cognitive	Candidate provides activities and opportunities that encourage curiosity, exploration, and problem solving appropriate to the developmental levels and learning styles of children.
	6. Communication	Candidate actively communicates with children and provides opportunities and support for children to understand, acquire, and use verbal and nonverbal means of communicating thoughts and feelings.
	7. Creative	Candidate provides opportunities that stimulate children to play with sound, rhythm, language, materials, space, and ideas in individual ways and to express their creative abilities.
III To support social and emotional development and provide positive guidance	8. Self	Candidate provides physical and emotional security for each child and helps each child to know, accept, and take pride in himself or herself and to develop a sense of independence.
	9. Social	Candidate helps each child feel accepted in the group, helps children learn to communicate and get along with others, and encourages feelings of empathy and mutual respect among children and adults.
	10. Guidance	Candidate provides a supportive environment in which children can begin to learn and practice appropriate and acceptable behaviors as individuals and as a group.
IV To establish positive and productive relationships with families	11. Families	Candidate maintains an open, friendly, and cooperative relationship with each child's family, encourages their involvement in the program, and supports the child's relationship with his or her family.
V To ensure a well-run, purposeful program responsive to participant needs	12. Program Management	Candidate is a manager who uses all available resources to ensure an effective operation. The Candidate is a competent organizer, planner, record keeper, communicator, and a cooperative co-worker.
VI To maintain a commitment to professionalism	13. Professionalism	Candidate makes decisions based on knowledge of early childhood theories and practices, promotes quality in child care services, and takes advantage of opportunities to improve competence, both for personal and professional growth and for the benefit of children and families.

Part 2

Documentation of Competence

Your final assessment as a CDA will involve a documentation of your competence. Five components make up the documentation:

> 1. *Early Childhood Studies Review*
> 2. *Professional Resource File*
> 3. *Formal Observation*
> 4. *Parent Opinion Questionnaires*
> 5. *Oral Interview*

As a Candidate enrolled in the CDA P$_3$, you have already completed one component of the assessment -- the Early Childhood Studies Review -- during your CDA Seminar. Now, you will complete the remaining components.

First, you will prepare to present evidence of your competence from the following (3) sources:

> 1. *Professional Resource File*
> 2. *Formal Observation by the Field Advisor*
> 3. *Parent Opinion Questionnaires*

Then, you will complete your Oral Interview during the Council Rep verification visit.

Professional Resource File

The Professional Resource File is a collection of materials that you will use as an early childhood professional in future work with young children and families. It is compiled for two purposes:

> 1. *It provides a picture of what information Candidates find valuable in their work as a basis for assessing competence as a CDA; and*
>
> 2. *It provides Candidates an important experience in locating resources and articulating their own view of the work in early childhood programs.*

The Professional Resource File is a working resource - one that should be USEFUL to you as a CDA during your career in early childhood education. The information it contains should serve as reference materials on a daily basis.

You have already collected most, if not all of the materials you need for your Professional Resource File and have drafted statements of competence for 5 of the 6 competency areas. Now it is time to revise and complete all three sections and arrange them in their final form.

Arrangement of the Resource File

The material in the Professional Resource File can be arranged in any one of many creative ways (e.g., bound in a notebook or contained inside file folders in a box). It should be professional looking and manageable in size. It should be organized and easy to add to or delete from. *There are no requirements about how it should look.* Whatever its physical form, the Professional Resource File should be portable — designed to be carried on a home visit, or to a meeting — wherever early childhood professionals work.

Contents

The Professional Resource File has three major sections: (1) *Autobiography*; (2) *Statements of Competence*; and (3) *Resource Collection*.

1. Autobiography: Write a statement about yourself of about 300 words. In the first part tell who you are, and in the second part, tell what things about your life influenced your decision to work with young children. *If you wish, you may attach a formal resume of your education and work experiences.*

2. Statements of Competence: In your own words describe the things you do with children and families that demonstrate your ability to meet the specific needs of children in each of the following six (6) Competency Goal areas. The description in each area should be 200-500 words in length and should state your goals for children and give specific examples of what you do to achieve those goals. *For bilingual Candi-*

dates, statements must be specific to the goals of bilingual programs and the statements in three (3) Competency Goal areas must be written in Spanish.

Begin each section by writing out the Competency Goal Statement:

1. Establish and maintain a safe, healthy learning environment
2. Advance physical and intellectual competence
3. Support social and emotional development and provide positive guidance
4. Establish positive and productive relationships with families
5. Ensure a well-run, purposeful program responsive to participant needs
6. Maintain a commitment to professionalism

Remember, your statement for each Competency Goal should contain no more than 500 words. Of course, you cannot describe everything you do in such a limited space. Choose the most important goals you have for children and the best examples of practices that you feel represent your competence.

Write about your *current practice*, using examples of your work now (within the past 6 months). As you review the draft statements you wrote when you first started the CDA P_3, you may need to revise them based on changes in your beliefs and practices as you progressed through your study.

3. <u>Resource Collection:</u> There are seventeen (17) specific items to be included in the Resource Collection. Even though you have collected them as you worked through *Essentials* chapter by chapter, you should check them again for completeness. They should now be organized by Competency Goal areas and numbered so that each item can be located easily during the Council Representative verification visit. *For Bilingual Candidates, the resources used directly with children and families must be in two languages (Spanish/English).*

COMPETENCY GOAL I
To establish and maintain a safe, healthy learning environment

1. Name of agency and telephone number to report child abuse concerns.

2. A record of Red Cross or other agency first aid class certificate of completion. Certification must have been issued within the past 3 years.

3. Agency name(s) that supply information on nutrition for children (e.g., Cooperative Extension Service).

COMPETENCY GOAL II
To advance physical and intellectual competence

4. Four songs including two from other cultures. Where available, include music along with the words.

5. Nine (9) stimulating activities that promote physical, cognitive and creative development — three (3) for infants, three (3) for toddlers, and three (3) for preschoolers. Describe the materials you use, the skills they encourage, and how you expect children to use them.

COMPETENCY GOAL III
To support social and emotional development and provide positive guidance

6. Titles, authors, publishers and copyright dates of 5 children's books (appropriate for the age group with whom you are currently working) that support development of gender identity by portraying males and females in diverse roles.

7. Titles, authors, publishers and copyright dates of 2 age-appropriate picture books that deal with disabling conditions.

8. Titles, authors, publishers and copyright dates of 3 books you would use with children, or recommend for parents that deal with separation, divorce, remarriage, or blended families. The books for parents may either be children's books or adult's books.

9. Name of local hospital and its policies about group field trips, orientation for children scheduled for hospitalization, and parents' presence during children's inpatient stays.

10. Agency name and telephone number for making referrals to family counseling.

COMPETENCY GOAL IV

To establish positive and productive relationships with families

11. Policies for your program that specify what parents should do and what program does for parents. Include also the flyer or brochure you use to advertise your family day care home, and description of your plan for emergency or substitute care.

COMPETENCY GOAL V

To ensure a well-run, purposeful program responsive to participant needs

12. Samples of 4 types of record keeping forms used in family day care programs: 2 small business forms, such as bookkeeping, insurance, and taxes; 2 program operation forms such as accident report and emergency form.

COMPETENCY GOAL VI

To maintain a commitment to professionalism

13. Name and contact information of agency that regulates family day care homes; copy of current regulations. If no regulation exists, a copy of the standards endorsed by a local, state, or national family day care association.

14. Brochure(s) and membership information from two or three national early childhood education associations, and one or two state or local family day care associations.

15. Pamphlet(s) designed for parents about how children grow and learn. (No more than 5)

16. An observation tool for recording information about children's behavior. One copy should be blank; the other filled out with a sample observation of a child. (Anonymous). Identify the age range of children for which the tool is appropriate.

17. Name and contact information of agencies in the community that provide resources for children with disabling conditions.

Formal Observation

A vital source of evidence of your skill is your actual hands-on work as primary caregiver with children and families. Documentation of these practices is collected through a formal observation.

You will be observed by your Field Advisor while you are working with young children in your field placement setting. This observation will be carried out exactly like your first formal observation conducted during Unit 6 of *Essentials* using the *CDA Observation Instrument*.

Your Field Advisor will arrange a time to conduct the observation. S/he may complete the formal observation in one visit or it may take several. Once the observation form is completed, it will be presented to the Council Representative during the verification visit. The instructions for your Field Advisor are included with the *CDA Observation Instrument*.

Keep in mind that the purpose of the observation is to rate your skill in the following specific performance areas. The items the Field Advisor will look for are listed on the next 2 pages.

In a bilingual setting, the Field Advisor will look for examples of your performance that show your skill in achieving bilingual development in children.

Candidate Performance Items to be Rated
by Field Advisor

Functional area 1: Safe

1.1   All toys and materials provided for use by children are safe.

1.2   Supervision is appropriate for developmental level of children.

1.3   Emergency procedures are well planned in advance and are well organized.

Functional area 2: Healthy

2.1   General hygiene practices are implemented consistently to cut down the spread of infectious disease.

2.2   Health maintenance habits in children are encouraged.

2.3   Diapering/toileting procedures are organized to maintain health.

2.4   Meals/snacks meet the developmental needs of children.

2.5   Pleasant and appropriate environment conducive to rest is provided daily.

Functional area 3: Learning environment

3.1   Well-arranged space is provided, which meets the developmental needs of children during routines and play.

3.2   A variety of developmentally-appropriate materials are made available.

3.3   Materials for play are well organized.

3.4   Schedule provided meets children's needs for routine and play.

Functional area 4: Physical

4.1   A variety of activities are offered which enable children to develop their large muscles.

4.2   A variety of activities are offered which enable children to develop their small muscles.

4.3   Program activities are adapted to meet individual needs and special needs of children with handicaps.

4.4   Opportunities are offered to help children develop their senses.

Functional area 5: Cognitive

5.1   A variety of age appropriate materials and activities which encourage curiosity, exploration, and problem solving are accessible to children throughout the day.

5.2   Interactions provide support for play, exploration, and learning.

5.3   Individual learning styles are recognized.

Functional area 6: *Communication*

6.1 Communication with each individual child is frequent.

6.2 Talk with children is developmentally appropriate.

6.3 Children are encouraged to talk.

6.4 Children's attempts to communicate are responded to positively.

6.5 A developmentally-appropriate, print-rich environment, in which children learn about books, literature, and writing, is provided.

Functional area 7: *Creative*

7.1 Individual expression and creativity are appreciated.

7.2 Many appropriate music experiences are available to children.

7.3 Art experiences are age appropriate and varied.

7.4 Dramatic play experiences, with a variety of age-appropriate props, are available.

7.5 Variety of age-appropriate block play opportunities are available.

Functional area 8: *Self*

8.1 Children are given the message that each is important, respected, and valued.

8.2 Individual children are helped to develop a sense of security.

8.3 Diapering/toileting procedures are developmentally appropriate and are organized to encourage self-help skills.

Functional area 9: *Social*

9.1 Each child is helped to feel accepted in the group.

9.2 Feelings of empathy and respect for others are encouraged.

9.3 Non-biased curriculum is used.

9.4 Children are encouraged to respect the environment.

Functional area 10: *Guidance*

10.1 Methods for avoiding problems are implemented.

10.2 Positive guidance techniques are used.

10.3 Guidance practices are related to knowledge of each child's personality and developmental level.

Functional area 11: Families

11.1 Various opportunities to appreciate children's families are part of the regular program.

11.2 Information about families' culture, religion, and childrearing practices is used in classroom experiences.

11.3 Various opportunities are offered to help parents understand the development of their child and understand their child's point of view.

11.4 Resources are provided to help families meet their child's needs.

In addition, the Field Advisor will rate your performance in the two additional CDA functional areas where it may not be possible to actually observe your behavior during the formal observation. The Field Advisor may need to ask you some questions in order to complete her/his evidence of your skill in the following areas:

Functional area 12: Program management

Candidate manages by using all available resources to ensure an effective operation. Candidate is a competent organizer, planner, recordkeeper, communicator, and a cooperative co-worker.

Functional area 13: Professionalism

Candidate makes decisions based on knowledge of early childhood theories and practices, promotes quality child care services, and takes advantage of opportunities to improve competence, both for personal and professional growth and for the benefit of children and families. Candidate keeps abreast of regulatory, legislative, and workforce issues and how they affect the welfare of young children.

Parent Opinion Questionnaire

Parent perceptions about your skills and knowledge are extremely important in assessing whether you conduct yourself in a professional manner. Your Field Advisor will assist you in this process of gathering parent opinions. Each parent with a child in your care will be given an opportunity to complete a questionnaire. At least 75% of the questionnaires distributed must be completed. Your Field Advisor may have to make follow up telephone calls in order to get the questionnaires returned.

The questionnaires are confidential and you will not be able to read the parents' responses. The Field Advisor will collect the questionnaires and place them in a sealed envelope for you to present to the Council Representative. Instructions for distributing and collecting the responses to this questionnaire are included in the *Field Advisor's Guide*, along with the following cover letter and questionnaire:

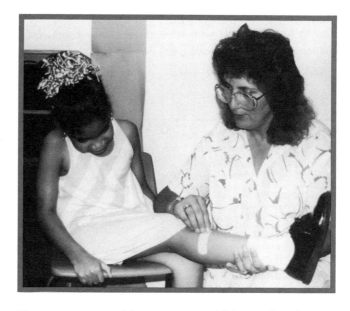

The more you are able to answer a child's need for help, the more parents have confidence in your abilities.

CDA PARENT OPINION QUESTIONNAIRE COVER LETTER

Dear Parents:

I am applying to be assessed for the Child Development Associate (CDA) Credential. The CDA Credential is awarded by the Council for Early Childhood Professional Recognition (*Council*), located in Washington, D.C. The Credential is awarded to competent caregivers and home visitors who have demonstrated their ability to meet the needs of children and parents on a daily basis.

The Council believes that parents have the right to know that the individuals caring for their children are competent. Therefore, parents have a very important role in the assessment of a person who wants to become a Child Development Associate. You can make an important contribution to a national effort to assure quality child care for young children by evaluating my work with your child and family.

As part of my assessment, I am required to collect the opinion of all parents who have children in my group. Therefore, I am asking you to fill out the questionnaire included with this letter. Your answers will be confidential. Please do not sign your name. Think about each question and answer it openly and honestly. Your specific comments at the end of the questionnaire will be very much appreciated.

I would be grateful if you would return your completed questionnaire to me in the enclosed envelope (**sealed**) by _____ .

If you have any questions, please contact me at _____, or you may contact the Council hotline at 1-800-424-4310.

Thanks for your help.

Sincerely yours,

CDA Candidate

Queridos Padres:

Estoy solicitando ser evaluada/o para obtener mi Credencial de Asociada/o en el Desarrollo del Niño (CDA). Esta Credencial es otorgada por el Concillo ("*Council*") para el Reconocimiento Profesional de la Educación Infantil/Pre-escolar/Temprana, localizado en Washington, D.C. La credencial es otorgada a personas que demuestran ser capaces de satisfacer las necesidades específicas de los niños, y quienes trabajan con los padres para fomentar el progreso del niño.

El Concilio ("Council") cree firmemente que los padres/madres tienen el derecho de saber que los individuos a cargo del cuidado de sus niños son profesionales competentes, es por eso que los padres juegan un papel muy importante en la evaluación de una persona que desea convertirse en un Asociado en el Desarrollo del Niño (CDA). Usted podría contribuir grandemente a este esfuerzo nacional, de asegurar la calidad en el cuidado infantil/pre-escolar, evaluando mi trabajo con su niño/s y su familia.

Como parte de mi evaluación, tengo la responsabilidad de recolectar la opinióm de todos los padres de los niños en mi grupo. Por esta razón, le pido que llene el cuestinario adjunto a esta carta. Sus respuestas se mantendrán confidenciales. Por favor no escriba su nombre. Piense y responda a cada pregunta en forma libre y honesta. Sus comentarios específicos al final del cuestionario serán apreciados.

Le agradezco anticipadamente se sirva devolverme este cuestionario completo en un sobre **sellado**, antes del _____ .

Si Ud. tiene alguna pregunta, por favor comuníquese conmigo al _____, o Ud. puede llamar a la línea de ayuda del Concilio (*Council hotline*) al 1-800-424-4310.

Gracias por su apoyo.

Sinceramente,

Candidata/o CDA

CDA PARENT OPINION QUESTIONNAIRE
CUESTIONARIO CDA DE OPINION DE PADRES

CDA Candidate's Name _____

Nombre del Candidato/a CDA _____

For each statement, circle the answer you think is best.

Haga un circulo alrededor de cada respuesta que usted considera como la más correcta

YES = CDA Candidate does this
NO = CDA Candidate does not do this
N/A = Do not know or does not apply

SI = La Candidata CDA lo hace
NO = La Candidata no hace esto
N/A = Ud. no sabe o no es pertinente

The CDA Candidate/ El Candidato/a CDA:

YES NO N/A 1. Reports accidents or any first aid given to my child.
SI NO N/A 1. Reporta accidentes o primeros auxilios dados a mi niño.

YES NO N/A 2. Requires my written permission to give any medication to my child.
SI NO N/A 2. Requiere mi autorización por escrito para poder dar cualquier medicina a mi niño.

YES NO N/A 3. Tells me about my child's eating, sleeping, and toileting/diapering.
SI NO N/A 3. Me dice como mi niño come, si duerme, sobre sus hábitos en el uso del baño, o cambio de pañales.

YES NO N/A 4. Follows feeding instructions for my infant or for my child with allergies.
SI NO N/A 4. Sigue instrucciones para la alimentación de mi bebé o la de mi niño que sufre de alergias.

YES NO N/A 5. Allows my child to be picked up only by people I have named.
SI NO N/A 5. Permite que a mi niño lo recojan sólo aquellas personas a quienes yo he autorizado.

YES NO N/A 6. Reports to me about my child's play and learning.
SI NO N/A 6. Me mantiene informado/a sobre el juego y el aprendizaje de mi niño.

YES NO N/A 7. Organizes toys and play materials so my child can reach them easily.
SI NO N/A 7. Organiza los juguetes y materiales de juego de manera que mi niño pueda alcanzarlos facilmente.

YES NO N/A 8. Provides a place for my child to store his or her own things and makes sure I can find the things I need to bring home.
SI NO N/A 8. Provee un lugar para que mi niño pueda guardar sus pertenencias y se asegura de que yo pueda encontrar todas las cosas que necesito llevar a casa.

YES	NO	N/A	9.	Has enough toys and materials so children do not fight over popular toys.
SI	*NO*	*N/A*	*9.*	*Tiene juguetes y materiales en número suficiente para evitar que los niños peleen por los juguetes más populares.*
YES	NO	N/A	10.	Takes my child outdoors to play every day, except in bad weather.
SI	*NO*	*N/A*	*10.*	*Lleva a mi niño a jugar afuera todos los días excepto cuando el tiempo esta muy malo.*
YES	NO	N/A	11.	Talks with my child frequently.
SI	*NO*	*N/A*	*11.*	*Habla frecuentemente con mi niño.*
YES	NO	N/A	12.	Listens with interest when my child talks and encourages my child to talk.
SI	*NO*	*N/A*	*12.*	*Escucha con interés cuando mi niño habla y lo anima a hablar.*
YES	NO	N/A	13.	Helps my child learn to control his or her own behavior without spanking or other harsh punishment.
SI	*NO*	*N/A*	*13.*	*Ayuda a mi niño a controlar su propio comportamiento, sin pegarle o sin usar castigos duros.*
YES	NO	N/A	14.	Reads to my child often.
SI	*NO*	*N/A*	*14.*	*Le lee a mi niño, con mucha frecuencia.*
YES	NO	N/A	15.	Provides many music, art, block and pretend activities that my child can do in his or her own way.
SI	*NO*	*N/A*	*15.*	*Provee muchas actividades de música, arte, bloques, actividades de pre tender, que mi niño puede hacer a su manera.*
YES	NO	N/A	16.	Helps my child feel proud of what he or she can do.
SI	*NO*	*N/A*	*16.*	*Ayuda a mi niño a sentirse orgulloso de lo que él puede hacer.*
YES	NO	N/A	17.	Encourages children to enjoy getting along with each other.
SI	*NO*	*N/A*	*17.*	*Anima a los niños el disfrute de llevarse bien entre ellos.*
YES	NO	N/A	18.	Gives me the feeling that she is truly interested in my child and me.
SI	*NO*	*N/A*	*18.*	*Me hace sentir que ella/él está verdaderamente interesada/o en mi niño y en mí.*
YES	NO	N/A	19.	Is pleasant and friendly with me.
SI	*NO*	*N/A*	*19.*	*Es agradable y amistosa/o conmigo.*
YES	NO	N/A	20.	Is available to discuss my concerns.
SI	*NO*	*N/A*	*20.*	*Esta disponible para hablar conmigo sobre mis preocupaciones.*
YES	NO	N/A	21.	Asks me for ideas to use with my child, including activity ideas.
SI	*NO*	*N/A*	*21.*	*Me pide ideas para usarlas con mi niño, incluyendo ideas sobre actividades.*

YES	NO	N/A	22.	Asks me what I think is important in raising my child.
SI	NO	N/A	22.	*Me pregunta sobre lo que yo pienso que es importante en la crianza de mi niño.*

YES	NO	N/A	23.	Talks with me about any fears my child has.
SI	NO	N/A	23.	*Me habla sobre cualquier temor o temores que tenga mi niño.*

YES	NO	N/A	24.	Maintains confidentiality; does not freely discuss my child or family in the presence of others.
SI	NO	N/A	24.	*Es reservada/o, mantiene información confidencial; no habla sobre mi niño o mi familia en la presencia de otras personas.*

YES	NO	N/A	25.	Encourages me to visit at any time.
SI	NO	N/A	25.	*Me anima a visitar en cualquier momento.*

YES	NO	N/A	26.	Lets me know of parent meetings and other ways I can become involved in the program.
SI	NO	N/A	26.	*Me hace saber cuando hay reuniones de Padres y me informa sobre otras maneras de participar en el programa.*

YES	NO	N/A	27.	Schedules conferences at times that are convenient to me.
SI	NO	N/A	27.	*Señala fechas para reunirnos, en días y horas que me son convenientes.*

Indicate language(s) you use at home_____. Language(s) you prefer Candidate to use with your child_____.

Indique el idioma/s que usted habla en su casa_____. Idioma/s que ud. prefiere que la Candidata hable a su niño_____.

Please write your opinion about this Candidate's work with your child:

Por favor escriba lo que usted opina sobre el trabajo de esta Candidata/o con usted y con su niño:

Part 3

Verification Visit

Once you have completed your Professional Resource File, Formal Observation, and Parent Opinion Questionnaires, you are ready for the Verification Visit by the Council Representative.

Your Field Advisor will notify the Council that these materials are complete, and the Council Rep will telephone you to schedule a date for the Verification Visit.

You will need to provide a private place for the Council Rep to review your documents and conduct the interview. It is preferable to locate space outside the family day care home, such as at a libray, community center or church. However, if no other space is available, the provider's home may be used, as long as the rooms are completely private and free from traffic, telephone calls and other interruptions, AND another adult is on the premises providing substitute care for the children. If you need help arranging a place, ask your Field Advisor to assist you.

Before the Council Rep arrives, prepare your documentation in the following way:

1. Put your Professional Resource File in final form. The Council Rep will check to see that all entries are complete and then return the File to you. *Make a xerox copy of your "Autobiography" and "Statements of Competence"* -- the Council Rep will mail these to the Council office in Washington, DC.

2. Get the completed CDA Observation Instrument from your Field Advisor. It should be in a sealed envelope for the Council Rep to mail to the Council.

3. Get the completed Parent Opinion Questionnaires from your Field Advisor. They should also be in a sealed envelope. The Council Rep will mail these to the Council.

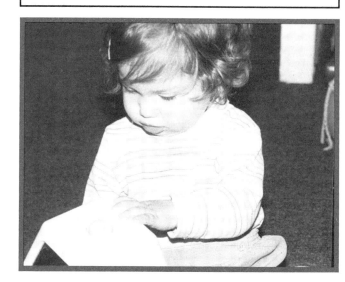

A competent caregiver provides opportunities for the development of eye-hand coordination in ways that are challenging and satisfying for the child.

During the Verification Visit, the Council Rep will:

1. Check the "Autobiography" in the Professional Resource File and send one copy to the Council.

2. Check the "Statements of Competence" in the Professional Resource File and send the copies to the Council.

3. Check the Resource Collection in the Professional Resource File and return it to you.

4. Check the Parent Opinion Questionnaires and send them to the Council.

5. Check the Formal Observation and send it to the Council.

6. Conduct the Oral Interview.

Oral Interview

The Oral Interview provides an opportunity for you to show how the information you have learned would be applied in a variety of early childhood settings.

The interview consists of 10 structured situations and takes about 1 to 2 hours to administer. The situations will be specific to your endorsement as a family day care provider, and if you have chosen the bilingual specialization, specific to bilingual programs.

For each situation, the Council Rep will show you a picture with a written description of the activity pictured. The Council Rep will read the description as you read along. Then s/he will pose a question and ask you to respond. As you respond, the Council Rep will listen, make notes and identify various aspects of your response. S/he may ask additional questions to help you give a clear and complete response. A sample interview question follows:

"It's not often that you find something that you love to do, do it well, and are rewarded for it. For me, the CDA Credential is recognition for doing well what I love to do -- and that's caring for young children. "

CDA, 1992

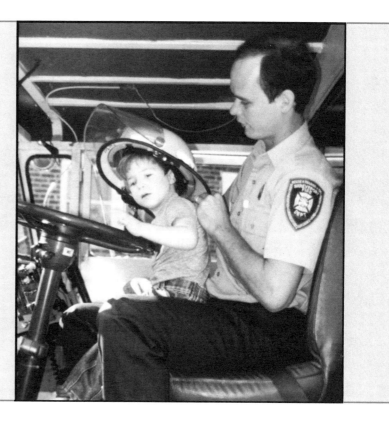

When the interview is finished, the Council Rep will score your responses and send the results to the Council.

After the Council receives the documentation of your competence, a committee will conduct a review and make a decision. If Credential award is recommended, the official Credential is sent to you, the new Child Development Associate. If the committee recommends more training, the Council will notify you and inform you of appeal procedures.

A CDA Credential is valid for 3 years from award, after which it may be renewed.

> *"Becoming a CDA is a process that you work at, learn, and nurture until it grows from within. It is a process by which you grow as an individual and as a professional.*
>
> *It is not a far-away dream that you cannot touch; rather, it is a process that is well within the grasp of reality."*
>
> *CDA, 1992*

CONGRATULATIONS!

You have completed all the requirements for the CDA Professional Preparation Program and have been assessed as a CDA. In just a few weeks, you will receive notification from the Council of the decision about your Credential award.

There are over 50,000 CDAs across the country, the Commonwealth of Puerto Rico, and the U.S. territories of Guam and the Virgin Islands. You will join their ranks, as well as the ranks of the early childhood education profession.

The choice to work with young children and their families is one of the most important career decisions that one can make in our society. Best wishes for a rewarding and successful career ahead!

Glossary of CDA terms

Bilingual Specialization—Open to Candidates who speak, read, and write both English and a second language and work in a bilingual program. Contact the CDA Candidate Connection at 800-424-4310 for more information.

Candidate— Individual enrolled in the Child Development Associate credentialing process through the Council for Early Childhood Professional Recognition.

Candidate Connection—A toll-free telephone number to find the answers to your questions about the CDA credentialing process. Call weekdays from 9:00 a.m. to 5:00 p.m., Eastern Time: 1-800-424-4310.

Child Development Associate (CDA)—A person who is able to meet the specific needs of children and who, with parents and other adults, works to nurture children's physical, social, emotional, and intellectual growth in a child development framework. The CDA Credential is awarded to child care providers and home visitors who have demonstrated their skill in working with young children and their families by successfully completing the CDA assessment process.

Council Representative—Person designated by the Council for Early Childhood Professional Recognition to verify successful completion of final phase of CDA Professional Preparation Program. The Council Representative records Candidates' successful completion of the CDA Early Childhood Studies Review. This Representative also interviews the Candidate and determines that the Candidate is applying the basic knowledge of professional practice.

Early Childhood Studies Review—Written assessment of knowledge about children from birth through age 5 gained from field experience, completion of *Essentials,* and participation in the CDA Seminar.

Field Advisor—Person who assists CDA Candidate in completing the self-study and final evaluation phase of the credentialing process. The Field Advisor is in touch with the Candidate at least once a week to discuss ideas and answer questions. The Field Advisor determines that the Candidate's responses to exercises are accurate and developmentally appropriate and verifies completion of designated exercises by the Candidate.

Professional Resource File—Materials and topics collected to use in teaching and for final assessment as a CDA. Includes regulations, policies, observations telephone numbers, teaching resources, and ideas.

Seminar—A group of CDA Candidates that meets with a Seminar Leader to deal with issues, sensitive topics and in-depth concerns related to teaching young children. At the completion of Seminar, Candidates will complete their written Early Childhood Studies Review.

Seminar Instructor—Individual who conducts Seminars for groups of Candidates. The group will discuss controversial, sensitive, and timely topics. Assignments will be made. The Seminar Instructor will advise Candidates of the date to take their CDA Early Childhood Studies Review.

Viewer's Guide—Ideas to think about while viewing the videotapes for Units 1 through 7 of the *Essentials* curriculum.

Index

clean child care settings, 123

cognitive development, 324
    discovery, encouraging, 324
    mealtime, using, 326
    teachable moments, 326–327
        strategies to support, 328–329
    The Discovery Area, 324–325

community resources, 385, 402, 436, 454, 489, 505

culture, children's families and, 209
    definition of culture, 212
    experiencing diversity, 215
        personal attitudes about, 215
        stereotypes. *See* biases and stereotypes
    identify and learn about various cultures, 209–210
    strategies for teaching about, 216–217
        art, 219–220
        children's games, 218
        languages, 217
        libraries, 218
        music, 218-219
        real objects, 218
    "Educating language-minority children," 213–215

curriculum themes, appropriate, 333–334
    infant themes, 334–335
    preschool themes, 337–338
    themes for daily activities, 333–334
    toddler themes, 335–336

D

death, teaching children about, 262–265
    animals in the program, using, 262
    funerals, 264
    questions about, 262

development, milestones of, 40
    children become aware of the world, 44, 52, 60, 66, 67, 76
        dramatic play, 67
        fears, 67
        taking responsibilities, 77
        words about time, 60
    children become more aware of themselves, 41, 48, 56, 64, 71
        body parts, 49, 57
        self-control, 64
        stranger anxiety, 42

children express feelings, 46, 53, 61, 69, 79
    aggression, 61
    fears, 61
    negative feelings, 53
    self-control, 61
    social contact, 46
    stranger anxiety, 47
    trust, 46

children learn to communicate, 44, 59, 65, 74
    babbling, 44, 51
    bi-/multilingualism, 51, 59, 75
    conversations, 74
    music, 66, 76
    picture books, 51
    play pretend games, 59
    telling stories, 59, 74
    vocabularies, 59, 66, 74
    written language, 74

children show interest in others, 40, 48, 55, 63, 70
    actions, 48
    cooperation, 55
    self-control, 56

children solve problems and use tools, 45, 52, 60, 68, 78
    counting, 68, 78
    tools, 68

children's muscles and coordination grow stronger, 43, 50, 58, 65, 72
    handedness, 58, 73
    large muscles, 65, 72
    small muscles, 65, 73
    toilet control, 59

development, observation of, 81–82
    techniques, 82
        interviewing children, 87–88
        keeping a diary, 82–83
        using a chart, 85–87
        writing on a specific incident, 83–85

developmental assessments, 89
    types of, 89

developmental hurdles, 235–236. *See also* separation anxiety
    egocentricity, 239–240. *See also* play, types of
    oppositional behavior, 237–238
        and toilet learning, 238–239

T

V

W

CDA progress record

Keep track of your progress toward your CDA by using this form. Each time you complete a milestone in your CDA Early Childhood Studies, check it off.

You are to be congratulated for each check—it shows that you are learning about how to be a better teacher of young children.

Phase of your CDA Early Childhood Studies

Section of curriculum	Self-Study	Video	Seminar
Unit 1. Introduction to the early childhood profession	❑	❑	❑
Unit 2. How children grow and learn	❑	❑	❑
Unit 3. Safe, healthy, environment to invite learning	❑	❑	❑
Unit 4. Children's social and emotional development	❑	❑	❑
Unit 5. Children's physical and intellectual competence	❑	❑	❑
Unit 6. Productive relationships with families	❑	❑	❑
Unit 7. Putting it all together as an early childhood professional	❑	❑	❑
Unit 8. Preparing for final assessment as a CDA	❑	❑	❑

Progress on other CDA activities

Date first-aid course completed_____

Parent Questionnaire discussed with Field Advisor on_____

Initial site visit and program observation by Field Advisor completed on_____

Formal observations by Field Advisor completed on _____